ALFRED BINET

ALFRED BINET

Theta H. Wolf

THE UNIVERSITY OF CHICAGO PRESS
Chicago and London

The University of Chicago Press, Chicago 60637
The University of Chicago Press, Ltd., London

Published 1973
Printed in the United States of America

International Standard Book Number: 0–226–90498–9
Library of Congress Catalog Card Number: 72–95957

To John

Contents

Preface

My first interest in Alfred Binet came in Florence L. Goodenough's graduate course in mental measurement at the University of Minnesota where even the timbre of her voice expressed admiration for his work. It impressed and puzzled me that, in light of the extensive applications of his intelligence scale and its use in countless research studies, so little was known about him. Of course, I did not decide then and there to fill the breach by investigating the career of Alfred Binet. Rather, a much later fortunate circumstance of my husband's fellowship grant for study in Paris allowed me to pursue this topic.

Works on Binet have indeed been minimal. There is one monograph in English, written in 1935 by Edith Varon as a master's thesis at Cornell University. It has had almost negligible recognition in bibliographies: even Edwin G. Boring in his 1950 edition of the *History of Experimental Psychology* and Goodenough in her *Mental Testing* in 1949 missed it. At the Bibliothèque Nationale I found two other general accounts of Binet's work: a 1925 thesis by a French student, Robert Martin, entitled simply "Alfred Binet," is delightfully discursive and even insightful, but more literary than systematic or detailed. A second, François-Louis Bertrand's *Alfred Binet et son oeuvre* in 1930, contains some interesting interviews with people who knew Binet, but it is unsystematic, disorganized, and incomplete, although the author did see that Binet deserved a book.

In addition to these general works there is a book by the Belgian François Zuza, *Alfred Binet et la pédagogie expérimentale,* which appears to be his doctoral thesis of 1948. It is a mine of painstaking scholarship in a limited area, but, despite the title, it contains no account of Binet's intelligence scales. More recently, in 1969, Guy Avanzini published *La contribution de Binet à l'élaboration d'une pédagogie scientifique*, an important book but also seriously circumscribed in scope.

The French have been slow to recognize Binet's significance and stature. They did not accord him distinction with a professorship in his lifetime, nor have they appreciated him substantially posthumously. In fact, even the famous Larousse encyclopedia called him a "physiologist" until I had the temerity to correct the listing. It still gives him only a few short lines. Belatedly, in April 1971, a plaque in his and Théodore Simon's honor was ceremoniously attached to the school rue Grange-aux-belles where in 1905 Binet established the first French laboratory of experimental pedagogy. There seems to be a curious lack of interest in Binet by a people who not infrequently exaggerate the importance of their distinguished citizens.

Clearly there was a place for new research. Indeed, once in Paris I found myself overwhelmed by the diversity and the sheer volume of Binet's writings. But one of my most fruitful experiences did not occur in the Bibliothèque Nationale. A month after our arrival in Paris I stammered through a completely unexpected interview with Dr. Théodore Simon, then eighty-six years old (see reference 305). He invited me to return and for several months I met with him regularly at his apartment near the Luxembourg gardens. Happily, Dr. Lucie Bonnis, a retired psychiatrist and Dr. Simon's former colleague, was also present. Although never speaking a word of English, she helped us understand one another's French and took notes, in barely legible French, for my later use.

On the basis of approximately eight months' work in Paris I prepared a long paper that embraced the first ten years of Binet's publications, from 1880 to 1890. The diversity, minute detail, and apparent unrelatedness of his projects were unsettling, but I was encouraged by Dr. Richard M. Elliott's remark: "Yet it is full of interest for persons who like to see the nursery of great accomplishment. I am one of these, and I thank you for letting me read the paper" (personal communication, 27 July 1962). Later visits to Paris provided opportunities for further study, and articles published in the *American Psychologist* and the *Journal of the History of the Behavioral Sciences* brought letters from Professor E. G. Boring and others urging me to extend my work into a book. The primary impetus, however, was the fact that I had become convinced that Alfred Binet had been strikingly, singularly, neglected in the history of psychology.

This book is an attempt to present the *process* of the development, through failure and success, of the lifework of an eminent scientist. It is an account of Binet's ideas developed from data that he hammered out of the raw material of human nature. It portrays the egregious consequences of his unwarranted belief that eminence and reputation should guarantee the rectitude of a "master's" precepts. It shows the unexpected influence of the institutionalization and bureaucratization of universities, and the group loyalties of administrators and scholars. It reflects the effects on a man's career of his personality and the personal events of his life. But most important is the attempt to show how Binet's ideas emerged from his experiments and to provide insight into the way his hunches, his sometimes brilliantly original ideas as well as his subjective assessments, affected his work. It also illustrates the unevenness of his achievements, his discouragements, his carelessness, his successes. In a word, it reports the lifelong labors of a productive man whose career throws light on the problems involved in creative scientific achievements.

Of course I owe much to many persons. In addition to those already mentioned I want to extend my really grateful thanks to the late Dr. Théodore Simon for the many hours of conversation and recall he accorded me, as well as for the use of publications otherwise unavailable, and for the little brochure *Inédits d'Alfred Binet* in which he acknowledged my discussions with him. Mme Simon was always a gracious hostess at these weekly meetings. Again, I am beholden to the late Dr. Henri Piéron with whom I had two interviews in 1963; he also sent me explanatory letters, loaned me his cards and letters from Binet, and made me a gift of the instructive volume *Centenaire de Th. Ribot,* which includes papers on Binet. The friendship with Dr. Lucie Bonnis has become precious to both my husband and to me, and she has assisted my efforts in French, discussed viewpoints by letter and on tapes, and answered innumerable questions. Not least, I wish to thank Alfred Binet's granddaughters, Mlles Georgette and Géraldine Binet, the daughters of Madeleine and Edgard Binet, whom I met in Paris, who have answered requests for information, sent reproductions of photos of their grandfather and his family, and have been very gracious in their interest in this project.

I must thank the Bibliothèque Nationale for its generous assistance, free of charge to foreigners. I am indebted not only for its great collection of printed books and journals, but also for the Salle des manuscrits where I found a few extremely valuable letters in Binet's script.

Other friends and colleagues should also be recognized: Professors Anne Anastasi, May Brodbeck, Terry Clark, Starke Hathaway, Mary Henle, and Harold Klehr generously took time to read and criticize parts of the manuscript, although they are, of course, not responsible for any of its faults. Mrs. Edwina Latimer showed intelligent forbearance in typing the manuscript.

My husband, John B. Wolf, has provided my most sustained support. Throughout its several revisions he has read and reread the manuscript as an editorial critic, with pencil in hand. His obvious confidence that I could and would complete this book overrode my occasional disbelief and discouragement. He praised warmly and criticized vigorously. I cannot count the ways of his assistance.

There are three pieces of general information of which the reader should be aware. First, I am myself responsible for all the translations, which I have tried to keep as close to the original as possible. Actually Binet was such a clear stylist that translations presented few difficulties, except the inevitable ones of making subjective selections among the several possible meanings of words. Second, although Binet had a number of close associates and coworkers, and although he acknowledged their coauthorship in all of the appropriate publications, I have frequently written as if he were the sole author. The coauthorship is indicated in the references, and this single use of his name prevents the awkward repetitions that would otherwise be necessary; it seems particularly legitimate, also, since Simon told me that Binet was always the man with the pen, as he was also most frequently the prime mover of the topic under study. Finally, in the text I have occasionally given English translations of the titles of books and articles in French that have not been translated. Thus the reader whose French might be insecure will find them easier to understand.

T.H.W.

1 Prologue: An Overview

A young French psychologist once likened the work of Alfred Binet to a magnificent *carrefour*, a crossroad from which avenues stretched out in many directions and yet not one of which was resolved into a true boulevard. This observation may be accurate for many men of science, but it is particularly true for Alfred Binet. His interests in psychology were so many and varied that he seems to have had several lives rather than one. As an experimental psychologist he encompassed many areas, from the study of protozoa to the study of suggestibility among schoolchildren. As an experimental pedagogue he measured mental fatigue and also attempted to evaluate teachers' effectiveness by means of achievement tests. As a reformer he stimulated legislative as well as educational changes for the benefit of retarded children.

He was original and inventive in his approach to the solutions he sought. Naturally his viewpoints and methods have a history of development, and, like other scientific ideas and achievements, they emerged from the intellectual milieu of his time and his own experiences.

The Young Binet

Alfred Binet was born in Nice on 11 July 1857, the only child of a father who was a physician and a mother who had modest artistic talents. The medical tradition was strong in this family: Binet's father, both of his grandfathers, and a forebear who served under Napoleon I had been medical doctors. His parents separated, and there appears to be no mention of his father in any documents, unless, as circumstantial evidence strongly suggests, the following unflattering quotation refers to him. It is very likely that Binet was speaking of himself when he wrote in the third person:

One of my friends, timid to excess in his childhood, had had a physician-father who, in order to make the boy brave, led him into a mortuary chamber, showed him a cadaver, and made him touch it; the child was overcome by an emotion from which he still feels the effects. Ten years later, in Paris, he could not enter the amphitheater [of the medical school] and renounced medicine as his professional goal [142, p. 149].

We assume that his mother, Mme Moïna Binet, took full responsibility for the boy's upbringing, but little is actually known about his childhood. He himself reported that from six to nine or ten years of age he went for two months each summer to the mountains to live at an English boardinghouse, which surely contributed to his later ability to read fluently English and American psychological literature. His "first memories" came from that experience: ". . . of waking up and finding myself alone in bed [after my mother's departure]: Tears!" (204, p. 195). A visit to the old city of Nice today makes it appear very probable that he bathed in the sea, ran along the wide sands, and explored the site of the ramparts set high up on the headland overlooking the Mediterranean. His residence in Nice, which had been a part of the kingdom of Piedmont-Sardinia when he was born, gave him a proficiency in Italian that in later years offered him easy access to Italian publications in psychology.

Young Alfred attended a lycée in Nice until the summer of his fifteenth birthday when he and his mother went to Paris to continue his education. Mme Binet obviously intended to provide the best for her son, since she sent him to the renowned lycée, Louis-le-Grand, which he attended for three years. His record at the school does not indicate a brilliant performance, but his three annual first prizes, "in French composition and discourse," and his lesser prizes, in "Latin translation," suggest that the fluent, clear, and colorful exposition that marks his later writings was already in bud during his adolescent years.[1]

[1] The headmaster of Louis-le-Grand, in a letter to me in May 1960, sent a list of Alfred Binet's "distinctions," which were

After leaving Louis-le-Grand he had trouble finding a career. He first entered a law school where he took his *licence* in 1878 and then began to study for the doctorate. This professional choice was not agreeable to him, and he could not take it seriously. Many years later he wrote: "As for the law, that is the career of men who have not [yet] chosen a vocation" (99, p. 14). He undertook medical studies, but did not complete them.[2] It is just possible that the conflicts aroused by this vocational indecision were an important factor in the temporary emotional difficulty that he recalled years later in a letter to a close friend who was ill. He wrote:

> When I was about twenty—a long time ago—I was myself very much overstrained [*surmené*] one winter. I had had cerebral anemia and had to take six months of complete rest and eat a rich diet to put me back on my feet [4, 26 February 1905].

The Early Psychologist

Binet actually found his career outside of any formal system of education. In 1879 or 1880 he began to read psychology in the Bibliothèque Nationale. Fifteen years later, in a letter to Professor Gaston Paris, he thanked that gentleman for having arranged his admission as a reader at the Bibliothèque (where a formal letter of recommendation is still required): "Your recommendation was sing-

---

prizes or ranks, for the three years that he attended that lycée, 1875–78.

[2] American sources particularly have repeated the error that Binet was a physician. His own writings may have been partially responsible, at least for the initial error, for he mentioned being a medical student (e.g., 13, p. 396, and 27, p. 149). Furthermore, he had a cousin also named Alfred Binet, and also born in Nice (1890), who became a medical doctor in Paris (1921); mistaken identity, therefore, is possible. But Zuza (311, note, p. 24), after searching for definitive information, wrote: "The Faculty of Medicine of Paris has been unable to give us any information about Binet's medical studies. Indeed, for the years *before 1900 it keeps the dossiers only of the students who finished the doctorate degree* [in medicine]" (italics added). Binet's name is not there.

ularly useful, for it was my studies [there] that decided my vocation" (2, 3 October 1895).

These years of his early studies were years of intellectual ferment all over Europe, and Binet easily became involved in the problems and postulates of this educated world. He may have started by reading Taine's widely known *L'intelligence,* which was then hailed in England as ". . . a striking statement and an admirably methodical exposition of the chief desiderata of psychological science at the present time . . ." (*Mind,* 1879, p. 291). Two books by Ribot provided excellent critical summaries of contemporary English (1875) and German (1879) psychology. He read in English or in French translations the current books of Herbert Spencer, Alexander Bain, and John Stuart Mill as well as some of Francis Galton's work, and Hermann von Helmholtz's *Optique physiologique.* Unlike many other aspiring young French scholars, he seems to have read little or no German. However, two major journals of that era, the *Revue philosophique* and *Mind,* offered him a broad orientation and acquaintance with publications from many European countries. He was caught up in evolutionary theory, French positivism, the controversy between determinism and free will. More specifically, in the psychological arena he was in fact completely absorbed by the ideas of the functional viewpoints and terminology, by concerns about the nature of consciousness, and by the need for comparative and developmental studies. And yet his first striking enthusiasm focused on associationism. This viewpoint was widely accepted by important men like Wilhelm Wundt, Hermann von Helmholtz, Hippolyte Taine, and Théodule Ribot, but it was John Stuart Mill who became his mentor. For three or four years after the publication of his first paper in 1880, Binet devoted his labors to extending this doctrine to an explanation of all psychology. Ribot, as editor of the *Revue philosophique,* offered his own personal encouragement to the young author by publishing his papers in this journal.

Binet must have been agreeably excited when, two years later, Joseph Babinski, a former classmate, introduced him to the Salpêtrière, the famous Paris hospital, where he met Jean Martin Charcot and Charles Féré. For the next seven years he spent much of his time in Charcot's "laboratory," observing and "experimenting with" hypnotized hysterics, publishing regularly, and uncritically adopting Charcot's methods and hypotheses about hypnosis.

In 1884 he married Laure Balbiani, the daughter of Professor E. G. Balbiani, embryologist at the Collège de France. Two daughters were born of this union, Madeleine in November 1885 and Alice in July 1887. These girls became known later as Marguerite and Armande, when they were subjects in their father's research.

Binet's first book, *La psychologie du raisonnement*, appeared in 1886. Its title, "of reasoning," has subsequently assured it more attention than it deserves, for it has been erroneously construed as Binet's debut into the study of intelligence when in fact this book's major objective was to demonstrate that the principles of the association of ideas could explain all psychological phenomena. One year later he abandoned that assumption as *sufficiently* explanatory of these phenomena when his observations of mentally disturbed patients and of hypnotized subjects forced him to focus on *disassociation.* In other words, the stark evidence of unconscious mental activity forced a change of his viewpoint that he acknowledged in a book called *Le magnétisme animal,* published with Féré (22).

In 1887 Binet was honored as *lauréat,* with a prize of 1,000 francs, by the Academy of Moral and Political Sciences. He must have been gratified since at thirty years of age he was just establishing himself as a psychologist, and this recognition would give him visibility. Since the prize-winning paper remained unpublished, the only information about its contents comes from the extended notes of the secretary of the Academy (23). Its 511 handwritten pages may have been a hindrance to publication, but perhaps Binet's own reluctance was even more weighty, for the paper contained rather astonishing statements that Binet himself disavowed within a few years. Very probably in trying to meet the requirements of the Academy he had allowed himself to go beyond his depth. One of his ideas, however, bears mentioning because of its great importance in his much later studies of the retarded: here for the first time he stressed the conviction that "doctors of psychopathology must start with the normal state before drawing conclusions about patients suffering delusions." This emphasis on the normal was to be constant in Binet's approach to human psychology.

The report of the prize paper provides a pen picture of its author in the statement of the evaluating committee. They wrote:

> ... This is the work of a mind that is very open, curious, searching ... of a man who has frequented laboratories and hospitals ... who makes methodical experiments, sometimes on sane subjects, sometimes on those with different degrees of mental illness. The Salpêtrière is his field of study. ... The paper shows an independent mind and effectiveness as an observer and experimenter. ... He manifests conviction in knowing how to use experiments that he has not done himself, and also dexterity in repeating them or substituting others. In these things lie his incontestable superiority. ... This *Mémoire* is distinguished. The author ... has a gifted and uncommon mind. He is at the same time broad and precise, bold and contained, firm in his ideas, but not at all intolerant or exclusive in them. He likes research and practices it as an observer and an experimenter. ... His style is natural, lucid, sometimes ingenious and piquant ... For these merits, he is worthy of the prize [23, pp. 643–65].

The committee actually required Binet to share the prize of 2,000 francs with another contestant because he had not developed the sections of the *Mémoire* on literature and philosophy fully enough to meet the formal stipulations of the competition.

In the year that he won the prize Binet's efforts included a bookish but lively discussion of normal and pathological fetishism and also a study of the "psychic life of microorganisms." Despite the possible inferences to be made from the title of the latter publication, it was in fact antivitalistic.

Beginning in the spring of 1888, while he continued his studies at the Salpêtrière and wrote articles on free will versus determinism as well as on the psychology of certain legal practices, Binet devoted much of his time studying in his father-in-law's laboratory at the Collège de France. He summarized Balbiani's lectures on heredity for publication (32). The bibliographical references provided by Balbiani were current and must have furnished Binet with a healthy antidote to Mill's flagrant environmentalist position.[3] Binet also entered a laboratory section in zoology where he practiced dissection for several hours a week, and he added a course in botany. He became especially absorbed in what he called "comparative psychology," doing research on the behavior, physiology, histology, and anatomy of insects. Some of these studies were published in brief notes in scientific journals, and, more important, in 1894 they furnished a thesis for his doctorate in natural science. The thesis, entitled "A Contribution to the Study of the Subintestinal Nervous System of Insects," is available in the Bibliothèque Nationale and is replete with handsome, detailed drawings of Binet's histological and anatomical studies. It appears that he drew most of them himself. It is highly probable that these years of experience at the Collège sharpened his observational skills and gave him a new vision of the possibilities of scientific controls.

In the meantime, while working at the Salpêtrière, Binet had accepted without question Charcot's assumptions about, and methodology in, the field of hypnotic phenomena. He even became their aggressive proponent in an acrimonious debate with professors of what was called the "Nancy school" and their staunch supporter, Professor J.

[3] The contents of this long résumé clearly show that in these lectures Binet was exposed to a genetic viewpoint that was very different from that of his "hero," John Stuart Mill. E. G. Balbiani evidently understood the mechanisms and significance of heredity according to current research, while Mill remained a complete environmentalist, refusing through seven revised editions of his *Logic* to admit the existence of any hereditary individual differences in mental characteristics (281, p. 270). While Binet recognized the role of experience, it would have been unfortunate had he assumed that this was the sole determinant of these differences.

L. R. Delboeuf of Liège. This debate continued from 1886 to 1889, with the young Binet naïvely attempting to defend Charcot's doctrines only to find himself in a completely untenable position. The counterattacks, especially on the part of Delboeuf, were devastating, and although as late as 1889 (34) and 1892 (43) Binet published two books that used illustrations from pathological and hypnotized subjects, the situation was so unsettling that by 1890 he broke his active connections with Charcot and the Salpêtrière. This humiliating experience left Binet with a compelling interest in the all-too-human trait of suggestibility. Thenceforth he frequently cautioned his readers about its insidious infiltrations into the work of unsuspecting experimentalists, especially psychologists and psychiatrists.

The Search for New Directions

After this unfortunate experience at the Salpêtrière, Binet cast about for valid methods, areas, and a location for possible further investigations. During this time his inventive mind was stimulated to make systematic observations of his little daughters. Their striking individual differences are apparent in three papers that he published in 1890, and his careful observations became important sources of his subsequent assumptions about cognitive processes. It has even been said that "the fact that Binet was married and had two daughters seems really to be a matter of some moment for psychology" (303, p. 25). This work was indeed seminal, and it is probably regrettable that he did not extend it, for it can be cited as a progenitor of some of Piaget's studies.[4]

Obviously, Binet needed an institutional association. Although generally reserved in manner, he took the initiative in the late summer of 1891 to approach Dr. Henri Beaunis, director of the Laboratory of Physiological Psychology at the Sorbonne, when they accidentally met in a

[4] Claparède could have drawn Piaget's attention to Binet's work, since he knew Binet for nearly twenty years and also worked as a student in Flournoy's laboratory in Geneva, where Piaget came under his influence.

railway station at Rouen. He asked Beaunis to take him as a member of his staff. In spite of the rancorous debates that Binet had carried on with the "Nancy school" and its supporters, among whom was Beaunis himself, the director held no grudge. He knew the quality and volume of the young psychologist's productivity and desperately needed staff for the laboratory. He was especially receptive since the appointment would not require nonexistent funds for a salary. Fortunately, Binet was sufficiently well-off so that he did not have to earn his living, and "psychology was his sole occupation" (248).

This first French psychological laboratory, instigated by Théodule Ribot and created by Louis Liard, director of Higher Education, had been formally established by a decree of the Minister of Public Instruction in January 1889 as a part of the section of the natural sciences within the School for Advanced Studies (L'École pratique des Hautes Études) in the Sorbonne. Beaunis, a physiologist and physician, had left his chair on the medical faculty in Nancy to become the director. With limited funds he tried to organize the laboratory on the model of Wilhelm Wundt's at Leipzig, but when Binet appeared he gave the young man a free hand to try new ideas. In 1892 he made him associate director, and in 1894 Binet became the director when Beaunis retired "to live the life of a sage, in the Midi" (271, p. 91).

Binet's activities for the one year 1894 illustrate his prolific output. In the year that he became director of the laboratory, he and Beaunis initiated and edited the first French psychological journal, *L'Année psychologique,* in which Binet himself published four original *mémoires* and about eighty-five reviews, from French, English, American, and Italian contributors. He was also appointed to the board of associates of the new American *Psychological Review,* and published two books, one an introduction to experimental psychology (48), the other on the psychology of master calculators and chessplayers (47). He also completed his doctorate in the natural sciences, researched the Müller-Lyer illusion, hypothesized about confusions in space orientation, developed an instrument for recording graphically techniques of piano playing, and began, with J. Passy, studies of dramatic authors. He and Victor Henri also studied schoolchildren's memories and their suggestibility. This fantastic productivity seems to indicate that Binet's genius was driving him compulsively.

L'Année psychologique

L'Année psychologique, the first French journal of psychology, published in 1895, was to be a lifelong professional obligation; nor should it be taken for granted that its editorship was something perfunctory and mainly left to others. Although the frontispiece of each volume lists coworkers, contributors, and *rédacteurs,* Binet was indeed the director and editor-in-chief. Since it was a continuous involvement, and has not been recognized even in so-called complete bibliographies of his work, it warrants some detailed attention.

Each edition of *L'Année* contained original articles, many from the staff of the laboratory, a large annotated bibliography with a broad coverage of areas, reviews of selected publications from several countries, and a "complete" bibliography of publications in psychology and related fields for the previous year. This bibliographical task was lightened after the second issue when Binet secured the right to use the bibliographies prepared for the *Psychological Review,* but the editorship was nonetheless a formidable one.

For the first two volumes, Henri, Ribot, and Beaunis were listed as coeditors, the latter two seemingly in honorary roles. From 1897 through 1901 Victor Henri was subeditor *(Secrétaire de la rédaction),* a task that the Swiss J. Larguier des Bancels assumed for the next six years, after which he shared the honors with Simon. Letters and large postcards that Binet wrote to Larguier, 1900–11, and to Henri Piéron, 1903–11, demonstrate unmistakably Binet's overwhelming involvement in the enterprise, and those documents that survive represent, of course, only a very small sample of his correspondence relating to this annual publication. While Henri and Larguier covered a large part of the responsibility for selecting the German contributors and the German publications to be reviewed, Binet seems to have been responsible for the rest.[5] In addition to his own contributions, he wrote innumerable letters to scholars requesting original articles or general reviews in their specialties. He was constantly planning changes in *content:* "Leave out the physiological, particularly 'visual sensations,' which are superannuated . . ." he wrote (4, 6 October 1908) ; in *length* of articles and reviews; and in *format.* Americans will be interested in his remark: "I have requested very few articles from American psychologists, for the simple reason that I have found little of interest in them!" (4, 1907). For one volume he suggested "numerous pictures," only later to regret the expense.

Binet was frequently worried about contributors' failures to respond: "I have written an unbelievable number of letters, with very little success" (4, 14 July 1903), or "I have received promises—only!" (4 December 1903) ; or he was "surprised that previous authors of reviews had responded so sparingly" (4, 1906). Sometimes his own friends let him down, as in the case of Victor Henri who seems to have done so a number of times after he left Paris. In fact, Binet once wrote of being "disappointed, and even hurt by his silence" (4, 1903). On the other hand, he was sometimes elated on receipt of certain agreements or excellent papers. Occasionally he expressed personal comments to Larguier: "I am tired out and rather concerned about the reviews. I fear I may be unable to do many of them" (4 December 1903). Again: "*L'Année* is going very well, but with a multiplicity of correspondence that no one can imagine" (4, 24 March 1904).

[5] Letters to Larguier in 1903 and 1905 respectively give lists of about a dozen and twenty-five possible topics along with their suggested authors. They included such areas as anatomy, pathology, and physiology of the nervous system, aesthetics, linguistics, pedagogy, statistics of crime, mental retardation, philosophy, etc. He wanted one in sociology, which was finally written by Fauconnet. One wonders why Durkheim was not represented, but for some unexplained reason, Binet wrote to Larguier: "I have heard that the school of Durckheim [*sic*] detests me. They are very good. What do you know about it?" (4, 21 December 1905).

In discussing the foreign reviews with Larguier (1908), Binet made a surprising admission that helps to make credible his great labors. Saying that Larguier had been translating German publications too literally Binet wrote: ". . . I use the English and Italian articles freely. . . . I simply summarize what I understand of the condensed commentary. In that way, the author's own ideas can be brought into play" (4, 22 March 1908). And again: "I have taken some great liberties, and believe that I was right. I read the commentary, responded to it in my head, and rewrote it. Do you not think . . . that the result is much clearer?" (4, 19 April 1908).

Binet also was completely accountable for business arrangements. In July 1903 he changed publishers from Schleicher to Masson, and, while his letters do not explain why he did this, he seems much distressed that Schleicher appeared to have been offended, for he would not respond to Binet's overtures. "To five letters," he complained, "*Rien! Rien! Rien!*—[Nothing! Nothing! Nothing!]" (4, 14 July 1903). His relations with Masson were apparently very cordial, but through the years the publication suffered some dark days. The sales were uneven, and sometimes disappointing. In 1904 Masson was "distressed" to find that only 372 copies of volume 10 had been sold and requested Binet to guarantee to pay for the volumes unsold after a certain minimum number. Although Binet tried some improvements for volume 11, he feared it would be the last. His letters reflect his anxiety and feelings of threat. He wrote to Larguier: "Picard has promised for next year. Ah! Next year *L'Année* will perhaps be dead! My heart is oppressed even to think about it!" (4, 1904?). Writing about his concern to attract new readers, he added: "We must do this or our twelfth volume will be the last, and I would regret that bitterly!" (4, 21 December 1905). The sales vacillated, but fortunately *L'Année* did not suffer demise and today is still very much alive.

The Laboratory at the Sorbonne

The history of Binet's laboratory within the School for Advanced Studies was something less than a success story.

When he became its director there were few students and even fewer distinguished visitors to use its instruments and build its reputation. After a few years, Binet spent less and less time there, and while he was the director the laboratory never achieved much recognition, either in France or abroad. There were many reasons for this. Henri Piéron suggests that Binet's dominating personality was the most important one, but the fact remains that the Laboratory of Physiological Psychology was never adequately supported financially or academically. Staff assistants there, in common with all others in the School for Advanced Studies, were so poorly paid that they had to take other positions to support themselves. But much more significant were the facts that the university awarded no diplomas or degrees to certify foreign students when they returned to their native lands, and that there were no positions in the French lycées for teachers of psychology. Binet could do nothing about employment for his students in France, but he did appeal to his former mentor, Dr. Gaston Paris, an administrator at the Collège de France, writing as follows:

I am writing to you in order to draw your attention to a question that, I know, appears important to you, that of the granting of certificates or diplomas by the École des Hautes Études [Sorbonne]. At my laboratory I often receive foreigners, notably Americans, who have studied psychology in their own country and who come to Europe to look for a complement to their education. You undoubtedly know that at this moment the number of laboratories of psychology in America is increasing rapidly and now surpasses thirty. However, the American students are not satisfied with diplomas given at these laboratories, and so they come to the laboratories of old Europe, seeking a title that has more prestige than theirs. For a long time they have gone to Germany, particularly to Wundt's laboratory at Leipzig,[6] and if they stop in Paris at all it has been quite simply to visit the opera and the museums.

[6] Victor Henri gave an enlightening account of Wundt's laboratory where the students were obliged to act as "voluntary" subjects for about six months, after which they could under-

But for the last year or two we have been receiving some of them at our Laboratory des Hautes-Études; they want to work here with us. Up to the present time I have had to clarify the situation for them, to tell them outright that our school does not confer any title, any diploma; thus, practical men that they are, they have drawn away after a short time, and have gone to enlarge the number of students at the German laboratories.

I have always thought that *we are at fault in not fighting against a state of things that assures an overwhelming weight to German ideas in psychology.* It is for this reason that I am appealing to your help to defend the interests of French science . . . [2, 3 October 1895; italics added].[7]

This last sentence is a reminder that French science, although beginning to rise in status, was in general held in comparatively low esteem in Europe, and also that in France itself it was less prestigious than the humanities. The rest of the letter bears witness to the power that administrative decrees can exert on the dissemination of viewpoints and hypotheses. Diplomas granted at the School for Advanced Studies in the 1890s might early have leavened American psychology in the direction of the experimental study of individual differences in complex processes.

---

take their own research (202; also 48, pp. 14 ff). Wundt's students then frequently completed these experiments and their degrees in a surprisingly few months, often not much more than a year. At the end of this time they were given degrees, signed and sealed. Both the short apprenticeship and the certificate added to Wundt's reputation and made his laboratory very popular, although there are some amusing accounts of frustrated and angry students.

[7] In a letter Piéron expressed his surprise that Binet addressed himself to Gaston Paris since the latter was an administrator at the Collège de France rather than at the Sorbonne (256). What Piéron seems to have forgotten is that Paris was also a major academic politician as well as an adviser of Louis Liard, a director in the Ministry of Public Instruction, which was the sole ministry empowered to create a new degree at the School of Higher Education, Sorbonne (T. Clark, private correspondence).

Binet continued to verbalize his complaints that French psychology was largely ignored abroad, and especially in the United States, yet his remarks were not entirely justified. Even though German psychology was clearly ascendant, there were many reviews of French articles and books in American journals, and even an announcement in the *American Journal of Psychology* of the anticipated first volume of *L'Année psychologique* in which the editor "assured both its character and its success" since MM. Beaunis and Binet were in charge *(Am. J. of Psychol.* 6 [1895] : 653). *L'Année* continued to be reviewed in *Science* and other journals, although not consistently. A number of Binet's own books were reviewed with reasonably balanced judgments. For several years the *American Journal of Psychology* listed Beaunis and Henri among its members of the editorial board, and Binet's name appeared in the same capacity from the first volume of the *Psychological Review* (1894) until 1910, when only Americans were appointed. Although these illustrations indicate that Binet had overlooked a considerable American attention to French psychology, he was warranted in deploring its eclipse by German work. For instance, in a book on *The New Psychology* published in the United States in 1897 (226), only the six pages written by Binet himself were devoted to French psychology.

Biological Sciences and Experimental Pedagogy

Binet's training in his father-in-law's laboratory, as well as his recognition of the close relations between biological and psychological processes, was reflected in his continued interest in biology and natural science. He not only wrote short articles for biological journals, but also, by means of reviews, tried to keep the readers of *L'Année* informed of findings in histology, anatomy, and physiology. Moreover, in 1895 the Société de Biologie recognized him by electing him to membership. Two years later he and Henri founded an abortive bimonthly, *L'Intermédiare des Biologistes,* subtitled "an international organ of the family of disciplines represented by zoology, botany, physiology, psychology, and medicine."[8] This was undoubtedly too broad, too ambitious, a project; it survived for little more than a year. Nonetheless, it is an indication that Binet was trying to see "man" more comprehensively than psychology alone could do.

At this stage in his career, Binet seems to have believed that he could make important contributions as an editor, for in addition to the review for biologists he also attempted to launch a series of books for educators that would bring together the fields of pedagogy and psychology. He and Henri wrote the first volume, *La fatigue intellectuelle* (1898). This series, or *Bibliothèque,* of these aspiring editors failed to continue, but the volume of 1898 was the first one in Binet's continuing publications in the field of pedagogy, and he did publish another volume in the *Bibliothèque* series (77).

Binet's own research at this time also took a physiological turn. Beginning in 1895, he spent five years seeking correlations among physiological, physical, and psychological data, thus displaying a persistence that one tends to overlook in a man of such diverse concerns.

Professor at Bucharest

In the spring of 1895 (27 April to 17 June) Binet, for the first and only time in his life, had the exhilarating experience of becoming a popular university professor. M. Take Ionescu, Minister of Public Instruction in Bucharest and a former classmate at Lycée Louis-le-Grand, invited him

[8] This was a journal of about twenty-five pages, divided into two parts: the first was devoted to questions asked by subscribers; the second, to answers given by experts. Among the latter were well-known men such as Hermann Ebbinghaus, C. S. Sherrington, James M. Baldwin, Ed. Claparède, Johannes Müller, J. J. van Biervliet. Among other articles Binet was himself cautionary about the use of "the questionnaire method of G. S. Hall—a preliminary trial method. . . . The future will tell us whether it is very useful to extend it on such a vast scale as Hall has done . . ." (1898, No. 11, p. 254). Baldwin even claimed that Preyer had informed him by letter that Binet's "method of recognition" of colors had been used by Preyer in 1882 (1898, No. 7, p. 153). Binet did not argue the point.

to the university to present a series of twelve lectures on experimental psychology (265, 266). He agreed, and Mme Binet, their two daughters, and a maid accompanied him to Bucharest, where they were most cordially welcomed, especially by the Maiorescus, the rector of the university and his wife. The families lunched and dined together frequently, often on the flower-bedecked terrace of the rector's home. It is probable that nine-year-old Madeleine's attack of pneumonia brought them closer together, since, because of her parents' overwhelming anxieties, Mme Maiorescu spent many hours daily with the Binets and often took little Alice, whom she called "charming" and "delightful," to her home.

The course of lectures progressed splendidly. The university had purchased the necessary apparatus and furnished technicians to show Binet's slides. The newspapers carried announcements, hailed Binet "as a representative of modern science, along with Wundt, Fechner, Ribot, etc.," and then reported the contents of the lectures in some detail. Indeed, these accounts are the only record that remains. The number of students, professors, and interested citizens who attended swelled beyond the limits of the lecture hall and forced a move to a larger auditorium. It must have been a heady experience for a man who had not achieved any professorial status in the academic community of his own fatherland.

The visit ended with a banquet, and subsequently Rector Maiorescu several times offered Binet a chair at the University of Bucharest. He did not accept it; like many Frenchmen, he could not believe that men could live far from Paris. Nonetheless, the two men carried on a sporadic but very friendly correspondence. These letters suggest the charm and playfulness that may have been characteristic of Binet before events at the turn of the century (his wife's illness, the deaths of his father-in-law and of his friend Marillier, his failure to win a French professorship) darkened his life. In October 1895, on his return from the family summer at Saint-Valéry, Binet wrote to Maiorescu:

How much we have been touched by the affection you provided during our visit with you! And how much we regret that friends like you live in Bucharest, because they did not think, like us, of being born in Paris! How often we speak of you two with our children, and even imagine ourselves still on the terrace of your pretty house Mercur. . . . We are counting on your promise to come to see us here next year. You must remain several days, and we must decide in advance our schedule for these happy days. As you did, we shall write little notes with an immense pencil, as happened there, near the flowering clematis. Recalling all these memories I press your hand with the assurance of my most sincere feelings attached. . . My respectful remembrance to Mme Maiorescu whom my whole family embraces tenderly . . . [266, p. 202].

There is no evidence, however, that the Maiorescus ever returned the Binets' visit. One of Binet's letters (1899) suggests that his wife's ill health may have prevented this. Or indeed the relationship of the two men may have cooled because of Binet's difficulty with Nicholas Vaschide, a student from the University of Bucharest who went to Paris, funded by his own university, in order to study "with the great French psychologist." The young man unfortunately seems not to have shared Binet's rigor as an experimentalist; there is a hint that he slanted some of his measurements in the direction of the hypothesis being tested (248). Their relations deteriorated to the point that Binet could not work with him; Vaschide withdrew from the laboratory (1899) and went to join Professor E. Toulouse at his laboratory (Villejuif). Earlier in that year Binet wrote Maiorescu his last gentle refusal of a professorship at Bucharest, and no further correspondence between the two men is recorded.

Collaborators and Confrères

Binet's methods of working and probably his personal predilections seem to have demanded that he should frequently have a collaborator who could act as a sounding board for his ideas and as a research associate in his investigations. In the years between 1890 and 1911 the names of at least eight young men appeared with that of

Binet on papers or books. The best known of the men who worked with him was, of course, Théodore Simon, but in the early 1890s Victor Henri, who took a Ph.D. under Johannes Müller, became the first to fill this function. He and Binet worked on many projects, but by far the most important was the famous prospectus for the study of individual psychology (1896). In this paper they outlined a possible program for research, which Binet later complemented with an article on measurement in individual psychology. There can be no question about the importance of this project for Binet's growth as a psychologist. It bore fruit in the 1900 studies of attention and suggestibility, in the 1903 studies of habitual orientations in thinking and of tactile sensitivity as well as in all the studies of intelligence. Henri, however, did not cooperate in these latter works. He found it difficult to decide whether he wished to be a psychologist, a philosopher, a physiologist, a chemist, or something else. Unquestionably his sporadic collaboration and final withdrawal were a disappointment to Binet. When in 1899 Simon proposed himself as a student-collaborator, Binet unwittingly found the man he needed (306).

Fresh from medical school with a thesis to prepare for his final degree, Simon had been so impressed with Binet's writings that, without any introduction, he appeared at the laboratory and requested to work under his direction. Since Simon was at that time an intern in the colony for retarded children and adolescents at Perray-Vaucluse, he rightfully assumed that, with over two hundred boys "entirely at his disposition" as subjects, Binet would be interested in accepting him. Indeed he was, but not without first putting Simon to some "tests" of competence, persistence, and good faith. Much later, Binet told Simon that he had so often been deceived in the men who had come to him that "he did not immediately accept the students who presented themselves, but rather tried to discourage them so that he himself would not be disturbed in carrying out his own work" (297, pp. 410–11). Probably he was particularly sensitive at this time when he had so recently dismissed Vaschide. Accordingly, Binet assigned Simon a whole series of measurements to make on his 223 boys at the institution, with instructions to extract from them means and mean variations for each measurement in each age group. "It was several months before I returned to the laboratory," Simon wrote. "Finally I presented my work, which became my doctoral thesis in medicine. And then I was adopted" (297, p. 411). This was the beginning of a collaboration that continued until Binet's death, one that provided the necessary support for the extensive experimentation and analyses upon which the intelligence scales depended. Only rarely touching on intimate or personal matters, the two men regularly walked, talked, and worked together as long as Simon was in Paris, and when Simon became *directeur-adjoint* of an institution in Rouen (1908), regular correspondence ensued, along with fairly frequent meetings.

Within a month or two of Simon's first appearance at the laboratory in 1899, another young man, nineteen years of age, presented himself. He was Henri Piéron, who later became both director of the laboratory at the Sorbonne and editor of *L'Année*. Unlike Simon's, his reception was distressing. He has written that Binet greeted him with a "closed, tight-lipped expression," and that he even disparaged the usefulness to the young philosophy student of studying experimental psychology. Since Piéron insisted, Binet set him to work on some reaction time experiments, and, as with Simon, put him through a grueling test of his "critical sense and ability as an experimenter." Piéron found the experience extremely frustrating and after a few months he left Binet's tutelage. Later, Binet and Piéron continued to exchange correspondence concerning editorial matters, but their relationship does not appear to have been very cordial. It is not unlikely that the 1899 encounter colored the subsequent ones. There was, too, an age difference of twenty-three years between the two men, but perhaps their relationship held some similarity to the one noted in Binet's last letter to Piéron. Commenting on the latter's disaffection with another psychologist, he wrote, "Isn't it curious that from the moment two scholars become occupied with the same questions, they understand one another so badly? It is both curious and disappointing . . ." (5, 7 July 1911). Be that as it may, at the centenary conference honoring Binet's birth, Piéron's *Souvenirs* lacked the enthusiasm of the other contributors (286).[9]

Society for the Psychological Study of the Child

At about the same time that Simon came to him with the offer of such a large number of experimental subjects at the colony of Perray-Vaucluse, Binet also had the good fortune to be asked to join the newly founded *Société libre pour l'étude psychologique de l'enfant* hereafter referred to as *La Société*. This gave him both a "cause" to support and an opportunity to be allowed to go into the schools for his own experiments. *La Société* was founded to give teachers and school administrators an opportunity to meet to discuss problems of education and to be active participants in research investigations. It was exactly the sort of forum that Binet needed, for here he could press his ideas about the need for a union of education and psychology. He had hardly become a member before he emerged as the prime mover of the organization.

It was not long before he persuaded the board of *La Société* to establish a publication, a *Bulletin*, which Binet edited. It provided a record of the so-called research carried out by the participant members, and of the monthly meetings that reveal Binet as a paternal and directing force. He cajoled and stimulated his *confrères*, guided and interpreted their studies, and infected them with his own enthusiasms and viewpoints. Members of this *Société* spearheaded the movement to arouse the Ministry of Public Instruction to do something on behalf of retarded schoolchildren. It was as a leader of *La Société* that Binet was appointed to the famous study Commission from the vantage point of which he saw the compelling need to find

[9] In 1964 Piéron's attitude was still generally critical and cool toward Binet (256), and there appears to be corroborative evidence for this antagonism in the fact that Reuchlin, Piéron's student, scandalously disregarded Binet completely in his article on "French psychology" (*J. of Hist. of Beh. Sci.* 1 [1965]: 115-23).

a way to differentiate those children who could learn normally from those who could not. As a result, he and Simon forged the instruments that became in turn the 1905, 1908, and 1911 exemplars of the metric intelligence scale.

Disappointment and Distress

The year between mid-1901 and mid-1902 was a time of deep heartbreak for Binet. In the first place, his close friend, Léon Marillier, a *Directeur des études* at the School for Advanced Studies and a philosopher with interests in psychology and primitive religions, drowned when his canoe capsized on the Côte du Nord. Simon believed that Binet was so greatly affected by this death that "his fun-loving nature was profoundly and lastingly influenced, so much so that he ceased writing the revues and vaudevilles that, in his leisure time, he had so much enjoyed creating both with and for his daughters and friends" (248).

At about the same time, Binet was trying to obtain a professorship, first at the Collège de France and subsequently at the Sorbonne. He had never been appointed to a professorship in France, and since he was the foremost, if not the only, French experimental psychologist, he must have felt that he deserved one of these posts.

As it is not unusual to do in European universities, and as it is required in France, Binet proposed himself for the two positions, and in close succession. In the spring of 1901 Ribot resigned his "chair of experimental psychology" that had been created for him at the Collège de France, and Binet sought this post. To his very close friend, Paul Passy, *Directeur des études* at the School for Advanced Studies, he wrote:

> You know perhaps that Ribot has just resigned, and that I am presenting myself against Janet Pierre [*sic*] to replace him. It will be a rough campaign, in which I am happily supported in the most vigorous manner, and if I lose, it will not be my fault. I have thought that among the professors at the Collège de France whose voices I am seeking, you have two friends, Chavaunes and especially Havet. I am asking you to approach them on my behalf. It is evident that they will not want to favor me solely

because you are my friend, but I do wish, however, that they will not commit themselves basically to Janet without having listened to the pros and cons and without having themselves conscientiously examined my record [*titres*]. It is over twenty years that I have been active in psychology, as you know; I educated myself all alone, without any teacher [*maitre*]; and I have arrived at my present scientific situation by the sole force of my fists; *no one*, you understand well, no one has ever helped me. I have done experimental psychology—the title of Ribot's chair—and I am really the only one in France who has done so. Neither Ribot nor Janet have done it; the former is a critic, and the latter carries on pathological psychology with hypnotism, hysteria, etc . . . [3, 4 July 1901. It appears that Passy sent Binet's letter on to Professor Havet].

Pierre Janet was elected to the post. This appointment left open his position at the Sorbonne as *chargé du cours de la psychologie expérimentale.* Binet then tried to secure this appointment. This time he wrote directly to Professor Havet, who seems to have had an influence with men at the Sorbonne who would vote for Janet's successor:

The post office has again made a stupid blunder in preventing your receipt of the letter that M. Rousselot has certainly written to you. Here is what it is about: I am presenting myself for the course in experimental psychology that Janet had at the Sorbonne. . . . I have as my competitor [George] Dumas, one of my friends, in fact; the vote will take place in the assembly of professors (titulary and adjoint) on Saturday, the 15th of March at 3:30 o'clock. I am no longer unknown to you; my friend, Passy, has spoken of me to you, and moreover you were at the Collège where you heard the discussion and report of M. Marey, which, I have been assured, was very favorable toward me.

I believe I have some chance of succeeding at the Sorbonne, where I shall be defended by M. Boutroux. I am older than Dumas, and I believe that I can say—for it is the exact truth—that he has neither my scientific titles, nor my authority, nor my age. He is, I am told, more scholarly than I. I am a doctor of sciences and am reproached for not being a doctor of letters; but a month ago I was exempted from obtaining the *licence* [roughly equivalent at that time to an American M.A.], and I shall deposit my two theses for the doctorate of letters *tomorrow*. I am then *en règle*.[10]

I had thought that you would be able to speak about me to some of your colleagues; I fear that the vote may be run through by [a margin of] two or three voices. Ms. Lafaye, Geuraud, Collégnoir, Thomas, etc., are inaccessible to me. Although time presses, if you can give me an appointment, I would be very willing to come . . ." [3, 11 March 1902].

But George Dumas was elected to the post at the Sorbonne.

It appears that Binet must have tried a third time, for among Havet's letters in the Bibliothèque Nationale there is the last page of a letter that suggests that Binet had again sought a professorial post. The date disappeared with the missing first page. On the last one he wrote:

. . . I have rather counted on you to insist on the very small importance of the titles of chairs. In a chair of medicine, Claude Bernard taught physiology, and d'Arsonval does the same. Marey, in a chair of the history of organized bodies, improved the technique of registering movements and analyzed the flight of birds. Just recently Tarde worked on sociology in a chair of modern philosophy. No one has complained. It is not the title that is important, but the personality of the professor. I truly believe that Bergson's scruples would yield if someone of your authority would press this idea in the assembly. . . . I am sending you with this letter my list of publications, hoping you will ask to read or to skim some of them (3).

Binet himself has unwittingly solved this mystery in two letters to Larguier. On 27 May 1904 he wrote: "I have presented my candidacy at the Collège de France. Janet is unalterably opposed. That saddens me, but does not stop me . . ." On 2 June 1904, he wrote again: "I have almost completed my visits. I would have presented myself for the chair left by Tarde, but I believe that Bergson is going to

[10] Simon recalled that Binet had written a thesis in Latin, but the records in the Bibliothèque Nationale have not disclosed any evidence of it.

take it in exchange [for his present one]. I will request for myself a change of his [presumably Bergson's] title to scientific philosophy or something like it. Now you know as much as I do. . . ." The letters say nothing more about the matter, but it is evident that his candidacy was again stillborn. In 1902 Binet had lost twice, once to a psychiatrist and once to a philosopher, whose chairs included "experimental psychology" in their titles! Now in 1904 his rejection by academia was complete.

Why was Binet rejected for three chairs? In the case of Ribot's professorship, the reason is not far to seek: Janet had been a "substitute professor" for Ribot at the Collège for a year or two, and "had worked with him for years" (256, 1960). When Janet was eighty years old, he himself wrote: "Ribot did me the honor of choosing me as his substitute at the Collège de France; he helped me to obtain his chair when he decided to retire; he also upheld my candidacy for the Institute" (271, p. 27). In other words, Ribot was Janet's *patron,* Janet was in Ribot's cluster of followers, and, according to Clark (273, pp. 55-58), a basic requirement for university promotion was membership in a cluster around a distinguished *patron.* Ribot's mantle, therefore, easily fell to Janet. Likewise, George Dumas was also in Ribot's cluster. He himself has provided this information in a commentary on his early years: ". . . as a former student of Théodule Ribot . . . I worked under his direction from the time of the normal school [École normale supérieure]. I followed his courses at the Sorbonne, and then at the Collège de France during all the time he was a professor there . . ." (271, p. 37). He had the further advantage over Binet of being an *agrégé* in philosophy, a doctor of medicine, and, of utmost importance, a doctor of letters. Terry N. Clark has furnished a bill of particulars of the qualifications for a professorship at the Sorbonne: "The ideal type included a brilliant secondary school record followed by study at the exclusive training school for future *universitaires,* the *École normale supérieure;* an *agrégation* in the subject which at the time enjoyed great prestige and attracted many of the best students—philosophy; several years' experience at teaching philosophy in provincial *lycées;* study in Germany with a Ministry of Education fellowship; completion and successful defense of two theses for a state *doctorat dès lettres.* Nonacademic, but far from negligible personal characteristics, were petty bourgeois family origins (ideally with a father as a primary school teacher), a strong sense of French nationalism and passionate devotion to the Republic, militant anticlericalism, and Radical Socialist or Socialist political preferences. . . . The overshadowing religious issue was Catholicism versus non-Catholicism, or more precisely, clericalism versus anticlericalism" (273, pp. 55–56).

Binet met none of these conditions, except probably anticlericalism. In fact, he was even nominally a Catholic. He did not attend the "right" university, he did not study philosophy, he failed to learn German and thereby to be in line for a fellowship to Germany, his family were among the upper classes and well-to-do, and no strong socialistic attitudes were visible. Indeed, he was too busy or unconcerned even to take much interest in the Dreyfus case, the cause célèbre that shook French academia perhaps even more than it did the rest of the population. He did write to Havet a judiciously composed letter to suggest that the defense should prepare a synoptic table of all the asserted proofs and pertinent refutations of culpability, so that it could be consulted readily, without relying on memory or the tedious consultation of the records (3, 19 August 1899). If political preferences were as significant as suggested, he was too neutral to satisfy the excited mood of the period.

On another level of discussion, Piéron felt that personality factors were prominent in Binet's rejection. He characterized him as "difficult, dominant—perhaps even domineering" (247) in the laboratory, a statement in which his bias is almost certainly manifest. He added a further pertinent fact by saying that Binet never left the country to attend meetings of any kind.[11] Ed. Claparède underscored this observation when he wrote:

[11] This contention has further confirmation in contemporary reports of several international congresses of psychology. With

With Binet I had much more lasting associations [than with Beaunis]. But it was certainly not at a congress that they were primed. The immortal author of the "tests" never attended any one [of the International Congresses held abroad], and I believe that he made only a brief appearance at the one in Paris, in 1900. When I urged him to attend the one in Rome or Geneva, I came up against his slightly enigmatic smile, and I had the impression that his mind was irremediably impermeable to a suggestion of this kind. Also Binet, whose name is one of the most universally known among psychologists, was himself little known personally by his colleagues. Undoubtedly, always taken up with some new problem, and convinced solely of the fecundity of experimentation, he rejected instinctively the thought of the "vain chattering" at the Congresses, which resolved nothing . . . (271, pp. 144–45).

It seems more probable that, without a solid professional status, he was ill at ease in such academic gatherings. In conditions in which he felt accepted and recognized he seems to have been very effective and quite comfortable, as in the leadership of *La Société,* where the members were largely school people rather than professional psychol-

---

regard to at least two, those in London in 1892 and in Rome in 1905, papers written by Binet were read by someone else; in Munich in 1896, we find that Binet and Courtier "collaborated on a paper—on 'the influence of the emotions on the capillary circulation' " and that "Binet presented a paper on individual psychology," stressing the importance of studying complex processes. But we also find: ". . . among the absentees . . . were Wundt, Sully, Binet, S. Hall, Delboeuf, and Müller" *(Am. J. of Psychol.* 8 [1896–97]: 142).

One wonders if Binet was also absent from the two International Congresses held in Paris in 1889 and 1900, where among the 203 present in 1889 were many whose names still ring: Helmholtz, Hering, Exner, Bechterew, Beaunis, Ribot, Bain, William James, Jastrow, Wundt, Münsterberg, Flournoy, Delboeuf, Freud, Babinski, Bernheim, Hughlings Jackson, Lombroso. Ribot substituted for Charcot as president, and Taine and Magnan were vice-presidents. By 1900 there were 529 members. Binet's name, along with those of Janet, Ribot, and Richet, was among the French group *de Propagande;* he may or may not have been present (285, p. 401).

ogists, and also in Romania where psychology was embryonic and he was heralded as an eminent authority. In fact, Simon has said that Binet was "lively when he was in a sympathetic environment" (296, p. 346).

Moreover, Binet's assertion in the letter to Passy that "no one has helped me" might have glazed the eyes of the voting contingent who could recall the kindnesses and influence of Ribot, Beaunis and others. It also underlined the fact that Binet had no *patron*. Nor was he even favored by the interested friendship of Marillier because of his premature death. Also, the "decline of the laboratory" mentioned by Piéron may have been a factor in influencing votes against him. Binet's own work was at full gauge, but he had largely moved out to the schools and institutions for his subjects and seems to have lost his drive to spark the laboratory into productivity. Whatever the reasons were, the first experimental psychologist in France was passed over for a professorship by its two greatest institutions of higher learning.

Great Productivity, 1901–11

The disappointment over his failure to obtain a professorship may have depressed Binet's spirits, but it did not dampen his enthusiasm for research. In fact, he seemed to be driven by a daemon. After 1901 article after article came from his pen dealing with many aspects of personality. Probably the most famous of these, apart from the scale itself, was *L'Étude expérimentale de l'intelligence*, a probing study of personality, for which his two daughters were again the subjects. One of his pressing preoccupations in this period was the effort to discover some way to distinguish between intelligent and nonintelligent children. "I shall strive," he wrote, "to judge childrens' intelligence by special tests" (82, p. 415). There was no area that he refused to consider. He spent many years trying to find physical indices: cephalometric studies, graphology, the shape of the hand, anthropometric measures, indeed any physical characteristics of individuals that could "reflect a personal style" and measurable differences. He had already studied psychological characteristics, and with members of *La Société* he was pursuing others, for example, memory. But his results were unsatisfactory and inconclusive. Early in 1904 he published a long, descriptive "psychological portrait" of the novelist Paul Hervieu, almost as an admission of his discouragement in failing to discover any "relatively short means of portraying personality characteristics by means of tests." At the same time Henri had reported the same failure in a joint paper written with Binet at a conference on experimental psychology in Germany.

That fall Binet was appointed to the ministerial Commission that was to report on the plight of retarded school children in France. He quickly discovered how blind the official attitudes were. The members were interested only in administrative problems, and were unconcerned with any objective means of selecting the retardates from among the normal children. Binet realized that he must provide this, and soon afterward came the flash of understanding that allowed him to see that an effective test must be oriented to "tasks or behavior" rather than to so-called faculties. The next year Binet, with Simon's help, published the first crude metric scale of intelligence. This and the two revisions of 1908 and 1911 were to make famous Binet's name. He himself knew better than anyone else the scale's limitations and imperfections, and understood the need for further research.

He was not a man to concentrate all his energies on a single idea or problem. In 1905 Binet and friends from *La Société* established the first pedagogical laboratory in France and attempted to create an international committee of pedagogy to coordinate work done all over the western world. The committee did not succeed in taking hold, but the pedagogical laboratory became a continuing responsibility. Nonetheless, this did not interfere with his writing and research, for between 1905 and 1908 he wrote on the psychology of court testimony and collaborated with Simon on a book about the mentally retarded and a long article on language and thought. He also edited *L'Année* annually, and the scale, too, was not forgotten, for in these years he and Simon completed the massive labor needed for the development of the 1908 revision. In light of these labors, it is amusing to find Bertrand (267, p. 325) and later Varon (303, p. 126) explaining that poor health prevented him from writing anything for *L'Année* in 1907! It is especially amusing in light of the fact that, in addition to all of this work, these were the years when Binet embarked on his first and only flight into metaphysics.[12]

After Simon moved to Rouen the projects that the two men worked on together were varied and on several levels. They made meticulous and exhaustive observations and tests both of imbeciles and of psychotics, drawing tentative hypotheses about the different natures of these psychopathologies. These long investigations resulted in instructive publications in 1909, 1910, and 1911 that seem to have been given little notice by students of clinical psychology.

During this same period the pedagogical "crusader" also published *Les idées modernes sur les enfants,* a popularly written book for teachers and parents and one that gives the reader a more personal feeling for the man than anything else he wrote. In fact, many years later a member of *La Société* wrote a little article entitled "After rereading *Les idées modernes. . . .*" in which he commented on Binet's "relevance and humanity," and his marvelous aptitude for being surprised and fascinated by his observations of childrens' behavior (*Bull.* [1958] No. 442, pp. 34–40). Despite its popular cast, *Les idées modernes . . .* contained many of Binet's hypotheses about intelligence, and in one chapter Binet expressed a hope and an intention to complement his work on intelligence with tests of special aptitudes. In 1910 he believed that he had made a noticeable beginning on this project, but his death in 1911 cut short any development.

[12] The vast bulk of Binet's work was in the field of psychology. This venture into philosophy does not fit into any of the categories needed to discuss his psychological thought. Therefore, in this book a short discussion of his metaphysics has been put into an appendix (pp. 339–47).

Some Personal Circumstances of Binet's Life

During all these years of intense mental activity, of course Binet also had a personal life. Regrettably the evidence to give a full description of it is meager and so it must be pieced together as well as possible from incomplete documentation. His marriage to Laure Balbiani, whose parents lived in Paris, plus the fact that Binet's mother and several other relatives also lived there, indicates a larger family relationship than that of wife and daughters. During the first years of their marriage the young Binets lived in Paris, on the rue du Regard and rue Madame, on the Left Bank. Later they moved to Meudon, a pleasant suburb, where they stayed until 1908; they again returned to Paris, to the avenue de Maine, where Binet died.

Simon described the house at Meudon as very attractive, set in the inevitable little garden, with four rooms on each of two floors and furnished with antique pieces. In the protocols of *L'Étude expérimentale de l'intelligence* Alice and Madeleine mention the servants in friendly terms and talk of pleasant experiences in the garden, of pets, bicycles, a new phonograph, and agreeable summer vacations at St. Valéry-en-Caux and later at Samois-en-Seine near Fontainebleau. Binet, too, liked to walk in the magnificent forest of Fontainebleau and was an enthusiastic bicyclist (142, p. 235). He once wrote to his friend Larguier that he and his daughters had ridden about sixty miles in one day (4, 12 July 1903). Evidently Samois also became almost a second permanent residence, for he was elected a municipal councillor there, and "took this work very seriously, for several years" (251, 10 December 1968).

There is other evidence that the Binet family had delightful times together. Alice shared in her grandmother's artistic talents as a painter, and Madeleine's daughters say that their mother was a talented sculptress (251, 10 December 1968). Binet also was interested in art, and mentions visits to the Louvre (*Psych. Rev.* 1 [1894] : 346). Later he even wrote two articles about painters, one of them with Alice (145 and 146). Family fun sometimes followed a hobby, common to French intellectuals of that time, which involved little vaudevilles, written by Binet for his family and friends; it apears that members of the family acted in some of them. In a letter to Larguier he excused himself for his delay in writing by announcing: "My *Revue* has been successfully played, with pleasure for the whole family" (4, 22 September 1906).

After about 1900, however, these relaxing, spontaneous self-expressions occurred less and less often (248). A sort of pall crept over the household. Madame Binet's father died in July 1899, "after five months of a very cruel illness" (3 August 1899), and apparently his death caused his daughter much distress. She herself was in ill health as long as the Simons knew her, beginning in 1899: ". . . depressed, sad, and languishing. . . . She almost never went out socially and rarely entertained others," although on the few occasions when the Simons did see her, they found her "sweet, gracious, and pleasant" (248).

In addition to the relative social insolation that their mother's ill health must have imposed on Madeleine and Alice, the two girls did not go to school; they were taught at home. There is mention of a tutor in German, but for the most part Binet speaks of giving the lessons himself (90). Perhaps he realized too late that this kind of training, which separated the girls from their peers, was a mistake, because in 1909, when they were in their twenties, Binet wrote the following:

> . . . The instruction of children must start with a study of individual psychology. Of course, if one exaggerates any good idea, one makes a mistake; no curriculum can be made to fit exactly the aptitudes of each child, *for we are not alone in the world. We live in a time, in a milieu, among individuals to whom we must adapt ourselves.* Adaptation is the sovereign law of life. Instruction and education, which have as an objective the facilitation of this adaptation, must necessarily take account of these two data together: the environment with its exigencies, and the human being with his resources [142, pp. 11-12; italics added].

Binet must have recognized how the girls' confined social relationships had affected their friendships. As they grew into young womanhood his anxieties about them began to weigh so heavily upon him that in his last years he shared his feelings with Simon, who, calling them "cruel cares," felt convinced that they had hastened, if not caused, his death. Simon added that "the illness of one of Binet's daughters"—almost certainly Alice—in several specific instances "caused her father to be beside himself with anxiety" (296, pp. 346 and 351; 248). Madeleine's marriage was also a cause of great distress to her father: "Much against his wishes, [in 1910] she married a cousin, Edgard Binet."[13]

In addition to his family worries, Binet must have borne many painful reminders of his failure to receive recognition through a professorial appointment and thereby a status that he justifiably coveted. Furthermore, his tests, so enthusiastically hailed abroad, were ignored, even abused, in France, except by some school people in *La Société*. Claparède reports a capital story:

> We know well enough that the schools were far from adopting the appropriate measures by which Binet's recent pedagogical psychology could have benefited them. In this epoch [about 1910] the lack of comprehension in school circles, their animosity to Binet's ideas, in France, were unbelievable! The famous "tests" were put up to ridicule. I remember a primary inspector whom I met in Lyon about 1911 who did not stop chaffing about the research of our illustrious friend, showing also his own self-conceited stupidity, for certainly he had understood nothing! It was he, I believe . . . who criticized the tests for including questions to which the pupils could not successfully respond, since they were not a part of the school curriculum!

[13] Simon indicated that Binet was particularly disturbed because of the hereditary dangers that he recognized as the possible consequences of such a consanguineous marriage. The two daughters who were its issue, however, are attractive and well-endowed. Madeleine's sister Alice did not marry until 1928, and there were no children.

Binet was at first amused by the grotesque criticisms, but I believe that after awhile he felt some bitterness at the deaf opposition that he received [271, p. 144].

The foreign appreciation was, of course, sweet for Binet, but who would not prefer the recognition of his fellow countrymen?

What sort of man was Alfred Binet? Obviously he had great driving energy. " 'One of my greatest pleasures,' " he told a friend, " 'is to have a piece of white paper to fill up. I work as naturally as a hen lays eggs.' Better still: work amused him . . . It was also play . . ." (271, p. 145). He must have been a prodigious reader to have gone through all those books and articles that he reviewed or discussed in reports of his own research. There are descriptions of him at his desk working out projects, discussing them with his assistants on long walks or in his study, and visiting schools and hospitals with his briefcase stuffed with papers. He was a formidable man at these times, for Binet seems to have been "all business," austere, and anxious to be on with his work. No matter who his coworker, Binet wrote the articles or books himself. Simon's amusing description of Binet's criticisms of the first piece he brought him is most enlightening. Binet was "brutally frank" in his comments; he incisively pointed out the errors in composition, and gave the young man a lecture on the necessity of writing with vigor, dramatic force, and clear direction (296, pp. 348–49). One needs only to read his writing to see that he followed his own advice. Perhaps this statement should be modified, for, although Binet did develop his material in the "positive fashion" that he urged upon the young Simon, he usually ended by admitting that more research should be done before definite conclusions could be asserted.

Binet was probably most happy when he was working with his collaborators or perhaps even alone. He did not like the company of strangers. He was a reserved man who, according to Claparède, "approached every unknown person with a sort of timidity that was basically an instinctive distrust of charlatans and bluffers, but who was most amiable upon further acquaintance . . ." (271, pp. 144–45). Claparède described the help that Binet gave him as a very young and inexperienced student researcher in psychology. Binet seems always to have had patience with bright and sincere young men. The English psychologist Sir Cyril Burt has written: ". . . I had myself taken the liberty of corresponding with Binet . . . and it is a pleasure to recall how fully he replied to the numerous inquiries of a young and importunate investigator [which Burt was at that time]" (271, p. 170). To the Americans Henry H. Goddard of the Training School at Vineland, New Jersey, and Edmund Huey of the Lincoln State School and Colony, Lincoln, Illinois, he gave agreeable receptions, both to their visits and their correspondence. And Simon claimed that he generously gave the young Lewis Terman the rights to publish an American revision of the scale "for a token of one dollar," although this may be an apocryphal story, since it has been impossible to trace any correspondence about the transaction. The aloofness Binet showed to strangers seems to have carried over to his relations with many of his peers in the profession, but this aloofness may have stemmed more from diffidence than from anxiety. It did, however, increase after his rejection from any professorial rank at the turn of the century.

Binet had few close friends. Even Simon was not often taken into his confidence about personal matters. Nonetheless, many times in letters to Simon and to Larguier his deep affection shows through his words. Since Larguier was living in Lausanne, Binet saw him infrequently, but his letters are full of "wishes" that he would hurry back to Paris, or of pleasure in having seen him there. In one letter he mentioned sympathetically Henri's injuries following a bicycle accident, Simon's "exhaustion" from long hours working in Saint Anne's Hospital, and Larguier's own painful indisposition, adding: "I can say that my three best collaborators, those whom I love most, or rather, the only ones whom I love, are suffering in poor health" (4, 14 August 1904). Concerning Henri's unreliability, he wrote: "I am very much annoyed, but I do not have the strength to hold a grudge . . ." (4, 1 April 1904).

Binet did have a large number of acquaintances with whom he sustained personal associations over many years and with whom he was more comfortable and spontaneous than with professors. These included both men in *La Société* where he was a mentor and those who were close to him in his other psychological labors. These people may not have loved this man, but he was admired and greatly respected in many quarters.

Institutionalized patients who were research subjects for Binet also must have seen another side of his character. Simon says that "to examine patients with him was always an extreme pleasure, for he brought to the situation so much imagination! In a happy manner, he seized every occasion to talk with a patient . . . He entered into the action with an infinite naturalness" (296, p. 347). And speaking of the long daily observations of imbeciles in the hospital, Simon continued: "What afternoons we passed with these subjects! What delicious conversations we had with them! And what laughs, too!" (297, p. 412). These descriptions provide an excellent reason for believing that work was also play for Binet.

A statement written by Madeleine two decades after her father's death provides a poignant, although rather formal, memory of him:

> My father was above all a lively man, smiling, often very ironical, gentle in manner, wise in his judgments, a little skeptical, of course—moderate, ingenious, clever and imaginative. Without affectation, straightforward, very good-natured; he was scornful of mediocrity in all its forms. Amiable and cordial to people of science, pitiless toward bothersome people who wasted his time and interrupted his work. His facial expression was sometimes meditative, sometimes smiling. He always seemed to be deep in thought [267, p. 63].

Binet's religious views were those of many French intellectuals of the late nineteenth century. While he was nominally a Roman Catholic, he did not take communion (248). Even in 1888 he openly and forcefully declared his adherence to "determinism" as a basic postulate about human behavior (31) and affirmed Huxley's position that consciousness is an epiphenomenon (19). In 1906, although his hypothesis about the nature and role of consciousness had become unsettled and undecided, he proposed a kind of monism for the relation of mind and body.

From personal comments that Binet wrote concerning Hervieu's views there is a transparent indication of some of his own beliefs. Reporting his psychological study of this dramatist, Binet explained that Hervieu "gives some examples of precocious good sense . . .," and added:

> Although raised in the Catholic religion, by a family in which the women were communicants, M. Hervieu never had the least possible understanding of what faith is. During instructions in the catechism—for he had made his first communion—like everyone, he became frightened by the idea of eternal damnation, but at the same time his good sense, already awakened, did not comprehend at all the following contradiction: "I will be damned if I do not believe, yet I cannot believe voluntarily." One is much struck to encounter such an example of resistance to automatism in a child so young; it must be added, perhaps, such an absence of emotionalism, for faith is not only a matter of suggestion, it is also a need for adoration and veneration.
>
> In the work of several American authors, I have found that, of one hundred children raised in the same religious conditions as M. Hervieu, there are not ten who succeed in freeing their thought, as he did, by the sole means of his own critical and skeptical mind which examined the problem and accepted a negative solution with resignation . . . [99, pp. 13–14].

Apparently Binet was fully convinced that religious belief is basically irrational. In one of his reviews he wrote: "Faith is an emotional state . . . that cannot be either shaken off or consolidated by reasoning" (63, p. 552).

Binet had one avocation that was closely related to his desire to understand the psychology of human beings. In addition to writing the vaudevilles for family entertainment, he had always been an avid theatergoer. Simon has told us that he knew the works of all the major French dramatists of the day (296, pp. 351–57). After he was forty-five years old he even tried his own hand at the production of dramas, which were enacted at theaters in Paris. Between 1905 and his death he produced at least four plays, which, according to Simon, provided "one of the rare occupations that could distract him from his cruel [family] cares" (296, p. 351). Of these, *L'Obsession* (1905), *L'expériment horrible* (1909), and *L'homme mystérieux* (1910)[14] were coauthored with André de Lorde, director and actor, whom Binet called "the French Edgar Allan Poe . . ." (129, p. 98). The fourth, which he wrote alone, *Les invisibles,* was first performed after his death in 1912. In 1923 de Lorde produced in London a drama called *A Crime in a House of the Insane,* naming Binet as coauthor. It was probably based on a story that he and Binet had at some time discussed. All of these plays deal with psychopathological problems in plots of suspense and usually of horror. In one a man tries to revive his daughter's corpse with an electric machine; in another, a doctor fails to understand a patient's pathology and so is inadvertently responsible for the patient killing his own son. The most popular one, which ran for twenty-five to thirty performances at the Sarah Bernhardt Theatre,[15] portrays doctors prematurely releasing a paranoid-schizophrenic patient from the hospital, only to have him strangle his own brother. Throughout all of them the themes of pathological behavior and of stupid medical men undoubtedly reflect Binet's own interests and attitudes.

By 1911 the uncertainly diagnosed illness that took his life also probably influenced his vision of himself and his

[14] With regard to this play Simon wrote: "I walked with Binet for an afternoon in the quarter of the agitated patients at the Bicêtre [asylum] so that he could study those with the same kind of illness he was representing in *L'homme mystérieux*" (296, p. 352).

[15] His exertions are manifest in letters to Larguier: ". . . The play will take place at the Sarah B. on October 31st—it has filled my time . . . Write me more often than I write you. I am overwhelmed" (4 October 1910). And a few days later: "Our piece goes on on Wednesday at Sarah, and I am fagged out" (29 October 1910).

profession. The issue of *L'Année* that carried the second revision of the metric scale (1911) also contained a leading article by Binet that was almost a cry of despair for the status and future of psychology. Previously having insisted on controlled, systematic introspection as a necessary concomitant of probing psychological experimentation, he now became convinced that, while necessary, systematic introspection was definitely not sufficient or complete; unconscious functioning would thwart even the most careful investigations of the real contents and processes of thought. He reached the conclusion that neither the subject nor the experimenter could induce the mind to give up all its secrets. He sought a name for this inextricable bond of emotional and cognitive functioning, and chose the ambiguous term "attitude." Around these so-called attitudes he hoped to build a more or less "unified account of normal psychology." "If I could only have had five more years!" he confided to Simon during his last weeks of fatal illness. His despair for the future of psychology appears to have become naïve optimism. How could he hope for a "unified account of normal psychology"—in five, or fifty years? But dying men often speak as though they had forgotten the complexities of the world that they are about to leave, and perhaps a man who must die at fifty-four has the right to believe that he could have solved the perplexing problems that disturbed him had he been given only a few more years in which to try.

2 The First Ten Years: Errors Compounded and a Time of Crisis

In the latter years of the nineteenth century a French student could study man as a sensitive, intelligent being by combining work in philosophy, medicine, or biology, but there was no curriculum in France for the study of psychology. Actually Alfred Binet ignored these alternative routes and became a self-made psychologist. It is small wonder that his first efforts were something less than extraordinary; indeed, they led him into blind alleys. His first ten years might be called an era of failure, of "errors compounded," were it not for the fact that they obviously contained seeds of his later growth. His first paper in 1880 was followed by many others, but by the early 1890s he had withdrawn from or become noticeably silent about most of the viewpoints he had upheld forthrightly and doggedly for a decade.

The Bibliothèque Psychologist: Advocate of Associationism

He began in 1880 as a library psychologist, and soon became a particularly ardent follower of John Stuart Mill whom he once astonishingly called his "only teacher of psychology" (90, p. 68). He also accepted wholeheartedly the belief in mental images as the necessary basis for thought. Although he reported phenomena that must have made him suspicious and uneasy about this widely held hypothesis, it had such an aristocratic patronage (Taine, Charcot, Galton) that he dared not deny it. In the field of hypnotic phenomena and its methodological controls, however, he fell into his most serious errors. Here, in published debate, his loyalty to eminence and reputation led him astray to wage rough battles for Charcot and the Salpêtrière—and to lose! Here he fought fiercely for the "facts," only to be rudely unseated in the fray that finally, and publicly, unmasked his unsuspected personal biases that were rooted in his loyalty to the renown and celebrity of Charcot and others of his distinguished colleagues.

With his first brief article on "the fusion of similar sensations" (10) Binet announced his entry into the arena of psychology as a dedicated proponent of associationism. He began categorically: "We know that the association of ideas by similarity is one of the two principles that assures the succession of our thought," that is, the present sensation, idea, or feeling recalls former ones that resemble it. His main thesis was that, to the degree that two impressions are similar, they fuse and give the effect of a single one. Binet did not claim any originality for "fusion" as a property of resemblance, since, as he said, Herbert Spencer had given it definite exposition,[1] but he felt that it needed emphasis and illustration. His data consisted of differential thresholds on various body surfaces for tactile impressions from an aesthesiometer. However, in giving easy and homely illustrations for the reader, Binet suggested that "perhaps the differential thresholds [for example, between the forearm and the mid-back] were due largely to experience and exercise." Unfortunately, the self-taught Binet apparently had failed to do his homework well enough, for this first article was immediately attacked by a venerable gentleman of Wundt's generation, Professor J. L. R. Delboeuf of Liège, who was to be Binet's severest critic during the next ten years.[2] Delboeuf not only pointed out errors in Binet's observations, but also objected to his failure to credit Delboeuf himself for the claimed importance of "experience" in differential tactile thresholds; Binet had written as though the ideas were

[1] Binet's reference seems mainly to be Spencer's chapter "The Composition of Mind" in his *Principles of Psychology*, especially p. 182.

[2] Boring has identified Binet's critic as follows: "Next to Fechner and Müller, the Belgian, J. L. R. Delboeuf (1831-1896) of Liège played the most important role in psychophysics" (268, p. 426)

his own.[3] This must have been a salutary experience for a young aspiring psychologist. In fact, his next article came two and a half years later, and showed more careful documentation.

In this article on "reasoning in perceptions" (11) Binet spelled out clearly his conviction that all problems in psychology could be solved by the twin functions of association by contiguity and similarity. A quotation clarifies this position:

> The operations of intelligence are only diverse forms of the laws of association: it is to these laws that all psychological phenomena revert, whether simple or complex. Explanation in psychology, in the most scientific form, consists in showing that each mental fact is only a particular case of these general laws; from the moment that this proof has been accomplished, one can consider the explanation as definite, and carried out as far as it is possible to go, for the laws of association are the most general laws . . . they embrace all of psychology. . . . In applying these ideas to the subject that concerns us, we conclude: to explain reasoning is to determine by what combination of the laws of association this mental operation was brought about; simple in appearance, it is complex in reality, and reducible, in the last analysis, to the two functions of similarity and contiguity [11, p. 412].

In this paper Binet turned once again to books and armchair speculation, and, again, the main explanatory principle was fusion. Here he applied it to perception and reasoning, a much more complicated subject than the tactile threshold. "All of today's psychology books," he wrote, "repeat that perception implies reasoning," but he emphasized that they were wrong to infer that the two are similar *only in the end results*. They are also similar *in the process*.[4] Both should be represented by a syllogism, which

[3] Delboeuf wrote this in a note in the *Rev. philosophique* 10 (1880): 644-48.

[4] Binet credited Helmholtz with a similar doctrine, namely that perceptions are "unconscious inferences," emerging from analytical induction. Binet, however, insisted that the process was one of deduction, and introduced the concept of fusion to account for the process.

might, for example, appear as follows in perceiving an orange: from past experience it is known that every visual impression having characteristics of yellowness, circularity, smell, etc., is given by an orange; the visual impression I now sense has this character; therefore, this is an orange. The difference between reasoning and perception was in the awareness of the units. In reasoning, the will and reflection play a conscious part in using the major and minor premises, or the past and the present sense-impressions, while in perception a spontaneous "work of the mind" *fused* the premises, giving an immediate closure that prevented awareness of the process. He cautioned that "language is powerless to describe what [really] occurs." The process is unconscious, and, furthermore, we often do not have the necessary information to frame a syllogism; nonetheless, we *can* and *do* frame the perception. And fusion, he announced, is the key.

There was, however, a paradox to resolve. A perception requires former experiences in order to take place. What was the source of the *first* sense-impression, upon which the first perception was based? Spencer had posited "racially inherited experiences." Binet made brief mention of this hypothesis, although he did not use it in an outright fashion. He accused Herbert Spencer's explanation of perception as being "vague and far-fetched—satisfactory to no one," and Alexander Bain's as "banal."[5] His own paper, stressing the involuntary fusion of sensory images, was clearly not superior.

An Alliance with Charcot and the Salpêtrière

At about this same time (1883–84) Joseph Babinski, Binet's friend of lycée days, introduced him to Charles Féré who in turn introduced him to Jean Martin Charcot. The clinic at the Salpêtrière was now open to him, and for the first time he had some subjects to study. The importance of these mentally ill persons as subjects may well

[5] Binet characteristically made no distinctions among the persons whom he criticized. These two men, internationally known through their writings, were about forty years his senior.

have been enhanced by Ribot, since he regarded the distortions of psychopathology as a primary means of enlightening psychologists. This idea fitted Binet's own concern with normal psychology. He did not look at mental pathology through medico-clinical eyes, for he was first and always a psychologist. In 1884, therefore, by studying these patients he sought insights that might present useful understandings of the normal state.

Binet's first paper thereafter was on "theoretical and experimental research on hallucinations" (13 and 14), a rather exaggerated title since both the theory and the experimentation were limited. In studying these phenomena he was continuing his concern with sensation and perception, though in a content-area that had been debated for many years and in which he was merely a novice. "But," he queried self-confidently, "what matter the length of discussions and the number of words if the last one has not been spoken?" His subjects were "hysterical-epileptic" patients whom, for the most part, he observed in a hypnotized state; only years later did it become obvious that his experimentation was polluted by suggestion. He concluded that hallucinations are a pathological form of perception, with the past impressions, that is, the major premise, arising from earlier experiences "which have been diverted from the normal by particular states of the nervous centers, perhaps an organic lesion." How could he have escaped that heyday of organic hypotheses for all mental illnesses?

He claimed that his original contribution lay in "discovering" that hallucinations always utilized external physical objects as reference points. Under hypnosis, and the experimenter's suggestions, the hallucinated perceptions changed when the subject moved, or when one eye was closed or ocular pressure was applied, or when the subject looked into a mirror or through a prism or opera glasses. In all of these conditions and more, the changes in the external object influenced the hallucinatory responses "just as they would under conditions of normal vision." Sometimes a simple piece of paper would suffice as a referent when the experimenter suggested that the subject was looking at a photograph of himself. An amusing incident was provided by Wit . . . , a "rather pretty patient" who gained some notoriety through the years in which she served as Exhibit A in Binet's and Charcot's experiments at the Salpêtrière.[6] When she "looked at her [hallucinated] photograph," she commented: "I do have a lot of freckles, but not as many as that!" Although Binet considered at length the possibility of simulated responses in these hypnotic séances, he dismissed it to his satisfaction. Regrettably, his "tests" for simulation were not adequate; the experimenter's unrecognized suggestions crept in to vitiate the results.

Binet did add a modern and instructive note by pointing out the influence of social and educational factors in his patients' hallucinations. The subjects' major interests, preoccupations, professions or *métiers*, or religious beliefs were frequently evident. He concluded that "the nature of religious visions varies with the times and the places, and conforms always to the prevailing mythology."

Other aspects of perception, for example illusions and perceptions of distance and their physiological counterparts, continued to concern him. In addition, he was interested in *inhibition* or the paralysis of movements and perceptions under hypnotic states when, at the experimenter's injunction, the subject could not move or was unable to see an object that was in front of him. His doubts of the sufficiency of associationism to explain psychology were taking root, for he queried: "How could the association of ideas account for *not* seeing an external object that was actually present?" Within the next six months he published papers that dealt with hypnotism and responsibility (15), with studies of nerve vibration that caused him to conclude that hallucinations, memories, and perceptions have the same seat in the brain (14),[7] and with demonstra-

[6] Delboeuf later (192) tells us that "Wit . . . was often used in Charcot's demonstrations." It is very possible that she was the major subject for the demonstrations that Freud saw Charcot conduct.

[7] One instance threw doubt on this seat-in-the-brain theory: a patient, color-blind in her left eye, while seeing a bright red

tions of "transfer phenomena" that "proved" that movements and perceptions could be shifted from one side of the body to the other by magnets and that emotions could be reversed by the same process (16). This latter idea was soon to be the core of a controversy that brought Binet little satisfaction and some ill-fame.

When Binet arrived at the Salpêtrière, Charcot's studies on hypnotism had only recently been responsible for readmitting "The Master" (Charcot) to the Academy of Sciences. Honored for putting hypnosis "on a scientific basis," he had described the "physical states" of three distinct hypnotic conditions, namely, lethargy, catalepsy, and somnambulism, plus some "mixed" states. These were called "physical states" because they were believed to be effected, and even changed from one to the other, by rubbing the vertex of the patient's head, putting pressures on one side of the head or the other, or manipulating certain muscles and joints. Féré and Binet obtained Charcot's results, on the same kind of subjects, if not indeed *on the same subjects!* The Salpêtrière was a natural setting in which to find appropriate subjects, since Charcot's theory included his assertion that hypnotizable persons had deteriorated or suffered from very unstable nervous systems. Binet and Féré followed all his conditions and claims literally, and in addition "discovered" transfer phenomena. Their data were published with dogmatic flair, initiating a running debate with the Nancy school and its ally Delboeuf that was to continue for several years and in which Binet was a doughty protagonist.

During January, March, and April of 1885, Binet and Féré presented the phenomena of transfer in full dress (14, 15, 16). Explaining their experiments, they insisted that an act or its inhibition or a visual, auditory, or tactile perception would move from one side of the subject's body to the other when an aesthesiogen or magnet, "unknown

---

hallucinated man with her right, saw him only in gray with her left eye. The problem was rationalized by concluding that the gray experience resulted from "laziness in the nervous elements." It is interesting to pick up these retroactive evidences of "Maier's Law"! (278)

to the subject," was placed near him on that opposite side. One droll illustration must suffice: the experimenters requested Wit in a posthypnotic reaction to thumb her nose at a bust of Franz Joseph Gall with her *left* hand. She did this several times. Then, with the magnet hidden near the *right* side of her head, her gesture became uncertain "as if atrophied," she became restless, looked at the bust, and called it "disgusting." Then, after scratching her ear with her right hand, she used it to thumb her nose at Gall: "transfer" had been victorious!

Binet and Féré excitedly and vigorously pursued their observations. Shortly the magnet "influenced" not only the described transfers but also the modification of nonbilateral responses—"polarizations" of perceptions and emotions, as they called them. Binet admonished his readers to recognize the import of these results, since they were "entirely unexpected, and issued therefore from nature itself, thus showing an inflexible logic" (16, p. 375). In this study of "psychological polarization" (16) he and Féré reported that an hypnotically induced, hallucinated *red* cross, "seen" by the patient on white paper, would, under the influence of the "unseen magnet," first become a red cross with elongated complementary green rays between the arms, and then would change to rose and to white, surrounded by green rays. The experimenters reserved their greatest excitement, however, for the field of complementary emotions. Under the power of their magnet, hallucinated fears, for example, stimulated by a piece of rubber called a serpent by the experimenters, were turned to caresses; hate responses turned to love; joy to despair. From these experiments came our authors' exclamation that they had reached "a conclusion of capital importance, but so completely unexpected that one will perhaps be shocked at its novelty. . . . Complementary emotions exist just as complementary colors do. . . . The magnet has permitted us to establish this parallel, although the simple observation of normal states makes it already predictable." In their reports "many unanswered questions" were posited, but the phenomena of transfer and of polarization by the magnet were not among them.

It must be understood that the experimenters saw nothing mysterious in these phenomena, nothing extrasensory, and *no effects of suggestibility.* The magnet was a physical force acting on the nervous system—like electricity—and the phenomena supported determinism. The experimenters believed that they guarded against their subjects' simulation by putting them into a state of somnambulism, one of Charcot's three "physical states that was most certainly unsimulated hypnotic sleep." To be sure, the Nancy school soon made strenuous objections, and insisted that suggestion caused it all. But Binet and Féré insisted equally that the Nancyians' failure to understand and to achieve Charcot's nosological categories was responsible for their inability to replicate the Paris experiments. They singled out Hippolyte Bernheim and J. Liégois, whose work, which ignored the Charcot categories, they called "a veritable anachronism"; they further claimed that their own acceptance of the aesthesiogens as physical agents capable of eliciting response-changes fitted the practices of the day. They pointedly indicated that noted physicians and psychiatrists used them widely as therapeutic agents to modify the nervous system.

The nature of hypnotizable subjects was another matter on which the Nancy and Paris schools differed. Binet and Féré again took Charcot's position: "As much as we can judge of them after long experience," they wrote "hypnotizable subjects offer stigmata of neuropathology either in their present state or in their antecedent ones, and most of them belong through their heredity to the neuropathic family" (15, p. 278). And the best of these were the hysterics.

The publication of the transfer and polarization experiments inspired disbelief in the Nancy school, and the growing controversy persuaded Delboeuf to enter the conflict with conviction. He had been interested in animal magnetism since his student days at the mid-century, and later, anonymously, had even tried to correct public sentiment about "miraculous" stigmata in a notorious case by pointing out that they were instances of autosuggestion.

He followed the literature on hypnosis, or animal magnetism, and had especially been impressed by the publications of the Paris and Nancy schools. He had found credible the physical categories by which Charcot defined differentiations among the three states, but Binet's and Féré's publications on transfer and polarizations by means of the magnet produced astonishment—and incredulity. He wrote, "One fine morning I could contain myself no longer: I wanted to see." In December 1885, therefore, he journeyed from Liège to Paris (192). He tells the story so vividly that nothing can provide an adequate substitute for his words:

All the way to Paris I was reflecting on the experiments to be made and on the precautions that should be taken to prevent error. On the day of my arrival I saw M. Ribot who presented me to M. Binet who, the following morning, presented me to M. Charcot. The Salpêtrière was open to me.

There I was witness to the famous three states—lethargy, catalepsy, and somnambulism; there I saw the half-states and the stupefying "mixed states" [combined lethargy and catalepsy] shown differentially on each side of the body, when one eye was closed and the other open; even those expressing two contradictory feelings . . . love on the right, hate on the left; there I was shown in action the neuro-muscular hyperaesthesias; there, finally, I was present at the experiments on transfer. But when I saw how they did these last experiments; when I saw that they neglected elementary precautions, for example, not to talk in front of the subjects, announcing in fact aloud what was going to happen; that, instead of working with an electromagnet activated without the knowledge of either the subject or the experimenter, the latter was satisfied to draw from his pocket a heavy horseshoe; when I saw that there was not even a *machine-électrique* in the laboratory, I was assailed with doubts which, insensibly, undermined my faith in all the rest [192, pp. 7–8. It will be noted that these particular paragraphs were written three years after the visit to Paris].

Delboeuf remained several days at the Salpêtrière, talking with Taine, and witnessing demonstrations by Charcot, Binet, and Féré. An interesting record published a year later presents a dramatic picture:

Let us continue the recital of what occurred that particular day among us four. I will never forget those delicious hours. M. Féré and Binet are both young, both tall; M. Féré more reflective, it seems to me, and more accessible to objections raised; M. Binet more adventurous and more affirmative; the former with serious physiognomy, and a clear and profound gaze, the latter, with fine features and a mischievous expression. Between them sat . . . the placid and "appetizing" Alsacienne Wit . . . not only wearing a complacent look, but finding visible pleasure in getting ready to do anything that should be asked of her; then myself, the old scholar, head full of reflections and questions, but never having had at hand this kind of experimental offering, a veritable human guinea pig [*grenouille humaine*]. Around us, the most vast silences . . . [190, p. 143].

If for no other reason than that his writings frequently show a fearless, blunt, straightforwardness, it seems probable that Delboeuf at once expressed some of his objections verbally. In a Belgian journal in 1886 he wrote: "Before even entering the Salpêtrière I had not hidden from M. Binet my doubts of the true reality of these phenomena." And in the same article he added: "Perhaps some doubts arose also in the minds of the two young savants . . ." (191, p. 143). During the days of the demonstrations Delboeuf himself taught a subject to write in reversals, but was unable to persuade her to *transfer* to normal writing either with his magnetized knife, an iron bar, or a horseshoe. "Now these gentlemen," he wrote, referring to Binet and Féré, "claimed that she had not been able to transfer because her other arm would always contract." Delboeuf concurred, "But," he added, "it contracted from *suggestion.*" He noted that M. Féré "played Wit . . . as if playing on a piano . . . a light touch on any muscle—or even pointing to it without touching—made Wit . . . contract any muscle, even in her ear." Delboeuf could not duplicate these maneuvers or fully explain them. But he did warn the experimenters to note that the patient was subject to hysteria, an illness not really understood, and that she was the only subject who was so wholly successful in their project. "It is this fact that Féré and Binet have hidden from themselves in the studies that they have devoted to her," he reported (191, pp. 258–59).

It seems impossible that Féré, Binet, Charcot, and others at the Salpêtrière could have failed to read these articles in the *Revue belgique,* but if they did read them, they gave no sign. In addition, Delboeuf had told Taine and Charcot of his doubts that their subjects could not, as they claimed, later recall what had transpired during their hypnotic sleep. In fact, he made some brief demonstrations before them that supported his contention that such subjects *could* recall. No one in Paris, however, seemed inclined to give any serious attention to their Belgian critic. It was to be three or four years before his coup de grâce.

When Delboeuf returned to Liège, assailed as he was with many doubts, he was firmly prepared to put various problems to the test. He states that he undertook these tests "with absolute faith" in the reality of the three states described by Charcot, and that initially, following Charcot's admonition about the characteristics of hypnotizable subjects, he had used a young female hysteric. On the other hand, he was already a true unbeliever with regard to transfer by a magnet. His sturdy empiricism is disclosed in the following words:

> It must be understood that I hold no belief [in transfer and polarization]. But nothing should be denied on an a priori basis. Many times the story has been told that Darwin, having one day heard someone speak of the influence of music on the germination of plants, charged a musician to play the bassoon throughout several consecutive days, sitting beside some bean seeds that had been planted. I do not know whether or not the anecdote is true, but I myself would be capable of playing . . . the drum or the barrel organ before the moon itself, if someone maintained that it would be influenced [by these instruments] (192, p. 21).

By the following May Delboeuf published the first results of his work (189). His initial and brief experiments on transfer gave inconclusive results. By August he published a strong, unfettered attack on the contentions and methods of the Salpêtrière (190), especially as they differed from those at Nancy. He also pointedly indicated that from the first he had been entirely unsuccessful in trying to use young women hysterics as subjects. His experience had rather supported Beaunis's statements,[8] namely that "*somnambulisme provoqué* can be obtained very easily with a great number of subjects . . that very often hysteria and neurotic conditions are *unfavorable* to its production . . . that peasants, soldiers, workers with an athletic constitution sometimes fall into somnambulism at the first *séance*" (190, pp. 151–52). Delboeuf's first successful subject was "a young peasant woman, strong, robust, and sane—she was asleep in seven minutes." Furthermore, his conclusions from many experiments performed in the presence of several of his colleagues were that the famous "three states" were neither inevitable nor clear-cut, and that there was no evidence of transfer *when the conditions were properly controlled.* He maintained that the purblind Parisians had been duped by their belief that their hypnotized subjects were unaware of what they, the experimenters, were saying and doing.

Delboeuf had come to a definitive conclusion: "Suggestion," he said, as Beaunis, Liégois, and Bernheim had long been insisting, "is at the bottom of it all. . . . At the Salpêtrière the *somnambules* have no difficulty receiving suggestions from [the assistant]" (190, p. 147). Although he did not mention any one person or place, it must have seemed to the men in Paris that he was firing his volley directly at them when he wrote:

> Without any doubt there is an undeniable influence of the hypnotizer on the hypnotized—like master, like disciple. But the subjects themselves, principally the very first one, train the experimenter who directs them, and, without being aware of it, determine his method and his

[8] This was the same Dr. Beaunis who was to become the first director of the Laboratory of Physiological Psychology at the Sorbonne in 1889.

maneuvers. In a way then, turning the proverb around, one could say: like disciple, like master. This action of the first disciple on the master is then reported to other disciples who adopt his procedures, and thus are created the schools that have the monopoly of special phenomena . . . [190, p. 149].

From these experiments that I have reported it is clear that the hypnotized are eminently easy to influence by example, by words, by simple wishes. . . . The existence of several schools of hypnotism is, then, nothing but natural and easily explainable. They owe their birth to the reciprocal action of the hypnotized on the hypnotizers. Therefore their rivalry has no raison d'etre: they are all in the right. One will never be able to apply to better purpose the eclectic axiom that truth is relative to the times and the places. We can even add: and to the persons [190, pp. 169–70].

He concluded that a subject, like the famous Wit, could perform all the requests if he or she could see them done, or even if told about them—"all except perhaps those related to neuro-muscular hyperaesthesias or the double-states."

In November Binet entered the controversy on his own behalf and that of his colleagues in Paris. Entitled *"Les diverses écoles hypnotiques,"* four notes were addressed to "mon cher Directeur" of the *Revue philosophique,* two from Binet, with two replies from Delboeuf (20). They disclosed a taut, dogmatic, unyielding, and even sarcastic Binet, while the much older man clothed his irony in some famous words and scenes of Molière. Binet complained that Delboeuf, in trying to evaluate the two "schools," had failed to make clear the real question that divided them. He agreed that "suggestion" *could* bring about hypnotic phenomena such as those reported at Nancy. But the point of dissension concerned the physical phenomena, stimulated by physical frictions specific to the various states, "described with such care by M. Charcot and his students," and which the experimenters at Nancy had not been able to reproduce. Beaunis and Bernheim had therefore failed to resolve the question, the former for lack of sufficient evidence, the latter, "less prudent," by asserting that the three states and their physical concomitants were simply and only the result of suggestion.

Now, Binet continued, Delboeuf was "entering into this grave question," and his insufficient evidence showed that he also demonstrated only imitation, example, suggestion. His very descriptions showed a lack of precision in his approach. This was a technical matter and, citing page and line, Binet pointed out Delboeuf's errors, his ineptness in trying to create the "three physical states." If he wished to resolve the debate he must first produce *by suggestion alone* the precise neuro-muscular and cutaneous-muscular hyperexcitabilities, the upheld limbs kept steady without trembling and without modifying the respiratory rhythms, and the different "mixed" states. Finally, however, even if he and the Nancyians *could* do all these things by suggestion alone, which they had not yet done, this still would not rule out the production of hypnotic phenomena by "physical maneuvers," which both Delboeuf and the Nancy school seemed unable or incompetent to reproduce. It was this failure, therefore, that made it impossible to reconcile the rival schools. These were some of Binet's arguments.

Delboeuf replied that as for the "astonishing" neuro-muscular phenomena that he had witnessed at the Salpêtrière, he doubted his ability to reproduce them because he himself was not an anatomist. He asked those at the Salpêtrière to reconsider the circumstances of their first trials. Was it not possible that during the early trials some verbal suggestions had been given that continued to influence the subjects' behavior, although only the "physical" frictions were later employed? Apropos of the transferences, was it not possible that some unconscious suggestion had been given by the hypnotizer? "I have repeated these experiments with *absolutely negative,* and I would almost dare to say, *conclusive* results," he wrote. "I fear that the subject—and it is almost always or principally the case of this celebrated W. . . .—guesses what is wanted of her."

Delboeuf's reply was not satisfactory to his antagonist. Binet now asserted that Delboeuf's attempt to extricate himself had not been a happy one. On the one hand, he now "confused catalepsy with contracture by suggestion . . . his subject, who appears to me to be a commonplace somnambulist, does not present the slightest trace of lethargy and catalepsy in the descriptions of the author." Moreover, the fact that Delboeuf was not an anatomist displayed an "incompetence" that prevented his doing what he flattered himself to have done, namely, to reconcile the rival schools. His examples were insufficient. His insinuation that suggestion explains all hypnotic effects was "not sufficient to resolve the question pending between the Salpêtrière and Nancy." Here Binet stopped, without any word concerning transfer, the characteristics of hypnotizable subjects, the controls of verbal or behavioral cues, or the almost singular use of "the celebrated Wit . . ." as the main subject of the experiments.

In the fourth letter of the interchange Delboeuf had his tongue in cheek. He did not want to deprive M. Binet of his great pleasure in holding him up to the readers as ignorant of the differences between lethargy and catalepsy and catalepsy and contracture. At this point he described what he had thought was a "classic example" of each condition, and asked:

> Wasn't this a "classic distinction"? I thought so. But it appears not; my honorable contradictor declares that it is not. So be it. . . . I would be very much distressed not to be wrong for fear of diminishing his [Binet's] triumph.
>
> I will go even further. I confess ingenuously that, in my mind, there is no *fundamental* difference between contracture and catalepsy . . . since a light modification of word or gesture produces the one or the other at will. My friend responds to me victoriously that the effects that I obtain by these methods are of a psychical and not a physical nature. I see this now very clearly. "I was speaking prose without knowing it" [quoted from *Le bourgeois gentilhomme*].
>
> Again, one thing is clear to me: the depth of the debate is above my competence. Sganarelle beat Martine, and Martine wished to be beaten. I am not going to play the part of the Roberts.[9] Therefore, I give M. Binet back to

[9] This reference is to Molière's *Le Médecin malgré lui* wherein Sganarelle, the husband, frequently beats his wife, Martine;

MM. Beaunis and Bernheim. *Ne sutor ultra crepidam.* In French *sutor* is translated by *anvil,* and *crepidam* by *hammer.* J.D. [20, p. 538].

Although Delboeuf had thus claimed that he would be neither an anvil nor a hammer, by the fall of 1888 he began to pound mightily.

In the same issue of the *Revue* in which the four "notes" appeared, Alfred Binet, in a review of five and a half pages of small print, attacked Hippolyte Bernheim's second edition of *Suggestion and Its Application to Therapy.* He boldly and angrily repeated some of Bernheim's criticism of the school of the Salpêtrière. "Under the harshly critical title of 'Experimental illusions,' " he reported, "Bernheim regrets that so many distinguished minds, misled by an initial erroneous conception, have been brought to a series of singular errors that no longer allow them to recognize the truth . . ." (21, p. 560). Among the "errors" mentioned by Bernheim and denied by Binet appeared the three supposedly clear-cut physical states of hypnosis, transfer by the magnet, the effects of prisms, opera glasses, and the like on hallucinated perceptions, and the polarizations of color and of the emotions by magnets.

In indignant rebuttal, Binet replied to several points that he had omitted in his altercation with Delboeuf. After lashing out at Bernheim's "professed claims of his own priorities" in the field of hypnotism, he affirmed that Bernheim had given only new examples of long-known phenomena. As for the three states: "Since Bernheim doesn't find them," he expostulated sarcastically, "they don't exist! . . . But what dominates the book," Binet continued, "is a theory of suggestion pushed so far that it ends up by destroying itself. . . . Suggestion isn't everything, but only a beginning; to stop there is to have the key in hand and not to use it." Bernheim had omitted *physical* causes: ideas aroused in hypnotism were only images of former sensa-

but Martine, although protesting, gets some masochistic pleasure from these beatings. Their friend, M. Robert, tries to interfere in Martine's behalf, but gets hurt himself in the process.

tions that had been aroused by stimuli *(irritations)* in the external world. "We see, therefore, that the psychic method can come only after the physical method." Even the facts of "suggestion" could not exclude other possible procedures.

Binet went on to assert that Bernheim had failed to achieve the results of the Salpêtrière because he had failed to replicate the conditions: he used only *somnambules*, because the rare *grandes hypnotiques* were not, as in Paris, at his disposal. Moreover, he had done only a minuscule number of experiments with which he claimed to refute "experiments that had been repeated in Paris a thousand times."

Again, how could Bernheim dismiss transfer by the magnet so lightly, "a problem that had been so seriously studied by so many distinguished men"? Binet agreed that it was necessary to control the experimental conditions, to keep the subject [*but not the experimenter!*] in ignorance of the presence of a metal magnet, but added:

> There is nothing mysterious about its action . . . it acts physiologically like a weak electric current. To deny the action of the magnet on the organism would be to deny the action of electricity. Will M. Bernheim go so far? . . . As for us, we take no stand in the midst of these controversies; more patient than M. Bernheim, we await the light of new facts, which are indispensable to cut a debate of this nature [21, pp. 562–63].

The latter assertion is surely commendable, but hardly consonant with his heated attack.

Bernheim's response was unruffled (174). He reiterated his criticisms of the Paris school and added more, concluding: " . . . most of the phenomena described as physical are essentially of a psychical order."

Binet's retort appeared only in a footnote (26, p. 496), but he retracted nothing. By the end of that year, however, in his book *Le magnétisme animal*, coauthored with Féré, he had softened his position considerably. Nonetheless, Charcot, to whom the work was dedicated, remained the high priest of studies of hypnotism. They wrote of him:

> By applying the nosographic method to this study M. Charcot has admitted to the domain of observational sciences phenomena that had hitherto been regarded as beyond its range. . . . The researches of the school of the Salpêtrière have been the point of departure for a new scientific movement that continues to the present day [22, pp. 60–61]. . . . Hypnotism is adapted to playing a considerable role [in the study of normal] psychology [22, p. 77].

These authors were also categorical in their claim of objective verification for their experiments (22, Preface). However, despite these and earlier dogmatic statements, especially in the controversies with Delboeuf and Bernheim, Binet and Féré qualified many previous viewpoints. Hypnotizable subjects could come from any kinds of persons if they were sufficiently "fatigued," although "the hysterics remained the most effective," and in any case hypnosis continued to be "pathological in nature . . . even if it should be discovered that no one is refractory to it"! The importance of somnambulism as a "test" to rule out simulation was now vitiated and could not be trusted. Even the three physical states described by Charcot, and hitherto so boldly supported by Binet, were found to have lost their specificity, although Binet still defended "the master" bravely:

> One could create six, nine, different states—and even a greater number . . . . Hypnotism is a nervous state in which the symptoms can vary with the maneuvers that effect them. . . . Is it then necessary to conclude that M. Charcot's description is artificial? Not at all. At the time when it was made there was a question of . . . demonstrating the existence of a nervous experimental state through characteristics so gross or obvious that they could escape no one. M. Charcot chose subjects who showed these characteristics under an exaggerated form, which left no doubt of their certainty. . . . The doctrine of the three states contains, then, only a part of the truth. But this part has opened the way. . . . As long as profound hysterics exist, we shall be able to verify most of the results obtained by the school of the Salpêtrière [22, pp. 119–20].

The quarrel with the Nancy school was still primarily joined on the matter of hypnosis by suggestion as compared with physically induced hypnosis. Binet continued to dig himself deeper into errors that he would regret. "The two modes of experimentation are parallel," he wrote. "It would be difficult to say which is the most extensive. . . . Paralysis effected by either method probably results from modifications of the cortex, and is consequently a cerebral reflex. But what a difference in the two cases!" One demanded the aid of intelligence, while the other, induced by physical friction or pressure, did not. The Nancy school would not accept the latter category "only because they do not find it. . . . Their observations do not amount to much," Binet insisted, "exclusive of the facts of suggestion. . . . If it is true that none of [Bernheim's] subjects ever presented . . . any physical characteristics of hypnosis, if everything is summed up as suggestion, we are compelled to conclude that none of his subjects gives scientific evidence of really having been hypnotized" (22, pp. 123–25).

The transactions of transfer and polarization received full treatment in *Le magnétisme animal,* manifesting the authors' undaunted belief in their scientific validity. Added to the former effects, the experimenters now found even consecutive oscillations in which the action of the magnet was continuous, first producing and then removing visual and other sensory "anaesthesias" and movements. They warned, however: "It is clear that aesthesiogens act only on a certain class of subjects. . . . We insist that our present and future opponents should perform their experiments exclusively on hysterical patients who display evidence of profound hypnotism, and in whom sensitivity and muscular strength are modified by the application of aesthesiogens" (22, p. 196). The experimenters appear satisfied that they had not been guilty of making unconscious suggestions, since they specifically cautioned against using "unconscious gestures and words." They warned: "We cannot too often repeat that *only the first experiments are convincing,* since, strictly speaking, only these are . . . safe from unconscious suggestion. Every time an experiment is repeated there are some spectators who comment aloud. . . .

Moreover, at the second experiment the subject may *recall* the first, and so contaminate this experiment" (22, pp. 142–43). One cannot fail to wonder about the many reports based on "the celebrated Wit. . . ." The experimenters intended to forestall this objection by a sentence that was supposed to quiet any such doubts: "For these reasons among others, we have always taken care in our papers on hypnotism to give the results of the first experiment . . ." (22, p. 143). But nothing is said about the effects of using the same subject for so many experiments, even "first" ones. The changes in viewpoints expressed in this book, however, definitely gave ground to Delboeuf and Bernheim, although no retraction is mentioned.

During the following year (1888), Delboeuf, "always as spirited a fighter as he is an indefatigable worker" (236), reversed his earlier assertion that he would leave the field to others and vigorously assumed the role of the "hammer." The blows came first in the *Revue belgique* in articles that were reprinted immediately in a small book (192). The occasion for these publications was a report of Delboeuf's visit to Nancy, and there seem to have been at least two instigating factors for it. Delboeuf had found the men at Nancy more and more congenial as his own research in hypnotism fell into accord with theirs. Furthermore, he had been engaging in strong altercations in print with members of the medical profession in Belgium concerning "free versus restricted" uses of hypnosis. Although until recently the physicians had scorned hypnosis and had produced no research to enlighten the subject, they now wished to restrict its use to their own profession. Moreover, they had mocked Delboeuf for maintaining that the origin of its curative effects was autosuggestion: "After all," they declared, "[Delboeuf] is not a doctor, that is plain to see!" (192, p. 25). In this matter, also, the Nancy school had publicly supported Delboeuf.

There was a second, although certainly not a secondary, purpose in his publication: a full-scale critical comparison between the findings and theories of the schools of Nancy and of the Salpêtrière. *Le magnétisme animal* must have aroused him anew. Only a few months before its publication Binet had made scathing attacks on Delboeuf and Bernheim. Now, in this book, although he and Féré had demonstrated several unacknowledged points of agreement with their opponents, they had also again presented the phenomena of transfer and polarization with the magnet, and with utmost confidence. These were the very data that had initiated Delboeuf's doubts, and had impelled him that "one fine day" in 1885 to go to Paris. Since that time he had used the magnet among his own subjects "with absolutely conclusive results—*negative*—equally successful with false or true magnets, or without any magnet at all" (192, p. 19). Now he could keep silent no longer. His publication contains interesting descriptions of Bernheim and Liébault and their clinics, allusions to Beaunis and Liégois, and careful reports of his own experiments performed at Liège. But his major emphasis was on highlighting the controversy between the two schools, which he did in the following very dramatic style:

> I finally decided that [these phenomena] were due to training and suggestion. The experimenter at the Salpêtrière had regarded as essential some altogether individual, even purely accidental, characteristics presented by his first subject. Unconsciously using suggestion, he had transformed these into habitual signs; he was certain, always without knowing it, to obtain them from other subjects who reproduced them by imitation, and thus the master and his pupils reciprocally influenced one another ceaselessly to feed their errors .... When I became convinced of this, I rallied myself to the affirmations of the Nancy school.
>
> ... And what has the school of the Salpêtrière replied to these deductions, so strongly upheld by facts? That my subjects and those of Nancy were only "commonplace *somnambules*," that Paris alone had access to "profound hypnotism," while we—we had only "*le petit hypnotisme*," a hypnotism of the provinces!
>
> It would be difficult to find in the history of the sciences another example of an aberration perpetuating itself in this way by pure overweening pride [*amour-propre*]. This

conflict between the two schools is now considered as ended, but it still continues, thanks to M. Charcot's prestige.

M. Charcot is perhaps the savant of all Europe who has studied nervous illnesses more than anyone else, and who has done the most to interest scholars in magnetism. Noticing an analogy between certain phenomena—hysterical and hypnotic—he assimilated hypnosis to hysteria. Imbued with this idea he drew from two or three hypnotized hysterics the results that he expected without suspecting—who would suspect at the beginning?—that he had effected them himself; and there it was—now his opinion sits on the experiment. His students are convinced, since they have seen it. And so, first by conviction, then by training, and finally through respect, not daring to contradict the master, and by a point of honor not wishing to contradict their own preceding affirmations, illusioned and fooling themselves, they go along beside the most vocal facts without hearing them; they close their eyes before the most astonishing manifestations, and become entangled in a physical theory of phenomena that is of purely psychological origin! They rub the top of the head to make the subject fall into somnambulism, they open his eyes to put him into catalepsy, or by opening only one eye, they impress catalepsy on him on only one side. . . . They raise the corners of his mouth and the subject laughs; they contract his eyebrows, and the subject becomes angry; they join his hands and the subject prays.

Certainly when one sees these things they appear demonstrable and clear. I returned from Paris absolutely convinced. It is lucky for me that, against my intent, my first subject did not obey my maneuvers . . . or I would perhaps still be turned into *"le salpêtrièrisme."* The fact that, imitating in every point the Paris procedures, I fell almost in spite of myself into agreement with the results of Nancy has a high significance. At the present time "profound hypnotism" still remains the privilege of the great capital, and of the five or six hysterics . . . of the Salpêtrière. Neither MM. Liébault, Bernheim, Beaunis, and Liégois at Nancy, neither MM. Fontan and Segard at Marseilles, neither M. Forel in Switzerland nor M. Morselli in Italy—none have encountered them. . .

However, there was a proof [for me] to administer:

this was to train a subject who could rival Wit . . . [192, pp. 10–12].

Delboeuf realized this objective to his satisfaction and to that of his colleagues. By intentional suggestion he reproduced most of the phenomena of the Salpêtrière, and, to his surprise, with a subject who showed no signs of hysteria. Thus he had demonstrated, "without the shadow of a doubt," that it was all done with autosuggestion (192, p. 24). "It is not my fault, I like to believe, that the facts are as they are. But to set one's self against the facts is to want to displace Mont Blanc with the force of one's arms" (192, p. 25).

This attack, of course, thrust further onus on Binet's still unyielding viewpoints, undermined the credibility of the data concerning his favorite subject, Wit, and particularly demolished the "facts" connected with the use of the magnet. It was the "facts" now—"the facts so seriously studied and wholeheartedly accepted by so many distinguished men"—that were tumbling down. He had to acknowledge it, and he did so [grudgingly?] in the preface of his book *Les altérations de la personnalité,* published in 1892 but completed during the summer of 1891. His capitulation to suggestion versus physical stimulation is clearly revealed in the following quotation:

At first, when these studies on hypnotism and somnambulism were returned to an honorable place by M. Charcot, there was a great movement of enthusiasm. Since then, we may as well admit it, the enthusiasm has diminished; it has been recognized that these studies present a host of causes of error, which very often falsify the results without the knowledge of the most careful and prudent experimenter, and no one can say that he has never made a mistake. One of the principal causes of unceasing error . . . is suggestion, that is, the influence of the operator by his words, gestures, attitudes, and even silences . . . [43, pp. 67–68].

Regrettably, Binet had been led to a "master" and colleagues who were both naïve and dogmatic about psychological investigations; moreover, he had been fiercely loyal to them. It is highly probable that he was chagrined by his role. Simon recalled that Binet had never discussed the Salpêtrière with him, because, he surmised, Binet realized that he "had been 'taken in' by Charcot's international prestige" (248).[10] Perhaps he had become the hero-image that Binet had wished for from his father. At any rate, Binet learned clear lessons about the need for careful experimental controls, and for skepticism toward the contentions of "famous men." There can be no doubt that he had been profoundly affected by the dismaying experience wherein his unwitting errors were so egregiously discovered and exposed. His continued interest in suggestibility from that time forward has a crystal-clear lineage.

Diversification of Interests, 1886–90

Binet's work during these years was not by any means limited to these controversies. His other publications about sensation, perception, images, and reasoning—questions prevalent in Western psychology and philosophy at that time—indicate the diversification of his interests. For about six years, after 1880, his key concept was the principle of the association of ideas, which was built upon recalled images and present stimuli, cemented by contiguity and similarity in various relationships. *La psychologie du raisonnement* (19) embroidered this theme. Using hypnotized hysterics as subjects, and deductive logic as the primary methodology, it vigorously reflected the heyday of images, which were basic to all propositions.[11] He repeated

[10] The legitimate origin of Charcot's prestige is evident through his extensive and pioneering work in clinical neurology and neuroanatomy. See J. M. Charcot, *Lectures on the Diseases of the Nervous System,* The History of Medicine Series issued under the auspices of the Library of the New York Academy of Medicine, No. 19, pp. 399. Translated and edited by G. Sigerson. Hafner Publishing Company, 1962 (note provided by Dr. John K. Wolf).

[11] In fact, commenting on Galton's questionnaire-inquiries about images, Binet went so far as to say that the savants who reported that they had no images, or only a few, simply refused to admit them because they did not *believe* in them. They were afraid, Binet averred, of making concessions to materialism! And after all, the naïve, unselfconscious people, that is, "women

his earlier hypothesis (11) that perception and reasoning are both constructed on the same model. He further argued that images have properties "just as chemicals do . . . and those properties, having been put in motion by external sensations, follow as the night the day. . . . Images merely have to be brought together for them to become organized, and . . . reasoning follows with the inevitable necessity of a reflex. . . . We reason because we have in our brains a machine for reasoning" (19, p. 3). To this assertion he brought Wundt's support: "The mind," Wundt had said, "is a thing that reasons" (19, p. 146). Because there had been reproaches against English associationism for the "passivity" that such descriptions implied, and probably also because Binet had himself felt the same criticism, he tried to correct the situation with the following assertion:

> Images are not by any means dead and inert things; they have active properties; they attract each other, become connected and fused together . . . . The image is a living element, something that is born, transforms itself, and grows like one of our nails or hairs. Mental activity results from the activity of images as the life of the hive results from the life of the bees, or rather, as the life of an organism results from the life of its cells . . . . In all perception [and reasoning] there is *work* [19, pp. 187–88].

This book has been carelessly cited as a forerunner of Binet's conception of intelligence, a farfetched statement unless it is assumed that his interest in reasoning per se, as a "superior mental process," might have had its seeds in this study. Actually Binet's experimentation even with hypnotized hysterics was meager and poorly controlled; and although he wrote with flashes of wit and ingenuity, the marshaling of arguments was treated with hypothetical deduction that sounded more like a debate than a scientific treatise.[12]

---

and the unschooled," overwhelmingly reported images; altogether they were too universal to be denied (17, pp. 805f).

[12] In his review of *La psychologie du raisonnement* Pierre

Binet followed the same approach in an article applying the laws of associationism to the effects of the intensity of images (26). Using nine kinds of stimuli, he concluded that in all of them changes in intensity affected the intensity of the images and the subsequent actions dependent upon them. As in the case of hypnotism, he was drawn into errors with his analogies to electricity: "Images," he wrote, "vary in intensity as do muscular contractions . . . the association of ideas becomes a veritable *line of force;* it can be compared with the metal wire that transmits the force of a magneto-electric motor" (26, p. 476). For example, motor responses, based on images, were stronger for a red disk than for a green one, and black effected no activity at all. Again, reactions were augmented by belief and diminished by skepticism; they were also increased as the result of a strong, authoritative voice on the part of the experimenter. Furthermore, concurring with the opinion of the day, Binet claimed that there is a sexual character in hypnotic phenomena, especially in somnambulism, which makes the subject ready to do what "the beloved, sexually attractive hypnotist" expects of her or him.

It thus becomes clear that Binet appreciated the role of suggestion in hypnosis, but in his opinion it did not account for the results of physical stimuli like red disks, magnets, or vibrations of the scalp and muscles. This

---

Janet stated: "The method was indicated, and M. Binet has the honor of having written the first work in psychology founded on experimental researches by hypnotism; this first application of the method can only encourage the hopes that have been founded on it" (205, p. 188).

It would seem that M. Janet's "hopes" were overenthusiastic, given the poor methodological controls of that time, especially at the Salpêtrière. Varon's conclusions about the book, with her fifty years' advantage on Janet, appear more appropriate: "All the former arguments were brought together, as carefully ordered as an offensive array of pawns on a chess-board, and greatly elaborated. . . . This careful order lends to the book a spurious air of inducing its conclusion from experimental results, whereas the history of it shows a strained effort to find in experiments as much evidence as possible to support what seemed to Binet like a foregone conclusion" (303, p. 8).

dichotomy died hard with him. Although he reported one subject who had been hypnotically "paralyzed" so often that she "could have given a complete course on paralysis by suggestion," nevertheless he still affirmed that he had effectively guarded against simulation by forcing the subject, under hypnotism, to exclaim *"Sapristi!"* every time he or she told a lie! This, he claimed, would prevent simulation *based on suggestion.* The *physical* phenomena, on the other hand, would take care of themselves. "After all," he had remarked, "a knee-jerk is not produced by imagination!" (13b, p. 494).

The grave problem of *inhibited* perceptions and responses arose again to plague explanations by means of associationism. When the hypnotized subjects were told that they could not see, hear, feel, or otherwise react to the appearance of some given cue, they did not do so. How could the association of ideas or images account for "no-reaction," since "no-reaction" had never been associated with the designated cue? Binet's limp answer illustrated his difficulty: "Probably the motor image was suppressed, the motor current dried up at its source, thus leading to the paralysis of the motor center" (26, p. 491).

By the time he had submitted his competitive *Mémoire* for the *lauréat* prize (1887) it was evident that his complete faith in the explanatory sufficiency of associationism was beginning to crack. In this *Mémoire* he explicitly brought up the question of "the passivity of mind" inferred by this doctrine, saying: "It tends to reduce the mind to a sort of passive automatism, that is, to a *spectator*-me rather than to an *actor*-me. . . . Yet, the most important phenomenon, in which the mind attests to its spontaneity, is *attention.* . . . A person's penchants (be he artist, sailor, or what) make his *attention* ready to react to the signs in the external world" (23, p. 650). Therefore, there was some active condition, a directedness of attention, that influenced the effects of contiguity and similarity and was not accounted for by the doctrine. Binet recalled that Mill "had admitted this weak point forty years earlier," and he himself still found it quite unresolved by associationism.

With the publication of *Le magnétisme animal* his uncertainty grew, and Binet abandoned the possibility of resolving all the problems of the association of images. For instance, in reexamining visual anaesthesia he argued: "The words 'Mr. X is nonexistent' cannot be associated with [an image] of the incapacity for seeing Mr. X. For a given object to become invisible, the subject must first perceive the object and then recognize it as the one that is not to be seen . . ." (22, p. 152). Having discovered that the same difficulties arose with suggested paralyses, he came full face with his problem:

> Perhaps this whole class of facts is subject to a general psychic law for which the most advanced psychologists have not succeeded in discovering the formula, and which may have an analogy with an *inhibitory action*. . . . Provisionally one could surmise that . . . the experimenter induces in the subject a mental impression that has an inhibitory effect on one of his sensory or motor functions; it should be definitely understood that it is not the mental impression that effects the inhibition, but the concomitant physiological process. It is necessary, furthermore, to remember that inhibition is a word that explains nothing, and cannot excuse us from seeking the true explanation. . . . Here the laws of association, which are of such great usefulness in resolving psychological problems, abandon us completely. This is probably because these laws do not give the explanation of all the facts of consciousness; they are less general than the English psychologists thought them to be . . . [22, p. 153].
>
> . . . Classical psychology, which does not speak of psychical paralyses, forgets half the story of the mind; it describes the active, impulsive forms of the intelligence [sensation, images, memory, reasoning, will, movement, etc.] without suspecting that the passive, negative forms are just as numerous; it represents *the side of the mind that is in the light, without taking note that there exists also the side in the shadow* [22, p. 227; italics added].

It is interesting to note these gropings for "light" that later stimulated psychologists to seek a solution in behavioral rather than only in ideational terms. The statements presage Binet's active interest in unconscious functioning that assumed full form a few years later in *On Double Consciousness* (1889) and *Les altérations de la personnalité* (1892). They also pry into phenomena that later (1903) led him to insist upon *imageless* thought.

In addition to *Le magnétisme animal,* a spate of other publications appeared in 1887. Binet was very active, but it appears that he did not find a satisfying orientation. More than ever it becomes clear that, in continuous contrast to the psychological "tradition" of French psychology, he was seeking to understand the *normal* rather than the abnormal. For example, there are the seeds of an interest that developed substantially a dozen years later: a note critical of the current methodology of graphologists, and a brief report of his own observations of the changes in the handwriting of hypnotized hysterics under conditions of excitation and of depression (25).

During the spring and summer of that year Binet also made a striking though partial change in his professional orientation. He became a student in Balbiani's laboratory of embryology at the Collège de France. He attended the professor's lectures,[13] undertook research projects with his guidance, and continued these studies actively and almost exclusively at least until early in 1889. While other concerns thereafter took precedence, these topics continued to stimulate papers, and a doctorate in the natural sciences (see chap. 1).

His first long publication based on the work in Balbiani's laboratory, "La vie psychique des micro-organismes," ap-

[13] Binet summarized Balbiani's course on modern theories of reproduction and heredity (32). The bibliography, taken from French and German sources, was very much up to date. In the section on heredity there are clear descriptions of the three layers—endoderm, ectoderm, and mesoderm—from which the differential parts of the body emerge, and also a recognition that an individual's heredity comes not only from the "nuclei" of the parents, but also from those of the four grandparents, and other progenitors, as well: "If this is true, it is not strange that male characteristics through the father . . . are formed of male and female elements combined." In other words, that era was knowledgeable enough to provide a credible basis for genetic individual differences.

peared first in the *Revue philosophique* in 1887, as the chapter of a French book in 1888, and in English translation the next year. The rather startling title has sometimes brought the onus of "vitalism" upon Binet, but the subtitle, "A study in experimental psychology," correctly dispels that possible inference. Binet considered it a venture into comparative psychology, which had so far largely been the domain of the English and the Americans. Now he was extending it to the "hitherto somewhat neglected area of microscopic organisms," bacteria and infusoria. It is a beautiful little study amply illustrated with Binet's line drawings, a considerable number of which were adapted from Balbiani. In addition to histological, physiological, and anatomical details, he reported the results of his own surgical interventions, and thus added behavioral descriptions that were as acute as the drawings. Again he had entered into an arena of controversy, especially with Charles Richet and George J. Romanes. Romanes maintained that only "irritability" was characteristic of these "homogeneous microorganisms," while Binet insisted that they showed a genuine "adaptability." "Every microorganism has a psychic life," he argued, "transcending the limits of cellular irritability . . . and we can conclude this from the fact that every microorganism possesses *a faculty* of selection; it chooses its food, as it likewise chooses the animal with which it copulates" (28, p. 109; italics added). The controversy, of course, was not resolved,[14] but Binet's monograph reflects a man who was broadening his experimental interests, becoming devoted to "observed facts," and, despite his use of the word "faculty," at least impli-

[14] It may be interesting to note that the point of real difference between Binet and the other men was applicable to *bacteria,* since Richet agreed with Binet's contentions concerning infusoria. Bacteria were another matter, however; Romanes and Richet insisted that they were homogeneous organisms, that is, undifferentiated. Binet countered that "our knowledge of morphology . . . depends upon the degree of *perfection* attained by technical science . . . which has not yet been able to show the presence of a nucleus in bacteria." He gave reasons for believing that this *perfection,* or improvement, would be reached, as indeed it has been.

citly exhibiting his attachment to the functionalism that later was so prominent in his work. He defined the psychic life of microorganisms in terms of "their life of relations," that is, of sensitivity and adaptive movement-responses. It is hardly surprising that he made no mention of the laws of the association of ideas in this monograph!

While working in the zoological laboratory, he also wrote several armchair or library researched articles and published a few "notes" on his observations of human subjects. For instance, he worked out a long article on fetishism in love (27). This should not be unexpected when one remembers both his own recent contention that hypnotized subjects are "in love" with their hypnotists and Charcot's interest in pathological sexual aberrations. The article acquires color from illustrations (for example, of Descartes "who is said to have had a taste for cross-eyed women," and of Rousseau, who was drawn to "imperious women, taking pleasure in their making him suffer").

At the very outset he indicated that his intention was to discuss the relationship of pathological to normal fetishism, and he wrote:

> Pathological fetishism is often distinguishable from the normal state only by small nuances. . . . M. Magnan considers most of the symptoms . . . as episodes in the hereditary insanity of degenerates. *But for the psychologist, the important fact . . . is found in the direct study of the symptom, in the analysis of its formation and its mechanism, in the light that these morbid cases throw on the psychology of love* [27, p. 146; italics added].

In everyday love as in religion, he claimed, fetishism plays a part "in our tendency to confuse [the loved one] or the divinity with the material and palpable objects that represent them" (p. 143). He also included homosexuality as an example of "the same kind of phenomenon. . . . Heredity," he added, "has played a capital role, but only to prepare the ground—making the subject susceptible to particular experiences."

His revision of the principle of associationism is shown in the following quotation:

In general [that is, among normal people], neither ideas nor perceptions [alone] profoundly modify the organism; the modification that persists comes . . . from the domain of *instincts, feelings,* and *unconscious impressions*. . . . It is necessary to have recourse to the law of the association of ideas *and of feelings* (p. 167; italics added).

Associationism was found wanting because it did not go beyond the realm of ideas, of images.

He concluded the essay with a long comparison of the essential differences between pathological and normal love. The primary difference lay in intensity or degree of symptomatology, but he added also: "Normal love is harmonious [all-encompassing?]; the lover loves all manifestations of the body and mind of the beloved. In sexual perversion . . ., the harmony is broken . . ., the part is substituted for the whole. . . . Perverted love is a theatrical presentation whereby a merely accessory actor advances toward the footlights and takes the major role" (27, pp. 272–74).

The subject of moral responsibility and the courts also claimed his attention (15, 18, and 31). His position, he stated, was the same as that of Mill, Adam Smith, and M. Tarde, as well as of the Italian "positivist school":

Moral responsibility should cease to be the basis for our penal legislation [and sentencing procedures]. . . . If a person has acted in accordance with his own character, that is, has not been coerced . . . at the time of the [criminal] act, then the object of our penal legislation should be to attempt with ever-increasing efficiency to defend society and therefore to eliminate harmful persons from it [31, p. 231].

Binet's viewpoint was explicitly deterministic. He asserted that freedom of the will, since it is attached to no determined antecedent, is truly a matter of chance. The article is particularly interesting for its psychological insights into prevailing processes for arriving at court decisions of guilt or innocence, which, as he described and illustrated them, became the result of a balancing of aversion to, and of pity for, the criminal. Binet set out clearly the consequent injustices and ineffectualness for society of such conditions. His illustrations could serve dramatically in current discussions of psychology as related to the law.

Among his shorter reports there appeared continued work on the relation of perceptions and images to cerebral correlates (29, 33). He also wrote with Féré a review of voluntary and involuntary movements among hysterics (24) and extended this work to include problems of the muscular sense per se (30), to which his hysterical subjects presented some perplexity. While unconsciously pointing or writing with a hysterically "paralyzed" arm, because the experimenter had suggested the actions, the patients, because of their assumed "paralysis," had no feeling of innervation and no experience of antecedent images. These unconscious actions obviously threw into a quandary the theory of the association of images as a basis for acts. Thus he continued to anticipate his definitive assertion in 1892 that the association of images and ideas is not a sufficient explanatory principle of psychological phenomena.

Upon returning briefly to Charcot's clinic in 1889, Binet became absorbed in problems of the nature and relationships of states of consciousness, and published a summary in his little book *On Double Consciousness.* This appeared only in English with the intention of "introducing English-speaking psychologists to the work of the French, which had been ignored everywhere and especially in those countries where they pretend to give a complete picture of the present state of psychological research" (34, Preface). This omission seemed all the more incredible to him since the Americans and the English had been much interested both in automatic writing and in "double personalities," which had been lengthily studied in France. He guessed that one reason for the oversight lay in the characteristic marks of French psychology: There was no "school," no body of accepted doctrines, so that the research appeared in separate monographs and almost exclusively in the pathological field. "We are dispersed," he wrote, "like skirmishers upon the field of research . . ." (34, p. 8). In *On Double Consciousness* he was trying to redress the balance by calling attention, for example, to his own work on automatic movements in which he used various distractors, and with normal as well as with hysterical subjects. He again discussed at length the problem that *inhibition* presented to explanatory principles. Shortly afterward he wrote a complementary article about this problem, with an analogy between physiological and psychological inhibition in which he used almost field-force, Lewinian vocabulary: "When an antagonism exists between two mental syntheses, each one jams, abates, or slides into the other in accordance with conditions of intensity, complexity, and degree of emotion or feeling" (41, pp. 155–56). He was clearly dissatisfied with this, however, and focused attention on the unresolved complexity of these inhibitory actions. Functionalism had indeed invaded the framework of his basic assumptions.

At the end of the summer of 1891, at the time Binet asked Beaunis to take him into the laboratory, he had completed writing *Les altérations de la personnalité*. This book was more judicious and less dogmatic than any of his earlier publications. The title, however, is misleading since the substance of the book includes, besides total successive personalities, diverse levels of unconsciousness such as automatisms, temperament, and memory, plus a section of discussions on experimentally induced changes through hypnosis and direct suggestion. It was a systematic, organized treatise that integrated the subject matter of plural (un)consciousnesses. Its importance probably lies in Binet's stress on the unity that existed within any of the diverse forms of conscious-unconscious activity; there was always an arrangement into some kind of a synthesis, both for the larger and the smaller event-units. In other words, for each class of personality changes, brief or prolonged, he noted a *unity*, which appeared to be cemented by "attention" or directedness, and determined or selected the particular individual responses to any given event. This characteristic of directedness became a constant in his assumptions about the nature of intelligence.

In two points Binet explicitly backed away from earlier positions: one was his admitted skepticism concerning the physical effects of aesthesiogens, and, second, his admission that he no longer considered it important or even especially relevant to search for physiological (for example, cerebral) concomitants of psychological experiences. "While seeming more exact [because they are physiological], they are really more hypothetical and false . . . [even than] the frequently indefinite outlines of the phenomena of plural consciousness" (43, pp. 70–71).

The classical law of associationism had suffered gradual attrition as Binet sought to apply it to unmanageable observations. By 1891 further data from "the side of the mind that is in the shadow" forced him to challenge it again. He now criticized the old psychology for its stress on faculties of the mind to account for the variety and nuances of mental life and for its countenancing of belief in *a* memory, *a* will, *a* reasoning, *a* perceiving. "Now," he wrote, "we know that that which is real and living in an individual are *acts* of memory, *acts* of reasoning, *acts* of will, etc., that is, little particular and distinct *events*. . . . What we must principally retain of all this is what we call our mind, our intelligence, a grouping of internal events, extremely numerous and varied, and that we should not look for the unity of our psychic being anywhere except in the arrangement, the synthesis, in a word, the coordination of all these events" (43, pp. 317–18). He credited Théodule Ribot with coming to the same conclusion: "the unity of the self—unity means coordination." Distinct acts appear, disappear, and reappear according to the "synthesis or coordination of the dominant ego"—a fact most strikingly illustrated by double personalities where an object or an event effects different behaviors in each of them: certainly classical associationism could not account for these personality syntheses.

Binet posited more profound causes whose nature could not be determined just because they were unconscious, "since they operate to apportion our ideas, perceptions, memories, and all our conscious states into free and independent syntheses." This problem continued to attract Binet's attention until, in 1911, he perceived it as precipitating a crisis for psychology: the nature of thought would always be elusive since its unconscious components were hidden from view. In 1891, however, when images were assumed to be a necessary concomitant of thought, any instances purporting to be without images were rationalized by saying that the images must exist "in the lower or secondary consciousness." The hypothesis that images are necessary to thought seems never to have been seriously questioned at that time.

Les altérations de la personnalité proved to be a watershed in Binet's career as a psychologist. After its publication the chastened Binet ceased to use hypnosis or to work with hysterical subjects. He no longer pursued research on the nature of perceptions, hallucinations, illusions, or inhibitions, since he had done this primarily to embellish the laws of the association of ideas that he had now renounced as a sufficient explanatory principle for psychological events. On the other hand, his fascination with the problems of consciousness, unconsciousness, and thought remained constant;[15] in fact, he had written that the question of consciousness is one of the most delicate problems that psychology could undertake to solve. For the most part, however, the problems that had occupied most of his attention and investigation for a decade came to a halt with the publication of this volume.

The Significance of the First Ten Years

An attempt to assess the importance of these years to Binet the psychologist presents something of an enigma.

[15] In fact, one of the first experiments that Binet carried out in the Laboratory of Physiological Psychology gave evidence of this interest. He studied thresholds of consciousness-unconsciousness among subjects who were asked to estimate elapsed time in several simple reactions. The number of errors made around each individual's *average* threshold brought Binet to the conclusion that for some persons consciousness begins at a definite point, while for others, who had large mean variations, the threshold is not a fixed point, but rather one of degree. The initials used to represent the experimental subjects make plausible a guess that they included Beaunis, Binet, an American E. B. Delabarre, and the laboratory assistant Philippe. As in Wundt's laboratory, they were all taking in one another's washing!

François-Louis Bertrand believed that they represented a transition from a psychiatric to a psychological orientation (267, p. 29), and Edith Varon suggested that, except for some experimental practice, they simply led to his repudiation of associationism (303, p. 25). These dicta are either evident misjudgments or too limited.

After reading psychology at the Bibliothèque Nationale and publishing his first papers out of that reading alone (10 and 11), Binet was, so to speak, "rescued" from several directions: Charcot's clinical laboratory gave him access to subjects, and "The Master" himself offered him some professional status that he had entirely lacked before. Ribot offered him a place for his writings in the pages of *Revue philosophique.* Delboeuf "taught" him to look into the appropriate literature before making rash statements, and even more important, to suspect his "facts" by suspecting his methodology and basic assumptions. Binet's work in Balbiani's laboratory acquainted him with developmental concepts about the growth of organisms, gave him an awareness of individual differences, of normality and variability, and experience with a biologist's methodology in establishing new "facts."

On the other hand, by succumbing to the viewpoints and influences of the Salpêtrière, Binet suffered a distressing personal humiliation. It is not strange that he had made this alliance, for it was a famous and prestigious one, but Binet had to learn the hard lesson that eminent reputation is not a valid basis for scientific claims; that, in fact, it may even contaminate the evidence. From this experience he also learned to beware of the insistent problem that is today called "the effects of the experimental setting," of the "expectations" of subjects as well as of experimenters, which may seriously falsify data. His own suggestibility in these experimental settings influenced him later to investigate suggestibility extensively, and he never again became anyone's "man."

It was difficult for Binet to admit errors. Indeed, in the discouraging year of 1889 he wrote: "I admit that this [abandonment of an opinion] cost me a great deal, for it is singular to observe how, in spite of ourselves and our desires to be impartial, we are so reluctant to surrender a first idea" (34, p. 39). And later he phrased this affirmation in more general terms: "[Experimenters] often make the error of throwing themselves too quickly, head lowered, into the facts for which they have an irresistible predilection. They should take more time to study the directing idea . . . before putting their hands to the work" (89, p. 477). Binet had also learned to discern some of the complexities of psychological phenomena that had been ignored in much of the literature. Moreover, he learned to be professionally productive during these years, a characteristic that grew to proportions that are rare in this field, and his writing improved with respect to clarity, organization, and exactness.

At the end of the decade, Binet had lost his first orientation without gaining another. He was compelled to search, even to grope, for valid methods and areas of investigation with normal subjects. Furthermore, for nearly two years after he abandoned his work at the Salpêtrière, he sought institutional footing, which was evidently important to him and without which he could not assure his career any solid achievement.

3 Experimental Psychology: Its "Fatherhood" in France

Ever since Newton proclaimed the law of gravitation as a key explanation for the organization of the universe, scholars in other disciplines have sought to discover equally simple, direct explanations as a key to their world pictures. The atom seemed to provide this for the chemists, the "economic man" for the economists, the struggle for survival for the biologists, and, at the end of the nineteenth century, psychologists hoped to find it in sensations and their mental structural elements. These would be "units" in the analysis of consciousness, and an immense amount of effort was expended to discover and describe these units, almost as though they paralleled the atoms of the physical world. After perceiving flaws in the hypothesis that the association of ideas sufficiently explained all psychological phenomena, Binet early distrusted these easy solutions to complex problems. He insisted that the understanding of human behavior could not be broken down into atoms, or small units, to be reassembled afterward. For him the activity of the human mind was essentially a problem of complex relationships, and solutions could be found only within a complex frame of reference. In his restless efforts to probe these problems, he explored the frontiers of intelligence, of learning, of perception, of suggestibility. Certainly Taine, Ribot, and others already mentioned added to his arsenal of ideas, but much of the credit must go to his own dauntless desire to understand.

Beginnings of Experimental Child Psychology

In a single year, during the period he was without a professional home, Binet published three significant papers that, although neglected in the history of child psychology, were unmistakably an original contribution to the experimental research on the psychology of children (38, 39, 40). At a time when the baby biography and the questionnaire were waxing brightly, Binet's reports were not in the least in these genres. He was recording certain behavior of his two little daughters. By systematically varying conditions, he began to study certain movements and cognitive responses. His experiences in Balbiani's embryological laboratory may have suggested these developmental studies, and his wide reading in the works of Wilhelm Preyer, Francis Galton, and G. Stanley Hall must have sharpened his perceptions of the two small girls whom he observed daily and whose individual differences struck him so forcibly. Unfortunately, he seems not to have recognized the seminal nature of these efforts, for he did not pursue them then, nor for that matter did his contemporaries hail them. It is clear now, however, that they contained initial intuitions and groping hypotheses about development, individual differences, and intelligence that became characteristic of many of his later contributions.

Although he did record among his daughters' behavior many of the same phenomena described by Preyer, he found a number of things more interesting than the ubiquitous attention then given to "the first time some action occurs." The 1890 papers most significantly emphasized developmental changes and comparisons between children and adults, thus leading Binet to recognize that *significant* differences lay only in *complex,* not in simple, functions. He also described some striking individual differences between his daughters; and yet, it is surprising that he was not struck by the age differences, since Madeleine was twenty months older than Alice.

Some details from these papers are important. The principal subjects were Madeleine, born 5 November 1885, and Alice, born 6 July 1887; in his published reports he used the pseudonyms Marguerite and Armande for these girls. Initially their individually different styles of "voluntary attention" intrigued him. Madeleine always concentrated firmly on whatever she was doing, whereas Alice was impulsive. "When [Madeleine] was learning to walk," he wrote, "she did not leave one support until she had discovered another near at hand to which she could direct herself . . . while [Alice], on the other hand, advanced into empty space without any attention to the consequences." Madeleine was "silent, cool, concentrated, while [Alice] was a laughter, gay, thoughtless, giddy, and turbulent. . . . Now [when the sisters were four years and two-and-a-half years of age] the psychological differences . . . have not disappeared. On the contrary, they have imparted a very clear character to their whole mental development" (38, p. 298).

Developmental changes per se interested Binet. For instance, he studied the bilaterality of hand movements as well as reaction times by means of a Marey tambour attached to a revolving drum. Indeed, he appears to have been the first one to use these graphic measurements with children as subjects. He reported the growing frequency of unilaterality between two and three years of age. Collecting similar graphic data from eight adults and six children (from forty-six months to nine years), Binet discovered that the two groups differed little in the simple responses of reaction times, duration of hand contractions, and the number of times a rubber tube could be squeezed during a given time interval. Next he compared the "two little sisters with a few adults" in their ability to recognize differences between lines of varying lengths drawn on cards, and between varying sizes of angles displayed on Beaunis's "ingenious instrument" of two demicircles. In both cases the children were only minimally less adept than the adults, thus persuading Binet to his growing certainty that significant individual differences lay only in complex processes (39), a radical departure from the measurement assumptions and practices of the day.

To expand his study of judgments of quantity beyond angles and lengths of line, Binet investigated them in two ways; the first suggests a parallel with Piaget's conservation experiments, and the second is now included in well-known preschool intelligence tests. Binet was impressed by Preyer's report of a child ten months old who knew when one of his nine bowling pins was missing, and who, at eighteen months, recognized perfectly that one of his ten animals was missing. "Now," Binet exclaimed, "it is worth trying some methodical studies." Putting similar objects together in two groups he asked Madeleine, four years and four months of age, to "point to the group having more than the other" and recorded the responses T and F. At this time Madeleine could *count* only three objects,[1] but he wanted to know how well could she *perceive* quantitative differences. Using sous, tokens, or bean seeds, he laid them flat and close together on the table. He tried a large number of comparisons; the difference between eighteen in one group and seventeen in another was fairly correctly indicated, but when asked to differentiate between twenty-two and twenty-one objects Madeleine's score was not better than half right. Seeking some explanation, Binet next substituted green and white tokens (*jetons*), one 2½ cm., the other 4 cm. in diameter. Now Madeleine was successful in indicating that five of the smaller tokens were "more than" four of the larger; however, when the groupings became larger, her success lessened, and only with nine larger and eighteen smaller tokens did the smaller win out, as "more than" the other group. Binet posited that the explanation was to be found not in the actual numbers displayed, but rather *in the space covered on the table,* an astute observation about perceptual development that unfortunately he failed to test further.

The second variation of number perception or judgment consisted in placing before the child a number of familiar objects that Binet then took out of her sight, putting them back one at a time with the query: "Are there any more?" The difference between the child's "No" and the correct number was the indication of the size of the error. For Madeleine at four years, five months the limit was five. He was satisfied, in light of these variations, that the perception of continuous size, represented by lines and angles, is

[1] Binet mentioned with satisfaction that Madeleine had not been coached either in reading or counting. A descriptive article that he wrote on "fetishism in love" (27) indicates that he had read Rousseau thoroughly, and the above remark probably reflects the latter's point of view.

easier and more exact than the perception of discrete objects, whether tokens or other small, familiar items. He also indicated the value of this method, which "permits the experimenter to determine number-perception with a fair certainty." He failed to see, however, the fertile implications and so failed to explore further by replicating these and similar stimuli with more children of various ages.

Binet also hit upon the idea of giving experimental dimensions to "intelligence," his vague definition of which opened his third 1890 paper on children's perceptions: "What is called intelligence, in the strict sense of the word, consists of two principal things: first, perceiving the external world, and second, reconsidering these perceptions in memory, recasting them, pondering them" (40, p. 582). He first examined at length the perception of colors. Taking exception to Preyer's method, he claimed that Preyer confused the ability to *name* a color with that of being able to perceive it well enough to remember it. He asked Alice to match from memory swatches of Holmgren wools. She must match one swatch at a time from among a group of nine; in doing this, of course, she performed much more accurately than when she tried to name the colors.[2]

Binet next observed his children's recognition of drawings "made with five or six strokes of the pencil" (and therefore without shadow, third dimension, or color). He drew simple, everyday objects like an umbrella, a ball, table, drinking glass, chair, hat, bottle, and horse. Two results appeared to surprise him: first, even at twenty-one months Alice could recognize and name these crude drawings just as well as she did the objects themselves; but on the other hand, "even at four years . . . [Madeleine] did not recognize isolated parts, like a nose, ear, eye, or parts of fingers . . ." This latter datum, he said, should be attributed to children's "lack of any talent for analysis. . . . Contrarily, we adults can recognize parts of the body as complete wholes, even though they are not copies of any

[2] Schallenberger (224) commented on Preyer's "insufficient method of naming colors," attacked Baldwin's methods as being all theory and no work, and commended Binet's refinement and real contribution through this "method of recognition."

[exact] perceptions formerly seen" (40, p. 592). Binet concluded that children recognize wholes before their parts, that they "fractionate" perceptions only much later, but he seems never to have quite perceived this observation as an important general principle of developmental growth, as we do today.

He attempted a test of what he called "interior perception" by asking his children to tell him what they saw in a set of Darwin's pictures of simulated emotions. Madeleine's "interior perception" at four years, three months was clearly differentiated only for crying and laughing expressions. His attempts to discern the beginnings of the awareness of the self were not more successful, but they did arouse some amusingly caustic comments from his nemesis, Professor Delboeuf (193); this time Binet did not reply.

The next test will be familiar to the reader who is acquainted with the Stanford-Binet scale: a vocabulary test, in which he pronounced a word and asked "What is it? Tell me what it is." He discovered to his surprise how "utilitarian" children are; the words were overwhelmingly defined in terms of use. His conclusion was that "a little child is clearly incapable of the kind of defining that requires comparison, reflection, elimination; the little ones respond without reflecting" (40, p. 606). He presented to each child separately the same list of words, it appears about thirty in all, over a period of nine months. Many sample responses are reported, for Alice from two years, seven months to three years, four months, for Madeleine from four years, three months to five years. It is not surprising, of course, that answers like the following continued to occur: "A snail is to step on," "A dog bites."

This harvest of papers shows major characteristics of Binet the experimenter, and it is so closely allied and related to his later work on intelligence that it belongs to that chapter as well as to this. These studies reflect his functional orientation and clearly portray the method that marked all of his successful research: he took the various stimulating conditions to the subjects and recorded the results as they occurred, however unexpected they were. A priori conclusions were already an anathema to him, to be displaced with just such experimental work. He also recognized the scientifically rewarding results of studying carefully a few subjects well known to the experimenter. Even so, he could not jump the barrier of faculties, *functional* faculties though they were; he was steeped in these response categories. Furthermore, despite his recognition of singular differences between adults and children, he did not then grasp a conception of age-stage growth. By concentrating on the individual personality characteristics of the two girls he failed also to discern the important maturational differences between children almost two years apart.[3]

Nonetheless, these 1890 papers can be looked upon as Binet's initial offering in "individual psychology," the phrase for which he later claimed priority in France (69, p. 113, n.). Simon was correct when he asserted: "Individual psychology is the originality of Binet"; others have emphasized the same point (for example, Paul Fraisse, 275, p. 110, and René Zazzo, 309, p. 114). Although he sometimes pursued the nomothetic or general principles of general psychology, one feels that he was doing so primarily as a backdrop and point of reference for individual differences.

Early Studies

After he joined the laboratory at the Sorbonne in 1891, Binet published alone or with collaborators a few papers on currently conventional topics—"colored hearing" (associations of certain tones with specific color sensations), reaction times, speed of movements. Their relation to individual psychology is shown by his concern for the differences displayed among his subjects. Although he had left the Salpêtrière, on Charcot's suggestion he also studied at length two men who were gifted as rapid calculators, In-

[3] These papers are more fully treated in Wolf (307) and are translated in Pollack and Brenner (287). They are also given an appreciative discussion in R. H. Pollack, "Binet on Perceptual-Cognitive Development, or Piaget-come-lately," *J. of the Hist. of Behav. Sciences* (1971) : 370–74.

audi and Diamandi. He compared them not only with respect to auditory and visual imagery, but also childhood backgrounds and the relation of their special ability to their other capacities. He concluded that these two men, earning their livelihoods by means of public performances, were actually rather ordinary persons who had had very special practice in their calculating precocities, with no evidence of genetically special aptitudes. In fact, Binet brought to the laboratory a mnemotechnician of his acquaintance who, by giving meanings to the numbers, demonstrated a more sensational memory than the calculators who used auditory or visual imagery. Concurrently he studied chessplayers who, blindfolded, could play several games simultaneously (47). Binet's "personal data" came from a small sample of letters, face-to-face interviews, questionnaires, and published accounts. According to the fashion of the day, as represented by Charcot, Galton, and Taine, he expected to find brilliant visual imagery among these precocious players. On the contrary, although there were individual differences, he found clear evidence that several players relied on what he called "the different lines of force" of the various pieces, the power and direction that they could wield, rather than on visual images of the board. This could have been a clue to "imageless thought," which Binet stressed so forcibly a decade later and for which he claimed priority over the Würzburg school.[4]

In 1894–95 Binet and Victor Henri published three articles on schoolchildren's memory, and one on their suggestibility (49, 51, 52, and 50). These studies, begun in 1892, belong for the most part to the area of general psychology, with individual psychology illustrated primarily

[4] Perhaps it should be noted that even as early as 1890 Binet was speculating about the problem of sensory images, and *possibly* of "imageless thought." He wondered, for example, whether the little girls were thinking of "a particular dog" or of "a generic" one. If the latter, what was the image that went with it? This problem was to become an important theme of his study of his daughters' cognitive and personality modes, published in 1903 (90).

in age differences.[5] Binet dismissed the significance of his study of memory for separate words, which treated "only relatively simple elements of consciousness," as those by Hugo Münsterberg, Mary Calkins, W. V. Bingham, and others had done. He argued that in the case of memory for sentences "we are entering into an entirely unexplored domain." He found the effects of age small but constant, and the memory for sentences "twenty-five times superior to that for isolated words." His analysis is interesting: in both short and long sentences, the children tended strongly to substitute their own familiar words for the more elegant textual ones, for example, they used *sauta* for *s'élança*, that is, "jumped" for "sprang." Of course, in the longer sentences they showed more "complete forgettings" of phrases as well as a tendency to simplify the syntax. He noted that some errors occurred because of emotional stresses, adding: "It is probable that in citations more moving than ours, this emotional character would have played a greater part" (52, p. 58). Although the illustrations are disappointingly brief, the reader may be reminded of the now well-known "leveling, assimilating, and sharpening effects" in recalled materials, which are foreshadowed here. As Binet pored over hundreds of these children's papers, impressions of individual differences must have affected his psychological conceptualizations, although his mention of them in this text was surprisingly shallow.

Binet's penchant for variations within a single problem area next moved him to study memory by substituting visual rather than verbal stimuli. This time he used lines of different lengths. He and Henri presented several model lines singly, asking their subjects to find the same length among twenty-one lines on a test card. The results showed expected improvement with age, which Binet saw even then as a clear indication of the importance of the memory

[5] The subjects in the various experiments ranged from 240 to 380 boys, seven to thirteen years of age. Sex differences were at that time out of the question, since Binet did not yet have permission to experiment in schools for girls.

function in intelligence. He added: ". . . the results appear to us to be due not only to the children's memory per se, but rather to their faculty of attention, judgment, and criticism; it is especially in these last points [or capacities] that a child of seven years differs from a child of twelve. . . . For example, the older children can observe, 'It is a very long line,' thus affecting their judgments" (49a, p. 169).

The same stimuli of lines were used for the study of "suggestibility," which included three conditions: the first, called "suggestion by preconceived idea," demonstrated three lines of increasing length, presented separately, each to be indicated from memory on the test card; then another series contained a line *not* appearing on the test card. Would the children fall into the suggestion, or would they say, "It's not there!" The second, called "status and verbal suggestion of the experimenter," added his misleading suggestions, such as, "Isn't the correct one the line *next* to that one?" In the third, called "suggestion in a group situation," Binet assembled groups of four children in the testing room to see if the others would follow the first one to answer. In his conclusions he clearly saw the effects of the experimental setting, and warned that in such experiments "the personality of the experimenter takes on an importance of the first order . . ." (50, pp. 346–47). Laboriously, he arrived at some conclusions about the nature and conditions of suggestibility among schoolchildren: "In order to overcome the obstacles . . . the child must have a certain hardiness of mind . . . ; a child of exaggerated timidity, although possessing an excellent degree of observation, would not come off well in this test. . . . To succeed it is necessary to have both intellectual qualities [attention, memory, judgment] . . . and also moral qualities: a firm character, and an assured self-confidence" (50, p. 340). These experiments were expanded later in his book, *La suggestibilité* (77).

During this same period Binet investigated children's fears by means of questionnaires addressed to teachers and a few other adults, and also by observations made on his own and acquaintances' children. The results were vague and inconsistent, but they represent an attempt to analyze the subject, providing a definition, contents of fears, signs in behavior, relation to health, moral and intellectual characteristics, and the incidence and causes of children's fears. With direct acknowledgment of suggestions derived from Rousseau's *Émile,* he added nine pages discussing possible treatment (58).

In another study of this period, which followed his own advocacy of studying people in real settings, Binet, both alone and with his friend Jacques Passy, undertook to investigate a number of creative artists, among whom were the novelists Edmond de Goncourt and Alphonse Daudet, playwrights Alexander Dumas, Victorien Sardou, and François de Curel, and the poet François Coppée (53, 54). He wanted "to try to clarify the very important, but very poorly known and little studied, question of the creative imagination" (53, p. 60), and used conversations and relatively systematic questionnaires to elucidate certain points. Although his objective was only minimally satisfied, he did record the artists' explanation of the sources of their inspiration and provided insight into their methods and hours of working. He also had some evidence on their reported pleasure or pain during periods of productivity, and especially on the degrees of voluntary or involuntary control they claimed to experience in the plot-development and writing. In the case of Curel, for example, Binet described the "spontaneous" nature of his inspiration. The playwright himself claimed that he was a "vessel through which his characters spoke," that he wrote what they were saying to him, as though from their dictation. "When I am in full production," he told Binet, "my mind manifests a phenomenon very analogous to currents of electrical induction. . . . Although I do not recall ever having dreamed of one of my plays, it is certain that during the night my pieces progress greatly. There is in the morning a superabundance of production . . ." (54, pp. 132–33). This long account of Curel's "spontaneous inspirations" dramatically illustrates the phenomenon of positive unconscious functioning.[6] Other authors included in these studies said

[6] A recent illustration of the involuntary sources of creative activity comes from the greatly gifted American author Saul

they planned and plotted their works very consciously, conscientiously, and even painfully. With all of them Binet tried to discover childhood influences, but he had only limited success because their efforts at introspection were not useful.[7]

Initial Explicit Formulations in Experimental Psychology

If the title of a professional treatise should point up the orientation of its contents Binet's *Introduction à la psychologie expérimentale* was misnamed—and perhaps as a result it was largely ignored or produced comments like the following from Princeton's H. C. Warren:

> It is to be regretted that M. Binet has not seen fit to lead the readers of the present volume to anything like a thorough and systematic grasp of the elements of experimental psychology. . . . One cannot help confessing to a feeling of disappointment when it is considered what even a short book like this might have been . . . [244].

This American judgment was undoubtedly influenced by the fact that E. C. Sanford's *Course in Experimental Psychology* that had run serially for over two years in the *American Journal of Psychology* was a meticulous and systematic manual with long laboratory exercises following the German model. Binet's book was no manual or handbook but rather a critique, an analysis, and an original, seminal contribution to experimental psychology. It

---

Bellow. In an interview taped for *Writers at Work: The Paris Review Interviews* (Viking, 1968) he describes how this process worked during his writing of *Henderson* and *Herzog*, "to tame and restrain the style I developed in *Augie March* . . . it has something to do with a kind of readiness to record impressions arising from a source of which we know little. . . . From this source come words, phrases, syllables, sometimes only sounds, which I try to interpret; sometimes whole paragraphs, fully punctuated. When E. M. Forster said, 'How do I know what I think until I see what I say?' he was perhaps referring to his own [similar] prompter." Aldous Huxley has urged the positive unconscious as a proper study for psychology.

[7] Binet's summarized conclusions can be found in (54), pp. 114-18.

included not only positive suggestions for programs of research but also harsh criticisms of current programs, especially those in "psychometrics" and "sensations, perceptions, and attention." What delicious, and probably alienating, fun he had with those "foreigners" who set up such "sterile experimental conditions," failing as they did to make use of their subjects' introspections to clarify the meanings of the experimental settings. America and Germany were singled out, as Binet wrote:

> . . . Subjects go into a little room, respond by electrical signals, and leave without so much as a word to the experimenters. . . . The latter want "simple and precise" results, even to carrying them to three decimal places and measuring them to 1000/seconds. Simplicity is in fact obtained and in some ways imposed by this method. If, however, in experiments on the time-sense the experimenter should ask the subject to report what he felt . . . he would certainly provoke many different responses, although he could not easily classify them, handle them, extract means, and establish mathematical formulas. . . . With the three choices only—"equal," "greater," or "less"—they often seem to set up the results of the experiments in advance. . . .
>
> Their aim is simplicity, but it is only a factitious one, artificial, produced by the suppression of all troublesome complications. This simplicity comes about only when we efface all individual differences, thus coming to conclusions that are not true [48, pp. 28–30].

Paragraphs like this could have added to Warren's "disappointment." He had been trained in Wundt's laboratory, which was one of Binet's special targets. This attack on the cowherds and the "sacred cows" of the day did not make Binet popular.

Most of the chapters of the *Introduction* were written in collaboration with one or another of Binet's colleagues or students, but in fact, this "collective work" was very evidently his. He tried "to indicate and make understandable the character of the [or his] new psychology, to define the principal methods that it employs, and the domain in which it carries on its research . . . in short, the experimental psychology of the normal individual" (48, pp. 1–2). The book included discussions on "The Laboratory," "Methods of Observation and Experiment," "Sensations, Perceptions and Attention," "Movements," "Memory," "Ideation," and "Psychometry."

Binet recognized and struggled with the insoluble problem presented by the overlaps among the so-called faculties. For example, he pointed out that "sensations, perceptions, and attention" also required "judgment, imagination, and reasoning" and concluded in his perplexity: "To understand these intellectual states . . . would be instructive . . . but they cannot be easily analyzed, nor can we submit them even to an approximate measure" (48, p. 44). He seemed most proud of chapter 5, "La Mémoire," written with Henri. Indeed, he fairly exulted in comparing his twenty-six pages, out of a text of 146 pages, devoted to methods of studying "memory" with Wundt's fourth edition of 1,350 pages, in which "600 pages were given to 'sensation' and only 11 to 'memory'!" He felt that the Wundtians were sacrificing all *important* measures "to their desire for precision" (48, p. 72). The novelty of his and Henri's proposals impressed him, and he claimed that ". . . here for the first time, and at our own risk and peril, we are formulating methods for studying memory. . . ." He believed that ideally methods should provide ways of studying changes in memory as influenced, for example, by age, profession, individual differences, race, sex, and so on. At that time he could not see ways of producing quantitative results for all these areas, but they did represent complex, real processes that "are significant even when not quantifiable." The chapter presented four methods for studying memory, and reported some crude data on individual differences between artists and nonartists, between rapid calculators and blindfolded chessplayers, and between adults and boys in repeating nonsense syllables. It suggested ways to test duration of memories, and deplored the necessity of using laboratory settings rather than spontaneous memories, since the latter could usually not be validated.

In the chapter on "Ideation" Binet suggested variations

of the experiment he and Flournoy had worked out (196). In addition to Wundt's, B. Bourdon's, and E. W. Scripture's word-association tests, he suggested what seems to be an ingenious predecessor to the present and popular "analogies" test. It consisted of series of two-word pairs for each of which the subjects were to indicate explicitly what relationship between the two words made their pairing appropriate. Were they linked by cause and effect, means to end, contiguity, or what? By this means he stated that "one would certainly arrive at a test of judgment and of other complex functions" (48, p. 102). He noted that this and any number of other tests of associations were highly open to chance, and that they also presented conundrums to the experimenter who must classify and score them.

Binet's criticism of the sterile methods of psychophysics was balanced by his suggestions that the study of reaction times could effect useful comparisons of individual differences in many categories and permit the discovery of the influence of drugs, alcohol, caffeine, and the like. In his brief "Conclusions" Binet reminded the reader that psychology had definitely achieved a status as a "distinct and independent science. . . . Psychology," he insisted in 1894, "is a natural science, nothing more."[8]

Although this book made very little impact at the time, it was fertile in conception and very characteristic of Binet. In this embryonic period for psychology he was proceeding in a very different direction from Wundt and, indeed, from English psychology as well: he was seeking to find experimental methods for studying individual differ-

[8] In a way this book dramatizes the similarities between Ebbinghaus and Binet: emancipation of experimental psychology from philosophy; pursuit of a wholehearted empiricism; application of experimental methods to "fleeting mental processes"; disapproval of the artificiality of Wundt's elementarism; anticipation of Gestalt psychology in stressing unity in variety; application of psychology to pedagogical problems; faith in scientific methodology to provide the basis for a scientific psychology (288). It appears that both men were aware of one another's work, but it is not possible to trace the mutual influences.

ences in complicated cognitive processes. Thus the *Introduction à la psychologie expérimentale* was really integrally related to three later articles that probably should have been bound together in one book, namely *"La psychologie individuelle"* (59), *"Connais-toi toi-même"* (or "Know thyself," 60), and *"La mesure en psychologie individuelle"* (69). These articles and the book are particularly relevant to the development of Binet's conceptions of intelligence (see chap. 4), and they are, of course, integral to Binet's studies of measurement in psychology. Unfortunately, their publication was scattered; even the famous Henri and Binet article in *L'Annnée* (59) was buried among "general reviews." It seems doubtful whether readers of the time would have troubled to put together the three, plus the *Introduction,* to follow his thought. Surely a part of Wundt's reputation rested on his concentration of results, while Binet suffered from diffusion of his efforts and findings.

In a study of the well-known Müller-Lyer illusion that varied the angles at the ends of equal lengths of lines, Binet continued to apply some of the methodology that he had proposed in the *Introduction.* He ingeniously varied every possible unit of the sizes and lengths of angles and lines. In both increasing and decreasing schedules he presented it to schoolboys[9] to determine the conditions under which they perceived the line between the obtuse angles as equal to the constants with oblique angles. His explicit and numerous conclusions stressed the unexpectedly wide individual differences that were apparent and, finding the illusion stronger among the younger pupils, he hypothesized that it was an "innate" rather than an "acquired" illusion.

In another experiment, "after long trials," Binet developed a method of recording on a graph performances on the piano, "thus," he claimed, "setting straight the ear's [subjective] witness." By means of a rubber tube fixed under the keys and attached to a graph, he recorded the

[9] There were sixty boys in the first and second classes who had an average age of twelve years, and forty-five boys in the fifth class whose average age was nine years.

duration and force of notes, the speed, the crescendoes and diminuendoes, and the rhythms of trills and intervals. His delight in such measurement is evident in his almost lyrical claims of its advantages over "the confused perceptions of the ear alone" (57).

Although Binet was unable to work it into the metric scale, another theme from this period became an integral aspect of his conceptualization of intelligence. He was then and always continued to be deeply impressed with the importance of individual, personal "orientations of thought." These were habitual personality patterns of the first order. Surprisingly, he first broached this subject in a popular article (60) in which he described a simple test he had given to children. He had merely asked them to write a description of an object. He assured his readers that the results "provided an understanding of the way a child looks at an object, how he observes and gives an account of it . . . to see if he has a tendency to describe, or observe, or imagine; he is earthbound [*terre à terre*] or idealistic, verbally effusive or reserved, reflective or careless, emotional or passive. . . . All of these mental qualities are certainly as important to recognize as memory . . ." (60, pp. 419–20). This was a better way, he claimed, to evaluate character than by means of handwriting, phrenology, or palmistry, and he urged that teachers capitalize on such personality differences in their approaches to their pupils. He elaborated on the experiment in *L'Année* by giving details, and by adding another sample, a group of young people whom he asked to "describe a cigarette" (62).[10] At all age levels and in both sexes he found qualitative differences that he called "natural families of character"—literary, scientific, emotional, aesthetic, sympathetic, and egoistical types—and he urged the necessity of thinking

[10] A picture of La Fontaine's "Laborer and His Children" was given to one hundred and seventy-five boys and girls between eight and fourteen years of age. They were allowed to look at it "carefully" for two minutes, after which they were asked to describe it in writing. The older group, who were asked to describe a cigarette, was composed of teachers in training and laboratory assistants.

up other tests to probe such types more adequately and also to assess the consequences of these differences "for the rest of intelligence." He found the teachers impressed by the differences "in the character and form of intelligence" that were evident in the many "protocols," and decided that this test, "to describe an object," was an excellent means of determining "personal styles"; he warned, however, that more than one test was needed. While his detailed illustrations of each type are fascinating, they lack something in preciseness, and yet they are obviously early probings with a projective instrument. He himself characterized the task as one in which "a pupil must withdraw into his own depth [self?]." Indeed, he perceived this "personal factor" as so important that he insisted upon "searching for the physical signs of [this personal] emotivity in changes of capillary circulation, heart rhythm, respiratory modifications, even if only artificially evoked" (69, p. 123). He published, with Courtier and Vaschide, a half-dozen articles on the physiological effects of the emotions, and of physical and intellectual work, saying of these relationships as he noted how much the results were affected by small changes in the conditions: "This is really psychology, make no mistake about it!" (266, p. 210). As his notes show, he began these studies in February 1895; he had been influenced by E. J. Marey, A. Mosso, and German and Italian studies (56), and had given some reports at the Society of Biology. His subjects were adults, including himself, and schoolboys. Putting all the data together he must have been disappointed with his general proposition that both the individual and group differences exerted on the various physiological variables were so small as to offer no significant generalizations (61). Yet he was not convinced that his conclusions were definitive, since he later urged further research in this area (69, p. 123).

Another group of experiments will be surprising to those who see Binet as a psychologist of cognitive-perceptual functions. He published hundreds of pages, representing thousands of work-hours, on a prolonged, multifaceted investigation of individual differences in physique and physical force. Binet, with Vaschide, published eighteen chapters in volume 4 of *L'Année* in which they reported their studies, for two different age-groups, of relationships among a large number of physiological, physical, and anatomical measures. The experimenters honed their measuring instruments so diligently that, for example, they used three sizes of dynamometers to fit different hand-measurements; they took sixteen anatomical measurements, and they set tasks of physical force that included spirometers, several tests of strength, reaction times, distance running, and rope climbing. They could not have been serious when they added "intellectual order" to these items among which they sought correlations, since their criteria were simply teachers' judgments and students' memory for digits!

Although they recognized flaws in the instruments and conditions in this study, Binet and Vaschide were fairly well satisfied with the results as a basis for correlations. After many trials and errors in computing results, Binet hit upon a method that was a form of rank difference. Each individual was given a rank order for each measure, after which the whole group was separated into four subgroups for each measure. The computed averages of the rank orders in each of these subgroups were arranged in a table so that by inspection the average rank orders for each subgroup could be seen immediately. The experimenters described their crude methods of determining mean variations, of what is now called "internal consistency," and of the order of significance for each variable as it correlated with "total physical force" (65, pp. 171–72). It is not surprising that "intellectual order" was near the bottom of the list, but only that it was included at all in such faulty guise.

Of course, this whole problem was much too ambitious for the methodological tools and even the instrumentation available at that time. The collaborators recognized some of their shortcomings and did not claim great significance for their long and tedious labors. They called them "suggestive," and concluded with "intentions of continuing on a vaster scale." Furthermore, when Binet explained some of the experimental weaknesses in the research plan, he mirrored the feelings of many another investigator with these words: "... We could not know this [disadvantage] in advance; it is only after having completed a piece of work that one sees how it should have been carried out" (64, p. 2).

These laborious studies had bad reviews, which surely did not help the cause of French psychology abroad. For example, Shepherd I. Franz, in the *Psychological Review*, was harsh and devastating. He pointed out first that the experimenters had not calculated mean variations for the raw scores, but only for "ranks." He went on to point out errors in calculations, specifying pages and tables, and noted that, although there were some typographical errors, these were not the cause of the erroneous calculations, since they were also reproduced on the graphs. Any reader can verify these criticisms with quick, simple arithmetic. Franz went on to say that "the whole series of articles shows the marks of haste" (197, p. 665). In fact, Franz reflected the impressions of the twentieth-century reader of these many pages. There is a disconcerting carelessness throughout the grueling labor of this research, combined with admirable and minute diagnosis of unsolved problems. Binet's work seems replete with this paradox: careful, determined, and inventive probing for data and their interrelationships, contrasted with employment of data reported in haste. This particularly striking instance was performed with Vaschide, whose calculations Binet probably did not verify; the two men parted company shortly after.

La suggestibilité and the Psychology of Testimony

Binet's next publication was *La suggestibilité* (77), a book about which one American reviewer, at the end of a six-page résumé, commented:

> ... This bare description of the facts conveys no adequate idea of the author's ingenuity, erudition, tact, and fairness in the manipulation of an experiment and the interpretation of its results. He is a worthy leader in this

field of research. He has proved more than he set out to prove. Not only has he demonstrated a relation between normal suggestion and hypnosis . . . but has contributed much to our knowledge of the child mind and the theory of applied psychology [227, p. 616].

La suggestibilité was the second book published in the *Bibliothèque de pédagogie et de psychologie* "under the direction of Alfred Binet."[11] The fact that he was his own editor, unrestrained by a blue pencil, helps to explain why this book is so exuberant not only in tone but in pages of detail. It is expansive and prolix to a fault, but it is also "dramatic and carries the reader through a lifelike experience face to face with the child . . ." (227, p. 610).

Binet's historical chapter included the then recent but limited work of some Americans: Thaddeus L. Bolton, B. Sidis, and also L. M. Solomons and Gertrude Stein, who were working on automatic writing at the Harvard psychological laboratory, but who, Binet complained, failed even to mention his related research published several years earlier. Binet especially complimented the work of E. W. Scripture and his two students, J. A. Gilbert and C. E. Seashore. He found it "the most important—very curious and new . . ." (77, p. 63). For the most part, however, this historical account sharply illustrated the fact that little had been done on "suggestion" as separate from hypnosis. This was to be Binet's particular contribution, since at the end of the nineteenth century this difference was frequently not recognized. Binet's proposal to develop methods to study suggestibility without recourse to hypnosis as well as his emphasis on individual differences were as important as the results per se.

The experimental studies in this book investigated suggestibility under the following conditions: "suggestion by a directing idea"; "by moral personal influence," including one outstanding section that Binet related to legal

[11] This book had been preceded by an article (70), almost every word of which is incorporated in the book, which, with its much larger scope, is more appropriate for our attention. About one hundred and fifty children took part in these experiments, with twenty-four to forty-five in any one subtest.

testimony given by children; "suggestion by imitation in a group of peers"; and "suggestion by automatic or subconscious movements." Binet strove to control the influence of the experimenter in all tests except where it became the explicit independent variable, but since he was always present he knew that he could not achieve this objective. He did produce experimental situations that "were nearer normal life than most" (216, p. 290).

Under the condition of a "directing idea" Binet used lines and little boxed weights in several variations that set up the idea in the subject's mind of expecting further increases, in longer lines or heavier weights. After the first four increasing stimuli he introduced a "trap" (*le piège*) by keeping constant the following stimuli and recording the responses of from ten to thirty-one such constant stimuli in a row. In order to arrive at numbers by which he could compare individual differences, he worked out a method for calculating "coefficients of suggestibility" for each subject. In the lines, for example, these coefficients ranged from 109 to 625; Binet could then put the results for each category of tests in ranks, comparing individuals or groups by quartiles or otherwise. In his first tests, and a replication with other subjects, he found relatively close correlations among tests and subtests, although he believed that his "new methods" required further refinements. He could not forego turning "moralist" toward his scientific colleagues by remarking that "directing ideas" influenced others than children. He wrote: ". . . It is indeed rare that men of science observe and experiment without being led by a directing idea, whose verification they are pursuing" (77, p. 86). Surely he was recalling his own misguided efforts at the Salpêtrière.

By the condition called "suggestion by moral influence" Binet referred to the effects of another person's persuasion. In one variation the experimenter introduced contradictions. Two or three times as the subject was writing the names of a series of colors shown to him, the experimenter would say in a neutral tone (*voix blanche*): "No! blue!" just as the subject was about to write "green." "The great majority," Binet reported, "wrote the name of the color suggested," although in subsequent interrogation they asserted that they knew better. In the second variation the experimenter showed lines, all 60 mm long, and alternated between saying, "Now the next one is 'shorter' " and "this one is 'longer.' " Sixteen students out of twenty-three "completely submitted to the suggestions."

A more interesting variation of "moral action," as Binet called it, introduced a little competitive spirit to motivate the subjects to greater accuracy. Six objects were attached to a cardboard. There was a whole but battered sou with several distinguishing features; a sales ticket from the lingerie department of the *Bon Marché* that had a pin sticking through it; a button with four holes, and pasted, not sewn, to a carton; a black and white portrait of a man with his mouth open, yawning or haranguing; an uncanceled postage stamp; and an illustration representing a postmen's strike in front of a gate set in a high wall. Of course, all the items had several features that could be erroneously recalled. The instructions are helpful in imagining the experiment:

> My friend, we are going to do an experiment together, to discover whether you have a good memory, a better memory than your comrades. I am going to show you a cardboard . . . on which some objects are attached, and place it before you . . . for ten seconds, which is a very short time. . . . You must look very hard and attentively at the objects, because after ten seconds I shall take them away and then ask you many questions about what you have seen. Do you understand? [77, p. 248].

He lengthened the time to twelve seconds, "while the student leaned forward, and devoured it with his eyes." Recording the responses himself, Binet first asked the student to tell everything he saw and then followed up with specific questions. He manipulated conditions to investigate three different degrees of "forced memory," using different subjects for each, of course. The first questionnaire asked straightforward questions, like "What color is the portrait?" "How is the button fixed to the carton?" "Is the stamp French or foreign?" "Is the sou old or new?"

Or: "Draw the sales ticket." He provided many pages of verbatim responses that fell into two main categories: logical—for example, if subjects judged that the button was sewn on; and inventive—for example, if subjects believed that the stamp was foreign. This latter category contained the largest number of errors.

The second questionnaire insinuated errors by "moderate suggestion" like "Isn't the portrait a dark brown?" "Isn't the sou a new and shiny one?" "Isn't the stamp canceled?" The third carried strong suggestion like "Is the [black and white] portrait dark brown or dark blue?" "How large was the hole in the [intact] sou?" Or "What color is the thread that fastens the [pasted on] button to the cardboard?" To the first two questionnaires Binet received both affirmations and doubts or negations of the suggestion, but to the third the suggestions took over almost completely. Not entirely satisfied with these results, Binet varied the conditions and used another group of children. After showing them the cardboard with attached objects, he asked them to *write* all their memories, including every detail noticed, and he allowed twenty minutes for this report. Of course the copies were differentially rich or poor in detail, but the number of outright errors was a third or less than in the case of the "forced memories." He thereby proposed that "if you wish to achieve maximum verity in children's testimony, do not pose questions to them, even questions devoid of all precise suggestion, but simply tell them to describe everything they recall, and leave them tête-à-tête with paper [and pencil]" (77, p. 294).

Perhaps the most significant result of this work was the finding that feelings of certainty and completeness of reported detail were not at all incompatible with errors; that is, reliability of testimony was not correlated with the subject's "certainty" or with his precision of recall. As Binet stated:

Specialization is a characteristic of the errors. A child's description can be exact on one point and false on another. . . . This dissociation of perception, this specialization of errors, has a double importance, both for psychology and for the practical science of testimony. . . . Practically, it proves to us that we would be wrong in believing that when a person makes one correct response from memory, he will respond correctly for the remainder. Often in judicial quarters one hears the reliability or truthfulness of a witness discussed; and if by chance his testimony can be verified on one point, he appears to acquire [in the eyes of the court] a status or reputation for much greater reliability regarding other points that cannot be verified.

We can formulate only general rules, but it appears that partial dissociations of memories must be admitted, and consequently, being given a series of memories—a, b, c, d, etc.—we cannot conclude that if "a" is found to be exact, this is proof that "b, c, d, etc." are also exact [77, pp. 285–86].

Binet took the same or similar tests to Versailles to a teacher-training institution and, while the number of errors among these late adolescents was smaller than among the primary school children, he judged that "the method of suggestion by means of leading questions is powerful enough to influence not only children but young eighteen-year-old men as well" (77, p. 329).

Binet's following chapter on "suggestion by imitation" deserves a place in any historical account of the psychology of small groups. Despite its poor controls by present standards, it is truly an attempt to measure the influence of children on their peers. He differentiated between "suggestibility" and "imitation" by saying that the former is "the induction of judgment by erroneous cues," while the latter is a subform, induced by "the repetition of the *same* detailed error as that of another person." Binet takes the reader through his several trials and gropings as he was developing his procedures. Trying to pinpoint "imitation," he took primary children into a room, three at a time, presented them with the six objects on the cardboard for twelve seconds, and then read questions one at a time to all three. He or an assistant recorded the order and content of each child's responses beside his name. Although the exceptions are instructive, he was surprised to find that most of the pupils wanted to be the first to answer, "thus hampering reflection," and he was "astonished" at their imitation. There were none who resisted suggestion by imitation less than ten times, and a fourth of the group yielded to it thirteen times. Some even drew the same kind of hat that the first respondent had drawn, or the same sou with its nonexistent hole, or the same erroneous postmark, and so on. Because some of the pupils tended always to answer last, he put the orders of the replies in a table for easier inspection, and concluded: ". . . these dry numerical results are nonetheless very interesting, since they show that each child in a group [tends to] take a position in the group . . . , which is maintained; [that is], the group organizes itself . . ." (77, p. 342). He felt that future tests of "imitation" would be improved by setting up competitive conditions among the groups, perhaps by rewarding the group with the most exact answers, so that accuracy would be more highly desired than in his testing situation where no group loyalty had been aroused.

This test presented one more illustration of Binet the experimentalist who allowed unexpected results rather than a priori contentions to speak to the problem posed:

> In imagining this collective experiment I had supposed that a group of children working together and judging memories common to them would, thanks to their collaboration, become less suggestible than children alone; I had supposed that this bringing together of three intelligences would augment the critical spirit of the responses, would dissipate also this feeling of timidity that is one of the most important adjuncts of children's suggestion. But the results have shown me to be completely wrong [77, p. 343].

Throughout *La suggestibilité* Binet's conclusions were hedged and cautious. In final form judgments about the group experiment on "imitation" were simple: "Grouping produces: 1) a division of functions, some children becoming leaders, others followers; 2) an increase of suggestibility; 3) a strong tendency to imitation" (77, p. 359).

To study suggestibility in unconscious movements, Binet used two variations: automatic writing, initiated by the experimenter, and a modification of a balance-apparatus from Wundt's psychological laboratory in Leipzig.[12] The chapter gives a vivid account of the difficulties encountered and, it appears, not satisfactorily overcome. Except for one or two of the most and the least "automatic responders," he found no correlations between the two tests.

At the conclusion of the book Binet considered that he had made two contributions. First, he had demonstrated to a large vocal group of doubters that an experimenter could investigate suggestibility without using hypnosis; and second, he had been able to imagine tests that could *classify,* not directly measure, individual differences in school children's suggestibility, *in the terms of the tests used.* That is, from the results, he made no general claims about suggestibility.

Although it seems bizarre today to believe that this first demonstration was necessary, it was a fact that he found the doors of many schools closed to him because of the headmasters' suspicions that hypnosis would necessarily be a part of his experimentation.[13] With the months of work with children that these experiments had entailed, he felt he had resolved this objection. But, in addition, the introspections that he had requested from his little subjects had provided him with insights on still obscure points about the mechanism of suggestion. On the one hand, he found a similarity with hypnotism in that the subjects underwent "suggestion with the intermediary of unconscious phenomena." He added: "He is ignorant of the origin of the idea that directs him, and does not know why he continues to submit; indeed, he even invents motives to explain his conduct" (77, p. 201). On the other hand, differences lay first in the fact that the subjects of a psycho-

[12] This apparatus was a hammer, held by the subject, but which could be raised and lowered by the experimenter in time with a metronome. After the experimenter had ceased his activations, he would record the subjects' continued responses.

[13] The difficulties of getting subjects, and of finding sympathetic teachers and principals, which Binet discussed at various times, must have hampered his plans. It should be recalled that he was carrying out these studies before the advent of *La Société.*

logical experiment, without hypnosis, become less suggestible as the tests multiply, while under hypnosis the subject becomes more and more suggestible as the experiences multiply, and "it is this condition that constitutes the moral danger of hypnosis" (p. 375). Secondly, the suggestible subjects in an experiment, through instruction and demonstration, can gain much more control over these "unconscious tendencies to suggestibility." Binet fairly belabored the experimenter's moral responsibility to explain his objective at the conclusion of the tests, as well as his pedagogical responsibility to help the students "cure" their suggestibility by calling attention to their errors and urging the development of habitual controls (77, pp. 375, 388).

Binet recognized deficiencies in the reliability of the tests as well as in their internal consistencies, and urged the development of a much wider variety of tests that could be validated with real-life situations. Furthermore, although he was devoted to measurable individual differences, the following characteristic and colorful quotation portrays his appreciation of the richness and complexities of human personality, the qualitative differences that no measure could yet encompass:

> . . . Whatever may be the manner of combining these different elements [that characterized the subjects' judgments], one feels sure that mere numbers cannot bring out . . . the intimate essence of the experiment. This conviction comes naturally when one watches a subject at work . . . as he is left to himself. What things can happen! What reflections, what remarks, what feelings, or, on the other hand, what blind automatism, what absence of ideas! From the subject's [seemingly simple] notations . . . the experimenter judges what may be going on in his mind, and certainly feels some difficulty in expressing all the oscillations of a thought in a simple, plain [*brutal*] number, which can have only a deceptive precision. How, in fact, could it sum up what would need several pages of description!
>
> We consider it necessary to insist that the suggestibility of a person cannot be expressed entirely by a number, even if the latter should correspond exactly to his degree

> of suggestibility. It is necessary to complete this number by a description of all the little facts that complete the physiognomy of the experiment [77, pp. 119–20].

Like the "Ninety-five theses" this statement should have been nailed to the church door for later experimenters and practitioners to read! It also represents Binet's attitude toward the intelligence scale.

His equivocation between "contribution" and "criticism" of his own work exemplifies Binet's personality: he always perceived and was compelled to note both his originality and his shortcomings. It is natural that his readers would do the same. This book is indeed so prolix as to discourage careful study. There are careless errors, both in printing and in recording data, and, of course, methodological weaknesses are very apparent. Yet the record provides a large residue of increased insights on the contagion within groups, on the psychology of children's memory as related to the psychology of testimony, on the fact of measurable individual differences in suggestibility, and on the ingenuous originality of applying experimental methodology to the study of such a complex and significant aspect of personality as suggestibility. Binet's own conclusions furnish a fair judgment. Although claiming that this work was "only a sketch, with everything to be completed," he also concluded:

> These experiments will render a great service to individual psychology. The degree of suggestibility is one of the most important characteristics of the individual. . . . Every time one tries to classify characters in a useful manner, according to real observations and not to a priori ideas, one is bound to give a large share to suggestibility [70, p. 84]. . . . This work represents a real, but small, part of a much more general plan . . . of a prospectus I published with Victor Henri in the name of "individual psychology" [77, p. 385].

This intrepid researcher, so well aware that "these studies are barely outlined here," considered analogous studies on imbeciles and idiots, who appeared to him as very suggestible. By this period Simon had come to work with him and undertook to apply the same methods to studies of inmates at Vaucluse. As far as possible he duplicated the tests, usually omitting written answers and a few other items that were too difficult for his subjects. He soon discovered that his "morons" were equal to, or even a little superior to, the normals in their control of suggestibility. Perhaps this was due to a growing lack of timidity, since Simon had lived among them for a year. They also showed few emotions such as blushing, embarrassment, or obvious frustration, which Binet's subjects had exhibited. Actually the results of this study of retardates are of little apparent value, except, perhaps, in demonstrating their social indifference, but they do fit appropriately into Binet's attempts to illuminate individual psychology.[14]

Regrettably, Binet failed to follow up this fruitful area of suggestibility and the related psychology of witness testimony that presented such an important scope for psychology. J. Larguier des Bancels (207), Ed. Claparède, and others have credited him with the first *experimental data* in the field, but it was Wilhelm Stern and his coworkers in Breslau who, two years after the publication of Binet's *La suggestibilité,* initiated studies and a journal on this subject, the *Beiträge zur Psychologie der Aussage.* In 1905 Binet, "with a little melancholy," reiterated his priority in this field, and blamed some of the failure to develop it in France on the inertia of the administrators of justice, whom he had approached to request permission to study jailed criminals and their dossiers. "Respect for the assassins!" was their reply. Binet's "melancholy" should have been enlightened by a realization that his work on testimony per se filled the pages of only one chapter of *La suggestibilité* and was not even given a title to identify the field. Furthermore, his explicit claim to breaking new and significant ground was buried in a footnote:

> The questions that we are treating here are so new that they shed light on some unnoticed, unexpected blind spots.

[14] These studies are reported by Th. Simon in an article entitled, "Expériences de la suggestion sur des débiles," *L'Année* 6 (1900): 441-84.

I want to point out in passing the usefulness that could come from creating a practical science of testimony by studying errors of memory, the means of recognizing them, and also ways of recognizing the signs of fact [or accuracy]. This science is too important for it not to be organized at some time or another [77, p. 285].

It is not surprising, therefore, that his priority was not credited.

Nonetheless, it should be added that, although Binet had not himself pressed forward, he conceived of the field as including much more than the psychology of court testimony. He also recognized its relationship to the psychology of making judicial judgments, of pronouncing verdicts and penalties, in fact of all formal judicial courtroom procedures. As a result he proposed the formulation of a *psychojudicial* science, and believed that only circumstances beyond his control prevented him from exploiting it (116).

Tactile Sensitivity: The Two-point Threshold

Sometimes the dispersion in Binet's coverage of topics for study seems more apparent than real. For the most part it revolved around the pole of individual differences, and not infrequently he returned to make a new attack on earlier topics. This is true of his studies of handwriting, of physical signs of intelligence, especially cephalometry, and of individual "portraits" of writers. In 1901 he returned to tactile sensations, especially to the establishment of the two-point tactile threshold. (The experimenter applies to various parts of the *blindfolded* subject's skin a compasslike instrument called an esthesiometer. The experimenter can change the stimulus by altering distances between the two blunted points, by one or two centimeters more or less, or can also apply only one point. The objective is to try to discover how small a separation can be detected as "two points" rather than being mistaken for one point. The smallest distance detectable as "two" is then called the two-point tactile threshold.) Far removed as it seems today, at the turn of the century it was a very conspicuous topic for investigation in Wundt's laboratory, and therefore among his former students in the United States. Furthermore, Binet's collaborator, Victor Henri, had not only completed his doctoral thesis in Germany in this field, but had also written a highly documented general review on tactile sensations for *L'Année* (203). *La fatigue intellectuelle* had also offered "promising uses" for tactile sensitivity in measures of fatigue in the schoolroom. Additionally, Binet had studied it in his report on "Attention et adaptation" (74) in 1899, the same year in which he published research on tactile sensitivity during states of distraction.

In 1901, Binet published in *L'Année* and the *Revue philosophique* over two hundred pages on the two-point threshold (91, 92, 93, 94, 95, 96, 98). A physiologist whom he called Dr. X had asked Binet to test him carefully with an esthesiometer in order to assist him in some of his work. In this subject Binet had a highly motivated individual. Although the doctor was acquainted with esthesiometers, he had not seen the one that Binet had improved and now used. There were two experimental sessions of two hours each. The most striking result was an increase in Dr. X's errors for the single stimulus; in fact, the longer the experiment proceeded, the more confused and doubtful he became. He even began to suspect that Binet had substituted a different instrument. Often he remarked about the form of the points, which appeared to him as "bizarre, unsolid, and changing." Binet remarked:

> When the two sessions were terminated, I showed him my instrument and his responses. At that moment he conceived a violent suspicion of the accuracy of the Weber method of measuring tactile sensitivity . . . It was evident to us that on this examination the role of interpretation, imagination, and [selective] judgment was considerable [94, p. 204].

Madeleine, then fifteen years old, gave Binet the definitive clue to the fact that individual *interpretations* were determining responses. He asked her to repeat similar experiments that she had performed six months earlier, and discovered that she improved noticeably and demonstrated the influence of her interpretations: "I knew better this time what the sensations meant," she said. "When a sensation was a little 'big,' I thought there must be two points, because it was too thick for one" (94, pp. 207–8). Binet himself then became a subject and discovered that he could control the number of his errors according to his own stipulations about his responses. Individual interpretation, therefore, became crucial to reliability.

These dramatic instances that challenged many of the results then being published about tactile thresholds led Binet to read and reread the literature on the subject. He felt the importance of starting "from the beginning" with Ernst H. Weber's original Latin monograph of 1834: *De Pulsu, Resorptione, Auditu et Tactu.* As the title indicates, it covered a lot of ground, and Binet could not refrain from pointing out that Weber's precise experiments on "the pulse" sounded much like the claimed "recent discoveries attributed to some of our contemporary physiologists. . . ." In his tactile investigations Weber had utilized introspective reports by asking his subjects to analyze four or five degrees of the "distinctness" of their sensations. These introspections became very significant for Binet, and he remarked that Weber had unfortunately failed to emphasize them sufficiently (91, p. 94), for Binet had discovered that these personal interpretations entered into the subjects' responses to feeling "one" or "two" points of tactile stimulation. Alerted as he was, Binet studied the literature with new insight. He recognized that other astute observers, especially Henri, his own student Clavière, who was then a professor at the college of Chateau-Thierry, and the American, George Tawney, had also noted that subjects reported intermediary sensations between "oneness" and "twoness" that would make the meaning of their responses equivocal. But he pointed out that they had failed to capitalize on the real significance of these subjective interpretations, as he proposed to do. Binet first reproached Gustav T. Fechner and Wilhelm Wundt, asserting that Fechner was so preoccupied with technical precision that he committed "some enormous errors" in subjective controls. He wrote:

I am alluding here to an error so grave that one would hesitate to impute it to the father of psychophysics if the written proof were not furnished. Fechner, working alone to compare two weights that he raised successively, knew every time in advance which of the two was the heavier! [91, p. 120].

Fechner also smoothed out troublesome results in "doubtful cases" by dividing them between the True and False categories: "Thus," Binet commented, "to have doubted twice is as if a subject had made one exact perception and one false one" (91, p. 125). He also pointed out similar "automatisms" in Wundt's laboratory. For example, his tactile thresholds were determined by averaging the data for increasing and decreasing minimal variations, yet each procedure was so open to suggestion that Wundt himself admitted to the "error of expectation," and resolved the matter by decree: two false computations, based on "expected errors," were averaged to determine a "true threshold." "A completely factitious result!" was Binet's incontrovertible remark (91, pp. 119–20). He maintained that such a technique that suppressed all responses except "True" and "False," or "one" and "two" was used only to quash more complex results that were too embarrassing to manage. After all, he himself had seen subjects who could not decide, and concluded that their "forced responses were simple guesses, given by chance, that raised the interesting problem of the unconscious" (91, p. 125).

Within this morass of unacceptable experimental conditions, however, Binet found one man whose probity stood out, and whose work was more impressive than he himself had apparently recognized. This was an American, George Tawney, who, although a student in Wundt's laboratory, had noted and reported individual differences and introspective responses, both of which were frowned upon in this "master's" domain. Actually as early as the mid-1890s Tawney had published several reports, in German and in English, and on one of them collaborated with Victor Henri. Yet Binet had failed to be impressed with their implications until Dr. X's reactions had borne in upon him.

Binet now commended Tawney for not burying his results that had disagreed with so many and better known men who insisted that practice makes the threshold more sensitive, and therefore more accurate. Tawney reported that practice brought improvement only for those who *expected* a practice effect, but not for those who, as Binet put it, "due to an infraction of the rule ordinarily followed in Wundt's laboratory, had not been told the true purpose of the experiment" (95, p. 235). When unaware of the objective, they changed very little, but then improved immediately when the experimenter told them that he was "seeking the effects of practice." Moreover, Tawney "had the probity to fix his attention strongly on a recurring error," that of the *Vexirfehler,* or the paradoxical illusion of feeling two points of the esthesiometer when in reality only one is applied. In the latter case Tawney found that instead of improving, "as the education [practice] of the subject is increased, the number of errors on the single-point also increases." This was true even of Friedrich Kiesow, Wundt's *préparateur,* an "esteemed scholar" and a most conscientious experimenter. Tawney reported that even after Kiesow was shown the single point he continued to feel its application as "two." Binet wrote that "Tawney's work is infested with [reports of] this 'error', which, like an evil weed, swarms all over a cultivated field" (91, p. 99).

Patently the effects of suggestion, of unreliable results, and of *Vexirfehler*[15] threw grave doubt on the many tactile thresholds that filled the monographs and texts. Binet wondered why Tawney had not pressed "the capital importance" of his results, but surmised either that the author himself had not understood their "revolutionary character" or that "perhaps he did not bring them to light through prudence, so as not to shock some local authorities in Wundt's laboratory, which is like a sanctuary where

[15] "The *Vexirfehler,*" Binet wrote, "have been the despair of some experimenters who are at a loss as to what to do with them, or how to represent them in their calculations; *some authors have even decided never to use the single point—a radical means to prevent the error!*" (92, p. 146; italics added). Radical indeed!

Weber's tradition is profoundly respected" (91, p. 97). In other words, while Tawney must have recognized that the experimental data on touch thresholds were demonstrably unreliable because they were influenced by "nuances of felt sensations," his discussions were muted and obscure. Most important, he had failed to press the "revolutionary conclusion" that these results compromised the whole measure of tactile sensitivity. This reticence did not affect Binet, who expressly and clearly converged on the "revolutionary conclusion." Strangely there is no recognition of this fact in the psychological literature.

Binet was not satisfied to rely on Tawney's results without testing them himself. His research plan to study tactile thresholds presents almost a model of critical analysis in psychological methodology. He demonstrated the importance of instrumentation,[16] and of an improved testing method, which he called "irregular variations," to reduce the interfering factor of "expectancies." In fact, since he noted that "the subject responds with his whole intelligence," he gave special attention to "the errors that form the personal equation," both by applying precise experimental explanations and instructions and by recording stenographic notes of all, "absolutely all,"of the words exchanged by subjects and experimenter. He ended his exposition with the words: "Don't forget that, when you are dealing with tactile sensitivity, you are right at the heart of psychology." He was clearly accommodating to what today are called "the demand characteristics of the experimental setting."

Binet used both trained subjects, as experimenters did at Leipzig, and naïve or unpracticed ones of various ages and educational backgrounds, since the preferability of the one or the other had not been determined. From the results of these heterogeneous subjects, even including eleven blind persons, he listed three categories of respondents: the simplists, the *distraits* or those whom he experimentally "distracted," and the interpreters. For the most

[16] He had himself constructed an esthesiometer that he believed to be more effective than any previously recommended ones.

part, although not exclusively, the schoolchildren were the simplists, who answered "I feel two points" only when they had no doubts. That is, they gave a "one" response until the difference clearly became "two." The thresholds for the simplists were quite distinct and even sudden. The *distraits* are not important for the main purpose of the discussion. It is easy to infer that it was the interpreters who cast serious doubt on the myriad experiments that had purported to establish tactile thresholds. Binet demonstrated that their responses were "reflective, more refined" and definitely the result of deciding upon judgments rather than of some state of [physiological?] tactile sensitivity. When the two points of the esthesiometer were close enough to confuse the respondent so that he felt "thick," "broad," or "dumbbell-shaped" sensations, but *not* two distinct stimuli, he might reply, "I feel 'one' or 'two' " according to his own personal interpretation. These subjective responses, plus the prominent *Vexirfehler*, brought such unreliability to the results that it was impossible to make any claims of established thresholds.

Since Binet's work with the results of practice on the threshold also were in agreement with Tawney's, without apology he stated his conclusions that the effect of practice on the threshold lay in the expectation of the beholder, and that "the threshold of a double sensation cannot be scientifically determined." The responses were instead determined by the direction of attention, and by judgments about the stimuli. Moreover, Binet further claimed that very careful attention and reflection on the part of a subject frequently befuddled or clouded the responses so that what was at first clear became vague. To this delectable datum he called to witness Fechner's own testimonial about some of his psychophysical experiments: the results, Fechner had admitted, were more effective when he did not conscientiously reflect upon them. "This remark," Binet added, "could be used as an epitaph for this chapter" (96, p. 247).[17]

[17] I communicated with Prof. E. G. Boring about these Binet papers, since in his publications he only briefly mentions Tawney's experiments, without noting their implications, and ig-

L'Étude expérimentale de l'intelligence

The studies on problems of tactile sensitivity were followed by *L'Étude expérimentale de l'intelligence,* a book that has been called Binet's masterpiece. In this book he returned to the careful study of his daughters who were then entering adolescence. Apparently he had been observing them continuously since publishing the 1890 papers,[18] but only after 1900 did he begin the concentrated, systematic work that produced this volume. He insisted that at that embryonic stage of psychology, results obtained by this method of intensive study of a few subjects, well known to the experimenter, were much superior to data collected from hundreds of subjects about whom the experimenter had no other knowledge. Like most of his other books, the title of this one should not be taken literally, at least not according to current usage. The word "intelligence" is misleading because for Binet this concept seems to have been correlative with the concept of "personality." He stated, in fact, that he was making a detailed study, through ideas, images, and words, "of what is truly personal in each of us." It is an experimental study of personality differences. His experiments also led to provocative

---

nores Binet's. Although he replied near the beginning of his fatal illness, he characteristically took great pains to include appropriate reprints and references. He did not, however, attempt to account for his failure to have noted Binet's work in this area, but wrote generously: "There has been very considerable writing on the *Vexirfehler* in the two-point limen, and I know quite a lot of it, but evidently not all, because you know more than I do about Binet and Henri and Tawney" (1 February 1967). Not knowing the work of these men, Boring actually gave the credit to Titchener for recognizing the role of interpretations in tactile thresholds (E. G. Boring, *Sensation and Perception in the History of Experimental Psychology,* 1943, p. 252, note to Titchener, *Proc. Amer. Phil. Soc.* 55 [1916]: 204–36). It is important to note the 1916 date of Titchener's observation.

[18] Binet speaks of studies carried out "*with two little girls . . . who have for a long time served in my research in experimental psychology*" (*L'Année* 6 [1900]: 405; emphasis added).

discussions of imageless thought, for which the Würzburg school, rather than Binet and Paris, became well known a few years later.

L'Étude . . . has never been translated into English, and, because of its prolixity, it is doubtful that it will be, but it is a study well worth the attention of a perceptive student. A generation ago Edith Varon wrote that "this book represents the greatest of Binet's attempts to study mental states by simple means, and also the most complete and careful attempt to characterize psychological types in accordance with the results of tests" (303, p. 70). In 1911 one of Binet's contemporaries lauded this book, while at the same time he disparaged the intelligence scale:

> Binet said that the results of *L'Ètude* . . . add up only to small partial "verities". . . . However, the facts, for the moment inexplicable, were so striking and so suggestive, . . . and they contained so many promises for psychology that they make the program of Toulouse, Vaschide, and [Henri] Piéron appear very poor, and the synthesis of Titchener quite incomplete. Unfortunately the author seems not to have followed up these very original beginnings . . . which reveal the mechanisms of thought. . . . He quit [to follow instead] the needs of pedagogy . . . to establish a metric scale of intelligence [206, pp. 64–65].

The late Florence Goodenough of the University of Minnesota, whose enthusiasm for Binet spilled over warmly in her graduate classes, perceived this study in its proper setting as "perhaps the earliest and certainly one of the best studies of projective methods that has appeared in the literature." She continued:

> Binet was interested in the qualitative aspects of thought and behavior. . . . *L'Étude* . . . is unrivaled for the masterly way in which facts of seemingly little consequence in themselves are marshaled, one after the other, in an array that eventually leads to a remarkably illuminating analysis of the fundamental differences in the attitudes and ways of thinking of the two girls. . . . At the end of his studies Binet emerges with one of the most convincing pictures of personality differences that has ever appeared.

... Compared with it, most of the modern projective methods appear superficial [276, pp. 416–22].[19]

But Goodenough's opinion has been slighted, as much as Binet's work has been.

Binet gave a very interesting foreview of his *L'Étude* ... in an earlier sketch, *"L'observateur et l'imaginatif"* (83). It was a happy chance that led him to his concentration on the tests finally decided upon, and that culminated in the book. He began during the family summer vacation, for he set the starting date as July 1900, when, "without any preconceived notion," he decided to try to delineate in some way the mental characteristics of his daughters, who were then about thirteen years and fourteen-and-a-half years old. He seems to have had in mind covering at least roughly the ten areas of individual psychology programmed by Henri and himself (59). "I continued almost every morning for five months," he wrote, "and then followed up at various times through 1902." Each day he probed and studied the results, comparing them continually, putting aside those that seemed insignificant, and "repeating, verifying, and modifying" anything that seemed particularly interesting. From his very numerous documents he began to perceive that the "individual psychology of the subjects was not by any means made up of bits and pieces, not a juxtaposition of disparate mental qualities, but governed by some *caractères dominateurs* . . ." These dominating characteristics brought him to abandon the idea of going from one trait to another in search of "the total individual psychology" of the girls, but instead to focus extensively on one of these dominating characteristics, *the habitual orientation of ideas* (83, p. 522).

These insights into dominant characteristics apparently came as the result of tests in which he had asked the girls to write several series of words that totaled about three hundred for each of them. They also may have resulted from studies of ideation that he had adapted from those

[19] Goodenough's exuberance caused her to state also that all the differences of his analyses "would meet even the most rigid of modern requirements for 'statistical significance.' " This is undoubtedly a case of hyperbole.

of B. Bourdon, G. d'Aschaffenburg, T. Ziehen, and H. Ebbinghaus. From these various items he had perceived that Madeleine showed a tendency toward "observation" and Alice toward "imagination." As he cast about for more effective items, almost as if by chance he suddenly recalled his earlier tests using "description of objects," and quickly included items in which he asked his subjects to describe pictures and events in addition to common objects. These items, he wrote, "supplied the keystone of the arch." And because they had accrued without any conscious expectation of their significance, he felt that they were all the more scientifically valid. He proceeded to gather dozens of these descriptive protocols, until he was satisfied that by means of a very great number of precise experiments, he had been able "to affirm that the types of 'observer' and 'imaginative' have an importance in individual psychology that has not been suspected up to now . . ." (83, p. 523). He continued to experiment, both to add further data and particularly to try to discover whether the subjects' discrete and impressively different patterns of thinking would leave their imprint on other mental aptitudes. That is, he wondered if one could discern their effects on the functions of reasoning, remembering, concentration of attention, and the like. The book takes the reader almost step by step through the processes of the three years of experimentation.

In setting up his conditions Binet stressed the control of variables and the systematic, extensive use of "attentive, detailed, and profound introspection," which enriched experimental understanding. He listed his apparatus as "only a pen, a little paper, and a great deal of patience." The girls were strictly forbidden to discuss the activities with one another, and he gave them no inkling of his objectives in order to guarantee that their responses would not be vitiated by autosuggestion, "that formidable psychologists' error, the hazards of which should be posted along all the avenues of our science, like signs put up for cyclists to warn of dangerous descents." He also followed inflexibly the practice of writing at once everything that was said during the session, "for one word uttered by the experimenter can completely change the mental dispositions of the subject, and to neglect suggestibility is to commit a negligence equivalent to that of the bacteriologist who carries on very delicate research in a dirty medium" (90, p. 300).

Binet justified his use of only two subjects by contrasting this method with the statistical one that he felt could give nothing but mediocre results. In his characteristic style he continued to give serious attention to psychological methodology:

> . . . The Americans, who love to do things big, often publish experiments made on hundreds and even thousands of persons. They believe that the conclusive value of a work is proportional to the number of observations made. This is only an illusion. . . . If I have been able to throw some light by the attentive study of two subjects, it is because I have seen their behavior from day to day and have probed it over a period of several years.
>
> . . . We should prefer experiments that we can make on persons whose character and way of life are familiar to us. Our psychology is not yet sufficiently advanced to allow us to disdain any source of information that may be provided to us from outside our experiments. . . . I believe that when we study superior functions we should address ourselves to persons whom we know intimately—to relatives and friends [90, pp. 297–98].

He added that this arrangement permitted the frequent repetition of an experiment, as well as intensive systematic variations in subtests, which could clarify the analyses and comparisons.

In order to simplify comparisons and discussion Binet numbered his tests one to twenty, although they are not, and were not to him, of equal importance. In general the first eight can be considered the most original and suggestive. For test number one Binet asked his subjects simply to "write twenty words," three times at a single sitting, and for five or six sittings. After each list he interrogated them about each one of the words, asking them to tell him whether it was written "without thinking of anything, that is mechanically; or while thinking of any object whatever in its class, or while thinking of a particular object." Each sitting lasted for about seventy minutes, and it is not surprising that Binet remarked that "these experiments were very long and hardly recreational." Neither was the experimenter's task "recreational" when he set himself to analyze responses to six hundred twenty words, the income from the two girls! He frequently used the phrase *"fouiller les résultats"*—to dig into the data—which is certainly appropriate to his painstaking search for meaning and significance. He first compared the results in six categories: unexplained responses; persons or objects in their present setting; things belonging or pertaining to the subject herself; memories, recent or distant; abstractions; and imaginings. The girls differed in all six areas, and their responses tended to fall into the categories of "introverted and imaginative" for Alice and "extroverted and observational" for Madeleine. Alice was less conscious of the sources of, and the transitions between, her words; that is, they had a more involuntary character than her sister's. Recent memories and present objects were also poorly represented, and in her three hundred words "she never named an object belonging to herself." She produced many more abstractions and even fictional situations than her sister. Madeleine, on the other hand, was in all things more in contact with the immediate exterior world; she could explain many more of the sources of her words, she included memories of very recent date, more concrete and real objects, and included visible stimuli. Her themes, or groups of associations that Binet discovered in the lists, were more regular, with little variation, and "even monotonous," while Alice's were shorter and showed "an incessant change in the direction of her thoughts, a zigzag route by little broken spurts—the unexpected, the original" (p. 68).

Binet's second test is reminiscent of Jung's word associations. He gave the girls twenty-five to thirty words at a sitting, and asked them what idea each word aroused. He had set up the same conditions in primary schools, but abandoned the experiment because he did not know the children well enough to assign significance to their responses. For his daughters he repeated this experiment "to satiety, for over two years; there were twenty or more sessions, and in each twenty-five to thirty words were used" (p. 72).

Again he made an analysis similar to the first one, and with similar results. For example, the immediate past was shown by Madeleine in her response to the word "crowd." She associated with it "the crowd at the dogmarket a week ago," while Alice recalled "the crowd acclaiming the Czar, rue Soufflot, several years ago." To "dust" Madeleine recalled "the dust of the forest when riding my bicycle there," while Alice remembered a small incident on the train two or three years before. To determine the intensity of images, Binet asked his daughters to rate their images of fifty words on a scale from 0 to 20; Alice's were the less intense. Finally, he asked them to follow his suggestions for changing their images: "Imagine a monkey who is smoking his pipe. . . . Now put a top hat on him and have him stand up," and so on. Alice could not do this; her images changed involuntarily and not at command. Madeleine was just the opposite; she continued to exercise a very strong voluntary action over the monkey that had been conjured up by her father's commands.

The third test varied from the first simply in a change from writing lists of words to writing lists of sentences. Again Madeleine's responses were more practical, more immediate, and Alice's more poetic and remote. For example, Madeleine wrote straightforwardly: "Today the weather is very nasty; it is raining and there is a lot of wind. This is indeed astonishing, for it was magnificent yesterday. Nevertheless, [Alice] and I went to the village on our bicycles, and we bought a yellow and green penholder for P . . ." The contrast with Alice's sentences is indeed striking. An example of hers is as follows: "In a gracious gondola in Venice we see the heads of some of the passengers." Or: "The funeral passes in silence and glides the length of the streets drenched with rain." Or: "The crows pass croaking in the night" (90, p. 173).

The fourth test consisted in asking the girls to complete

sentences, after the fashion of Ebbinghaus. A few illustrations will be of interest:

"I went into——"

Madeleine wrote: "a bakery and bought some chocolate for two sous."

Alice wrote: "the countryside by way of a covered path."

"The house——"

Madeleine finished with: "is warmed by a good stove."

Alice wrote: "is raised up on a height from which one sees a precipice, then a town whose distant noise comes feebly to us."

In the fifth test the girls were asked to write themes about given subjects, for example, "The death of a dog." Binet found this exercise too much like a school task to be useful, yet the same differences between detailed observation and vague, rather emotional responses were evident.

In the sixth test they were asked to write ten memories at a sitting, excluding only memories from the same day. Again the orientation of Madeleine's ideas was practical and of more recent events, while Alice's was more and more distant in time. Although it later becomes apparent to the reader that Madeleine appears more advantageously than Alice in her father's eyes, in this instance he remarked that "[Alice's] ideas are more reflective, more complicated than [Madeleine's]."

Binet states that he went thus far in his tests without trying one that had already given him notable results with schoolchildren and teacher trainees, namely, descriptions of pictures and objects. Now, in his seventh test, he asked his subjects to describe a picture. It is the same one that appeared later in the 1908 scale, with a boy and his father straining through a pelting rain and dragging all their ragged possessions on a peddler's cart. The girls also wrote descriptions of a box of matches, a paper-covered book, a leaf from a chestnut tree, a watch, a sou, a pen, a question mark, and others. It was this test that furnished "the keystone of the arch." A few illustrations will convince the reader that these two teen-agers looked at the world from different perspectives. When Binet presented the leaf of a chestnut tree, Madeleine wrote:

The leaf that I have in hand is a leaf of a chestnut tree picked up in the autumn, for the folioles are almost all yellow, except for two, and one is half green and yellow.

This leaf is a leaf composed of seven folioles attached to a center that ends in the stem called a petiole which holds the leaf on the tree. The folioles are not all of the same size; out of seven, four are much smaller than the other three.

The chestnut tree is a dicotyledone, which one can recognize by looking at the leaf; it has ramified ribs.

In several places the leaf is touched with points of rust color. One of the folioles has a hole.

I don't know any more to say about this leaf from a chestnut tree.

Alice's response was the following:

This is a leaf, from a chestnut tree, which has just fallen with the autumn wind. The leaf is yellow, but still stiff and straight, perhaps there yet remains a little vigor in this poor dying thing! Some traces of its former green color are still imprinted on the leaves, but yellow dominates: a brown and dark red trim its edges.

The seven leaves [folioles?] are all very pretty still, the greenish stem has not at all detached itself.

Poor leaf, now destined to fly along the streets, and then to rot, heaped up on many others. It is dead today—and yesterday it was alive! Yesterday hanging on the branch it was waiting for the fatal *blow* of wind that would loosen it and carry it off; as a dying person awaits his last agony.

But the leaf did not know its danger, and it fell softly onto the ground [90, pp. 216–17].

The request for a description of a sou brought the following:

[Madeleine]: This piece that I have under my eyes is a sou, it is brass, tarnished from long use. The edge of this piece represents an eagle with wings spread out, for it dates from Napoleon III emperor.

On the back is written: French Empire, five centimes.

On the face is the head of Napoleon III, encircled with these words: Napoleon emperor, and below, the date when the piece was struck, but it is too worn away, and I cannot read it.

This piece is not thick, almost 2 mm [90, p. 217].

[Alice]: It is an old sou worn by time; the head of Napoleon III is still distinguishable, most clearly on this tarnished background. What stains of *vert-de-gris* decorate some of the words: Napoleon III emperor, then the date. On the other side of the piece the letters are more worn, so that one distinguishes almost nothing more. . . . How long it would take to tell its story, this sou! Where does it come from? Through whose hands has it passed?

People don't even think of this in looking at a humble sou, they don't look for its history, Heavens, no! It appears so simple to look at a sou, it is so common! Sous pass along unperceived like so many things that one is used to seeing everywhere [90, 217–18].

The request for a description of a pen evoked the same kind of contrast: Madeleine again described every detail she could think of. For example: "This pen is a Blanzy-Poure pen, it is called that because it must have been fabricated at the house Blanzy-Poure. It is fairly long, it has not a very pointed end, but it is very good for writing. It is hollowed out from one end to the other. . . . At the end of the place where it is stuck into the holder, it is larger . . . I do not exactly know how to explain it. . . . This pen is about 3 cm long."

Alice imagined it as having a life of its own. She wrote: "It has not yet been used, it has then no history at all, it has not passed over any paper, it has not left the black marks that are so expressive. It is shining and very new, one guesses its whole story; it has remained peacefully in a box, while those like it went away, each in its turn. This is a very ordinary object, this pen! It can go with the box of matches and the old stamp, these objects will never draw any particular attention, they pass unperceived . . ." She then added a few of the details similar to those given by Madeleine (90, pp. 218–19. The girls had already written descriptions of the match box and the stamp).

One more illustration is the description of a question mark drawn on a piece of paper: [Madeleine]: "This piece of paper is in squares, gray on white. On this piece is written by hand in black ink a question mark, it is not quite in the middle, but a little to the left, and higher than the middle. This sheet can be about 15 cm by 10 cm." [Alice]: "This is an enigma, this piece of squared paper in the middle of which someone has drawn a question mark. The sheet is not large, the question is not by any means long, one is astonished and surprised to see this question point in the center of a white sheet . . . and there is nothing on the back" (90, p. 221). Binet pointed out that Madeleine started with a description, while Alice started with "an enigma," absorbed by the meaning. Alice, unlike Madeleine, was also inexact and inaccurate about the position of the mark on the paper, and about its being "drawn." He wondered if she was not speaking in a literary sense when she wrote, "the sheet is not large," because she went on to say, "the question is not at all a long one."

Binet repeated descriptive exercises for over two years, with similar results. He used a large variety of stimuli. For complicated prints and designs, however, the individual differences were small. Also, strangely unsuccessful were the girls' responses to ink blots, although he stated that he had earlier collected "some very interesting results" from a few schoolchildren, which it is regrettable that he did not publish. Those used with his daughters, at any rate, did not strike any provocative differences; perhaps his undoubtedly homemade ink blots evoked only the popular responses of butterflies or bats.

When he came to test number eight, Binet widened the base from the descriptions of pictures and objects to those of events. He asked each girl separately to write her memory of a train ride from Paris to Meudon the previous night; her memory of events at home during one evening, concerning which, parenthetically, Alice omitted the most important event, the registering of the family's voices on their new phonograph; and her memory of all the objects on the walls of the girls' bedroom. Again Madeleine was precise, and in the last assignment she proceeded in an orderly fashion, listing the objects as they existed around the room, while Alice had no regard for order nor position, nor did she ever enter into the details of any given subject matter as Madeleine did in her very conscientious, if not compulsive, way.

The remaining test items, from the ninth to the twentieth, were even at that time rather familiar in the psychological literature. There were five on attention, five on memory, and two with the curious rubric of "the interior life." These twelve tests, therefore, are less original except in Binet's discussions of them. They constitute his attempt to discover whether these ideational functions mirror in some way the "styles of thought" of the two girls. The account of them represents less than 20 percent of the book.

For several years Binet had been concerned with the nature and mechanism of voluntary attention, as well as its necessary relation to intelligence. "The force of voluntary attention" was the topic of tests numbered from nine through thirteen, and he borrowed several of the items from his work on "attention and adaptation" (74). For test number nine he asked his daughters to cross out specified letters on a sheet of text; for example, they were to draw a line through the a's, e's, d's, r's, and s's as fast as possible, without error, and usually for a ten-minute period. Madeleine was always on top. Poor Alice! The reader continues to hope that she never read the book, since her father made the comparisons very explicit.

Number ten required the familiar immediate repetition of numbers: twenty trials of five numbers each showed Alice with two errors more than her sister. The errors mounted perceptibly for both on the six-number lists, although Madeleine's accuracy was greater. Binet considered this as "uniquely a test of voluntary attention," and it is well known that it was an item that he used repeatedly in the scale.

In numbers eleven and twelve the subjects were asked to copy words, long lists of numbers, and complicated designs while the experimenter recorded the number of times they looked at the model as they copied it. Thus the number of elements apprehended at each glance provided an attempt to measure the *span* of attention. Alice almost always looked at the models more frequently than Madeleine.

In number thirteen Binet tested reaction times to tactile stimuli. At that time reaction times were reported ad nauseam throughout the psychological world, but probably none were reported in such individualized detail as those of Madeleine and Alice. Binet commented that it was "with some melancholy" that he occupied himself with reaction times, since "this research, with its immense number of studies, is one of those which has perhaps promised the most and delivered the least" (90, p. 240). And yet he believed that everything had not yet been said on the question. Introspection surely could add dimensions and interesting facts to broaden the problem, but more important, reaction times could be useful for individual psychology if they were related to the mental temperaments of the subjects. In about a week and a half, he took over three hundred reaction times of each of his daughters.

Binet provided carefully detailed descriptions of the conditions and results of each test as well as an analysis of his daughters' reactions to them. Madeleine was faster than Alice, and distinctly improved her responses, which was evidence of the "adaptation" that Binet had earlier attributed to better intelligence (74). Alice remained almost stationary, since her occasional spurts were balanced by slow motions. There were also strong differences in the girls' attitudes. He probed their feelings and manner of concentrating their attention; recorded their remarks, and their sighs. As usual Madeleine was very self-critical, "zealous, taking the exercises to heart, with feelings of regret and distress" when she thought she was inept. On the other hand, Alice was always "tranquil and indifferent"; the experiment became monotonous and she acted only out of politeness. "That," he wrote, "is what partially explains her slow reactions; . . . in other words, the curve of her reactions is also in part a curve of her character" (90, p. 250). He had observed the same heedlessness in everyday life. Reflecting on the significance of these character traits to measures of attention, Binet was not willing to say that his results were therefore vitiated: "After reflecting well on my results . . . I do not believe that there is a very great difference between not being able and not wishing, but only a difference in words. When [Alice] fails to make as vigorous an effort as her sister, it is proof to me that that is her nature . . . that there exists a constitutional difference between the power of attention of the two girls" (90, pp. 255–56). One wonders at Binet's lack of insight. The girls were then in their early teens, about fifteen and thirteen and a half. Their relationships, and intrasister competitiveness, especially with a father who, even in the pages of this book, seemed consistently to favor his elder daughter, could have made differences not hard to conjecture.

Binet's analysis of the girls' reaction times showed incontestably that their adaptation and attention had to be considered in any assessment of the results. The data forced the conclusion that studies of so-called simple reaction times are contaminated by emotional or temperamental attitudes, a finding that challenged Wundt's and Titchener's efforts to establish "pure" generalizations about such measures. The results of these tests, in which he had taken into account these individual differences, made him willing to conclude that Madeleine's power of attention was superior to her sister's, since she had demonstrated it in so many different tests (90, p. 255).

The five variations of tests of memory presented sore perplexities. Binet admitted that he had a "directing idea" that Alice simply had a memory inferior to Madeleine's. After the first test it became obvious that this observation was partially false. The expected consistency of Madeleine's superiority did not hold. "The question appeared well settled," he wrote, "when an altogether new test came to demolish my edifice of conclusions." In the initial one the girls learned verses, which Binet remarked "presented no difficulties of meaning" since they were frequently taken from the tragedies of Racine. Madeleine learned faster and recalled more accurately, both immediately and after a time lapse. He was sure that he was simply piling up more instances when he gave the girls lists of twenty and forty unconnected words to be learned within stated time limits. But the results were so puzzling that Binet repeated these lists for several months, sometimes reading the words aloud, sometimes giving them to the girls in writing. He seems almost chagrined to find the two subjects equal in their success. He then tried what he called "easy prose," extracts from letters of Mme de Sévigné and from the second volume of a French translation of *Nicholas Nickleby* that the girls had not heard previously.[20] He had two stipulations for the learning of Dickens' detail-packed lines: first, that his subjects should reproduce the meaning, and then give a word-by-word reproduction. They had only five minutes to study the passage. Again they were equal in reporting the meaning, and again Madeleine was superior in literal recall. There was, Binet felt, the same difference in their ways of learning their lessons, and a significant parallel in their "descriptions of objects": Madeleine was more literal and attached herself to the material character of the object, while Alice described the meaning and ideas evoked (90, p. 275).

Binet next attached various objects to a cardboard and asked the girls to recall as many as possible. In general both of them remembered eight or nine objects. Binet exclaimed in surprise, "After that, who would believe that [Madeleine] would learn textually sixteen lines of verse to [Alice's] eight!" He also remarked that this chapter was one that he had believed would be the easiest to write, while in reality it was the "one that has cost me the most trouble . . ." (p. 257). After painfully puzzling over the results he finally concluded that the difference must lie between voluntary and involuntary attention. The items in which Alice equaled her sister "required no particular

[20] The family had a habit of reading aloud, and were at that time reading the first volume of what Binet characterized as "the delightful *Nicholas Nickleby*."

effort on her part," but could be accomplished with spontaneous, perhaps mechanical attention. Alice had already been shown to have less force of voluntary attention. When things required more effort, she recalled them less well because of less attention, and not because of "a memory which, as a plastic force, is clearly weaker than [Madeleine's]."

With this directing idea he tried to introduce differential amounts of voluntary attention. He asked the girls to learn a series of English sentences, which would be completely devoid of sense for them. After a two-minute exposure Madeleine could write an average of fourteen words and Alice of nine words. Substituting complicated designs to be reproduced from memory, he found that Madeleine was again superior. Binet was now satisfied that he had made a correct differentiation between memory "as a plastic force" and attention, and he warned other experimenters to correct their mistakes made from a wrong premise, mistakes that combined the two functions (or faculties?). Adults, he said, did not, as was usually supposed, have better memories than children, but more matured and disciplined attention. For example, he and Larguier des Bancels had found that, after really learning pieces of verse, children retained them for a longer time than adults. He cited other instances in which he believed that plasticity diminishes with age, while the force of attention increases to compensate for this diminution. Later he acted on this hypothesis by putting various tests of memory and of attention into the mental scale. Whatever the reader may decide about Binet's differentiation between "attention" and "memory," or whether certain items given to the girls required only "involuntary attention," he must agree that Binet had provided evidence that people have *memories*, different kinds of memories, rather than *a* memory, an important point to make in the experimental study of individual differences.

The last two tests in the series included in *L'Étude* . . . attempted to compare directly the "interior life" of the girls. Binet used variations of tests of the reproduction or estimation of lengths, or spatial orientations, and those of intervals of duration, or time orientations. He concluded again that Madeleine was more externally directed, while Alice had a more internalized life experience. These tests and the results seem too lame for discussion.

At the conclusion Binet was obviously ambivalent about what he had done. He had certainly been "patient, through three years of studies." He had shown the usefulness of controlled and systematic introspections. He had not only repeated a single test many times, but had also varied each one a little, to clarify its meaning further. All the same, he wrote, "with the study of what is personal in each of us as the principal objective of the book, we have succeeded in finding only some little partial truths. . . . With the use of new approaches in psychology, we have found that undoubtedly there exists a mental continuity among the modalities of the functions that we have explored" (90, p. 300). But this continuity did not show an "ideal consistency" and "the words we apply to them are only labels, and not explanations." For instance, he noted that he had tried repeatedly to find a single word that would be applicable to each of the girls, but had found nothing satisfactory. The best seemed to be "stability" for Madeleine and "variability" for Alice. He qualified "stability" with the words "practical, reflective, ordered, conservative, balanced, uniform, serious, regular, precise, and so on" and "variability" with "idealistic, impractical, mobile, original, inventive, capricious, and so on." He also pointed out such contrasts as attachment to, or detachment from, the outside world; literal orientation versus imaginative; simple modes of association versus complex ones; memories for recent versus past events; practical versus poetic expressions; clear and intense images versus weak and imprecise ones. He regretted that his account was "more literary than scientific"; that it was not in any way explanatory. On the other hand, he believed that he had made a contribution by demonstrating a "harmony" or "unity" of individual thought modalities.

It is apparent that Binet was as disappointed as he was exhilarated. Indeed, he seems to have had some masochistic tendencies in his scientific honesty, for in a short footnote in his pages of "conclusions" he wrote:

I would have had pleasure in continuing my experiments on my two girls if I had not perceived that age had brought some changes in their character [they were about fifteen and a half and seventeen years old at the conclusion]. The psychological portraits that I have traced of them have become less characteristic today than they were three years ago; and it seems probable that more important changes will be produced in ten years [90, p. 298].

A few years later, however, he reported to the English psychologist Cyril Burt that the major characteristics he had described were largely unchanged.[21] And his discussion gave evidence that he thought the differences were genetic, since the girls had been brought up in such a homogeneous way.

Binet added some confusion for the reader by putting a discussion of imageless thought in the center of the book, in chapters 6 through 9. Up to that time the authority of Taine, Charcot, and others had kept alive the hypothesis that images are necessary for thought. Data from his daughters' protocols had convinced him that this was not true. Not infrequently he had found, through sudden and precise questioning, that they had no image at all, or had one that did not parallel the thought, or that was much thinner or simpler than the thought. For example, Alice did not have any image of the maid they had had for a half-dozen years; and she had no image for the word "tempest." When asked to think of Bouquin, a carriage driver in Samois, Madeleine thought only of his name and

[21] A personal communication from Sir Cyril Burt, 5 August 1969, referred me to his article "The Inheritance of Mental Characters" (269). In this he reports a note from Binet as follows: "In answer to a letter, [Binet] replied, not long before his death, that the characteristics of his daughters had persisted comparatively unchanged, and were therefore presumably innate . . ." (269, p. 190). The daughters were then young ladies in their middle and early twenties. It is possible to make several alternative guesses to acount for Binet's contrasting judgments, in 1903 and 1911, but they would serve no useful purpose.

an "impression" that he lived in a small house set back from the road. Again, with the proposed theme "a planned visit to the country," the accompanying image was hardly more than that of a green field. Again, when the word "elephant" was given to Alice, she imagined children ready to climb on the beast, but did not see the latter at all. Given the name of neighbors who had a large garden, Alice thought only of the unpeopled garden. Binet also gathered reports of his own and others' reactions to reading richly descriptive passages in books, and found that the meaning was much larger and more comprehensive than the related images. In fact, he concluded that "if one had only images as documents, it would often be impossible to reconstitute the *meaning* of a sentence or a paragraph." Furthermore, he hypothesized not only that "images do not have the primordial role that has been attributed to them," but also that even words, widely considered as "interior or verbal images," come *after* the thought, not with or before it. They provide feedback and exactness, but the thought precedes them, and is represented by a "directing, organizing force, which we call variously 'voluntary attention,' 'choice,' or 'adaptation' " (90, p. 69).

In this work Binet anticipated that of the so-called Würzburg school, to whom the credit for this aspect of the nature of thought and the method for determining it has been assigned. In fact, Binet was later so disturbed by this attribution of priority to Würzburg that several times he urged that the designation of origin should be changed to "the Paris school." Regarding this matter of priority, Ed. Claparède may have found the correct solution when he said that the systematic introspection applied to the study of thought, and which led to the principle of imageless thought, was used simultaneously and independently by the Paris psychologist and his German contemporaries. Yet he also believed that the Würzburg school had a right to the title because they had posed more explicitly and fully the principles of the method.

A report of a visitor to Binet's laboratory, however, has added another dimension to this story. In a 1911 letter to Larguier Binet wrote:

Imagine my receiving a visit from this Frenchman who had written me from Würzburg that Külpe and his students were robbing us [of our recognition or credit]. The man is a priest, professor of philosophy at Stanislas. He said that Külpe had protested against the reproach—which had been made against him by authors other than I. He [the priest] is convinced that [Külpe's] protestation is not founded in fact, and he knows that it is the reading of my book [*L'Étude expérimentale de l'intelligence*] that inspired them. [The priest said that] Bühler admits it himself. As you know well, I attach to all these points only a secondary importance; I have protested once, and I shall not go back to it again [4, 4 June 1911].

This occurred shortly before Binet's death. However, despite that 1911 assertion that he was not moved to protest any further claims for priority, he and Simon had worked sporadically on the topic for several years, perhaps in part to establish Binet's right to recognition. Their joint paper on language and thought is a particularly striking example of this work (140).[22]

This section on imageless thought seems to be an interjection in this book whose main objective was an analysis of Madeleine's and Alice's habitual modes of thinking. Yet this study obviously emerged from the long and searching investigations of their ideational responses. Binet's work on both of these topics offers important suggestions about the psychology of cognition, and also provides fertile ideas for projective methods in the study of the thought processes.[23]

[22] Binet's subsequent nonrecognition for this work is the more surprising since, for example, Th. Ribot and J. R. Angell, although disagreeing with his conclusions, gave him high credit for his investigations. Angell concluded that Binet was really presenting a doctrine of subconscious intellection in which the images were simply not *detected* (260). Ribot wrote: "This problem is very recent and has been treated by very few authors, among whom the regretted Alfred Binet is of the first rank," although he too felt that Binet's subjects had simply failed to recognize their images (289).

[23] Although Binet was for years devoted to the method of systematic introspection, there was one indication as early as 1903 that he had already recognized its shortcomings in the pur-

The Study of Creativity: Paul Hervieu

These studies of his daughters seem to have inspired Binet to reconsider the question of literary creativeness that he had pursued a decade earlier with his "dear friend, now deceased," Jacques Passy. It also represented a link in the long chain of studies of individual psychology that he and Henri had proposed in 1896 and that Binet had pursued in different ways "to establish *experimentally* the classification of individual psychological characteristics" (99, p. 3; italics added). He should have written "experimentally *or* systematically," for he studied creativity by the method of systematic interviews, which brought him to admit that he did not claim "to have succeeded in producing a really refined or subtle process of investigation . . ." (99, p. 5).

Despite the disadvantages of the method, Binet underlined the very important significance of investigating the extremes of the population, particularly the outstanding men of talent and genius "who serve better than the average to help us seize upon the laws of character, since these men present traits in a more accentuated way" (99, p. 3). His regret over the inchoate status of character study at that time was reflected in his fifteen-page review of P. Malapert's book, *Le caractère* (102, pp. 492–507). Here he took issue with the minute and subjective classificatory recommendations then in vogue, and concluded that "we do not have at hand the appropriate method for studying character." He added some suggestions for improving these studies, even proposing a series of artificial circumstances to which such outstanding persons should be asked to respond (102, p. 507). He also urged taking as many data from real life as possible.

In his own study of Paul Hervieu, dramatist, except for some brief tests and anthropological measurements, Binet

---

suit of the nature and functions of thought. In *L'Étude* . . . he concluded that "the frequent indeterminateness of images . . . is contrary to the opinion, truly superannuated today, that introspection is infallible as a direct method of studying knowledge" (90, p. 134).

relied on a mixture of considered inquiry and observation. He would have liked to add an analysis of Hervieu's vocabulary, grammar, and syntax as evidences of his manner of thought, but lacked the collaboration of a linguist (99, p. 53). M. Hervieu's "portrait" fills many pages, for he was very conscious of his actions and articulate about his reasons for them. He was also a critic and logician. As he put it, "my characters are persons who discuss." He was devoid of mysticism and superstition, characteristics that Binet urged as significant topics of inquiry for individual psychology. Hervieu did not believe in "fate," or even in "inspiration." He was compulsive in keeping his work schedule, and found his creative work "painful." Binet's analyses of his plays convinced him that his major personages reflected the author's own traits. Unlike François de Curel, there was no free-wheeling in his writing; his role of critic strongly controlled his imaginative output.[24] Binet cautiously concluded that Hervieu's whole span of "faculties" was at the same high level as his literary ones, "unlike certain mathematicians, painters, and musicians who showed only specialized genius . . ." (99, p. 16), although he furnished no evidence for this last statement.

There were other later reports of creativity. For example, a discussion of Rembrandt's greatness in collaboration with his daughter Alice (146), and an article describing the working methods of a talented nineteen-year-old painter (145). These articles are interesting, but too brief to be very instructive.

Of course Binet continued his experimental and sys-

[24] Binet's omitted observations are surprising in light of twentieth-century psychological hypotheses. For instance, he failed to comment on the probable influences of the following facts: Hervieu was the fifth of six boys in his family, with the four then living his elders by ten to fifteen years. His father had died when young Paul was thirteen years old and his mother only forty-nine years of age. Hervieu had reported to Binet that he "had his father's physique," never married, and "grew up near an excellent mother, living with her up to the moment when he lost her" (99, p. 11). The dynamic theorists had not yet invaded French psychology.

tematic studies, but most of them should be included with his work on "intelligence," "mental alienation," and "pedagogy," which ties this chapter pervasively to the next three that discuss these areas.

4 The Emergence of the First Useful Test of Children's Intelligence

The Binet-Simon intelligence scale of 1905 was a fundamental breakthrough that has had important influence on the subsequent development of both psychology and pedagogy. And yet a recent book on Binet's pedagogy omits any reference to the scale (311), while another that presents a competent account of it barely mentions his work as an experimental psychologist (262). Such treatment obscures the processes of Binet's research and the evolution of his ideas and interests. He was both an experimental psychologist and an experimental pedagogue. Without seeing these two roles within the same framework, his discovery cannot be understood.

The development of the intelligence scale was, of course, not a fortuitous event. Indeed, for over two decades some such instrument to differentiate children and adolescents on the basis of their ability to learn had been the objective of researchers in many countries, but everywhere this work seemed to lead to no useful results. Binet's path to the successful discovery also was beset with many difficulties. He did not unfold the scale as the result of a series of orderly, planned research projects. Almost the contrary is actually the case. Many of his leads were unfruitful; he followed paths that led into blind alleys; and he was frequently perplexed by baffling problems that seemed insoluble. Thus any reconstruction of the processes by which he finally succeeded in solving a part of the problem must follow his work as a psychologist, as an educational reformer, and as a man living at the turn of the twentieth century in a social milieu that was becoming concerned about the retarded children.

His own writings demonstrate almost step by step his dilemmas and solutions, his ambitions and failures, his persistent and diversified experimental trials of an idea, his inspirations and hesitations, his inconsistencies or unexplained changes in viewpoint that puzzle his readers, his agonizing questions, sometimes resolved practically but not theoretically; as well as problems that he raised and that have not been resolved even yet. On the other hand, some of his solutions seem so obvious now, "so clear that we are astonished that people were able to be astonished by them" (310, p. 14), and so patent that it is difficult for us to apprehend those earlier frames of reference.

On the very eve of his striking discovery Binet was almost ready to admit defeat. In April 1904 Victor Henri presented a joint paper for himself and Binet at the First German Congress for Experimental Psychology in Giessen. He spoke of their discouragement about finding any relatively brief measure of important individual differences. Their joint 1896 project on individual psychology was therefore unfulfilled. Charles E. Spearman's summary of this paper presented at Giessen simply stated that "Henri enumerated the various brief tests that they had used for this purpose, following the pattern of the 1896 program; all, however, had proved unsatisfactory, and now they could only recommend long systematic investigations of each person studied" (234, p. 448). The American J. W. Baird repeated essentially the same story (171), while the Swiss Claparède went into a little more detail:

> The experiments made since [the 1896 program] in the schools have shown that it is premature to look for tests permitting a diagnosis during a very limited time (one or two hours), and that, much to the contrary, it is necessary to study individual psychology without limiting the time—especially by studying outstanding personalities . . . [182, pp. 315–16].

Binet himself explained his disbelief in the possibility of assessments by tests in his lengthy study of the dramatist Hervieu, published in 1904; this was the type of study of individual psychology with which he and Henri felt they must settle (99).

One year and one month later, however, Binet and Simon published the 1905 scale of thirty items (118). Actually its now famous publication in *L'Année* in June 1905 was preceded in Rome on 28 April by an announcement made at the Fifth International Congress of Psychology where Dr. Henri Beaunis read the paper prepared by Binet and Simon: "New Methods for Diagnosing Idiocy, Imbecility, and Moronity" (123). The first announcement of this "giant step" in psychological innovations should have occasioned some excited responses from the audience:

> The two authors of the present note have especially preoccupied themselves with methods that could be used to make the distinction between normal and abnormal children . . . methods that will permit a clinician to separate the subjects of inferior intelligence into categories of idiots, imbeciles, and morons by using objective, known characteristics verifiable by all; and second, that will permit commissions who decide on the admission of children into special schools to make an exact distinction so that only really abnormal children will be sent to the special schools. . . .
>
> It is easy to demonstrate that these very useful methods have not existed up to the present time and have not even been formulated. The best works on idiocy contain only very vague definitions of the different degrees of mental inferiority . . . and cannot guide practice [because] there are no means of agreeing on these degrees. . . . Now we have studied these questions with real children (*d'après nature*), normal and abnormal. . . . These examinations have permitted us to organize a *method of differential diagnosis*. . . . This method is composed of three parts: psychological, pedagogical, medical. We enumerate them here in the order of their decreasing importance [for] it is psychology, we insist, that ought before all to furnish the characteristic and differential signs of the idiot, the imbecile, and the moron . . . [123, pp. 507–8].

The paper included a few examples of the test items, and indicated the "normal" mental levels of the idiot (to two years), the imbecile (to five years), and the moron (to nine years).

What an important contribution! This scale carefully described criteria that allowed diagnosticians, especially physicians and psychiatrists, to agree essentially on their diagnoses of three levels of retardation: idiocy, imbecility, and moronity, with some subdegrees indicated. Even though the Binet-Simon criteria fell short of experimental requirements, since, for example, the samples of subjects and of items were very limited, and the ages of "normal" children were spaced at two-year levels, the essentials of their method were inherent in this scale. This was a study of multiple complex processes with an empirical approach that presented tasks to the subjects and gathered up the results as they fell. The use of rough barometers scaled on "normal" children as points of comparison with the retarded as well as the establishment of precise directions for giving and scoring the items so that independent raters could make comparable judgments were unique achievements in 1905. Superficially this first scale appears to have been germinated within a year. It was, of course, the result of over fifteen years of development.

On the day after the announcement of the first metric scale of intelligence it would have been easy to look back to 1890 and announce that Binet's experiments with his small daughters had been the start of the process that had produced this useful instrument. Did it not include a number of items that he had first used to study his daughters' ideations? The naming of objects, responses to pictures, repetition of digits, the definitions, and even the comparison of length of lines were all part of both the 1890 studies and the 1905 scale. Obviously the two seem closely related. But this assumption would overlook the chasm that really existed between them. Binet's experiences in 1890 had been intuitive and had contained germs of ideas, but they lacked an integrated and hypothetical base. He had characterized intelligence in terms first of perceiving or sensing the external world, and then working over these perceptions to recast them; with this first so-called definition he also included uncertain thoughts about its measurement. He wrote that it would not appear absolutely impossible to him that sometime in the future "one could succeed in measuring intelligence, that is, *reasoning, judgment, memory, the ability to make abstractions . . .*" (39, p. 74; italics added). Furthermore, his experiments had even then convinced him that the important differences were in the complex mental processes,[1] and that qualitative as well as quantitative differences existed at widely separated mental levels. He mulled over the problem of these differential mental levels, and remarked almost cryptically:

> It would be interesting to know . . . whether intellectual development begins in the inferior functions, which may attain a very high degree and even terminate their evolution almost at the moment when the superior functions are still in a rudimentary state. . . . This is a new idea that future observers should note [39, p. 75].

He had no clear idea of maturational changes that would move with some predictability from stage to stage, and he seems to have had no suspicion that he had been investigating responses in his daughters that *could* represent intellectual status. Undoubtedly these homemade experiments continued, but he did not mention them again for nearly a decade.

In fact Binet's next book, on the alterations of personality (43), returned to his continued concern about the relationship between unconscious and conscious mental processes, as well as the thorny problem presented by the synthesis or coordination of "extremely numerous and varied internal events," which were generally called faculties. He wanted to understand this synthesis of faculties that represented for him intelligence or personality. Although he himself was caught in a vain attempt

[1] These striking data had convinced Binet. Yet psychologists in the United States, Germany, and England, including C. E. Spearman with his incredibly shaggy experimentation initiating his 1904 hypothesis that intelligence is composed of "general" and "specific" factors, continued for another fifteen years to look for the key to intelligence measurement in simple sensory and motor responses.

to set usable boundaries among them, he criticized the concept of faculties that treated them as "entities." He argued that *a* memory or *a* volition, for example, is imaginary and does not exist. The reality lay in *acts* of memory, *acts* of volition, or little "particular and distinct events." Yet the nature of the variables continued to baffle him. He persisted in speaking of faculties of memory, attention, imagination, volition, and the like, but he was perplexed by the problem of their relation to the whole or unified personality, and also by the overlaps between some faculties, as, for example, the ambiguities presented by attempts to differentiate imagination and memory.

One of the "acts" or "faculties" that always interested Binet was memory. Beginning in 1892–93 from the investigations that he and Henri carried out in the Paris schools, he concluded that the primary condition "for the mode of awakening memories" was the particular *direction of attention* that the subject had given to the original. Binet's conceptualization of intelligence later included this *directedness* as an intrinsic part of his schema. His satisfaction with his proposals for studying memory as an important area of the experimental psychology of the normal individual had already been evident in the earlier discussion of it in his *Introduction* (48).[2] Here he urged using the methods of description, recognition, recall, and reproduction, and cited examples of his own and his colleagues' work for reference. His experimental astuteness made him realize the need for a variety of tests in each category, because of "the probable effects on individual differences of varying the stimuli presented." In this little book, in which he proposed to make understandable the

[2] The development of psychology in the twentieth century indicates the importance of this emphasis. Binet also placed much stress on memory in the measurement of intelligence. The contrast between Wilhelm Wundt's and Binet's viewpoints about memory is well illustrated by the fact that H. C. Warren, a student of Wundt's, failed even to mention this chapter in his review of the book.

character of the new psychology, its principal methods, and its appropriate domain (48, pp. 1–2), he did not include a chapter devoted to "intelligence" per se, yet its traces are evident in the chapters on sensation and perception, memory, and ideation. In his discussion of memory, that process which later became such an integral part of his mental scales, he repeated his concern with qualitative data that he felt were so significant in that early era of psychology. He wanted to understand the mechanisms and the nature of the phenomena, and to observe their complexities close at hand; opportunities for such close study were lost in large statistical experiments.

This book and the article on individual psychology, published with Henri two years later (59), undoubtedly marked a turning point in Binet's career. In them he proposed avenues of investigation and methods of research that became characteristic of all his later work, and offered them in confrontation to the leading research hypotheses of that time. One can do no better than to allow Binet himself to explain his purpose, as he stated it in the article on individual psychology:

> We are approaching here a new, difficult, and very little explored subject. . . . If one looks at the series of experiments that have been made—the *mental tests*, as the English say—one is astonished by the considerable place reserved to the sensations and simple processes, and by the little attention lent to superior processes, which some [experimenters] neglect completely . . . [p. 426].
>
> The objection will be made that the elementary processes can be determined with much more precision than the superior ones; this is true, but people differ much less in these elementary processes than in the complex ones; there is no need, therefore, for as precise a method for determining the latter as for the former, a point that is often forgotten. Anyway, it is only by applying ourselves to this point that we can approach the study of individual differences [p. 429].
>
> Let us recall once more that the objective sought is not to determine *all* the differences among the psychic faculties of individuals, but to determine the strongest and

most important ones. . . . This is a rule that has not been considered and followed by anyone. We must expend our attention on superior psychic faculties . . . [p. 435].

From the literature he had reviewed Binet found just cause to criticize the popular quantitative emphasis on individual differences that had ignored qualitative analyses. He cited work at Yale in which J. A. Gilbert had described age differences only in degrees or amounts. The younger child, Binet insisted, differs distinctively from the older child in "his *manner* of thinking or reasoning, of willing, or of remembering."[3] The article continued with a detailed examination and critique of the tests of James McK. Cattell, Hugo Münsterberg, Joseph Jastrow, Emil Kraepelin, and J. A. Gilbert, after which Binet presented his and Henri's own ambitious research plan within the framework of three main points: first, the study of individual differences that would consider class, sex, race, occupation, criminology, psychopathology, and the like, as well as a quite different consideration of the relationships among the several faculties to permit predictions from one to the other, and to discover the most important characteristics to study; second, the testing of the hypothesis that significant differences are always found in complex superior processes rather than in elementary ones; and last, an attempt to devise mental tests with a number and variety of items for each faculty represented, in order to allow approximate evaluations of individual differences. The whole series, he hoped, could be arranged to take no longer than one and a half hours for each individual tested, and, since environmental influences were always present, he added a limiting condition that the tests should be "appropriate to the milieu to which the individual belongs."

Binet saw clearly that he had not resolved these problem

[3] Although Binet did not specify individual "styles" or "types" of responses, he was aware of their significance for personality assessment, for he wrote: ". . . If it is a question of a criminal having committed an act materially proven, it becomes of primary importance to study this act that, better than any examination [by tests], can reveal a part of the personality of the author of the act" (59, p. 435n.).

areas, that his plan was in the nature of a hypothetical beginning, but it was, he believed, the beginning of a new kind of program in that promising field of individual differences. Since it is uncommon to find a summary of the ten processes proposed, undoubtedly students who know the intelligence scale will be interested in the brief résumé that follows.

He suggested items to test "*Memory*" for designs, sentences, musical phrases, colors, numbers, and other variations that appeared effective. His brief rationale for including memory was this: "The study of memory can teach us about the faculty of comprehending: memory in fact is not a simple fixation of sensations; it is a more intellectual process that consists of coordinating the sensation and penetrating it with intelligence; one retains especially well what one has understood" (p. 437).

He made suggestions for testing the primary *Nature* of individuals' *mental images,* but perhaps the brevity of his treatment reflected his feelings of doubt about their importance.

He thought that the faculty or process of *Imagination* could be assessed by responses to inkblots and to thoughts aroused by such abstract words as "justice," "infinity," "force." Other clues might be provided by asking for a ten-minute theme on a given topic, like "A child lost in the forest," or for the construction of a sentence with three nouns or verbs provided by the experimenter.

He thought that *Attention* could be approximately measured by calculating the mean variations of a series of tactile stimuli, counting metronome beats, and other rhythmic tasks; or by carrying out several acts simultaneously. He added: "Attention is not a state *sui generis*. . . . It consists in the manner in which a function is carried out. . . ." (p. 445).

He had very few suggestions to test the process of *Comprehension,* but they are familiar in the scale. He requested subjects to define abstract words, and to give differences and similarities between two or among several synonyms, such as "goodness," "tenderness," and "kindness." And he added a series of phrases or sentences that contained some errors in terminology, some sophisms, or errors of reasoning, and asked the subjects to make the appropriate corrections.

To estimate *Suggestibility* he proposed tests that he had used in his school experiments, and added some on perceiving odors, imagining a stimulus that is made expectant, including a fear or apprehension of being hurt, and involuntary movements. His own feelings about this characteristic are found in his following remark: "Among the different indications forming the characteristics of an individual, that one relating to suggestibility should figure in the first line" (p. 449).

He wished to test the *Aesthetic sentiment,* or the "golden section" as he called it, but was obviously at a loss to find good examples for measuring it.

His examples of the *Moral sentiments,* too, lacked practicability. For instance, he thought of the presentation of a series of photographs representing views of Bukhara, with surprise photos of decapitations of criminals hidden among them to discover responses as a test of "emotivity." There was no hint at this time of the later tests that queried: "What should you do if. . . . ?"

He dipped into the popular interest in *Muscular force and strength of will or persistence* by proposing dynamometers and other tests of strength, with several suggestions for varying conditions. For example, he thought of introducing girls into the testing room to discover the effect of self-pride on the boys' attainments; or of adding fatigue and pain as independent variables.

For *Coordination skills and quick visual judgments* he mentioned the threading of a needle, the determination of the number of times a given line was contained in a longer one, plus similar tests that could be used for this function. It is at once obvious that Binet and his collaborator Henri were thinking in much broader and more inclusive terms than about intellectual differences, and, indeed, although its presence is certainly implicit, "intelligence" is not included among the processes suggested for study.

This seminal paper, coming from France instead of Germany and buried as it was as a special report in the last section of *L'Année,* aroused almost no attention among psychologists. Binet's disappointment is evident when some months later he remarked: "Our article is still too recent to have been able to influence other experimenters who are interested in individual psychology; the year that has just passed has not brought any very important contribution of works directed to this question" (62, p. 296). Even Binet's own next study within the framework of "individual psychology" was not inspired by the program outlined in 1896, but rather was directed to styles of thinking, habitual orientations of mind. This work was discussed at length in chap. 3.

Nonetheless, in 1898 in two articles, Binet returned to the theme of measurement. In one he urged his readers to "know thyself" (60), and for a more sophisticated audience he seriously extended his earlier publications with an article on measurement in individual psychology (69). For some reason he published the latter in the *Revue philosophique* instead of in *L'Année* where the line of relationship would have been more direct. In this important article Binet's introduction shows how fully cognizant he was of the immense problem presented by the nature of intelligence. He knew that James McK. Cattell and a committee of the American Psychological Association were not approaching insight when they simply filled hundreds of columns with measurements of "simple responses" of college freshmen. Emil Kraepelin, Hugo Münsterberg, and others were, Binet said, "doing a little, but not much, better." Apropos of the work of these men he pointed out:

> There is no difficulty in measurement as long as it is a question of experiments on . . . tactile, visual, or auditory sensations. But if it is a question of measuring the keenness of intelligence, where is the method to be found to *measure the richness of intelligence, the sureness of judgment, the subtlety of mind?*

And he modestly added:

> I hasten to say that I bring no precise solution; any systematic measurement at the present time could be con-

structed only by means of *a priori* ideas, which probably would not be applicable to *the immense variety of expressions of intelligence.* We must proceed *a posteriori* after collecting some facts. Forced to make some prescriptions [*dosages*], to give some coefficients, I have had recourse to empirical and provisory processes that have come to me while collecting observations or putting together some experiments. I will *"force" two categories of measurement* [on the diversity] [69, p. 113; italics added].

The first category included numerical measures of responses *when the tests remain constant,* and Binet gave examples from the faculties or processes of memory, suggestibility, speed, or fluency that represented the abundance of words used, muscular force, physiological responses, comprehension, and morality. Several new items were included that are now familiar in the Stanford-Binet: for example, the paper-cutting tests, which were suggested by V. Henri; putting jumbled sentences in correct order; comprehension questions like "What should you do when someone hits you without meaning to do it?"; and the request to give the sense of a difficult paragraph translated from John Stuart Mill.[4] Binet was vexed that he could assign to these last two tests only plus or minus values, but he hoped that weighted numerical values sometime might be determined.

The second category included tests of graduated difficulty, with numerical results as simplified as possible. This presented a more difficult problem, but Binet did suggest such tests for memory, suggestibility, and for motor skill (for which he developed his own apparatus for measuring the stability of the hand). But he concluded that this category was especially difficult in measuring intelligence. It took too much time, and much research was

[4] Binet presented this item to his subjects as a "test of memory" rather than of "judgment" to permit those who failed to save face. He recalled the aphorism of La Rochefoucauld: "A person is [always] willing to complain about his memory; but he will not complain of his judgment" (69, p. 119). He later substituted a paraphrased statement from Hervieu on "the value of life" (165, p. 158). An exact translation of this still appears in the Stanford-Binet test, even in the 1960 revision.

needed to determine empirically degrees of difficulty, for example, from the less to the more abstract, or the relative and real difficulties in sentences presented for immediate recall.

In these suggestions for gathering objective data Binet showed an increased facility for developing test items, and he continued to press the point that the results offered *classifications* among individuals, not true measurements. Nonetheless, his "mental set" made him continue to search for faculties, with the implicit assumption that, for a satisfactory individual assessment, all the significant faculties should be represented and tested. As if this task were not formidable enough, he added further complications by positing types of thinking, such as the literary, scientific, emotional, aesthetic, moralistic, and egoistic, since he felt that "the consequences of these types for the rest of intelligence present a question of capital importance for individual psychology" (69, p. 123). He could not, however, propose any way to put the separate items together to represent any individual's status.

In 1899 an American investigator, Stella Sharp, who was a graduate student in Titchener's laboratory, was bold enough to try to test Binet's and Henri's 1896 program in the very heart of the elementaristic prescriptions of the German methods (228). She wanted to discover whether different tests of any complex faculty would show internal consistencies, and also whether there were correspondences among several faculties. Her subjects were seven graduate students, so it is not surprising that the small sampling and general homogeneity resulted in disappointingly small correlations among the tests or within any category except in the matter of types of thinking. Sharp felt that her results lent support to the concept of faculties, since she was "inclined to the hypothesis of the relative independence of the particular mental activities . . ." (228, p. 389). Lack of correlations even within the single faculty being tested meant that this study yielded no practical results. This fact may be partly responsible for the eclipse in the United States of the Binet and Henri proposals for the study of individual psychology. Although Sharp was obviously disappointed at the confusing results of so much detailed labor, she also concluded, most agreeably for Binet, who reviewed her article (75), that "individual psychical differences should be sought for in the complex rather than in the elementary processes of mind, and that the test method is the most workable one that has yet been proposed for investigating these processes" (228, p. 390). Perhaps the most important part of her results, showing individual consistencies in habitual modes of thinking, was the fact that they gave Binet strong encouragement for his own investigations in this area (75).

Binet's next effort to implement the 1896 program came in a paper on "attention and adaptation" (74), called by an American reviewer "an important contribution to both individual and pedagogical psychology" (178). Here Binet sought to organize methods to estimate and measure voluntary attention, to which he added the measure of "adaptation" because he found this variable important in differentiating between a group of five students whom he called "intelligent" and six whom he called, by comparison, "unintelligent." These pupils had been selected for these categories on the basis of their teachers' judgments, which is astonishing since Binet actually suggested in his paper that a more valid selection could be made on the basis of age-grade placements. This latter process was more advantageous because children were placed in the various grades according to their school performances, which meant that by and large the younger children in any grade were the brightest children because they had progressed faster; teachers, on the other hand, tended to think that the older pupils were the brighter.[5] Although Binet did not have the courage in 1900 to use this age-

[5] Of course Binet never subscribed to a really close correlation between intelligence and school achievement, since, for instance, great effort or careless arrogance could influence the latter, but this criterion was better than teachers' judgments. It is an enigma why Binet not only did not use this criterion in the present study but why he *ignored* it; an inspection of the ages of his subjects quickly shows, for instance, one nine-and-a-half-year-old in the "unintelligent" group, although he was in the average grade for eleven to twelve-year-olds (74, p. 250)!

grade criterion, which he advocated nevertheless, he did use it later for his norms for the scale.

Despite these obvious uncertainties in the criterion for intelligence, Binet spent two months making the tests and another two months working through the data. He claimed that, in some particulars, the results differentiated *groups* of children at higher and lower intellectual levels. Because he believed that "raw attention" had an existence apart from the attention required by comprehension or reasoning, he searched for test situations that exacted absolute concentration on specific details but no selective judgments. The battery of tests required the subjects to respond to tactile and auditory stimuli, to count dots on lines of varying lengths and metronome beats at different speeds, to copy long lists of digits, nonsense sentences, and complex, unsystematic designs, for each of which the experimenter recorded the number of times each subject looked at the model to reproduce his own copy. There were tachistoscopic exposures of words of different lengths and of designs of different complexities. One test required the subject to correct a text and another to do rapid addition.

Binet discussed the results at length. Only half the tests showed even a reasonably detectable advantage on the part of the "intelligent" children. What he found as most significant was that, since repetitions of the items brought the "unintelligent" nearer and nearer to the performance level of the "intelligent" in all tests, it was the bright children's first quick "adaptability" to the initial conditions that differentiated them from the "unintelligent," a datum that made him caution other experimenters to take adaptation into account in their experiments. In the résumé of his data he also concluded that certain tests could offer clues to broad *group* differences in intelligence, but that there was not the slightest evidence that individual comparisons could be made.

The Search for Physical Signs of Intelligence

In the same period Binet's restless search for signs to indicate differences in intelligence took him into the area of physical or anthropological measures. He felt that an understanding of intelligence is so complicated that no procedure that might enlighten its study should be overlooked. Indeed, in a deep substratum of his own theorizing he seems to have been convinced of an essential unity between intellectual processes and all other aspects of a "person." Within this framework he gave years to an attempt to correlate cephalometry with intelligence and to discover whether or not physiognomy, handwriting, or the form of the hand could possibly be used to differentiate signs of character and intelligence.

To test his hypotheses he needed "extreme cases," since, as he said, normal persons differ too little to furnish discernible results. Thus since the schools could not supply him with the needed preliminary subjects, Simon's arrival at the laboratory with access to subjects at the Vaucluse institution allowed Binet to plan his first experiments in cephalometry. Under Binet's direction Simon wrote his thesis for his medical degree based on a long series of anthropometric studies of two hundred and twenty-three retarded boys. He tentatively concluded: "While waiting for more data it appears that the chances are greater of finding a strong intelligence in well-developed bodies and heads, while a general [physical] weakness is already by itself a presumption of insufficient intelligence" (229, p. 247). These were arresting data since experimenters at that time were divided on the question. Simon extended these studies for another year (230, 231) during which he and Binet collaborated on many aspects of cephalometry after practicing together to perfect their technique in order to make reliable comparisons.

A study of Binet's statements in earlier papers on head measurements reveals his almost anguished wrestling with the data in one very perplexing problem. Although large individual differences were apparent in the records of retarded and normal individuals, the *averages* in several of the age levels were almost the same for the two groups. The answer now seems easy, but when Simon was eighty-six years old he still recalled with a kind of reverence Binet's persistent grappling with the records until he discovered that the retarded must be divided principally into two categories: those with heads notably larger and notably smaller than the normal. It must be presumed, therefore, that the degrees of retardation in the Vaucluse group were not severe enough to provide readily observable examples of macrocephalics and microcephalics, as in fact we may infer from Simon's statement that this institution "received mostly those who appear apt enough to be employable in fieldwork" (229, p. 191). Yet the dichotomy of head measurements finally became apparent in the data that had led to the misleading averages.

Binet and Simon published more than a dozen articles related to cephalometry. They produced norms for the growth of the cranium and face between four and eighteen years; critiques of other studies in the field; and measurements of deaf mutes and the blind as well as those of retarded intelligence (72, 78, 79, 80, 81, 82, 84, 85, 86, 87, 88, 100, 105, 106, 107, 154). Binet also directed a number of other studies within *La Société* (177, 200, 242) in which severely retarded children were compared to normal children in height and five head measurements; on the basis of these he proposed a new technique that he called "anthropometric frontiers." If the physical measurements, noticeably cephalometric ones, fell below the critical points for the child's age, and if there were other indices of retardation, these measurements could be considered as presumptive signs of retardation.

In his final article about physical signs of intelligence Binet asserted that measures of physique, especially of the head, could offer only a means of confirming a diagnosis based on other and better methods, and concluded almost apologetically:

> When a child, according to tests made in class or in a regular psychological examination, appears to have little intelligence, *this judgment, always delicate and complicated,* can be weighed and confirmed by cephalometry. . . . A retardation [from the average] of six years or more appears to me to be significant [154, p. 11; italics added].

These studies, although always inconclusive, were extended throughout a decade. While the endless hours of tedious work testify to Binet's belief that the results would allow positive differentiations among individuals, he was also undoubtedly challenged by the bewildering variety of physical differences that might be made to give up some as-yet-undiscovered meanings. Binet openly admitted that his results were negative and that the relationships were so small that they were only minimally useful. Over two decades later the American professor of psychology, Donald G. Paterson, particularly recognized him for acknowledging this, and pointed out that others, like C. B. Davenport, J. M. Baldwin, and G. D. Stoddard, were still "exaggerating the relationships" (282, p. 276).

Binet's pursuit of external signs of intelligence and character also took him into investigations of physiognomy, the form of the hand, and especially graphology. He insisted that the general unpopularity of these areas among psychologists "has no importance whatsoever." What he wrote apropos of studying the possible significance of hand-forms is applicable: "Trying to unite into a synthesis all the little exterior physical signs that permit us to guess or to assess the intelligence and character of a person . . . we cannot refuse to study [any of them]" (141, p. 394). In fact, he took graphology so seriously that, in order to bring together the work that he and others had done, he wrote a 257-page book "on a subject that," he remarked, "has interested me greatly." He investigated the problem at several levels. First he asked members of *La Société*, people who were uninitiated in graphology, to distinguish differences in sex, age, and intelligence by examining handwriting specimens; members of the Parisian Society of Graphologists provided "expert" judges. Judgments of sex were made first, since they could be readily validated. He next presented writing samples of "the most and least intelligent pupils in several primary grades" with the request that the judges distinguish the most intelligent. "Of course, many errors were committed," he wrote, ". . . but the number of exact determinations was constantly superior to that of false ones, and sometimes an uninitiated 'judge' made almost no errors"

(101, pp. 191–92). In one of his tests Binet gathered fragments of letters, and then, in order to restrict clues from content, used only envelopes addressed by "great scholars, great writers, and great artists," as, for example, Poincaré, Claude Bernard, Ribot, Charcot, Bergson, Dumas, and Hervieu. He combined these specimens with those of "men of average intelligence" whom he described in surprisingly recognizable detail. The various judges, expert and naïve, continued to estimate the differences by better than chance, although the self-styled graphologists usually had a higher percentage of successes.

There was one amusing incident. Binet presented to "expert" graphologists handwriting samples taken from the prison files of convicted murderers, mixed these with samples from "good citizens," and requested character assessments. The graphologists were understandably angry when in some cases even the best-known "experts" furnished some disastrously false assertions (129, chap. 21). One convicted murderer, for instance, was reported to be "generous, socially conscious, and gentle." Binet concluded that graphology was much less advanced in assessing character than in determining sex, age, or even intelligence.

Binet's general results, however, convinced him that "assuredly there is something in graphology," although he became increasingly aware of the meticulous demands of experimental controls, which he discussed at some length. He also recognized the incompleteness of his own research in the following remark:

> Our principal objective has been to show the way to methods of demonstration for the study of moral [psychological] phenomena. Handwriting has been only an example related to my former research: *the exterior signs of intelligence*. . . . I foresee other research relating to the revelatory value of gesture, intonation, timbre, vocabulary, syntax. A little, very little, has been accomplished. Much remains on the drawing board. In graphology, in cephalometry, and possibly also in hand-formations there is something valid . . . but these studies [are surrounded by errors of all sorts] . . . the most dangerous of which is

suggestion, that cholera of psychology, and after suggestion, the evils of chance are most to be feared [129, pp. 251–52].

Binet saw no hope for scientific advance among the "expert" graphologists. They were not at all willing to submit their "art" to scientific tests. "Instead they resist criticisms and, [if faced with errors], reply: 'It is I who am in error—not graphology.' " He distrusted their reliance on intuition and authority, but, calling it a "vast domain," he predicted that, with appropriate research, it could be an "art of the future."[6]

Binet actually arranged a few tests in which "experts" and uninitiated teachers attempted to distinguish between intelligent and retarded children on the basis of their hand-forms and their physiognomy. Both groups were successful beyond the expectations of chance, but Binet seemed happy to report that a psychiatrist who had boasted that he could "tell children's intelligence merely by looking at them" made many errors. The high percentage of successes, however, led him to conclude that "both professionals and 'the uninformed' arrive at a sureness of observation that is not to be disdained" (130, p. 273). Thus he left incomplete his research on external signs of intelligence, but certainly with a conviction that the matter could be approached scientifically and that, if it were, some "revelatory values"—some signs of character and intelligence—could be discovered in these very individual, visible expressions of personality.

Deliberations on the Nature of Intelligence

Binet's extended and earnest interest in external signs was always paralleled by his search into the nature of thought

[6] Although graphology seems to have made little progress since then, we are told that it is at the present time finding growing favor in personnel offices, that the CIA uses it among its character tests, and that an affluent businessman asserts that "he considers handwriting analysis more accurate and reliable than just about any other personality probing device he can think of" (*Wall Street J.*, 11 September 1967, by staff reporter J. Gardner).

and intelligence. His conviction that intelligence is embedded in the total personality must be kept constantly in mind. It is indeed ironic that his tests later became instrumental in giving to "intelligence" a relatively independent existence in personality, since the weight of his writings stressed the unity of functioning in each individual. From 1897, when in the protocols of "the description of an object" he unexpectedly discovered "types" of thinking, these types became an integral part of his hypotheses about intelligence, although he was unable to give them any explicit place in the scales. They represented habitual modes of orientation or a *directionality* in thought patterns that once again, in Binet's opinion, undermined the explanatory power of the association of ideas. Failing to catch measures of habitual modes, however, he did stress complex ideations that went beyond simple, mechanical processes. He singled out Taine's hypothesis for particular criticism:

> Taine remained faithful to his beautiful theory of intelligence, so similar to the mechanism of a clock, where nothing represents *effort, direction, adaptation, choice,* where *attention itself is reduced to the intensity of an image. . . .* The existence of themes of thought [so dramatically illustrated in Madeleine's and Alice's protocols] is inexplicable by the automatism of associations. . . . In order for a theme to develop, *a selection of ideas is necessary, a work of choice and rejection. . . .* Association is intelligent only when it is *directed* . . . [90, p. 69; italics added].

Thus in 1903 Binet stressed, as a necessary factor in thought, the significance of direction, of intention (*intentionisme* as he called it in a newly coined word). Proposing imageless thought as a basic premise, he added: "A thought is a *directing, organizing* force, which I would compare—probably only metaphorically— with a vital [physico-chemical] force . . . [acting] like an invisible worker . . ." (90, p. 108; italics added). He strained for more insight. During the same year, 1903, as a result of the incredibly long and painstaking experiments on tactile thresholds, he was so struck with the great variety of individual differences even in this simple process that his concern to discover the "forces" within individuals that complete the intercourse with their environment became a persistent drive.[7] He realized that to the activity of an individual's taking in sensations there must be added the inseparable process that is "properly called judgment . . . with its operations of *inventiveness, adjustment,* and *realization* that cut into the sensation and modify it profoundly. . . . The stimulus receives the imprint of each personality. . . . External perception does not dominate us; it is rather *we, intelligence,* that dominate it" (98, p. 618; italics added). In 1903, therefore, he conceived of thought or intelligence as something—an act, a process, a force—that takes in external stimuli, organizes, directs, chooses, adapts them, all in ways that differ greatly among individuals. It appears that he had the ingredients to make a measure of intelligence, but how was he to put them together in a framework of the many "faculties" that, although representing *acts* rather than *entities,* were still acts that, in the minds of Binet and other psychologists, required separate and distinct testing?

Activities on Behalf of Retarded Children

While he groped for understanding of the nature of intelligence, Binet also sought to apply his knowledge to the problems that concerned *La Société.* The one that affected him particularly was well known, for retarded children had raised difficult questions in the schools ever since the administrative decision to enforce universal education in

[7] After crediting many philosophers and scientists, particularly Helmholtz, with the observation that our individual intelligences interpret in various ways the "signs" from the external world, Binet directed attention to the consequent error in psychophysical experiments that extolled the stimulus and the "homogeneous" undifferentiated responses among the subjects. In fact, he labeled the study of the relations between external excitants and their internal intepretations as "one of the most important problems of psychology" (98, p. 618). It was a central topic of his *L'Âme et le corps,* which, although neither a very original nor profound book, brought to the attention of psychologists the significance of epistemology for their science and implied the importance of individual differences.

1881. It was this issue that finally led to the appointment of the Ministerial Commission for the Study of Retarded Children, and also impressed Binet with the need to develop some instrument that would distinguish differences between the children in question. One of the study commissions within *La Société* had concentrated its efforts on retarded children. The members' assertive and persistent pressures on their behalf provided the final impulse that moved the French public administration to action. The protests of these members, of course, did not occur in a vacuum but were a part of the larger world where activities on behalf of retarded children were moving apace. In fact, they gained a kind of tempestuous fervor by virtue of the contrast between the enthusiastic activity on behalf of these unfortunate children in the rest of Europe and the United States and the apathy in French administrative quarters. These French advocates of action could point to the progress in other countries in support of their cause. In England, Belgium, the Netherlands, Italy, Norway, Sweden, Denmark, in Switzerland, Austria-Hungary, in Germany, and in the United States there were important beginnings—special classes and special schools for the retarded and legislation to insure continuance. Furthermore, these efforts began in the late 1880s or early 1890s. But even more than a decade later no special education existed in the homeland of J. M. G. Itard, Edward Séguin, and Jean-Étienne Esquirol whose writings on the mentally retarded were nevertheless read and quoted abroad. Although some French voices, and passionate ones, had been raised here and there, especially by doctors and teachers who were face to face with these problems, the French government had taken no action.

During the years 1899–1904, however, there was a forum where Frenchmen could express their opinions and publish their studies. Called the *Revue internationale de pédagogie comparative* (221), it was devoted "to the international clinical, therapeutic, and pedagogical study of retarded children." This *Revue* reflected not only French frustration but also the fact that the teaching methods used and the appropriate legislation passed elsewhere were far in advance of diagnostic methods for determining retardation. In fact, a cursory examination of this *Revue* reveals that selection and classification of the retarded were done intuitively and crudely; no one needs to be reminded that an instrument like the Binet-Simon scale would bring necessary relief. The *Revue* also presents evidence that protests failed to move French public administrators. Obviously the action of *La Société*, as well as Binet's research, stemmed from this unhappy situation.

All over the Western world some men were trying to do something about the problem of determining degrees of retardation. In the United States W. S. Munroe thought that physiognomy might serve as diagnostic of mental anomalies if facial dyssymmetry was noticeable (221a, pp. 2–6). A California institution developed a battery of questionnaires about the behavior of the child and his family history (221b, pp. 70–78). In Brussels, J. Demoor, while unable to distinguish the retarded from the "morally deficient," sought to identify retardates by their inattention and also their inability to demonstrate "illusions of the muscular sense" as do normal children over six years of age (221c, pp. 209–21). In Sweden G. Hellström had no difficulty differentiating adult imbeciles, which is neither surprising nor useful, but he saw the problem as insoluble when it was a question of differentiating morons from normals in school (221d, pp. 161–66).

The confusion was highlighted, but hardly explained, by M. Manheimer-Gomès, clinical chief of the Faculty of Medicine in Paris and author of a book on retardation, when he wrote: "Morons show a backwardness of the faculties; imbeciles, more deficiency; idiots, cerebral deformations and no possibility for any social life" (221e, pp. 42–48).

In France the protests for some action that might bring relief finally persuaded the government to transfer the responsibility for retarded and unstable children from the Ministry of the Interior to the Ministry of Public Instruction where at least some consideration of their rights to an education might be found (221f, pp. 100–101). M. Baguer, a very active member of *La Société* and director of an institute for deaf-mutes in Paris, broadened the problem by pointing out that the "[education] law of obligation of 1881 made it a public duty to provide primary instruction for all children," and that this must include the retarded and unstable just as it had been applied to the blind, the deaf, and the idiots (221g, pp. 29–38, 117–22, 169–78). Others soon joined him and insisted that the law simply was not being implemented. For those not so seriously afflicted that they could be sent to Bicêtre or the Salpêtrière, there was "Nothing! They make trouble in the schools and will themselves become desperate. Nothing is done for them. They end up either in prison or a padded cell. The state has a duty to them not only out of pity, but also out of social justice . . ." (221h, pp. 161–64).

More group pressure was exerted in June 1903, this time by the Third National Congress of Public and Private Welfare at Bordeaux. The representatives resolved that Parlement should with the least possible delay vote obligatory assistance to the retarded and arrange for facilities for special education at least in all the larger cities of France (221i, pp. 311–12). A director of this assembly reported statistics gathered by a Dr. Blin of Vaucluse "in which France appeared in the last place in assistance to the retarded. . . . It has been impossible to vanquish the benevolent inertia. . . . Any reasonable assistance . . . is almost entirely lacking in the country of Séguin" (221j, pp. 75–78). He pleaded for government action. Others joined him forcefully as notices appeared in the *Revue* about conferences on the education of the abnormal scheduled, especially in Belgium and Switzerland, for 1903, 1904, and 1905. These announcements and subsequent reports were also carried in a number of other French-language journals to keep the agitation alive even after the *Revue*'s demise in July 1904 closed that avenue to further developments. During that same year, however, *L'Année* published a *Revue de pédagogie des anormaux* (194), which emphasized both some problems and public ignorance about them.

La Société also moved into this stream of action. As early as 1901 three of its members, M. Baguer, Joseph Boyer, and J. Philippe, had urged that it should work in the area of the psychology of abnormal children. The board of *La Société* apparently responded favorably, but activity pursuant to it was slow until the meeting on 10 December 1903 when Baguer proposed that the Commission of Graphology should also include studies of the retarded among its projects. At this same meeting Mme Marie Fuster, Professor agrégée at Collège Sévigné, reported on her recent visit to German and Belgian schools for the retarded, especially emphasizing the work of Demoor in Brussels. She was followed by J. Boyer and M. Baguer who reminded the group of France's inactivity in the midst of so much concern in other countries. J. Philippe added: "Frenchmen must learn that from all sides the care of the abnormal is the order of the day." Baguer's remarks are worth reporting:

> People knew so little [as recently as 1898] of what constitutes a retarded child that they proposed at that time the establishment of classes in discipline, of classes of reform, with a severe regime for the children whose application and conduct left much to be desired.
>
> It is in France that all the ideas concerning the education of the retarded have emerged; it is sad to see our country so deprived now. It would be so easy to save these little children from the fate of the prison or the asylum for the insane [220, p. 390; meeting held in December 1903].

He went on to assure his fellow members that "the organization is ready and the place for starting easy to find. The only need is to begin. . . ." He began cautiously by proposing a resolution that the Administration for Public Welfare or Public Instruction permit the opening of a special class for the retarded, presumably a demonstration class. Various members agreed but obstructed action by bringing up ancillary problems such as the separation of the retarded from the delinquent, the most advisable kinds of facilities and instruction, and the stony indifference of the public administration. Finally, however, there was a unanimous motion that Baguer's proposal for a resolution was so important that it should be punctiliously formulated by a committee of the Commission for the Retarded. By the time of the February 1904 meeting this commission had grown to sixteen members, almost all professional people working with abnormal children. They produced their resolution without taking a stand on any hotly debated but secondary issues about facilities and methods. In a consideration of the important priorities they resolved:

> That in the primary schools, the children judged refractory to education, to teaching, or to the discipline of the school should not be sent away without being submitted to a medico-pedagogical examination, and
>
> That these children, if considered as educably retarded, should be grouped in a special class annexed to the regular school, or in a special establishment, and
>
> That a special class for the educable be opened for the present in one of the Paris schools, as a demonstration.

The resolution was adopted unanimously, and three members, J. Baguer, M. Albanel, and Dr. Voisin, were then appointed to take it as a proposal from *La Société* to the Ministry of Public Instruction (184, pp. 407, 429).

The commission of *La Société* then, at Binet's request, turned to the problem that he defined as "establishing scientifically the anthropometric [*corporelles*] and mental differences that separate the normal child from the abnormal; of making these differences exact, of measuring them in some way so that their assessment ceases to be a matter of tact and intuition, but rather becomes something objective and tangible . . ." (183, p. 408). Sometime afterward this commission, also in line with Binet's thought, projected investigations of "measures of perception, attention, memory, intellectual activity, judgment, and so on." It should be noted that the language was still couched in words of separate faculties or categories of functioning, the point of view that probably prevented the achievement of a serviceable scale up to that time. Parenthetically, the Commission on Graphology had reported essentially negative results for differentiating by handwriting the more from the less intelligent.

In July 1904 *La Société*'s Commission on Memory, under

Binet's tutelage but chaired by P. Malapert and J. Laguier des Bancels, published the details of an experiment that set out to determine whether the most intelligent children also had the best memories. Parison, the main teacher-experimenter, took as his criterion of "most intelligent" the judgment of all the teachers who had taught these children, rather than only the current ones. The tasks assigned were learning twenty-one digits and some prose and Latin verses in five- and ten-minute sessions. Parison decided that the results showed a positive relation between the children's memory and the teachers' judgments of their intelligence (215). Binet commended him for "the enormous work" undertaken, and then added: "On reflection . . . one could ignore the teachers' judgments . . . and compare the children of *the same ages who are in different grades*" (italics added).[8] Since Binet had seen the earlier data on the "memory" tests, he had already asked some other teachers to carry out the same experiment with children in two different grades in two different schools, with particular care given to providing him with the ages of each of the children. His observations at this point are most interesting for his subsequent research. He was surprised at the differences, and added:

> The children in the 7th and 8th grades retained double the prose and verse *than did their comrades of the same age* in the 5th and 6th grades. The difference is indeed enormous. . . . Are the latter generally more unintelligent? Or are they retarded because of illness? . . . Or from the carelessness of parents who keep the child at home? Many causes could interfere with advances in grade. . . . It would be necessary to examine each case. How interesting this would be! We are here at the very heart of psychology [*en pleine psychologie*]; and the results obtained are so important that they encourage a very long and difficult study [215, p. 488; italics added].

[8] We have seen that he suggested this method in 1900 (74) but failed to use it. Actually the idea was not original with him; he admitted to having read the suggestion "somewhere," and Professor M. C. Schuyten of Antwerp later resentfully reminded him of the source!

Binet's train of thought is not difficult to follow. If the age of a child according to the grade attained is roughly a measure of ability, and memory is also related to this age-ability, then perhaps measures of intelligence could be set up according to age units, a crucial concept for the final development of the scale. Binet's sentence, "We are here *en pleine psychologie . . .*" suggests that he had had the experience of sudden insight.

The results of this little experiment were published in the November 1904 *Bulletin* and, although exasperatingly without a statement of the number of subjects in question, they presented astonishing comparisons:

	Average number of lines retained	
Ages	*5th and 6th grades*	*7th and 8th grades*
10	5½	18
11	7	16
12	7	13½
13	4½ [?]	15½
14	9	18

A question was raised by members of *La Société* concerning the mean variations of the results, and Binet assured them that the groups were "very homogeneous" (219, pp. 507–8).[9] In the discussion that followed on the question of determining criteria for unintelligent and intelligent children, Binet's reply reflected his earlier thoughts about intelligence. He acknowledged that this was a very serious question for experimental psychology and continued:

[9] During 1905 the Commission on Memory of *La Société* organized a new experiment to retest this data. Two hundred and thirty pupils, nine to thirteen years of age, in six schools were given twenty-eight lines to learn in fifteen minutes; they were then asked to write them immediately and, without any warning, again a week later. In five of the six schools the results supported the conclusion that the pupils in the highest grades for their age gave the best performances. This suggested, therefore, that a good memory is not only an important input in school success, but also that it is a reasonably useful criterion for intelligence. When the experimenters examined the recalcitrant sixth school, the data "were even strengthened" by the observation that at that school "the most intelligent pupils" had quit at twelve years of age, and so had escaped the sample.

"One cannot measure intelligence without establishing some distinctions . . . relating at least to the functions of understanding, judging, inventing, or imagining" (108; 219, p. 508).

In the same issue of the *Bulletin*, without fanfare, Binet made a simple and straightforward announcement of the event that was to provide the impetus for the development of the scale, namely the appointment of a Ministerial Commission for the Abnormal by the Ministry of Public Instruction. The decree was issued in October 1904. A part of Binet's less-than-one-page announcement follows:

> We are happy to let our colleagues know of a very recent ministerial decision, proof that the questions to which our *Société* addresses itself are of highly practical interest, and also that the efforts made by our *Société* to bring about important reforms have not been useless . . . [109, p. 506].

He recalled that three members of *La Société* had personally taken the resolution to the appropriate public administrators, and added:

> It is then with a profound satisfaction that we announce the decree by which M. Chaumie has just organized a commission charged with studying the question of abnormal children. This commission . . . counts among its members four of our colleagues, MM. Baguer, Binet, Lacabe, and Malapert . . . [109, p. 506].

Binet promised to keep *La Société* abreast of the work of the new commission. Although disappointingly little appeared in succeeding issues of the *Bulletin*, Binet offered a glimpse of the familiar actions of such bodies when he wrote in *Les enfants anormaux:*

> I cannot express the profound impression left on me of the memory of the ten months during which my colleagues, multiplying the meetings of the plenary commission and of the technical sub-commissions, the visits to the principal establishments of the abnormal, the consultations, and the examinations of notebooks, elucidated every day a point of the problem, and hastened the time when the solutions

given for them could be translated into laws and regulations [134, p. vii].

The January 1905 *Bulletin* briefly reported two meetings at which the decision was reached to begin the work of the commission with a statistical study of the number of "backward and other abnormal children" in France. A questionnaire prepared by Baguer, Binet, Bourneville, and Robin was sent to teachers and principals throughout France to seek aid in distinguishing among the medically abnormal, the intellectually retarded, and the unstable. Binet drew up a long commentary, but did not publish either a copy of these notes of instruction or of the questionnaire itself. They were first sent as a pretest to teachers and principals in the second and tenth *arrondisements,* under the aegis of Binet's ever-loyal collaborator A. Belot, the primary school inspector for those districts. Apparently either the respondents did not read the directions carefully or found them too vague, because their definitions of the abnormalities were often amorphous, and in one school 25 percent of the pupils were considered abnormal, while in a neighboring one, not a single pupil was so designated. This evoked the ironical remark of M. Bédorez, director of primary teaching for the *département* of the Seine: "That makes an average of 12½ percent!" (134, p. 61). Binet generously noted that he could not criticize the teachers too harshly for their ineptness, "since the specialists, that is the alienists, have not succeeded any better in defining abnormal children." Clearly the commission was unable to formulate any useful conclusions about the number of abnormal schoolchildren in France.

"There is nothing like necessity to make new methods surge forth"

Binet has said that the ministerial commission was concerned only with administrative and pedagogical questions. When it came to problems of actually discriminating between the normal and the retarded, most importantly the morons, they were satisfied to recommend a "medico-pedagogical examination" for which they could offer no criteria for methods to be used, observations to be taken, questions to be posed, or tests to be originated: "The commission has not believed that it ought to answer these things; it did the work of administrative regulation, and not the work of science" (117, p. 163). Binet and Simon, therefore, decided to undertake this task themselves. "This problem," they wrote with superb understatement, "presents difficulties, both theoretical and practical" (117, p. 164).

In January 1905 Binet was still grasping at straws. For instance, when two members of *La Société* reported at a meeting that the great majority of their retarded pupils learned to write before they could read, Binet took the floor and observed that this "writing" was really "copying a model" and not writing words spoken or heard. Then he wondered aloud if one could possibly use "this fact of skill in simple graphic design accompanied with an inability to read as a sign of intellectual retardation" (111, pp. 563–64). It is to be presumed that an age level around seven or eight years was implicit here. In his casting about for differential items he also asked a teacher of idiots and imbeciles what games these patients played.

Yet there is evidence that Binet's creative activity had indeed been at work. When he noted that a measure of intelligence is not "established by distinctions in school subjects," he began to search about for independent measures of these school subjects as compared with mental processes like "understanding, judging, inventing, or imagining." Under his coaching his collaborator V. Vaney, principal of Grange-aux-belles school, produced the first of his "achievement" tests that he called "tests of the degree of instruction," a sort of "barometer."[10] The first one

[10] Binet seems to have got the idea from J. Demoor of Brussels who admitted to special schools children who were "two years or more retarded pedagogically." Since the assessment of grade-retardation was left to the teachers, a more precise barometer was needed. V. Vaney supplied this; his was not the first "achievement test" (see 311, pp. 110-11), but it was a very early one. It, too, has been unheralded in France.

estimated achievement in arithmetic, and covered the end of the first year to the end of the seventh school year, presenting items that "ordinary" or "average" pupils should have acquired for each grade. For example, the first graders at age seven were asked to read numbers from one to twenty, to write them from dictation, and to add and subtract them orally. The third graders, at nine years, should perform the four operations with large numbers and use them to solve simple problems requiring one operation each. At age ten, in the fourth grade, the problems became more complex since the pupil had to use decimals, divide by two numbers, understand measures and their multiples, and resolve problems requiring two operations each. By grade seven, at thirteen years, the pupils must convert an ordinary fraction into a decimal; must know the relation between measures of volume and of capacity; solve problems that required the addition and subtraction of fractions, and perform more complicated operations.

Vaney carried out this research project in his school of three hundred pupils in seven grades, from families of workers, small shopkeepers, or employees. It allowed Binet to draw two conclusions. The first was that a retardation of two years in grade for children in the first to third years or of three years in grade for children of the fourth to sixth years indicated a retarded child unless there were extenuating circumstances causing an irregular school attendance. The second conclusion was that the completion of the third school year appeared to be the upper limit that the retarded could reach. Among the population studied, he and Vaney found four seriously retarded children and one doubtfully so (239, p. 660). On the importance of this investigation Binet wrote: ". . . It is one of the best contributions to pedagogy that our *Société* has inspired, and I am extremely happy to tell M. Vaney how much I appreciate it." Vaney went on to produce other achievement tests for reading and orthography. Other members of *La Société* promised tests for various areas, including "everyday knowledge," but failed to produce them despite Binet's urging and encouragement.

This hopeful beginning in achievement measurement

was not, of course, paralleled at that time by equal progress in the measurement of intelligence. The incredible confusions in the medical profession about the diagnosis of mental levels created amusing distinctions. For example, idiots of the second degree have a "fleeting attention," imbeciles of the lowest degree "a momentary attention," and of the higher degree "an attention that can be fixed for a short time"; these were the conclusions of Dr. E. Bourneville, a physician who worked at Bicêtre. The psychiatrist P. Sollier also emphasized the faculty of attention: "weakness," "instability," "difficulty of attention" characterized for him the different degrees of retardation. As Binet observed: "One searches in vain for precise observations of idiots and imbeciles" (117, pp. 180–81). He agreed with Dr. Blin's complaints of the "regrettable contradictions" among his colleagues, recalling that in the Vaucluse one child was diagnosed as "imbecile," as "idiot," as "moron," and as "degenerate" by four different doctors.[11] Diagnosis was little if any better in other European countries and in the United States.

By 1905 Binet had been experimenting with and testing individual differences for about fifteen years. He had much information about functions or faculties, and had found, with roughly forged "tools," some *group* differences between "intelligent" and "unintelligent" children. He knew that only complex functions yielded significant differences; he had seen the importance of age-grade relationships in memory tests and had "discovered" that single tests of any function are useless—that they must always include a number of measures of each. He also had become convinced that "direction," "organization," and "judgment" were

[11] Binet complained that doctors made these distinctions without knowing what normal children can do. He wrote: "They talk of 'light' and of 'complete' morons, and give handsome percentages" with no indications of how the distinctions are to be made. "What arbitrariness! And when these vague notions are accompanied with figures, how comical! It is not our fault if, in the presence of these grave medical statistics, we think irresistibly of Molière!" (139, p. 85n.). It was Molière, of course, who made so many gravely comical comments about medical doctors and so devastatingly portrayed their foibles.

important intellectual operations, and he and Simon had observed idiots and imbeciles in institutions and had already noted similarities of behavior between adult imbeciles and young children. Furthermore, as crucial as any other point, his anthropometric studies had made it clear that, in order to make meaningful comparisons among individuals, indicators, norms, or benchmarks must be established by measures of "normal" children at different ages. Indeed, his own cephalometric measures represented such norms (85). There were also socially accepted age-norms at which children, on the average, should have completed grade-levels in school. Therefore, the need, the experimental discernment, and the hypotheses were there. Was there also a catalytic agent to set off the necessary insight?

There have been some speculations about the source of this agent. Although Binet did not state it explicitly, all the evidence points to the work of Blin of Vaucluse and of his student, Henri Damaye.[12] Binet remarked that "with regard to precision, the Blin-Damaye method appears superior to what went before [it]," and he presented their investigation in *L'Année* in considerable detail (117, pp. 182–90) directly before and in juxtaposition to his 1905 article offering the first scale. Its probable influence can be judged only by examining it at least briefly.

Blin and Damaye used twenty themes, each with a varying number of subquestions, in a "questionnaire" given orally to each child. The "themes" included evaluations of general appearance, articulation, personal and family data about age and place of birth, the children's ideas about age ("At what age is one a man?"), about objects (shown a key, pin, pencil, book, sponge, and so on the child was to name them, and also was asked to give the use and color of other objects), about the body ("Show

[12] Without seeing the original thesis of Henri Damaye, Varon nevertheless guessed that the Blin and Damaye effort may indeed have influenced Binet's insights (303, pp. 79-80). Damaye's doctoral thesis, of course, gives this guess much stronger support. Also Binet's review of this monograph, while critical, provides enthusiasm for the method (*L'Année,* 10, pp. 517–18).

me your hands, tongue, foot, eyebrows, eyelids. . . . Put your finger on your right ear"), about internal sensations, about time, about geographical features of France, about military service, about trades ("What does a butcher, baker, mason, do?"), about religions. The children were asked to reproduce four simple designs; to read, write, and do arithmetic; and, tests which Damaye credited Binet with suggesting, to perform motor skills, which included making dots as fast as possible and threading a needle. Blin and Damaye also graded each subject's general attitude. To establish a test score they alloted zero to five points for each of the twenty themes, thus giving a global or overall assessment to the several subquestions in each theme, with one hundred points (20 x 5) representing the maximum score.

Although Blin and Damaye examined 250 subjects seven to twenty-six years of age, their claim that ninety points was "normal" and that score-ranges represented various levels of retardation was arbitrary.[13] The doctors reported that, after submitting their work to Binet for criticism, "the first thought of this distinguished master of the school of the Hautes-Études [Sorbonne] was that it was necessary . . . to experiment . . . on normal children in order to have points of comparison" (184, p. 109). Since this occurred in 1902–3 it is clear that Binet had the chronological mental level well in mind some time before he produced the scale. The doctors Blin and Damaye were satisfied that they had met Binet's requirement: they said that their "normal sample" consisted of *moral* degenerates—pyromaniacs and kleptomaniacs, pederasts, and violent reactors—"whose intellectual sphere can be considered intact" (184, p. 36)!

Binet's criticisms of these studies seem wholly justified (117, pp. 189–90): in addition to failure to establish standards on "normal" children, many of the questions were at best academic; for example, "What is the chief city of a

[13] Blin and Damaye quite arbitrarily labeled those who earned between 60 and 90 points as morons, with 50-60 "doubtful"; those between 30 and 50 points as imbeciles, with 20-30 as "doubtful"; and those between 10 and 20 points as idiots.

given *département* of France?" The "Yes" and "No" answers were "unhappy" in form since chance could favor success, and the total evaluation was quite subjective because of the global assessments made for each theme-with-variations, even though the two doctors had compared to their own satisfaction their separate scorings which they arrived at independently. Moreover, since all themes were of equal value, and each was given a single composite score, the results presented no analysis of the kinds of successes and failures; for example, there were no comparisons of the relative difficulties of response to abstract versus concrete materials. Finally, their claim that items within each theme were ordered according to difficulty was subjective and not clearly delineated. "It appears to us as having come out all armed from the brain of a theoretician," Binet concluded. "Yet," he added, "like the [Binet-Simon] system it is essentially *psychological* . . . and it has the advantage that all the questions are fixed in advance and so are not influenced by the bad humor or the indigestion of the examiner" (117, p. 190). All the same, this method of testing was considered by its authors to be sufficiently effective and promising to be reported at the Fifth International Congress of Psychology in Rome in April 1905 at the same meeting at which the preview of the Binet-Simon scale was also presented (185).

Although the reader must have noted that a few items in both studies are the same, the Binet-Simon scale of 1905 was very different in content, in scoring, and in methodology. It seems most likely that the important impact of the Blin-Damaye study, as the catalytic agent, might have come in Damaye's following words: ". . . *The different faculties are thus no longer studied separately, in an experimental dissociation, we can even say dissection, but instead in their observable behaviors and tasks according to popular and varied notions* . . . The method appears to us to have a completely clinical character" (184, p. 47; italics added). Did this break the mental set, this viewpoint that avoided the "experimental dissociation" represented by tests of separate faculties and sought instead to test responses to "notions," to "tasks or behaviors," whatever their psychological components might be? It appears very likely that this was so. At any rate, Binet and Simon set to work to find intellectual *tasks* that would fall in a hierarchy of difficulty according to the ages at which about 80 to 90 percent success was achieved. Their method for selecting these tasks was empirical: they took many test items to dozens of children, tested individually, and recorded the responses "live." In contrast, they pointed out, that a priori, subjective methods were similar to "men who colonize Algeria on a map while sitting comfortably in their studies" (118, p. 195). "The scale that we are going to describe," Binet wrote, "is not at all an a priori work; it results from extensive trials made first at the school of the Salpêtrière and then extended into the primary schools of Paris on both normal and on backward children . . . All the tests that we propose have been tried out many times and are retained from among many that were eliminated" (118, p. 195).

Simon (297) has given a somewhat different picture of the early trials-and-errors. He stressed the initial work with *adults*: ". . . to this methodical examination of adult retarded subjects," he wrote, "the metric scale undoubtedly owes its birth, its form, and consistency . . ." (297, p. 412). He believed that the multivariables inherent in the children's ages and the unknown degrees of retardation would never have yielded the hierarchical data of the 1905 table. Even so, he stressed in their trials their "continual coming and going" between adult retarded and normal and retarded children. His description of the early efforts is intriguing:

> . . . We moved along somewhat at random, always with the same preconceived idea of discovering how, intellectually speaking, one subject, appearing more developed, differed from another subject, older by one or more years, but no further advanced. We tried things that occurred to us, or reactions that one of our subjects had by chance revealed; or even some incident that the parents related to us, like the impossibility of their child's carrying out three requests that they had given him simultaneously.

We abandoned the tests that did not demonstrate patent differences. But we never applied the rule of three-quarters [only 75 percent success?], which, after us, was demanded *to place a test at a determined age.* This rule was formulated by a German author, O. Bobertag. It is convenient, but for my part *I do not believe it very good. . . .* There are some tests whose results improve year by year; some that give only a mediocre result for many years, and then abruptly the number of successes increases. These are much the best . . . and as much as possible we kept them . . . [297, p. 416].

In another place Binet and Simon together discussed the subjects used in the tests of infants:

Our tests of three months to two years were derived in a *crêche. . . .* Our series represents not a development of the élite, but an average of children of the people; *even from this age, extreme poverty, the absence of fondling and being played with, already makes its mark and retards the awakening of intellectual faculties* [143, p. 4; emphasis added].

The collaborators had also set other criteria for the tests: "They must be simple to give, convenient, precise, heterogeneous, keeping the subject in continuous contact with the experimenter, and bearing principally on the faculty of judgment." Binet was still captive to the word "faculty." Data on the performances of "normal" children carrying out tasks that cut across these misleading faculties proved to be the breakthrough. Throughout the whole process Simon's assistance was very important. The amount of work necessary for the first scale obviously was great, but for the 1908 revision—the really influential one—it rose to immense proportions. There is convincing evidence that Simón's aid both in giving the tests and in analyzing and working through the data was crucial to its achievement.[14]

[14] In fact, Simon not immodestly corroborates this opinion. He wrote: "It is possible that Binet would never have established this Measure of Intelligence that has become his principal claim to fame if chance had not brought us together . . ." (*Bull.*, 1954, No. 418, back cover).

The two men spent hours, days, weeks going from schools to asylums, to *crêches* and hospitals. They studied their subjects' actual abilities to perform tasks, rather than assuming that they *should* be able to perform them. Where they drew upon samples of "normal" children in the schools they first consulted the teachers to help identify the children with regular attendance records who were in the regular grades for their age and "within two months of their birthdays." After much testing Binet and Simon arranged thirty items roughly in order of difficulty to test both infants and children three, five, seven, nine, and eleven and twelve years of age or older, as the difficulty of the last several items indicates.

But what did Binet think these items really tested? The word "intelligence" meant a number of things in 1905, and he hesitated to commit himself to a precise definition. As he wrote:

> We must make known the meaning we give to this vague and very comprehensive word "intelligence." Almost all the phenomena that occupy psychology are phenomena of intelligence. . . . Should we therefore bring into our examinations the measure of sensation, after the example of psychophysicists? Should we put all of psychology in the tests?
>
> A little reflection has shown us that this would be time lost. There is in intelligence, it seems to us, a fundamental agent the lack or alteration of which has the greatest import for practical life, and that is judgment, otherwise known as good sense, practical sense, initiative, the faculty of adapting one's self. To judge well, to understand well, to reason well, these are the essential springs of intelligence. A person can be a moron or an imbecile if he lacks judgment; but with good judgment he will never be one. The rest of intellectual psychology appears of little importance beside judgment. For example, what does it matter whether the sense organs function normally? . . . Laura Bridgmann, Helen Keller, and others with the same misfortunes were both blind and deaf-mutes, which did not prevent their being very intelligent. . . .
>
> Therefore, in the scale that we present we accord first place to judgment. It is not simply any errors whatsoever

that are important, but absurd ones that prove a lack of judgment . . . [118, pp. 196–97].

Before describing the items of the scale, and by way of introduction, Binet insisted that this "measure" was really only a classification, although a measured one. He also made it clear that it did not analyze special aptitudes, although he mentioned their probable intrusion into some items. Indeed, there is every indication that he and Simon realized that they were only sampling intellectual behavior. An example of the latter point appears even in the 1911 scale when Binet recognized the roughness of the measure by his reluctance to recommend the use of fractional parts of a year in computing mental level, because he was doubtful that the scale "warranted that much precision" (165, p. 149). There can be no doubt that Binet understood many of the limitations of the instrument. He was quick to point out that the first six items could not pass for tests of judgment. They were assigned to the "normal" level for the first two years, but in older children and adults they also reached the upper limit of idiocy. These tests required coordination movements of the head to follow a lighted match, unwrapping food done up in a piece of paper, and, the most difficult of the group, the imitation of gestures and following of simple commands like "Sit down." Binet commented that even though idiots cannot communicate with words, their ability to imitate gestures and follow commands "represents the first degree of communication between individuals—the beginning of interpsychology."

A presentation of the other items of this hierarchy with some of Binet's explanations will help to clarify his conceptions of the scale in 1905, and at the same time show the scope of that earliest scale.

Items seven, eight, and nine test "the degree of communication beyond infancy or idiocy." The child is first given the name of one of several objects before him, or shown a picture and asked to point out objects: "Show me the cup," "Put your finger on the window in the picture." Then, what Binet believed to be a rather big step, the examiner pointed out objects in a picture and required the child himself to select the correct word for the object. Binet commented: "If the child says 'I don't know' this is a good sign, for an imbecile rarely says that whole little phrase, and the avowal of ignorance is a test of judgment. . . ." The experimenters retained all three items because "they constitute the frontier between idiocy and imbecility, and this frontier should be very solid. . . ."

Items ten and twelve required the subject to compare lines and weights. Binet found that failures were not due to errors of selection but to inability to understand what was required. He discovered that in item eleven, repeating digits, the *kind* of error is important. For example, the answer is absurd when a reply of "1, 2, 3, 4, 5" is given for the stimulus of "0, 3, 7, 2, 8," or if the child is satisfied with his wrong answer, for he has then shown a lapse of judgment. Item thirteen, testing suggestibility, was "not a test of intelligence . . . it tries out his character instead." Item number fourteen required definitions of words, to which the younger children usually gave "a definition only by use," and to which absurd replies must indeed be recorded.

In the fifteenth item, repetition of sentences of fifteen words, Binet found that the difference in number of successes between seven- and nine-year-olds was not very apparent, but that the "sevens" gave many more absurdities in their replies. For the sixteenth test that asked for differences between "paper and cardboard," "a fly and a butterfly," "wood and glass," and so on, Binet cautioned the examiner to be sure that the child knew the meaning of the words. This test differentiated between the "fives" and "sevens," thus presenting one frontier between imbeciles and morons, in favor of the latter. The difference between "sevens" and "nines" was too subtle for the items, thus "requiring more difficult propositions."

The seventeenth test that required naming from memory as many as possible of thirteen objects displayed for thirty seconds on a board was later dropped because "there are too many possibilities of distraction" and therefore of chance failure. In the eighteenth item the experimenter asked the subject to reproduce from memory two designs shown for ten seconds. These same designs appear in the 1960 revision of the Stanford-Binet test for years nine and eleven. Binet had found a similar test that required copying from a tachistoscopic presentation to be very discriminating between his "intelligent" and "unintelligent" pupils (74), but he was distressed by the extreme delicacy required to evaluate the results. The nineteenth test presented longer series of digits than number eleven, to test immediate memory, and the twentieth required the subject to report resemblances between "a poppy and blood," "an ant, an insect, a butterfly, and a flea," and "a newspaper, a label, and a picture." It is interesting to find Binet remarking that he was surprised to notice that the children had much more difficulty in explaining similarities than differences. In fact, he said that "one must insist and keep on insisting to show them that, however different, two dissimilar objects can be a little alike."

The twenty-first item asked for a comparison of lengths of lines, shown in couples, with one easy series, and a second much more difficult, so that even many adults failed it; and number twenty-two required a comparison of five blocks, which were to be put in order of weight: "This exacts a continuous direction of attention, an appreciation of weights, and memory with judgment." The twenty-third item asked which weights from the previous test the examiner had removed.

Number twenty-four turned to different problems. The subject was asked to find rhymes for given words. That is, "... *grenouille* [frog] rhymes with *citrouille* [squash], because it has the same sound, *ouille*. . . . What rhymes with *obéissance*?" It does not seem surprising that this proved difficult, as Binet noted: "No seven-year-old succeeded, one nine-year-old and one eleven-year-old did a little better." Number twenty-five was a word-completion test, revised from those "imagined and proposed by Professor Ebbinghaus," and the twenty-sixth asked the subject to put three nouns—"Paris, river, and fortune"—or three verbs into a sentence. "This test may be passed at several levels . . . the examiner should note the quality of the response."

The twenty-seventh was labeled an "abstract question," or as later called, "a comprehension question." For example: "When a person has offended you, and comes to offer his apologies, what should you do?" Binet and Simon had prepared twenty-five questions like this one. "This test," Binet wrote, "is one of the most important of all for the diagnosis of the upper limit of the moronic level. . . . Any mind not attuned to abstraction succumbs here." The researchers spent many heavy hours analyzing these replies in an attempt to arrive at comparative values, finishing with five degrees of satisfactoriness for each question; eleven-year-olds' responses were used as criteria for the younger children. In the final "grading" the silences, ambiguities, and absurdities counted most in the negative direction. These questions are fascinating in light of their continued use in the Stanford-Binet test and could provide a mine of test items in this area of cognitive activities. This item was used importantly to separate morons from "normals."

In the twenty-eighth, the subject was asked to invert the hands of a clock with no visual aids permitted, and the difficulty was increased by asking why the inversion is never exact. The twenty-ninth required a drawing of what a folded and cut paper would look like when unfolded; and number thirty requested the subject to define abstract words by designating the difference between such words as "esteem" and "friendship," "boredom" and "weariness."

There seemed to be as many questions raised as answered in this first sketch of tests. Binet wondered, for instance, if the tests of sensory intelligence such as comparing lines and ordering and comparing weights "would not be better as tests of aptitudes, since morons are sometimes highly successful with them." Results from numbers twenty-four to thirty, with the exception of twenty-seven, were inconclusive, and possibly were left in only for future reference. After all, the population sample of the "normals" was scanty indeed: only fifty in the experimental group—"about ten each" from the preschool, and five-, seven-, nine- and eleven-twelve-year groups. Binet admitted his disappointment at not having extended the "cumbersome, time-consuming testing" to each age level between three and twelve, and to many more children. But he was in the process of doing this. Binet and Simon could also take some satisfaction in the control of the milieu: ". . . all were chosen from the same social condition, and the same educational milieu" (119, p. 298).

Binet and Simon took their instrument to the Salpêtrière to try it out with the retarded at that institution. Could it differentiate degrees of retardation? Binet did not wish to calibrate these degrees more finely than into the three widely accepted categories of idiot, imbecile, and moron, although he recognized that this was an arbitrary classification. "It has been proposed," he mused, "to designate the idiot [in subclasses] as 'complete' or 'extreme,' but . . . it is not easy to say which would be more serious for the idiot—to be complete or extreme!"

The "frontier" that favored the imbecile over the idiot was represented by tests seven, eight, and nine. The experimenters were not satisfied with the "frontier" between imbeciles and the lower level of morons, although the key item seemed to be the "test of differences," which they set at five years in 1905 and changed to seven years in 1908. They concluded that "the tests passed by the morons seemed to exact more initiative . . . more invention or judgment," and presumably they would look for more tests to meet this requirement. The major intent of this instrument was to differentiate the morons, who needed special education, from the "normal" school population, which was the reason one commentator called it "a test of *un*intelligence" (310, p. 17). They made clear their difficulty in delineating this level; at this time they put the upper limit at the "comprehension questions," to which the morons made unsatisfactory responses.

Perplexing Relationships and Problems about Mental Growth

Binet's experience with abnormal children gave him new

vision of the nature of intelligence. For instance, the reader feels the excitement of sudden insight on his part in the following words:

> After finishing with the children [at the Salpêtrière] we recognized that it is almost always possible to equate them with normal children who are much younger. . . . We have been especially struck with the resemblances, which are so numerous, so curious, that really, to read a description of a child whose age was not given made one unable to tell whether he was normal or abnormal [119, p. 321].

Binet's inference from these observations was not as clear-cut and sure as his statement above might imply, for on the same page he also questioned and pondered details of the *differences* between children of different ages who tested at the same mental level. About this observation he added the following caution:

> It can also be true that certain differences are hidden under these resemblances, and that some day we shall succeed in making them out so plainly that we can find signs of psychological backwardness quite independent of age [119, p. 321].

And a further statement indicates that his use of the concept of "mental levels" was expedient and not to be confused with any hypothesis about the basic nature of mental retardation:

> *Being ignorant of the exact nature of this mental inferiority, we wisely refuse at this time, without other proof, to assimilate it to an arrest in normal development.* It seems in fact that the intelligence of these retarded persons has undergone a certain arrest; but it does not follow that this disproportion between their degree of intelligence and their age is the sole characteristic of their state. There is also, probably in many cases, a deviation in the development, a perversion. . . . There exist differences, apparent or hidden. An attentive study shows that among some idiots [imbeciles?] certain faculties are almost nil, while others are better developed. . . . If they were all examined carefully, probably many examples of partial aptitudes would be found. . . . This will be the object of

some later work. At this time we are limiting ourselves to measuring intelligence in general—indicating *mental level. And to give an idea of this level we shall compare it both to normal children of the same age, and to those of an analogous mental level at different ages. The reservations expressed above* about a simple arrest of development *will not prevent us from finding great advantages in these methodical comparisons* [118, pp. 192–93; emphasis added].

When he compared a twelve-year-old retardate who was just struggling to read with an average six-year-old who was also just learning to read, he discussed differences that went beyond a simple arrested development for the older child, and yet he also stressed the similarities in mental level. Furthermore, Binet refused to make any predictions beyond the "present mental level," since at that time so little was known about the mental development of normal children, let alone of abnormal ones. It could take years to produce such data, and his prescription for remedying this situation follows:

> It would be indispensable to follow individually many subjects through their developmental years to discover whether these states of mental inferiority are 1) arrests of development, or 2) evolutions—very slow, continuous or perhaps saccadic and intermittent, or 3) whether some essential faculties can grow, while others remain asleep. We cannot, therefore, compare these subjects to normal children, age by age, year by year, detail by detail. Without facts to affirm it, we have no right to conclude that the cerebral defects . . . will be a definitive obstacle [to further development] [119, p. 298].

As an example he pointed out that a twelve-year-old and a four-year-old retardate might both be barely talking, but there would be no reason to assume that the four-year-old would not learn more in the next eight years than the twelve-year-old had done in that time. In other words, it might be possible for a child once diagnosed as an idiot to become an imbecile, or for an imbecile to become a moron, and therefore any diagnosis based upon present levels must be tentative.

Binet recognized that diagnosis must take into account both the mental level and the chronological age of the subject, but he had no satisfactory way of putting the two together. He suggested that a subject could be described as "*x* years in retard or in advance of normal," but he did not believe that the scale was exact enough to warrant its use in the establishment of a mathematical formula like, for example, the IQ, which he would undoubtedly have rejected.

At this point in his thinking Binet was also convinced that he could not postulate retardation as a global phenomenon. A retarded child might be at a very low level of intelligence in one area and near his age level in another. If this were true, his development would be characterized as an "unequal and partial" retardation, rather than a global one. Furthermore, he believed that the inequalities varied from person to person. Nonetheless, in each case they produced a "rupture of equilibrium" that constituted the abnormality. Some three or four years later he changed his mind about this problem, perhaps because it would be impossible to apply it to the processes developed in the scale.

Binet's absorption in the nature of intelligence, and his recognition of its complexity, far beyond the contents of his own attempted measurements, is also illustrated even in the very different context of his philosophical treatise *L'Âme et le corps,* in which he wrote the following:

> ... At one moment it, intelligence, apprehends an object, and it is a perception or an idea; at another time, it perceives a connection, and it is a judgment; at yet another, it perceives connections between connections, and it is an act of reasoning [113, p. 117].

At the same time, in another statement, he expressed his notion of the pervasive unity of intelligence within the total personality:

> Our motor is the will, the sentiment; it is the tendency, the direction. The will is perhaps the most characteristic psychological function. . . . Let us not separate it from intelligence, let us embody the one in the other, and instead

of representing the function of the mind as having as its objective *to* understand, *to* forejudge, *to* predict, *to* adapt itself, we shall be nearer the truth if we represent a being who *wants* to know, who *wants* to predict, who *wants* to adapt himself, for basically, he *wants* to live [113, p. 172].

The originator of intelligence measurement, therefore, was not at all unaware of the limitations of his instrument for assessing individual differences.

Applications of the 1905 Scale

Despite the embryological nature of this first scale, Binet and Simon considered it as representing the "psychological aspect" of their recommended three-pronged study of retarded children. The other two aspects of the assessment vehicle were "pedagogical" and "medical" examinations. The former was represented by Vaney's barometers of instruction, including the expected extensions into added areas of the school curriculum, and of "everyday knowledge." The "medical" was scarcely developed, beyond some height and weight tables and the norms of head measurements that Binet had furnished. He urged the medical profession to provide normative data for other physiological and physical measures, and to find some way to bring together the indices of each measure into a medical coefficient.[15] In evaluating the three aspects that were necessary for an assessment, he was straightforward in comparing their usefulness; he remarked that "the psychological method . . . can reveal almost *certain* signs of

[15] Binet had definite and explicit ideas about the normative barometers for genetic, physiological, and anatomical data; he insisted that ". . . these values must be fixed without preconceived ideas; and the sole means of achieving this is to make a comparative study of the normal state. This is a directing principle that is forgotten too often in medicine. It is, however, so important, so fecund for consequences, that a psychiatrist would make his name illustrious by doing nothing more than penetrating into the mind of his contemporaries with the idea that the study of the abnormal is possible only by comparisons with the normal . . ." (118, p. 243). The use of such normative data among doctors, geneticists, and others has become commonplace today.

retardation . . . the pedagogical method . . . *probable signs* . . . and the medical method . . . only *possible* signs" (118, p. 244).

Embedded in other somewhat caustic comments about the medical profession, such statements may have cost Binet acceptance of the scale in France, where its appearance raised scarcely a ripple. Even the Ministerial Commission for the Retarded seems to have been largely immune to it. Nonetheless, Binet's prediction about the usefulness of the scale came to be accepted by most of the Western world. He wrote:

> When the work only sketched out here becomes definitive, it will permit the solution of many current questions, since it is no less a matter than the measurement of intelligence, . . . permitting comparisons not only according to age, but also according to sex, social conditions, race, intellectual status, . . . and normal and criminal anthropology [119, p. 246].

The most notable immediate reaction to the 1905 papers appeared in an article by O. Decroly, director of a Brussels institute for the retarded, and his assistant, J. Degand (186). After a lengthy critique of the many inadequate tests previously tried out in Europe and the United States, they turned to the Binet-Simon investigation, which they commended for its originality as well as its usefulness. Far from ignoring it, they had already put it to a test with twenty-seven subjects, and concluded with emphasis:

> Despite some faults and flaws, *we are persuaded that these tests can already render service in making classifications of pupils for a school or classes in special training. . . .* Thus we advocate their immediate use from the beginning of the school year to reduce trials that are harmful to both students and their teachers [186, p. 130].

Although the Ministerial Commission did not understand or seek to understand the scale as an important diagnostic instrument, its members were cognizant of their responsibility to do something for retarded children. Therefore, they made it possible for Binet to organize a few special classes for them, and asked him to prepare a book for the public on retarded children (134). He and Simon subtitled it "A guide for the admission of retarded children into special classes" and were thus able to press the need for assessment. Limited action was therefore underway.

Thus by 1905 after years of efforts in many countries to find some objective measurement that would differentiate the several levels of retardation, Binet and his co-worker Simon had found an instrument that promised to develop into a suitable test to solve this baffling problem. In that year it was still in embryonic form, and indeed its authors were not yet fully convinced of its possible usefulness. There remained much work to be done, and for Binet, unhappily, the time was short that would be allowed him to complete it.

5 The Emergence of Binet's Conceptions and Measurement of Intelligence

In 1908 Binet and Simon produced a revised scale that represented a salient change in viewpoint and was, of course, the result of an incredible labor. From the titles alone the shift in viewpoint is apparent: in 1905 the scale was called "New methods for the diagnosis of the intellectual level of the abnormal"; in 1908, "The development of intelligence among children." Thus a method of assessing the lack of intelligence was transformed into a method of assessing or classifying the intelligence of a fan of children—retarded, slow, normal, and even above normal, since a few children were reported to be three or four years in advance of "normal." Undoubtedly even in 1905 Binet had had the idea of a more "global" instrument, for at that time he wistfully deplored his very inadequate sample of normal children and also predicted the usefulness of his scale, after improvement, to test many areas of differences (119, p. 246).

Of course, this change required a drastic revision of content. Of the thirty tests published in 1905, Binet and Simon retained only fourteen without change, dropped nine, modified seven, and added thirty-three new items. These were "standardized" on about three hundred children from three through thirteen years of age. The numbers of items at the several age levels, however, varied disconcertingly from two to nine. Binet issued some warnings: this was uncertain research (*tâtonnements*), he wrote, and in a complex area that "made it regrettable that our minds always simplify nature," a fact that interferes with true understanding. He discussed the tests as an attempt to discover a schema of children's mental development, but again he warned that the measures could not be exact like height and weight. Instead they were somewhat arbitrary since they depended upon the particular convention chosen to "grade" them and also upon the particular items selected, since special aptitudes and other unknown factors would influence results. Furthermore, a child might be retarded in some tests of his age and advanced in others. This, he remarked, gave a kind of artificial character to the process of assigning a number representing the retardation or advance in intelligence, since it would be in part a function of the conventional procedure adopted by the tester. Binet decided on a convention that would credit the child with all items passed: he started with the age at which the child passed all but one test, and then advocated adding a year's credit for every five items successfully passed thereafter. Since he and Simon believed that the measure was too approximate to calculate months more precisely, they presumably noted the fractions of years in the protocol that they insisted should accompany each test report.

The advantages of the scale, they said, lay in the fact that ". . . it runs its course according to an unvarying plan, it takes express account of age, and it assesses the responses by comparing them to a norm that is a real and living average" (139, p. 60). Examples of Binet's discussions of the probable significance of items will throw further light on his reasons for including them. For instance, he wanted his reader to recognize that it is "much more painful" for a child to have to name an object pointed out by the experimenter than to choose his own familiar name for any familiar object he sees in a picture. He and Simon had also discovered by this time the developmental significance of the three levels of responding to a picture, namely, enumeration, description, and interpretation, which they set at three, seven, and twelve years respectively. "This item," they indicated, "makes it possible to observe what strikes the child most, what idea directs him . . . how he reasons. . . . We place this test above all others; if it were necessary to keep only one, we would not hesitate to choose this one" (139, p. 8).[1] Nonetheless, Binet accorded almost as high a value to the absurdities and the "comprehension questions."

Binet went on to note that they had learned from the imbeciles that copying a diamond is more difficult than copying a square. The item of giving two memories from a paragraph that the child reads "has," he said, "a sort of solemnity for us. It serves as a limit between imbecility and the moronic status. Every moron is capable of communicating with his peers by writing and reading with understanding . . . [imbeciles are not]" (139, p. 32). By putting this item at the eight-year-level, the collaborators were influenced to set the top level of imbecility at seven instead of five years. The tests at this "frontier" between the two categories of retardation are interesting enough to be listed:

Seven years
(top level of imbecility)
Showing what is left out of pictures
Telling how many fingers he has
Copying a written sentence
Copying a triangle and a diamond (here "one-fifth fail")
Repeating five digits
Describing a picture
Counting thirteen cents
Naming four pieces of money
Giving definitions superior to use

Eight years
(evidence at least of moron status)
Reading a passage, and giving two memories
Counting nine sous, three simple, three double
Naming four colors
Counting backwards from twenty to zero
Comparing two objects from memory
Writing from dictation

[139, pp. 58–59]

[1] In the 1966 reconstruction of the scale (310, pp. 126-28) the French authors report small correlations between responses to the pictures and the whole scale, especially at twelve and fourteen years of age. They believe that the Binet-Simon pictures, each one of sad and deprived persons, arouse emotional and socially relevant responses that are more related to children's "social experiences" than to their cognitive ability. Of course the same criticism would not apply to the pictures used in the Stanford-Binet revision.

Two "good frontier tests" to assist the difficult distinction between the more effective morons and normal children were "comprehension questions" ("Before taking part in an important matter, what should you do?") and absurdities ("There was an accident yesterday, but it wasn't serious; only forty-eight people were killed." Question: "What is foolish about that?"). It is obvious that Binet was much impressed by these "comprehension questions" for the light they could throw on a child's reasoning. As an example he wrote:

> In a general way . . . these "questions" dissipate all doubts of whether or not children are abnormal . . . a very slow child, with little facial expression, did not know what day it was nor the day after Sunday, although he was 10½ years old. Yet when asked: "Why should you judge another person according to his acts rather than his words?" he was able to respond: "Because words are not very sure, and acts are more sure." That sufficed. . . . This child was not as stupid as he gave the impression of being [139, p. 47].

He also discussed the absurdities, giving other examples, such as "I have three brothers, Paul, Ernest, and me"; or "They found yesterday on the fortifications an unfortunate young girl, cut into eighteen pieces. They believe she killed herself." These absurdities are direct progenitors of some of Piaget's work; in fact, in his *Judgment and Reasoning in the Child* he wrote and analyzed many pages about Binet's "three brothers" absurdity. Binet had noted that a child can sometimes *feel* that a sentence is absurd when he may not be able to give the reason. "All this," he added, "could give place to many interesting analyses of our manner of understanding and explaining [cognitive processes]" (139, p. 48).

The comprehension questions and absurdities were added to the picture interpretations at the frontier where morons over nine years of age were clustered with normal children. Distinctions were made by responses to these several items. Binet also believed that making sentences with three given nouns or verbs, rhyming words, and defining abstract terms were important in the distinction, but he needed more data to make the frontier firm.

In addition to the test items Binet gave a "social definition" of moronity that sounds so modern as to arrest attention today, but one that is useful only for adult subjects:

> The general formula is that an individual is normal when he can conduct himself without having need of the tutelage of others, when he earns sufficient income for his needs, and finally, when his intelligence does not take him into work of a lower classification than that of his parents [like the son of a lawyer reduced to being a petty clerk]. . . . In a word, *retardation is an idea related to a host of circumstances that must be kept in mind in judging each particular case. The decision must be made on a synthesis of resultants* [139, p. 88; italics added].

As a general principle, Binet recommended the presumptive diagnosis of retardation for a child who, without undue absence from school, was two years behind his expected grade before nine years of age, or three years behind after nine years of age; or who was two years below average on the psychological test (134, pp. 57ff.; 139, p. 92). Yet the test alone was never sufficient to "convict" a child if he was in the appropriate grade for his age; in this case "he is always protected against suspicion" (139, p. 92). The data indicated that among the "normal" mental retardation of only one year was "so frequent as to be insignificant," while a retardation of two years was rare, or about 7 percent.

Binet felt that he should say something about the nature of the process that he and Simon were measuring, that is, general intelligence. Although he consciously hedged, he did note:

> It is a problem frightening in its complexity, and if we wished to take it in its totality, we would be obliged to state some a priori views *the least danger of which would be to lead to some distinctions and subdivisions that, while seeming important to us at the time, would perhaps not be so at all.* . . . Therefore, we want to confine ourselves to examining the facts that we have collected, thus presenting

no general theory of intelligence, but rather a detailed examination of some special and [until now] poorly known facts [139, p. 74; italics added].

The wide variety of different ways in which children approached the items ("constantly novel," Binet remarked) made him realize that the problem of special aptitudes was also one that must be solved, and, although he undertook it in earnest before his death, he achieved no success. Nevertheless, in the case of general intelligence, despite arresting qualifications made in a footnote,[2] Binet and Simon boldly concluded:

> . . . We possess at the present time an instrument that allows us to measure the intellectual development of young children whose ages are between three and twelve years . . . to know summarily whether a child has the intelligence of his age, or is advanced or retarded . . . [139, p. 82].

They felt convinced that they had an instrument for the individual and the social good. "But," they added, probably thinking of the school problems, "its most important applications lie in the determination of inferior degrees of intelligence" (139, p. 85). Once again Binet remarked that the two important factors to be considered were chronological age and mental level. Once again he was unable to find any appropriate way to combine these two elements. In his opinion this solution must wait upon the extended collection of data about the course of mental development, especially prognosis at inferior levels.

The repercussions of this 1908 revision were "tremendous." Overnight, Binet's name became well known in Europe. In Brussels O. Decroly, who had already hailed the 1905 scale, introduced the new one to Henry Goddard who brought it to the United States. John E. Anderson, of the University of Minnesota, then a student, later wrote that "it is impossible, unless we lived through the period,

[2] They wrote: "These tests are not the first ones we thought of; we have kept them only after long trials. But we are far from pretending that they are the best. Those who take up this work further will find better ones . . . elminating those influenced by instruction . . ." (139, p. 59n.).

to recapture the enthusiasm, discussion, and controversy that the Binet tests started" (259, p. 183). These tests made it possible to show that measurable differences in mental levels, rather than voluntary and thus punishable "moral weakness," could be responsible for children's school achievement. As Anderson went on to say: "Clearly [Binet's work] substituted for the onus of moral blame a measurable phenomenon within the child's resources that [was] to be studied henceforth in its own right" (259, p. 183). To Binet's satisfaction, the American psychologist G. M. Whipple also gave attention to the Binet-Simon tests in his 1910 *Manual of Mental and Physical Tests* (165, p. 145). The English also quickly recognized "the originality and ingenuity of the tests," as Sir Cyril Burt remarked over fifty years later when he recalled visiting Binet and Simon in Paris "to watch these men at work." He was "impressed not only with their scientific and metrical methods (a novelty in those days) but also with their delightfully intimate and sympathetic way of handling children" (254).

While America and the rest of Europe accepted the scale as an important contribution, it was largely ignored in France, and indeed sometimes ridiculed and scoffed at. Goddard was in Paris before he went to Brussels where he learned of Binet's work. He visited Janet there, and also Bourneville, a psychiatrist who headed a special school for the retarded children of wealthy parents. If either of them mentioned Binet's tests, Goddard's 1908 "Diary" failed to mention it. On the contrary, after visiting them he wrote that "there are no special classes in French schools for the retarded" (*sic!*) and he reflected the idea that there was almost nothing going on in France in their behalf except "a meagre sort of psychological examination and some neurological work at the Bicêtre." Another entry records: "Visited the Sorbonne. Binet's lab is largely a myth. Not much being done, says Janet" ("Diary," 1908, from Archives of History of American Psychology, University of Akron, Akron, Ohio). He had to go to Brussels to learn what was being done in France. After all, Binet did not have a professorship, and his association with other French psychologists and psychiatrists was not cordial or close.

The Psychogenetic Method: A Study of Adult Retardates, and Its Implications for a Schema of Intelligence

In October 1908 when Simon left Paris to codirect a mental hospital near Rouen, geographical separation did not end his cooperation with Binet. Although the two men could not continue the day-to-day collaboration necessary for the next revision of the scale, nonetheless they did keep in close contact with one another and undertook several serious projects. A very important one of these was a minute, highly instructive, and ingenious investigation of the development and functioning of institutionalized adult imbeciles (144).[3] The 1908 scale provided the underpinning for what Binet called "a really new research approach: the psychogenetic method." It is an example of comparative psychology that offered a method for differentiating normal and retarded children and normal children and retarded adults.

This article is ample evidence of Simon's observations about Binet's qualities as an observer. Binet began by making long naturalistic observations of his subjects and by asking them questions that would elicit spontaneous responses. Without such initial procedures to obtain an idea of the whole person, he remarked, "one's work would be as ridiculous as studying geography with a microscope." These regular and frequent observations and interrogations seem to have convinced him that such marked retardation accompanied a reduction of all the faculties—global rather than partial. For example, "the imbecile for the most part never voluntarily gives an account of anything because he does not take the initiative to speak. Therefore, he must be questioned, and his responses, more or less influenced by our questions, must be carefully studied." Only after such general investigations, he be-

[3] The reader is referred to the original article if he wishes to discover new insights into the nature of adult imbeciles, both in descriptions and in photographs. It was translated by E. S. Kite, Vineland Press, 1916 (277).

lieved, could "precision on particular points be achieved by detailed analyses" (140, pp. 329ff.). Binet and Simon then used the tests to group the inmates of the institution in the order of their intellectual levels according to the scale, so that they could study according to intellectual level the "evolution" of the following phenomena: character, attention, effort, movements and writing, perception, the feeling of pain, the association of ideas, intellectual activity as distinguished from level of intelligence, the "arithmetical faculty," reasoning, suggestibility and docility, and false judgments. Out of this ambitious initial study they arrived at a schema of thought that integrated, first, a kind of behaviorism, because it is a psychology of thought as action; second, of *Gestaltism*, because the hallmark of mental evolution is the process of differentiation from the general (undifferentiated) to the specific; and, third, of functionalism, because adaptation provides the central objective of the behavioral matrix.[4] Their main reason for choosing to make this extensive study of adult imbeciles rather than of children at similar stages of development was that the imbeciles had stopped changing. Their development was arrested and presented reactions that were stable over long periods of time, thus offering opportunities for minute comparisons. The study resulted in a schema of thought applicable to normal as well as to retarded individuals. It included three main operations: direction, correction or criticism, and adaptation. Among imbeciles all of these operations were dis-

[4] The reader may be interested in the words used by Binet that have influenced me to apply these terms to the schema. For behaviorism: ". . . the essential of the new theory looks for the essence of thought in a system of actions" (144, p. 146); for *Gestalt* theory: "Thought tends toward determination . . . it begins from chaos, where everything resembles no matter what, to end in a realization that resembles reality; then [by an integration of] such individualizations, it becomes a general idea" (144, pp. 132–33); for functionalism: "This adjustment of the means to the ends . . . is the proper work of intelligence, and constitutes adaptation. . . . All thought is like a key that must fit exactly in the hole of a certain lock" (144, pp. 133–34).

covered, although only in minor or simple expressions, which were contrasted strikingly with the same operations in "normal" children.

Binet entitled his first subdivision "direction" or "directedness" because thought is a system of actions in the process of attempting to find appropriate means to ends. "The objective must always be kept under control," he wrote. "One must work from a *directing idea*. . . . The power of direction in thought is manifested in two ways: by its complexity and by its persistence" (144, p. 131). He called the second "correction or criticism," "an apparatus of control . . . that is a kind of standing back to look at the exterior world, while also making reflections within one's self to judge the capability of the means for attaining the end. . . . Without this selection, no adaptation would succeed." He reported that the imbeciles' failure to judge the appropriateness of a response is a frequent symptom of their condition. They are satisfied to give *any* numbers in a digit series, or to point out "anything at all" in a picture, and to do this without giving any sign of having made a mistake. A lack of self-criticism also appeared strikingly in their daily conversations.

The third subdivision was "adaptation," which is the key to all action and works intimately with all other processes. In the march of thought there must be progress by means of appropriate *selectivity* (criticism) in the *directions* it takes. "In order to evolve, thought . . . consists in choosing constantly among several states, several ideas, several means that present themselves, like routes diverging from a crossroad. . . ." Appropriate adaptation works within a well-defined hierarchy of possibilities, for example, "as with the locksmith . . . who does not try out every key on his ring, but only certain ones." Furthermore, there is an abundant multiplication of intellectual activity (*pullulement*). An imbecile, on the other hand, will try almost any response, within a very broad hierarchy, and also only one or two responses rather than a number. Binet called this characteristic *n'importequisme* (no-matter-what-ism) and described it in his inimitable way:

. . . A close analysis would show that this *n'importe-quisme* is very complex; we suppose that its essential condition is an absence of a critical sense; the imbecile does not recognize the insufficiency of his response, but is content with a very gross approximation . . . and his thought does not evolve or multiply abundantly. . . . For example, in the game of "patience"—putting together [eight to ten pieces of a card] to make a rectangle. . . . A normal child shows an abundance of ideas . . . his intelligence meeting an obstacle makes an effort against it. With an imbecile the slow production of ideas is indeed striking, and the number of attempts [to solve] "patience" is extremely small. It is no longer living water that flows, but rather a rivulet of wax that congeals. . . .

It is indeed this paucity of ideas that makes a conversation with an imbecile so insipid. Recall our friend Albert who, when we asked him . . . after a week's absence: "Well, friend Albert, it's been a long time since we met. What have you been doing all this time?" replied simply: "I have been sweeping."

In looking at pictures, there is a lack of differentiation of thought. . . . Many imbeciles can say only one thing: "That, that's a man; that's a woman"—thus showing a lack of penetration. There is no evocation of the appropriate idea that belongs exactly to the particular picture, no interpretation that belongs to it alone . . . no differentiated response, no evolving adjustment. . . . It is the same for defining words, almost entirely by use. . . . Briefly, the imbecile tries only one or two keys to open a lock, and even these fit badly . . . [144, pp. 137-39].

These continuous and abundant observations brought Binet to a conclusion that reversed the earlier one that hypothesized a "rupture of equilibrium," an unevenness of capabilities, among those seriously retarded. Now he declared that *"there is at least some harmony in their rudimentary mental states."* In other words, ". . . if imbeciles lack judgment," he observed, "they lack it no more than they do direction, adaptation, and the rest. . . . One feels that it is especially the superior parts of intelligence, the most delicate and the finest, that are not developed in them. . . . They are reduced to what is . . . the simplest, the most elementary, the most general in man. . . . In the final analysis they are beings who are mentally poverty-stricken" (144, p. 123). Therefore, rather than the earlier "rupture of equilibrium" in mental faculties, he substituted for it a hypothesis of a "harmony of deficiencies." Either Binet had changed his mind after his extensive two years' experiences with these abnormals, or, in contrast to the partial aptitudes he had once recognized, by 1909 he was thinking primarily of the retardates' ability to function in some degree, however inadequately, in the general operations of directedness, critical capacity, and adaptation. In the latter case, he found them "harmoniously" in arrears. Whatever the reasons, there was a clear inconsistency: in the one instance, Binet had explicitly claimed that the state of being retarded was an uneven one, and in the later one he saw it as manifesting fairly equal weakness in all mental operations.

The Significance to Binet of a Contrast: Mental Level versus Mental Age

In this difference of opinion Binet was caught in a paradox between his theoretical hypotheses and his practical requirements. If the scale was to be used to distinguish among all levels of ability, the similarities among them, except in *degrees,* must be maximized to permit the same instrument to measure and compare the total group. This practical requirement would then influence Binet to stress "the harmony of deficiencies" among imbeciles. On the other hand, if Binet was to continue to opt for special methods of education for the retarded, and if his former emphases on qualitative differences were to be considered, he must point out basic differences between the retarded and the "normal." If this situation was a paradox in Binet's own mind, he did not explicitly point it out. Nonetheless, it seems plausible that his consistent use of the term "mental *level*" (*niveau mental*) instead of "mental *age*" reflected and symbolized his uncertainty. Moreover, he had explicitly said that he and Simon were ignoring special, partial aptitudes in their scale, and were limiting themselves to measuring intelligence *in general* and indicating it in "mental levels." Furthermore, Binet had said that despite reservations about qualitative differences between persons of similar mental level but dissimilar chronological ages, he felt that the advantages of comparing "mental levels" between retardates and "normals" justified the use of these "methodical comparisons" (118, pp. 192–93). "Mental level," therefore, was a more global, less detailed expression than "mental age," since the latter presumably would require precise knowledge about inclusive and representative cognitive processes at each chronological age. This he could not offer; it must wait on prolonged, developmental research. In fact, he had pointed out that never in his experience had an eight-year-old, for instance, passed all the tests at that level and failed all those for nine years. He gave many examples of these uneven performances among normal children, in which successes and failures would be averaged out, thus resulting in an average *level.* It appears therefore that he could not call this average level a mental *age,* which would imply a rather ordered, probably genetic, developmental progression that he had not demonstrated. The incompleteness of his instrument, which provided only samples of behavior, and the uncertain impingement of special aptitudes on results, also worked against achieving precise specifications of mental *age.*

This conceptual problem is very complex. Two French pedagogues, René Zazzo (310) and Guy Avanzini (262), should be credited with the discovery that Binet never actually used the phrase "mental *age,*" which has been erroneously inferred by many writers who have mistranslated Binet's actual phrase *niveau mental* or who have copied earlier authors who have made that understandable error. Actually the difference is very considerable, if not quite as much as Zazzo has claimed: "Age," he wrote, "implies growth, level implies nothing" (310, p. 33).[5]

[5] It has appeared unfortunate to the French educator René Zazzo that Binet did not suggest a quotient since in Binet's own *L'Année* a certain Ganguillet (Swiss or German) in 1904 and 1906 (198) had calculated a "mental quotient" by dividing the amount of schoolwork accomplished by the number of years it took a pupil to accomplish it. For example, four grades in four

Avanzini believes that Binet could not accept the theoretical position implied by "mental age" because it represents, in rather large part, "an endogenous and ordered dynamism" that has not been verified (262, p. 126). In other words, "level" was more noncommittal than "age" and so avoided prescriptions based on experimentally unconfirmed data about mental development. Therefore, it seems obvious that the honesty of Binet's convictions prevented him from being able to put together those "two important elements of chronological age and mental level" so that they could be expressed in some meaningful symbol. These delicate and significant reservations, however, did not affect Wilhelm Stern, the distinguished German investigator, who in 1911 proposed the popular concept of mental age (M.A.) and therefore of the intelligence quotient (I.Q.). Although so practically useful in giving notations to degrees of mental difference, it thus greatly transcended Binet's and Simon's claims of precision. Simon continued to think of the use of the I.Q. as a betrayal (*trahison*) of the scale's objective (248).

Intelligence Reexamined: Les idées modernes sur les enfants

The 1909 article on "the intelligence of imbeciles" included a statement about mental measurement that previews Binet's 1911 formulation. He wrote then:

> . . . We predict a new method for measuring the phenomena of consciousness; instead of measuring their *intensity,* which has been the vain and foolish ambition of the psychophysicists, we shall measure the useful effects of acts of adaptation, and the value of the difficulties overcome by

---

years could be represented by 1 or 100; two grades in four years, by ½ or 50; six grades in four years by 1½ or 150, and so on. Zazzo noted that with these quotients Ganguillet had surprisingly approached Terman's I.Q. categories for normals, idiots, and gifted. He apparently felt that this formulation should have suggested to Binet a quotient reached by dividing mental age by chronological age (310, p. 33). Our discussion, however, suggests strongly that a lack of necessary evidence made Binet shun any such formula.

them; there is here a measure that is not arithmetical, but one that permits a lineal seriation, a hierarchy of acts and of different individuals judged according to their effectiveness [144, p. 146].

He gave no hints of the means to this vague end, but with this point of attack he foresaw psychology as forging a synthesis among the disciplines of ethics, pedagogy, and philosophy. *Thought as a system of adaptive actions* was the key. Accordingly he paid a debt to American functionalism for this comprehensive conception, which forced him again to conceive of intelligence in a much larger framework than his tests encompassed.

During the same year, 1909, Binet published *Les idées modernes sur les enfants*. While it is a popular, almost a chatty book whose primary purpose seems to have been instructive for both the school and the home, he included in it some of his significant thoughts about intelligence that do not appear elsewhere. In the first place, without giving any evidence beyond the continuous observation of children that was his preoccupation, he recorded an intuition that has now been supported by evidence:

We must recognize that intellectual development does not follow a regularly ascending direction; the curve [of growth] has plateaus, and this is normal. From time to time a child stops developing, he rests in some way. Perhaps during this time the physical organism is growing in its turn; we actually know almost nothing of it [142, p. 106].

This quotation appears among pages of discussion about the various conditions, at home, at school, and within children's personalities, that can affect the proper assessment of a child's intelligence. He introduced his readers of *Les idées modernes* . . . to the 1908 Binet-Simon metric scale as a systematic aid to this process, remarking as follows about the nature of intelligence:

We are a bundle of tendencies; and it is the resultant of all of them that is expressed in our acts. . . . It is, then, this totality that must be evaluated. . . . The mind is one, despite the multiplicity of its faculties; it possesses one essential function to which all the others are subordinated. . . . Considered independently from phenomena of sensitivity, emotion, and will, *the intelligence is before all a process of knowing that is directed toward the external world, that works to reconstruct it in its entirety, by means of the little fragments that are given to us.* . . . Since all this ends up in inventing, we call the whole work an *invention,* which is made after a *comprehension* . . . that necessitates a *direction.* . . . It must be judged in relation to the end pursued; therefore, we must add *criticism.* Comprehension, inventiveness, direction, and criticism: intelligence is contained in these four words [142, p. 117-18; italics added except in the case of the four operations].

Adaptation had plainly become *comprehension* and *inventiveness,* and all were intricately rolled together with the emotions and the will. If the reader is puzzled by overlaps among the four vectors or operations, he will probably not be able to find relief in Binet's pages. They do, however, provide ample evidence that his concern with qualitative differences did indeed prevent him from using the phrase "mental *age*" as though it were a known and actual phenomenon. In discussing these four operations he compared adult imbeciles and children of the same mental level and normal children and adults. The brief examples that follow suggest that it is unfortunate that *Les idées modernes* . . . has not yet been translated into English:

Comprehension: the child is superficial . . . he can be struck by a small detail, but will not see the whole, the pattern, and he is especially incapable of differentiating the essential from the accessory. Ask him to recount an event, and you will see that he has had only a superficial view, that he was struck by the *décor,* and not by the hidden sense. . . . He is essentially sensory . . . employs few adjectives . . . rarely any conjunctions, those little words that are perhaps the most noble parts of the language, for they express subtle relations of ideas. He uses concrete rather than abstract words—has a comprehension that remains always on the surface . . . [142, pp. 120–21].

Inventiveness: his power of invention does not evolve, does not show differentiation. . . . The meaning of words is limited and banal . . . his responses to pictures would fit all sorts of pictures, and not particularly those shown to him. . . . To enumerate, to describe, to interpret—these are the three steps of evolving thought . . . from the "whatever" to the special; the young child is on the way to achieving this passage [142, p. 121–22].

Direction: The child is unreflective and inconstant; he forgets what he is doing . . . lets himself be carried away by fantasy, by caprice. . . . In a conversation he jumps from one subject to another according to any chance associations . . . Watch him go to school, making a "*voyage en zigzag* . . ." [142, pp. 119-20].

Criticism: The power of criticism is as limited as the rest . . . he does not know that he does not understand. . . . The *whys* with which his curiosity hounds us are scarcely embarrassing, for he will be contented naïvely with the most absurd *becauses*. His lies may be explained by his weak differentiation between the real and the fantasied. And finally, everyone knows of his extreme suggestibility that lasts up to about the age of fourteen years [142, p. 122].

Of course, Binet pointed out that in all this behavior the normal child resembles closely adult imbeciles. But he stipulated some differences, at least *one* of those he had hoped to find that are "independent of age":

The imbecile adult has completed his development, the child is at the beginning of his. . . . The child has a prompt and durable memory, even better than that of an adult. . . . He has an excess of activity . . . that makes him mobile and buoyant . . . and very refractory to the discipline of silence they want to impose on him at school. . . . Finally, *the child abandons himself to an incessant succession of attempts of all sorts in order to get acquainted with exterior objects or to exercise his faculties; as a very small infant, he takes up objects, handles them, strikes them, sucks them* . . . *and later he spends hours and hours absorbed in play; the child is essentially someone who plays* . . . play distinguishes and signalizes all beings who are in the process of developing. We scarcely need to add that the adult imbecile does not play . . . [142, pp. 123-24; italics added].

Parallels with Piaget's infant investigations and with

White's "competence motivation" are obvious in these observations.

Surely any author of "modern ideas about children" could not forego discussions and proposals concerning their proper education or consequently escape hypotheses about heredity and environment. Binet had attributed largely to heredity the differences in "habitual modes of thought" between Alice and Madeleine. His qualifications apropos of intelligence are important:

> . . . anyone's intelligence is susceptible to development; with practice and training, and especially with appropriate methods [of teaching] we can augment a child's attention, his memory, his judgment—helping him literally to become more intelligent than he was before . . . right up to the moment when he arrives at his limit. Thereafter progress is ruled by a law of remarkable fixity; the ordinarily great progress at the beginning diminishes little by little . . . and despite great efforts, the moment arrives when it becomes practically equal to zero. At this point the person has attained his limit, for incontestably there is a limit. It varies according to the persons and the functions under consideration . . . [142, p. 142].

Then follow Binet's fascinating pages of "mental orthopedics" (pp. 150–61) for retardates ("but also useful for normal children"). He stressed training that

> . . . teaches children to observe better, to listen better, to retain and to judge better; they gain self-confidence, emulation, perseverance, the desire to succeed and all the excellent feelings that accompany action; they should especially be taught to will with more intensity; to will, this is indeed the key to all education (142, p. 154).

In this program there were bowls of water filled to the brim for the child to transport without spilling over various distances and various obstacles; there were the immobile stances called "a game of statues"; dynamometer and *petits points* competitions; complicated exercises with corks, and so on. Binet made much of "learning how to learn" and of "learning by doing"; he acknowledged his debts to Rousseau, Spencer, F. Froebel, Dewey, G. S. Hall, G. Le Bon, and others.

It is surprising to see that Binet was willing to list the tests of the metric scale in this book intended for a popular audience. He not only listed them but went on for nine pages to discuss the items and the various responses that children frequently make. One must ask how he could suggest that his readers could use the list to discover the "limits" of a child's abilities. It is true that he warned his naïve public about the problems of using the scale, but the warning seems something less than sufficiently prudent. He wrote:

> . . . Every scientific procedure is only an instrument that must be directed by an intelligent hand. With the new instrument we have just forged, we have explored more than three-hundred subjects, and at each new examination our attention has been awakened, surprised, charmed by our observations of the different ways of responding . . . the thousand particularities that show us the impressive sight of an intelligence in action [142, p. 137].

While this comment may not have been an adequate warning against unsophisticated uses of the scale, it is convincing evidence that, had he lived, Binet would probably have continued his research and improved the instrument, for it underscores his explicit concern with special aptitudes on which he started work by 1911.

Binet considered the opposed positions of E. Thorndike and C. Spearman on the nature of intelligence but would not opt for either one[6] because he believed that extant evidence was too complex to fit into either extreme (142, p. 242). He himself was more interested in studying the

[6] Binet was justifiably very critical of C. Spearman's 1904 paper on "general intelligence" (120). Noting that Spearman found the correlations between teachers' judgments and simple sensory experiments "so great as to be almost identical," and that Spearman "judges this conclusion as *profoundly* important," Binet continued: "We ourselves are *profoundly* astonished at this because of the very defective character we find both in the sensory experiments of the author, and also in his method of estimating . . .the total intelligence. Before pronouncing judgment it is necessary to wait for other investigators to obtain similar results" (120, pp. 623-24).

manifold forms, the nature and development of intelligence, with the result that statistical studies and well-formulated theories engaged him only tangentially.

Binet's "Still Unfinished" Last Revision, 1911

For his 1911 revision, without benefit of Simon's active assistance and without his name as coauthor, Binet relied upon the collaboration of colleagues in *La Société,* at the laboratory, and others to "assemble new facts that have permitted us to make some important modifications. . . ." The number of "new" subjects taking part in the testing is not clear, except that there was at least one group of twenty each at ages six, seven, eight, nine, ten, and twelve years from a primary school in a lower middle-class neighborhood in Paris, probably at Grange-aux-belles (165, p. 153). Others may have been added from the 1908 sample. Most of the changes were technical in nature: certain tests were moved, especially where they had been too difficult at the upper levels; fifteen-year and adult levels were added, and the eleven-year level omitted. The twelve-year tests were moved into the fifteen-year bracket. He established the basal year at the age where all tests were passed, and granted two-tenths of a year for each test passed in addition. Nonetheless, he added the following arresting caution: "These calculations permit the assessment of the intellectual level with fractions . . . *but they do not merit any absolute confidence, for they certainly vary from one examination to another*" (165, p. 149; italics added).

Binet made no further changes in his schema of intelligence, although he shifted his central emphasis from "judgment," which had been the major intellectual variable in 1905, to "adjustment to the environment." He had asked dozens of teachers to reply to his query concerning the bases on which they judged children's intelligence, but he agreed wholeheartedly with one teacher who responded: "Intelligence serves not only for learning; it serves especially 'to make one's life. . . .' " He commented: "Thus we return to our favorite theory: intelligence is marked by the best possible adaptation of the individual to his environment . . . to this we really do not want to add another thing" (165, p. 172). How strikingly inept is such a pronouncement if we think of the excellent "adaptation" to their environment of mice and moose! Conversely, one wonders about the "adaptation" of paranoids whom Binet himself called "sometimes very intelligent" and whose illness "does not lower their mental level." Presumably by "adaptation" he implied adapting to a complex environment, and also "adaptation" made precise by the operations of comprehension, directedness, critical capacity, and invention. And yet the vagueness and uncertain applicability of his "meaning of intelligence" surely created that vacuum that was unhappily filled by others like Goddard and Spearman whose hypotheses were so questionable or so incorrect and misleading.

The revision was widely hailed.[7] The use of the scale had spread to Belgium, Germany, Switzerland, Italy, and Russia, with its heaviest acclamation in England and the United States. In fact, in 1915 Goddard wrote:

> It may seem exaggerated to say that the whole world speaks now of the Binet-Simon scale; but the laboratory at Vineland alone has already distributed 22,000 copies of

[7] Burt has said that Binet generously accorded him permission to translate the 1908 scale for use with retarded English children. He had in fact concluded that in order "to avoid the multiplicity of versions our investigation was the only one which received this agreement from Binet and Simon for the countries using the English language" (270, p. 244). Indeed, much later Burt wrote that "Simon and Binet had been 'much distressed' by the fact that Terman and several other compilers had published translations without his permission, and that they 'had sometimes misunderstood the intention of the tests' " (254). Burt added, however, that he believed that "later Binet appreciated the excellence of Terman's work."

After the publication of the 1911 revision, and after Binet's death, Burt received permission from Simon to make some small alterations, provided they were first submitted to him for his approval. Due to the disruption of World War I Burt and his collaborators' final revised version "did not appear in print till 1921, after receiving due sanction and agreement from Dr. Simon" (254).

the brochure describing the 1908 scale [sic] and 88,000 answer blanks [270, p. 246].

Thought, or Intelligence, as Action, Not Needing Images or Words: "What is an Emotion? What is an Intellectual Act?"

Despite Binet's devotion to application,[8] which he naïvely separated from theory, his concern for theoretical hypotheses was always apparent. He had long stated that acts or behavior result from an integration of intelligence, will, emotions and feelings, and habitual modes of thinking. In 1903 he prepared a strong case for the proposition that thought occurs *without images* (90). In 1908 he and Simon insisted as energetically that thought also occurs *without words* (140). Their main evidence lay in the data collected by their "psychogenetic method" with conclusions based on comparative reports of normal children, imbeciles, and, tangentially, of aphasics. Binet noted that the relation between language and thought is very complex, "one that only candidates for the baccalaureate degree are able to treat in a cavalier manner." He pointed out that children understand words and sentences many months before they can use these same words and sentences. His illustrations are reminders of what today are called the "one-word sentences" of the toddler: "Milk!" meaning "I want my milk!", "Bring me some milk!", "I see the milk!" Binet indicated that it had been easy for theorists to claim that children's failure to utter the words lay in their inability to articulate, their lack of practice in

[8] In his preface to *L'Année* Binet wrote: "Our intention is to give henceforth a preponderant place in this journal to a psychology oriented toward practical and social questions" (14 [1908]: v, vi). This viewpoint follows a familiar pattern; for over a decade he had written fairly popular articles about some of his investigations for *Revue des deux mondes, Revue des Revues,* and even for the *Popular Science Monthly.* In a book review in 1895, Binet expressed his conviction that "those who make science are the ones who should take the trouble to popularize it" (review of Queyrat's *De l'abstraction,* reported in *Psych. Rev.,* 2 [1895]: 100).

speaking, or their lack of any need to speak. Here the "psychogenetic method" intervened to serve the cause of developmental understanding: the imbeciles operated in a similar manner, even at twenty-five or thirty-five years of age, when "articulation, practice, and need" had had years to mature. For example, Denise, a low-grade imbecile, at twenty-five years could speak only a dozen single words, yet she understood the meaning of many. When she was asked who gave her her ring, she answered "Mama," as she happily showed it; she meant "Mama gave me the ring," but *she could never say so.* Again, when she said "Pee-pee" to the experimenters, she gave every indication of meaning that she wished to go to the toilet, but she could say only the one word. There could be no question of internal speech. She did not lack articulatory apparatus, but rather *developmental maturity* to give her the capacity to speak. Asking "What then *is essential* to spontaneous speech?" Binet answered that it was the knowledge that words stand for objects, a fact that Helen Keller dramatically discovered when she was seven years old. The essential condition for speech was, then, to know that everything has a name and to be able to associate the appropriate words with their objects in some functional manner. Nonetheless, the illustrations of the toddler, the imbecile, and even of lower animals indicate that they can think, or understand meanings, presumably without the necessity of images, and evidently without the necessity of words.

"Then, in what does the remainder of thought consist?" Binet asked, and answered in part:

It consists of an intellectual feeling, consequently very vague in its nature, but we perceive its presence, and particularly its effects—it is especially by its effects that it is revealed to us, for thought is not a *state*, but an *action*. . . . American psychologists understood [this difference] well when they established their antithesis between the psychology of *structure* and of *function*; . . . the second emphasizes action; it puts the accent on what serves, what is useful, what is accomplished. . . . Confused and often emotional perceptions . . . constitute the thought.

This vague sentiment is made more precise when it is

also completed by images, words, and acts; the images, the interior language, and the acts are the conscious forms of the thought; they are its light; they render the thought visible to us, they reveal its details to us. . . . But they come only *after* the thought, they are its results; before the images, before the words, the thought is understood, it is performed. This feeling dictates the words and suggests the images; and, in their turn, the images and words react on the feeling, amplify it, make it precise or modify it by a reciprocal work [feedback?] where the cause becomes effect and the effect cause. . . .

We believe that we have established beyond any doubt, by precise observations, that *there is thought without images, that there is thought without words, and that thought is formed by an intellectual feeling*. These findings are completely simple, elementary, demonstrable, and will serve later as a basis for new experiments and theories upon thought [140, pp. 338–39].

Thought (intelligence) is action, with or without images or words, with or without conscious elements. Actions are observable, and therefore to some extent measurable, by others. Since "adaptation" is the crucial core of effective action, it should therefore be the central objective in determining intellectual levels. Although Binet recognized that many of his test items could not meet this criterion, this was his theme for the 1911 revision. It also became the logical outcome of his last essay: "What is an emotion? What is an intellectual act?" (163).

Binet's concept of the influence of unconscious factors had been growing for twenty years. Now in 1911 he seemed overwhelmed by the realization that these unconscious processes were undermining the very roots of the psychological method that he had promoted for two decades: namely, systematic, planned introspection to search out the nature of higher thought processes. He now concluded that the method was clearly exposed as "full of lacunae in all their amplitude": ". . . completely insufficient, it has given truly curious, disquieting indications of the small scope of introspection, and even of the meager logic of thought. In summarizing it we are, in a manner of speaking, making a visit to some ruins" (163, pp. 6–7). After mentioning a long list of researchers who had used this method both in Europe and in America ("it presently fills all the American *revues* of psychology"), he singled out the German K. Marbe as being "among the first" of many to show that introspection does not, and cannot, "seize upon" the mechanism of thought, because "there are very great portions of our psychic life that are by their very nature inaccessible to consciousness" (163, p. 9). He continued: "To say that thought [intelligence] is a force that directs and chooses does not [really] clarify its nature," since so much goes on that influences action but cannot be discovered. In other words, he concluded that thoughts and emotions, conscious and unconscious, are pervasively interdependent, and even systematic introspection cannot disentangle or isolate them.

Binet's attempted resolution of this problem, for which he did not claim originality but only acknowledgment for particularizing it, lay in "attitudes" as an organizational hierarchy. "Attitudes" represented the inseparable union of emotions and intellect that combined to tend toward, or to effect, action: "There is a complete assimilation between being convinced of a thing and presenting a certain disposition to act in the defined direction of the conviction." Adaptation, therefore, would represent the externalized aspects of attitudes.

Binet compared and contrasted the emotional and intellectual processes. An "attitude" in which the emotional nature is uppermost "appears to be especially of a corporeal nature; it is more individual, personal; it has qualities of agreeableness or disagreeableness." When the intellect is uppermost, it is "less personal, colder, more distant from pleasure and pain" (163, p. 33).[9] In passing

[9] In this combination that integrated intellectual and emotional organizations, Binet had incorporated so much of behavior that it is surprising to have him practically equate his seemingly more inclusive "attitudes" with Bühler's "unconscious actions," Ach's "determining tendencies," and Kries' *adjustments cérébrals.* In fact, this essay is confusingly vague. Ribot was perhaps right when he claimed that "Binet's *attitudes* are only modes of motor activity" (290). Even this con-

from one of these processes to the other, the balance of organic sensations is changed, but the substantial unity of the mind remains. Binet recognized that he could not prove his hypothesis, but offered the belief that he could observe degrees of the two aspects: "The greater the organization [of a directed act], other things being equal, the more it will be intellectual in character; the weaker the organization, the more we shall have a phenomenon of pure emotion" (163, p. 36). Also, the more habitual an act becomes, the more unconscious it is, although *still influential:* "It is here that one sees introspection in all its powerlessness; one meets the limits of psychology . . . so near, so strong, so unshakable that one wonders if this science is not indeed very much limited" (163, p. 40).

For two decades Binet had been attempting to reconcile multivariant psychological processes with the unity that appears in behavior. His election of "attitudes" was, of course, of the same genre as his discovery of thought without images and thought without words. Now he had come face to face with the implications of this position for the discovery of the nature of thought, of intelligence. In his final sentences he fairly agonized:

> This viewpoint separates the old rational theory from the new theory of action, according to which the psychic life is not at all rational, but a chaos of shade crossed by illuminations, something bizarre and discontinuous, which has appeared continuous and rational only because, after the event, one recounts it in a language that puts order and clarity everywhere; but it is a factitious order, a verbal illusion, that does not resemble real life any more than the purring of a classic tragedy resembles the unbridled acts of [real] passions. There, perhaps, is the most beautiful idea, the most captivating, the most profound that we have achieved, thanks to these very careful results of introspection on the processes of thought. What a sub-

---

clusion, however, would not have prevented Binet from expanding his samples of such "activities," especially since he had asserted that "the essence of thought [lies] in a system of actions."

ject of meditation for those who love to philosophize! [163, p. 47].

We do not know what Binet would have done with this insight had he been given the time to develop its meanings. He did not, however, despair for in the preface to the last issue of *L'Année* that he edited he announced that he had in mind the preparation of a synthetic psychology that would present a hypothesis about "the manner in which the mental machine functions" (1911, p. xi). He also had in mind some sort of aptitude test that would be "the logical complement of the measure of [general] intelligence." Nothing came of either proposal, for his terminal illness affected his productivity to such a degree that even the notes he left were too chaotic to be preserved (248).

Conclusions and Hypotheses

Up to the time of his death Binet felt that the lack of sufficient evidence justified his avoidance of a definition of intelligence or of broad hypotheses about its nature. He felt that this was a scientifically, and indeed morally, correct attitude, since both definition and hypotheses could not escape a priori considerations. Yet his reluctance to speculate left a vacuum that cried to be filled—and allowed Spearman's theory "to constitute the conceptual basis for Binet's test approach" (301, p. 504). This fact is ironic, for Binet had openly stated that he could not accept either Spearman's or Thorndike's hypotheses (142, pp. 242–43). Nor did the unfortunate results of this turn of events end there. Goddard was most influential in introducing the tests to the United States, but, as R. D. Tuddenham remarked, "the devoted disciple [often] transforms the ideas of the prophet in the very process of transmitting them. So it was in this case." Goddard presented Binet's empirical method, but "substituted for Binet's *idea* of intelligence as a shifting complex of interrelated functions, the concept of a single underlying function (faculty) of intelligence" (301, p. 490). Furthermore, since Goddard believed that this function of intelligence was largely determined by heredity, he provided a basis for the belief in "the constancy of the IQ" that is directly at odds with Binet's view about the importance of the environment.

Perhaps even more at variance with Binet's conceptions about his discovery has been the fact that the scale has not been appreciably or importantly changed by the men who gave it so prominent a place in the United States. Binet's discussions and reflections about the nature and measurement of intelligence seem to be clear indication that he was not satisfied with the scale. At the time of his death he was talking about adaptive, inventive responses, about "attitudes in action" that had not yet emerged in the tests of intelligence. Surely he would have added questions that sampled them, for he did not believe that he had found the answer to his great question: "How shall we measure the richness of intelligence, the sureness of judgment, the subtlety of the mind?"

It is interesting to see that a half-century after Binet's death Dr. Anne Anastasi finds it necessary to urge that the development, use, and interpretation of tests should be reunited with the mainstream of psychology (258, 249). This surely is a frame of reference congruent with Binet's own tortuous experimental ventures and his basic assumptions. Did he not urge the study of the ways that "abilities become organized"? Did he not ask what "changes take place in the composition of intelligence over time"? Even as early as 1896 he was seeking ways to determine "the organization of intellectual functions in different cultural milieus, including national cultures, [and] socioeconomic levels." He also sought to know what might be the effects of "typical problem-solving styles . . . or response styles" on mental organization when in 1903 he made the masterful study of his daughters' habitual orientations of thought. Furthermore, his certainties about the pervasive nature of the emotions on intellectual acts can be translated into the current belief that "the separation between abilities and personality traits is artificial and the two domains need to be rejoined in interpreting an individual's test scores" (258, p. 304). His penchant for improvement strongly suggests that he would have deplored "the built-in inertia of tests," perhaps especially of his own. Indeed, the fact that so many of his ideas emerge as important problems a half-century after his death underlines the unhappy conclusion that his disciples often failed to appreciate, perhaps even to understand, the real bases for Binet's psychological methods and thought.

6 Alienation

An Attempt to Span the Field of Mental Abnormality

At the turn of the century French psychology was much concerned with psychopathology or alienation.[1] Taine, Ribot, Charcot, Janet, to mention a few of the more distinguished names, were fascinated by its problems, and Binet did not escape this influence. Yet his interest in mental pathology lay in his efforts to understand the normal. His investigations of imbeciles (144), for example, proved fruitful for the development of his hypotheses about the nature of intelligence and probably served as instigation for his study of other forms of mental abnormality. These inquiries in turn provided the inspiration for an attempted synthesis of all forms of this pathology that he published in a series of comparative papers entitled "Alienation."[2] He regarded this synthesis as a continuation of his former work and prefaced these papers with the statement that they were definitely related to five previously published articles, which the reader should perceive as a bridge to the synthesis. Four of these are

[1] F. G. Alexander and S. T. Selesnick report that J. P. Falret (1794–1870) was responsible for applying the term *aliénistes* to the physicians who worked with the mentally ill. Recognizing that estrangement from society is the most striking sociological fact of the condition of the mentally ill, Falret proposed that they should be called *aliénés;* their condition, mental *aliénation*; and hence the physicians who treated them, trying to resocialize them, should be called *aliénistes* (257, p. 138). We have obviously taken the words directly into the English language.

[2] As early as July 1903 Binet had requested Simon to prepare an article for *L'Année* giving a clinical résumé of mental illness "for the benefit of psychologists who do not have opportunities to see such patients face to face" (232). Representative of that era, Simon's classifications and descriptions were disorganized, which even then may have suggested to Binet the project on "alienation" that he published with Simon in 1910–11 (155 through 161).

familiar and have been summarized in chapters 4 and 5: the work on the intelligence scales of 1905 and 1908, "Language and thought" (140), and "The intelligence of imbeciles" (144). The fifth, "A new psychological and clinical theory of dementia" (149), admittedly provided the final impetus for the integrated series. Binet and Simon were trying to bring some order into a chaotic field. At this time amentia and dementia were not characteristically differentiated, descriptions and categories of alienation were rife with subjectivity, and lists of symptoms blossomed luxuriantly but were common to virtually all categories of mental illness and therefore specific to none. Binet proposed to trim them logically and psychologically so that there would be specificity for the different syndromes.[3] It was a herculean task that he posited, indeed one that psychologists have continued to work on since his death, although his efforts have been almost completely unnoticed.

"A new psychological and clinical theory of dementia"

The fifth article that Binet designated as a forerunner of the synthesis on "alienation" dealt at length with general paralysis (the French term for paresis), briefly with senile dementia, and it ignored dementia praecox, which was added to the later papers. First, Binet and Simon protested that the two most prominent current theories of dementia, which were a "defective mental synthesis" and "incoherent ideational associations," were vague, uninformative, and equally applicable to "maniacal, hallucinatory, or confused states." Furthermore, the accepted clinical "signs" of the dementia of general paralysis (G.P.), which were pupillary inequality, speech impediment, and a weak intellect, failed to provide a distinction from imbeciles, since these signs are frequently found in both. Thus the collaborators began the search for "psychological formulas" specifically fitting dements, paralytic and senile. They ex-

[3] These papers are so replete with descriptions of directly observed institutionalized persons that they might provide useful supplementary reading in a course on abnormal psychology.

amined about forty patients whom they met as often as possible in an informal setting, which Dr. Lucie Bonnis, Simon's former student and colleague, has described as follows:

> Binet very often went to Saint Yon [where from 1908 Simon directed the women's wards; Binet had already visited Saint Anne's and other hospitals where Simon had earlier been a staff psychiatrist]. He and Simon observed patients with great care, and took pains never to intimidate them. Since the interrogations were unstructured [*libre*], they did not wish to make them in forbidding medical offices. Therefore, they had asked Mme Simon to receive them in her dining room—not as patients, you see, but as visiting acquaintances [252, 15 December 1968].

"The work was vexatious," Binet wrote. "We were slow in formulating the idea that crystallized the interpretation, and were able to see it clearly only after groping in the dark for a long time" (149, p. 171). They used their 1908 scale to evaluate the degrees of the weakening of intelligence among the dements, a method that they considered not entirely adequate, but "much preferable to the usual assertions that one patient is 'very weak mentally,' and another 'less so' " (149, p. 172). Such objective measures could, they believed, "help to determine whether intellectual disintegration is gradual or saltatory," whether it occurs in particular functions or in all of them, and could furthermore dispel some uncertainties arising from the patients' articulatory disturbances alone. Later Binet became more and more convinced that observations of the daily behaviors of the patients were as significant as the tests.

The men gave close attention to differentiating dements from developmental retardates, a distinction that they thought was important. Binet used homely similes to portray it:

> Compared with one another, the imbecile and the dement are like two poor hikers who have different reasons for not completing a long walk—the imbecile because his

legs are very short, the dement because he is constantly falling down [149, p. 246].

With such analogies he was indicating that, while a dement and an imbecile could achieve the same mental level on the scale, qualitative differences would be evident, "similar to the [physical] differences between a dwarf adult and a child of the same height." He added: "It is often said that the dement is a rich person who has squandered his fortune, while the imbecile is poor from birth and remains so all his life . . ." (149, p. 183).

Binet and Simon wondered whether the deterioration of the G.P.s represented a systematic regression, presenting in reverse order the normal developmental stages of young children. They reported a negative answer for they discovered not only a global mental weakening but, significantly, a feeble evocation of responses, "an inability to make the machine play"—either at all or in any appropriate way. They noted in the patients' responses what they called *accrocs,* "rips," "tears," "blunders," "irregularities."[4] They analyzed these weak evocations and judgmental blunders (*accrocs*) in several categories:

Failure and extreme slowness in evoking even "old" memories: for example a forty-two-year-old man could not state how long he had been married, his earnings, or a correct list of the days of the week or the months.

Very slow responses—three or four times the normal time—to familiar questions.

[4] Dr. Lucie Bonnis has written me at length about the translation of this word, *accroc.* In part she writes: "If we judge by his mental level, the *malade* [*dement*] should respond almost correctly to certain questions. But his response does not correspond to his level or to his knowledge. All happens as if in the functioning of his intelligence there is something that rips *(accroche)* accidentally—it is an accidental tearing of the material." Or again: "The use of *accroc* is more literary than scientific, given our ignorance of the functioning of intelligence. But it can be justified. For example, a G.P. who has been a coal-merchant may declare euphorically, 'I am the Emperor'—yet with much tranquillity he also mentions his sacks of coal. The idea of his being the Emperor is a kind of *accroc,* a tearing of the web of his intelligence" (252, 18 December 1968).

Omission of parts of written words or sentences, which was "very frequent among G.P.s but infrequent among morons."

Arithmetical blunders: for example, requested to add 36 and 29, they might write down "15," and then, adding the 3 and 2, give 515 as the answer.

Directional weakness: for example, in the course of naming colors or counting pennies, they would stop and then start doing something else. Or if asked, "What is a fork?" they might reply, "A fork is a fork. I have three silver ones, but they are scratched." Binet went on to say: "There is an inertia in their responses—given an impulse, the billiard ball continues to roll" [149, p. 208].

Fragmentary perceptions: for example, asked to find a nine of clubs in a deck of cards, they might offer a seven or ten, saying, "The nine isn't far away." Or seeing a lamp-post in a picture as a spoon, they could not be dissuaded differently. When asked for his date of birth, the patient might instead give the place; to the question, "Are you a boy?" he might reply, "I have none."

Of this latter characteristic Binet wrote:

> To our knowledge these [fragmentary, incomplete perceptions] have not been pointed out previously; they have undoubtedly passed unperceived. . . . For awhile we ourselves failed to note them. . . . Collected in our stenographic notes we thought them fortuitous or unimportant, perhaps arising from distraction [149, p. 204].

The collaborators concluded that, while there is a general affliction in all of the G.P.'s mental operations (such as comparing, judging, combining, amplifying, analyzing, and the like), their most characteristic attribute was an inertia in evoking responses. The definition of inertia included failure to respond, incomplete or very slow responses, and incongruous, inappropriate errors. For a long time Binet and Simon had thought this resulted from a lack of effort, but further observations convinced them that it must be attributed to mental weakening. They also found much variability in individual G.P. productions, "unlike those of individual retardates." For example, when prodded sufficiently, a G.P. might succeed in a task formerly failed; asked to count backward from twenty to zero, one patient finally did so after six trials and urgings. In other words, she knew how to do it, but the request did not at first suggest the appropriate progression. Likewise, the apparent "psychic deafness" noted in incongruous replies could sometimes be destroyed by the experimenter's raising his voice, insisting, exciting the patient's attention. Again, the G.Ps also made some errors way out of line with their test-determined mental level: for example, a house painter mistook simple, basic colors; a patient with a nine-year-level agreed that the date was "the 50th" of the month. On the contrary, the *form* of their verbal responses might be considerably above their mental level; that is, the shades of expression, gestures, choice of words, would reveal residues (*réliquats*) of former abilities. They lacked the ability to make acceptable judgments and to solve problems. The more differentiated, essential, and adaptive responses, the more abstract ideas, disappeared first, leaving the simple, concrete ones accessible (149, p. 220). The patients' differential responses to pictures furnished crucial data. "The imbecile says over and over, 'It is a man,' while the paralytic may at least say, 'It is Victor Hugo'—an abyss of difference." The paralytic was, however, losing this differentiation, this ability to select the focal part of a picture rather than the accessory, while the imbecile had never attained it beyond a very limited degree (149, p. 243).

Binet and Simon felt that in their analyses they had improved on the current classical theory that presented the symptoms in long inventories without indicating any significant interrelationships. For their part they had "sought to classify the signs, to interpret them . . . to offer a psychological analysis. . . . The deficiency of evocation as broadly defined makes the errors of G.P.s different from those of epileptics, senile dements, [or retardates]" (149, pp. 244, 246). They gave a much briefer, but as significantly focused, portrayal of the dement suffering from senility. While admitting that he also may show a lack of evocation due to "a gross lesion of memory," and that he is also unable to make "reasoned judgments," they did find a major contrast between him and the G.P. The senile dements seem to have preserved what Binet called their "instinctive judgments,"[5] which might be translated from the context as their "superego" or social and moral habits of conscience that produce feelings of "ought" and "ought not."

Word by word conversations with several patients illustrate these "instinctive judgments," these "oughts" that persisted even when the names and number of their children were forgotten. One woman refused to take a piece of fruit from a bowl, remarking, "When I eat fruit, I pay for it." Another time, when Binet playfully asked her to lend him some money, there was a real skirmish. She indignantly denied that she had any money, and then grumbled that she would not lend it if she did have some, becoming intractable to the point of refusing to speak to Binet or to let him take her picture. The dialogue went on for forty-five minutes during which the patient, her rancor mounting steadily, never for an instant forgot the point that her money was wanted. Binet commented that "this directionality of thought was interesting in a patient suffering from profound amnesia." At another time, when an imbecile, Denise, laughed loudly and giggled inappropriately in the experimenters' presence, the same senile dement roundly criticized Denise, telling her to keep quiet, to be more respectful, and to stop acting like a child.[6]

[5] It seems unimportant to give much attention to Binet's use of the word "instinct." It was prominent in the literature at that time and he wanted to use it. He stipulated that he did not attribute to it "qualities of innateness, infallibility, specificity, unimprovability, or necessity but there is present a lack of logical perception, of verbal reasoning . . . " (149, p. 266).

[6] Binet's distinction between the two kinds of judgment, instinctive and reasoned, are forerunners of his "attitudes," developed in his article "What is an emotion? What is an intellectual act?" (163) In both he stressed the role of *feelings* in the act of making judgments. He presented these *feeling*-judgments in simple illustrations: for example, he reminded the reader that if you give normal subjects a list of one-hundred words to study, and then ask them to recognize those same words in a second, larger list, they will make these recognition-judgments immediately, without having to run through the first list

Binet and Simon found this "instinctive judgment" present in several other patients, and characterized it thus:

> It consists essentially in an emotive and motor tendency to approve and to disapprove; it may never manifest itself in ideas. . . . One has a certain feeling toward or against an object . . . or that a certain course is unreasonable or immoral, and be stimulated by a feeling of disapproval without any clear idea about it, without attempting any justification, without referring to any norm of things possible, unreasonable, or immoral [149, p. 262].

While the collaborators occasionally found instances of "instinctive judgment" among G.P.s, their firm conclusion was that given the same mental level, the senile dement preserved much more of it than the paretic. Furthermore, they had observed that the seniles were much more likely than the G.Ps to be conscious of their sad state of deterioration.

The general dramatic summation follows:

> If one compares a paralytic with a senile dement, both having the same mental level, one has the impression that in the case of the senile one is in the presence of someone, a person, while with the paralytic no one is any longer there [149, p. 270].

Binet stated explicitly that this article had inspired him to study mental abnormalities "by multiplying the points of comparison among them, to make the study more profound." It set off that series of "a well-ordered sequence of works . . . as a stone placed in an edifice serves as a base for new stones" (149, p. 272).

---

in memory; that is, they *felt* the familiarity. Or he noted that a painter says, "That doesn't go! It's idiotic!" in a quick response, without taking time for a considered judgment. So it was, Binet insisted, with the senile patient, who "along with her profound amnesia can judge [or feel] the proprieties of situations, their 'truth,' their 'justice' " (149, p. 263). He added also that " 'true judgment'—the flower of the process—seems to be a synthesis of 'ideational' and 'instinctive' judgments."

Alienation: A Broad Overview of Mental Abnormalities

Although Binet initiated and guided the work and wrote the reports, Simon's collaboration in these studies was very substantial. In fact, the psychiatrist became the seeing-eye for the psychologist.[7] Some sixty letters and postcards that Binet wrote to Simon from 1909 to 1911 testify that the men frequently visited one another, Binet going to Saint Yon, Simon to Paris or Samois, and exchanged many letters considering the work in progress. Simon, of course, was on the grounds of the hospital that furnished the bulk of the subjects, and consequently Binet sent him many questions about particular patients, whom he usually called by name, requesting observations and reports of their daily activities and behavior at the hospital, photographs of them, and data on their life histories. He also asked Simon to send him pertinent references, noting if possible the particularly important passages for him to read, to prepare comparisons of viewpoints between their own and those of other specialists, to list typical and atypical symptomatic behavior from published reports and from life, of patients within diagnosed syndromes, to list symptoms that were so common to all categories that they would be useless to particularized diagnoses, to prepare detailed bibliographies, and more. Binet occasionally grumbled ("*je vous gronde*," he wrote) when Simon's replies were delayed or too laconic, but the tone of his letters was consistently friendly. They showed concern for Simon's health or overwork and always ended with greetings to Mme Simon, but did not contain a single detail about his own family. Primarily the two men exchanged manuscripts for criticisms and additions. They set up plans of attack, and Binet himself constantly organized the material at hand to set the stage for the most effective use of their time when they met. The letters

[7] Although Binet was a psychologist, he made no apologies for entering the psychiatric field. On the contrary, he stated that "psychological thinking imposes itself today as the very basis of the psychiatric method" (168, p. 344).

reflect the great pains they took and their heavy workloads.[8]

Binet perceived that there was much disagreement among the "experts" in the field of alienation. He wrote: "Their propositions for revision, annexation, and dismemberment [of the field] that have been propounded at many congresses reflect the vivid preoccupations of our contemporaries." In his mind their differences offered a picture of the seething efforts of psychiatrists to arrive at an acceptable nosology of mental abnormalities, "a domain of shifting sands upon which each alienist seeks to build [his reputation]" (155, p. 70). Binet and Simon laid no claims that they had achieved a universal, or even a truly original, solution to this problem, but they did hope that they had substituted specificity and particularity for vagueness and intersyndrome overlapping.

They established six categories of mental abnormalities: hysteria, "lucid insanity" (obsessive-compulsive, psychasthenic, phobic), manic-depressive insanity, systematized insanity (paranoia), dementia, and retardation. The next step was to describe differentially the symptoms as well as the attitudes that characterized each of them, "constantly confronting each with the others, to obtain a clear view of the essential differences among them, [and] to get hold of a definition that belongs to each malady and to it alone" (161, p. 361). Without comparison and contrast, it was impossible to seize the essence of each category, because "otherwise, despite one's self, unconsciously, one adopts some conception that is so broad that it belongs to several different maladies, and therefore so commonplace that it explains none" (155a, pp. 61–62). Their "directing idea" was two-pronged: after giving a brief history and summary of current theories for each cate-

[8] In June 1909, Binet wrote: "I have not yet had time to read Kraepelin. If only you knew how I have labored, deleted, recommenced!" In August 1909 he remarked about the article on dementia praecox: "I have begun this article now four times!" —and he was to do so several more. Other tasks evinced dour words: "I have worked like a horse on this *folie* manic-depressive" (6, undated).

gory, they would, first, find distinct differences among the mental states and then divide these mental states into a) *symptoms* and b) *attitudes,* which were the modes of response of the total personality toward these pathological symptoms. Characteristically, Binet showed his pervasive inclination to understand the normal by adding to each chapter "remarks for [normal] psychology." The collaborators intentionally omitted any but the most cursory attention to problems of etiology, pathological anatomy and physiology, and treatment. In light of present, twentieth-century debates, even about the legitimacy of the term "mental illness," and also of recent avoidance and rejection of distinct, specific diagnostic categories, it is hardly surprising that Binet and Simon could not produce definitive results.

When Binet turned to *hysteria* he was critical of his first "master," Charcot, who had long believed the symptoms of hysteria were physical and should be studied as such. Charcot had taught his students that the scientific method consisted of moving from the simple to the complex, and, since he believed that "physical phenomena were much simpler than those of the mind," he concentrated upon them. But in doing so he mistook very complicated mental symptoms for physical phenomena. Binet could not resist including in his criticism the fact that Charcot's use of hypnotism had been somewhat less than happy. Even so he did admit that, toward the end of his life, Charcot changed his ideas about the mechanism of hysterical symptoms, basing them on the psychological phenomena of suggestibility. Binet added that Charcot took the credit for the changes in his ideas that really should have gone to his students.

Binet examined two principal current theories of hysteria: one based on the idea of suggestion, and the other related to "a [unique] mental state" or condition. Hippolyte Bernheim, Joseph Déjerine, and especially Joseph Babinski represented the former. From the 1880s Bernheim had stressed the role of autosuggestion in hypnosis and hysteria, a novelty at that time, "even a heresy," Binet commented. Now in 1910 Babinski was claiming that suggestion alone explained hysteria, and he created for it the term *pithiatisme,* meaning "curable by persuasion." His methods and dogmatic theory were "the order of the day" in Paris (155, p. 86).

The second group of theorists emphasized unconscious states. "Sketched out by Josef Breuer and Sigmund Freud," Binet wrote, "they have, however, been much more clearly and fully formulated by [Pierre] Janet." Binet's knowledge of Freud's work must have been limited, because he gave only two pages to an analysis and critique of psychoanalysis. Because of their unreliability, he criticized the use of dream reports as a basis for theoretical hypotheses and seemed almost amused at the many possible affective inversions and transformations credited to sexual repression. Thus he himself failed to recognize the significance of repression for a plausible hypothesis either of the development or the relief of hysterical symptoms. In fact, Binet thought that Freud owed a considerable unpaid debt to Janet's thesis that stressed a "lack of mental cohesiveness" that in turn led to a "splitting off," or a plurality of consciousness.[9] On the other hand, Binet complained that Janet's inventories of hysterical symptoms were common also to many other mental illnesses. Janet had studied only "a little corner" of mental illness at a time, first hysteria, then psychasthenia, "instead of running through all the phenomena of alienation . . . in order to give to each morbid state its true place, its true evaluation, its true definition" (155, pp. 104–5).

Apparently there were no patients diagnosed as hysterics at Saint Yon because Binet tells us that he had not seen hysterics for many years (155, p. 105n.), and therefore that he had taken most of his data from memory and published reports; in fact, he seems to have relied for much of this chapter on material in his own *Les altérations de la personnalité* (43). Cautiously he attributed the cur-

[9] Alexander and Selesnick have expressed the opinion that "Janet's theory, an innovation in psychopathology, did not include the concept of repression and thus did not concern itself with the significance of the dynamic unconscious" (257, p. 173).

rent lack of cases either to their having become more rare than in Charcot's time or to a change of label.

Binet concluded that there are two unique characteristic symptoms of hysteria, and with trenchant insight in the first he described the effects of the culture upon this illness:

> The primordial, specific characteristics are symptoms resulting from a special degree of suggestibility.... The environment constantly impinges on the patients' minds. . . . Therefore, the hysteria of one epoch does not resemble the hysteria of another. . . . In the Middle Ages beliefs in the devil prevailed; in the twentieth-century a reflection of our customs, discoveries, ideas. And furthermore, it is an affliction that follows the theories of the doctors who study it: Charcot saw symptoms especially interesting for their physical attributes—attacks, contractures, paralyses. Janet approaches these same patients as a psychologist . . . finding phenomena of subconsciousness, of double personalities, of dissociation: impulses, fixed ideas, weak wills. . . . Babinski, on the other hand, since for him the symptoms are the products of suggestion, seems to think that they do not exist. . . . He suppresses the hysteria in some way, reducing to a minimum its external manifestations . . . [155, pp. 109-10].

Of the second characteristic symptom he remarked:

> The suggestibility is carried out to a complete realization in sensory and/or motor consequences. Where a neurasthenic may have the *idea* of vomiting or of being pregnant, with its attendant anxieties and rationalizations, the hysteric, by contrast, would actually vomit or show signs of growing larger [155, p. 112].

Binet approached the problem of contrasting the *symptoms* with the *attitude*, or "the general personality reaction to the symptoms."[10] This is a difficult conception and one

[10] Binet used the word *attitude*, in contrast to symptoms, until he realized that he wanted to use this same word for normal functions; he called the combination of emotions and intellectual acts *attitudes* (163). Therefore, he decided to substitute the confusing word *accueil* for *attitude*. The translation, however,

that never becomes very clear, although Binet himself thought that the dichotomy between "symptoms" and "attitudes" was a "luminous division" of mental states. At one point he gave the following explanation of the possible meanings of the word "attitude":

According to different circumstances, we mean by "attitude," in a broad sense 1) the whole of intelligence, opposed to a portion of it . . . ; 2) the sane part of the intelligence as related to the sick part; 3) the voluntary and reflective part of our functions as compared with the involuntary . . . ; 4) the function of inhibition, direction, censure as compared with the functions of imagination and invention [sic!]. According to the particular case, it is now one of those meanings that dominates our explanations, now another [161, p. 368].

In a probably concurrent letter to Simon he added: "*It is all that, and it is still something else, and it is not always that.*" Perhaps his heavy underlining also revealed his uncertainty, which was at the same time mainly a strong conviction, a feeling-judgment.

Binet stated that the prevailing *attitude* of hysterics was characterized by their unconsciousness of the significance of their pathological symptoms. "They present a singular *attitude* of indifference, or rather of disinterest," he wrote. "The latter word is more appropriate, for it is not at all a question of willed indifference, commanded by stoicism, but a simple state of detachment. . . . They do not feel the very legitimate concern that a normal person would in thinking of their future; they act, indeed, as though a paralyzed limb did not belong to them" (155, pp. 114–15).

Binet's "remarks for [normal] psychology" naturally accentuated the importance of the unconscious, a concept

---

as "welcome," "acceptance," "reception," is so ambiguous that I shall continue to use the word *attitude*. Binet's conception—whether called *attitude* or *accueil*—is suggestive of Kurt Goldstein's discussion of the abstract and concrete attitudes, where a change from one to the other cuts across the entire personality, and all forms of behavior.

that had, of course, been cited by many persons for a long time. As Binet expressed it, "It is not only yesterday that one has made psychology with 'hysteria.' In France, almost all pathological psychology has been developed with this malady as a base, and the hysterical woman has become a laboratory frog for psychologists" (155, p. 120). Normal unconscious activity, as well as pathological, can be illustrated endlessly, of course, but for Binet Poincaré's sudden, so-called intuitive mathematical discoveries in which "the unconscious collaborated" remained the most striking example of the positive effects (155, p. 121). It was the nature of the unconscious, he added, "never to furnish precise details, but rather a direction, a matrix-idea containing many seeds that must later be developed by reflection" (155, p. 121). It appears that he hypothesized some kind of relativity on the conscious-unconscious spectrum.

For each of the six abnormal categories included in this series, Binet resorted, perhaps unhappily, to a one-word representation. For hysteria he chose the word "separation," which does indeed fit the concept of the "splitting off" of an impulse or impulses. He expressed his final definition as follows:

> There exists in hysteria a state of *separation* of consciousnesses by which the subject remains a stranger to the perception, memory, judgment, and will of the phenomena taking place in him as a result of his extreme suggestibility, and which end in their complete realization [or fulfillment] [155, p. 121].

He had already mentioned that the level of intelligence among hysterics is not lowered from their normal state, but "remains bright," a statement without accompanying evidence. This conclusion seems puzzling, in light of Binet's claim for "adaptation" as the major criterion of intelligence, until one realizes that the hysteric might indeed be making a very good adjustment to the total demands of his environment.

While Binet in his historical research did not explore

all the available literature, he did provide a reasonably intimate view of psychiatric activities in France. He recognized J.-E. Esquirol as the first to describe, in 1832, *lucid insanity* or *insanity with consciousness*, when he stressed that it was limited with regard to its object, and also that the patients preserved their intellectual level. Esquirol also included certain monomanias that were combined with compulsive and homicidal orientations. Benedict Morel, an Austrian trained in France, had imputed some emotional factors to this illness, although, in line with his times he still believed that it was due to a hereditary malady of the visceral ganglionic system.

"After Morel [1809–1873]," Binet claimed, "in a period when the analysis of symptoms [in mental illnesses] led to a crumbling, piecemeal approach, the insanity of consciousness also lost its unity." A plethora of monographs refllected the great diversity of forms. Psychiatrists recognized a multiplicity of phobias: for example, nosophobia, agoraphobia, claustrophobia, erythrophobia, and so on; of manias: kleptomania, pyromania, onomatomania; and of overwhelming doubts, tics, and other compulsive-obsessive afflictions. The point of agreement, at least among French and English writers, lay in the lucidity of the patients' consciousness of their disturbed and pathological ideas and drives. In fact, Binet wished to call the syndrome *folie lucide*, and would have done so had he not found the phrase too little used to be understood (156, p. 125n). The categorization of "insanity with consciousness" simply pointed up the condition in which the patient was unhappily aware of his troubles and conflicts, but was still unable to control them. It was this general lucidity that also bemused court magistrates who "indulged in endless discussions" because they could not understand how good sense and reasonableness could exist along with irresistible and conscious antisocial impulses: a "cloudy intelligence" was supposed to differentiate the mentally ill from the criminals.

Binet seems to have been either amused or irritated at Antoine Magnan's attempt to make all the symptoms fit into his system, which actually had the appearance of a dumping ground. Since he was head of the central bureau of admissions for the hospitals of the Seine, a one-time vice-president of the First International Congress of Psychology in Paris in 1889, and Simon's supervisor in psychiatry at Saint Anne's Hospital, Magnan's ideas could not be brushed aside. He claimed that there were two degrees of mental illness: the one, a simple, vulnerable "predisposition without degeneracy," illustrated by mania, melancholy, intermittent insanity, and chronic delusion; the second, a "predisposition with degeneracy," which included most other forms, and were also, in his opinion, frequently accompanied by physical and mental stigmata. By the process of elimination he argued that if a patient did not fit into one of the four forms of simple predisposition, he was degenerate. In summarizing Magnan's work, Binet somewhat ironically remarked, ". . . in his system all difficulty vanishes. No patient remains unclassified. It is a great practical advance, but basically artificial and contrived" (156, p. 129). He went on to point out that Magnan had ignored the lucid awareness of the patients in the category of lucid psychosis, and furthermore that neither he nor anyone else had tested the hypotheses about the hereditary nature of this illness.

Binet thought it equally imperative to examine Janet's theories, since he was even more influential than Magnan and since the syndrome of lucid insanity, along with hysteria, represented the professor's most ardent enthusiasms. He called the syndrome "psychasthenia," and included in it neurasthenic hypochondrias of pain and fatigue as well as obsessions, compulsions, and phobias. The term had a heuristic value, Binet thought, since no patient would be frightened by such an incomprehensible word: "It thus becomes an anodyne." He himself still preferred "lucid psychosis," adding the surprising assertion that the word "psychosis" would frighten no one (156, p. 132n).

Janet underscored "incompleteness"—of feeling and of behavior—as most characteristic of this illness. As Binet interpreted him:

These patients complete nothing, they remain always *en route*, consumed in projects, agitated in many ways, complaining and whining in the presence of their intimates, striving in sterile activities, in useless ruminations; they cannot arrive at a conviction; they doubt ceaselessly.

Janet describes the accompanying feelings: of difficulty, incapacity, indecision, worry, automatism, discontent, intimidation, revolt . . . of strangeness, of the "already seen," of disorientation in space and time, of uneasiness. . . . There are also some very strange feelings of double personality, of transformation, of degradation and even of death. . . . One has only to read the author's list to see how very rich his documentation is [156, pp. 136–37].

The symptoms and disturbances were most acute in situations when the patients were in contact with real life, especially social situations with their exacting and complex relations with other individuals (156, p. 137). Accordingly Janet, with his organic orientation, concluded that all the symptoms were the result of "nervous force discharged at inferior levels, because it could not mount higher." This led ". . . to a lowering of psychological tension with noticeable oscillations of mental level" that resulted in a range of behavior from serious attention to useless reveries. The wonder grows that anyone could find such an amorphous theory useful in any way.

Binet's first and gravest criticism was his usual one: these symptoms are common to other categories as well as to lucid insanity. Janet had occupied himself only with psychasthenia, "thereby concluding with imprecise notions . . . so that one does not know clearly what the exact relations of this malady are with those of other mental diseases—an ambiguity that he has never dispelled . . ." (156, pp. 141–42). Furthermore, the distance between Binet's conceptions of intelligence and Janet's is considerable. For instance, among Janet's lengthy lists of actions by which to judge degrees of psychasthenia, he had relegated "abstract reasoning" to a low function, on a par with free reverie.

In fact, recognizing the intersyndrome commonality of obsessions, anguish, bizarre gestures and feelings, and many other symptoms, Binet had to look elsewhere for specificity in lucid insanity. He found it in the *attitudes* of the patients in reaction to their disturbing symptoms. The contrast with other illnesses clarified this distinction. For example, if the patient with essentially the same symptoms were a manic or a melancholic he could "become the victim of this emotional storm," losing the clarity of his judgment; if a systematized paranoid, he would, while maintaining his usual level of intelligence, concentrate on directing his "reasoning" according to his special emotions; if a hysteric, he would lose his unity, would "be broken into fragments." But the patient with lucid insanity, face to face with his symptoms, would present a very different *attitude:*

> . . . He recognizes, judges, suffers [his symptoms], and forces himself to resist. . . . On the one hand is the morbid trouble; on the other, the whole personality that feels the urgency to resist the morbid impulses. . . . He can recount his troubles in infinite detail if they are not of a sexual or horrible nature that makes him ashamed [Binet did not ruminate on the possible role of these latter conditions]. . . . The critical sense is conserved. Apart from moments of exacerbation when the patient seems to lose the feeling of reality, he judges his trouble very well, understands its absurdity and pathology. . . . He knows that he is sick. . . . If he has delusional obsessions, they are not a true delusion to him, for he doubts them; . . . a true phobia requires that the patient be aware of its absurdity. . . .
>
> His attitude is not at all disinterested; this patient tries with all his strength to oppose these accidents. . . . This is especially true for obsessions that he feels coming on and wants to prevent, never being their [willing] accomplice. Not infrequently he implores to be committed. . . . Some even use sacramental [magic] formulas [to ward off these impulses] . . . Always there is an effort to fight. . .
>
> The best definition of this complex situation is that of a conflict. It is a conflict of ideas, of feelings, of tendencies, of will between the whole intelligence of the patient and the morbid, unfortunate event or situation. In this conflict we find consciousness conserved, memory conserved, judgment conserved, desire to fight against the trouble con-

served—but a will that has become ineffectual (156, pp. 146–48).

These patients are torn apart, then, with such self-destruction. Binet felt that this illness was much less curable than hysteria, for example. A hysteric may carry out categorical suggestions made to him, while the same suggestions made to a phobic may simply feed the morbid turn of mind. He felt that psychiatric aid for these patients was for the most part only supportive, ". . . helping them to consolidate their normal activities, and giving them exact knowledge of the nature of their problem."

He formed his "remarks for [normal] psychology" around the question of making judgments and executing them. These patients had shown that the conflict between the symptoms and the rest of the personality is less simple than it seems. "Censure" or self-criticism appears to be not a single, global act, but rather a dual one, with a judicial and an executive power. These patients *judge* their impulses, but cannot *act* on their judgments. Among normal persons these two performances tend to go together, but it is now strikingly apparent that agencies in the personality that perceive, judge, and desire are not one with agencies that will and act.

Using *conflict* as the most representative one-word characterization of this syndrome, Binet made the following definition:

> In insanity with consciousness there exists a mental state of *conflict* through which the subject preserves consciousness [of his plight] and judgment, but loses his will in relation to the [particular] troubles that are produced in his mental functioning [156, p. 163].

Binet added the further comparison that the hysteric carries to completion his morbid troubles, while the lucidly insane is "constrained from such achievement." Of course, criticism of this latter statement was inevitable, since compulsive, "lucidly insane" persons may indeed "achieve" or carry out their impulses, for example, when they murder someone. What they fail to achieve or carry out are their judgments and desires for the control of their actions.

When he discussed the *manic-depressive psychoses,* Binet claimed that the intermittent nature of this affliction was first irrefutably demonstrated by Jean Pierre Falret and Jules Baillarger in 1834. Magnan later tied the manic and depressive manifestations together so that the idea of this progression was so much stressed in France that it acquired the name *la folie intermittente.* Emil Kraepelin, utilizing "profound mental analysis" so praised by and dear to Binet, noted exceptions that challenged its general characterization as "intermittent." He found instances of single attacks followed by apparently permanent recovery as well as attacks that continued without abatement or change in their affective forms, and he even admitted involutional melancholia to the category of manic-depressives. Kraepelin found unity *in the disease* rather than in "intermittence" or "evolution." He also noted *mixed states,* in which combinations of melancholy and mania existed—for example, a sad mood with rapid ideations, or a "mute mania." Binet applauded his careful descriptions that threw into justifiable doubt the principle of a necessary intermittence in this syndrome, and he also praised his observation, previously overlooked, that, despite the fast flow of ideas in mania, the products were usually inferior to the normal intelligence level of the patient.[11]

Although Binet had insisted that he would not attempt to "explain" any of the maladies, he could not resist demonstrating "verbalisms" among the theories about this little-understood syndrome. He pointed out that psychiatrists in France, despite their alleged hostility to psychology, had surprisingly grasped hold of the James-Lange theory of the emotions, and had concluded therefrom that melancholy is the *consciousness* of the miserable state of the body—of the physical ills that so often ac-

[11] Some doctors had even claimed that the mental level was raised during an attack.

company it: dryness of skin, lowered temperature, coated tongue, constipation, and so on. Then, Binet asked, how do they account for mania, which presumably would require a different physical substratum? Another current theory attributed the so-called cyclothymic state to a flow in the equilibrium of affective feelings, with tendencies to brusque changes. This seemed hardly more than a description of observations, and could, of course, apply equally well to depressions and moods in other abnormal mental states.

Recognizing that "there is a lot of work to do" to differentiate both the manic and the depressive moods from those shown in other insanities, Binet began by saying that these patients have two particular characteristics: a provisional lowering of the intellectual level and a definite mood either of excitation or of depression. In his words:

> These manifestations are ordinarily simple; there is no complicated reasoning, no long reflection or scheming; there may be, for example, a series of cries, exclamations, a string of words pronounced in haste, complaints of being insulted; or perhaps a song, a dance, a collection of grimaces; or complaints, groans, repetitious grievances; or a scattering of unrelated, pointed remarks about people who pass by; or violent acts without any preparation, brusque attempts at suicide and theft, breaking things, immoral acts. All these acts are ordinarily short, summary, explosive. They do not constitute an adaptation of means to an end . . . but are rather exterior manifestations of an emotional state. They stem from a rather low intellectual level. . . . The emotions we find here are not just any emotions; they are not emotions of character, of passions, of calculated feelings, kneaded with ideas and reasoning, like hate, or envy, or avarice; they are emotions of mood, changes of affective tone, such as gaiety, sadness, anger, produced among these patients for most futile reasons [157, pp. 175].
>
> The nature of the ruling emotion is secondary; if any unity exists between attacks of such different emotional tones [as excited or depressed], it exists negatively in the absence of a state of calm . . . by brusque thrusts of mood

that alone occupy the scene and dominate the patient [157, pp. 197–98].

Binet discussed three types in this manic-depressive category: manics, melancholics, and apathetics. Of the *manic* he wrote:

> The state of excitation takes over the whole apparatus—intelligence, movement, affectivity. It is witnessed at once in his appearance—eyes flashing, head thrown back forcefully, step firm and wide, forehead shining, mouth alternatively nuanced with irony, with high distrust or anger, gestures rapid and sharp . . . [157, p. 176].

Binet's sparkling style is shown in the continuation of the description that, if included in a textbook of abnormal psychology, would surely etch "the manic" unforgettably on the student's mind:

> Now listen to him speak; there is a flow of words that you cannot interrupt. At our request, he makes a first response: there is a short silence; but almost immediately that disappears and speech is reanimated in an inexhaustible jet. . . . Free propositions, crude and gross terms, sometimes obscenities teem as in Rabelais. For the observers to be heard it would be necessary for them to join in unison, to cry and abjure, to strike a fist on the table like a tribune who, in a public meeting, wishes to dominate a tumult. Try and you will see what effort you must expend to attain the same degree of emotional intensity as is discharged here. Moreover, the activity of the patient will rise to a crescendo if you resist him. But it is only when patients of the same kind collide that one sees where they can go.
>
> One day we were witness to a very curious scene. We had had a submanic [?] brought into our office; our examination finished, she refused to leave, even after we opened the door to indicate more clearly what we wanted; then, like a blast of wind, in came another patient of the same type, but diminutive in size; immediately catching on to what we wanted, she took our part, and substituted herself for our authority. . . . At once she issues the order; the other responds peevishly, retires into a corner of the room, bar-

ricades herself behind a heavy table; the little one continues, her voice raised by one more degree, drawn up to her tallest height; like a cock after a first attack, she made so much noise that you might say she was addressing a whole battalion; she struck her chest with great sonorous blows the better to punctuate her commands, she advanced menacingly, precipitously tore at the table, threw it aside and brought the resistant patient out by force. The two had to be separated to prevent a real fight [157, pp. 176-77].

Binet recommended as another source of insight the careful reading of patients' letters, which would provide a new method of examination:

> The number and length of letters they write already speak eloquently. There are no pieces of paper that they do not use and do not cover—even the inside of envelopes, and postscript is added to postscript . . . [157, p. 177].[12]
>
> They are useful to follow the patient's evolution, his progressive deterioration or maintenance at a constant level, and the mechanism of his difficulties. Only . . . one must not become absorbed in the analysis of any isolated piece of writing, but rather take a whole series, which gives a global impression [157, p. 201n.].

He went on to indicate that there is often a great changeability of moods, from high excitement to tears: "ideas," he remarked, "jump about like butterflies." Everything —voices, gestures, facial expressions, body movements— all "attest to the real paroxysm of the emotional life." He practically said that they have to be seen to be believed, since in records, and even in letters, the vividness of responses is lost.

The elementary nature of the patient's ideas betrays a temporary poverty of the intellectual level, and at least a temporary state of affective and moral degradation, apparent in the absence of proprieties, or the loss of the so-called instinctive judgments. While this characteristic also fitted the G.P.s, according to Binet's schemas the difference between the two pathological categories would

[12] Binet mentioned one patient who wrote one hundred letters in nine months, without receiving a single response.

lie in the permanence or temporariness of intellectual lowering and in the quality and sustained presence of excitation or depression or its relative absence. Binet adopted the convention that a patient was a *melancholic* or depressive if the predominant emotion was sad or painful, in either an excited or an apathetic way. The melancholics tend to complain, to detail their woes, to gripe about food and surroundings, perhaps to expect terrible personal punishments. Like the manics, they too jump from one idea to another, although perhaps more slowly and with a certain self-pity. With no evidence indicated except natural observation Binet claimed that there often was a lowering of intellectual level during attacks, although he described some doubtful cases.

Binet felt that the category of *apathetic* patients among the manic-depressives had been overlooked in the literature. Nonetheless, in many characteristics he himself thought them actually more clearly in contrast to the manics than the melancholics were. They showed motor, intellectual, and emotional inertia, even stupor. Nevertheless, when he could get through to them with items of the Binet-Simon scale, he found some of these patients "normal—but tainted with apathy."

There were, of course, difficulties in testing these manic-depressive patients. In the case of manics Binet had success during periods when the patients were relatively calm, but was surprised by two observations that seem contradictory: first, despite their exuberance, the manics were almost incapable of sustained effort, stopping, for example, after giving two or three words when asked to name as many as possible. On the other hand, they could sometimes be bluntly surprised into reasonable replies. An illustration of this second characteristic was furnished by the story of the patient who was displaying extreme incoherence, emitting animal cries, rolling on the floor or chewing at a tableleg, but who nevertheless answered to the question "What should you do when a comrade hits you without meaning to do it?" by the response, "You must excuse him." This response is checked at the ten-year level in the 1908 scale (157, p. 188). The melancholics' responses to testing were more unpredictable. Sometimes they answered easy questions like giving their age, naming colors, counting pennies, but made no effort to repeat long sentences or to reply to abstract questions, ". . . although," Binet added, "one has the impression that they could if they would." These patients had lost reasoned judgment since they had lost the power of voluntary direction, of the continuous oriented control "that requires the effort of his whole intelligence or personality" (157, p. 193n.).

In his discussion of the *attitudes* of the manic-depressives in reaction to their symptoms, Binet urged the reader to "go to see them, and talk with them!" Otherwise he felt that his following exclamation might not be believed:

> When you visit with them you will ask "Where are they? Where is the personality of the patient? Where is that person whom one could hope to talk with?" He does not exist, he has disappeared; he is reduced to his morbid accidents; he is all words and gestures, if he is a manic; all groans and complaints, if he is a melancholic. . . . The essential thing remains a suspension of all the faculties of direction, of self-criticism, and of inhibition, accompanied with incoherent expressions of emotion . . . to express this suspended action, this psychic paralysis, we use the word *domination*. . . . There is an invasion of the whole personality, the mastery of the self is lost, the patient is governed, *dominated* by his morbid state [157, pp. 186–87].

He also added that during his attacks the manic and the depressive feels that his fantasies and recriminations are legitimate, that he is justified in his responses. Binet tried to correct "the widespread opinion" that the melancholic believes himself blameworthy. Instead, in many cases he had observed melancholics who, during the most vivid anxiety, affirmed their honesty and innocence: "No!" they exclaimed, "that is not just; I have never done wrong to anyone." Was Binet's observation in error? A recent book on depression cites among the five defining attributes of this pathology: "A negative self-concept associated with self-reproaches and self-blame." There is a question, therefore, as to who failed to observe reliably.[13]

The study of manic-depressives furnished Binet with a few interesting "remarks for [normal] psychology." In discussing the forms that emotions take he compared the patients' "oscillations of emotional acuteness, their ceaseless emotional imminence, sort of under pressure like bottles of Leiden water . . . ," with normal situations of great stress. For example, in the case of a mother whose child has just died, there are times of apparent calm, but particular situations, like visits of condolence, religious services, visits to the cemetery, and the like produce exacerbations of the emotions. For the patients, of course, the particular stresses were not obvious or discernible. He also pointed out the independence between the intensity and the kind of the emotion. That is, both sadness and joy can be active as well as passive in expression.

Binet and Simon felt that they had improved on the James-Lange theory by including a discharge of *ideas* as well as of *actions* as the excitants of emotions. Presumably one might be afraid not only because one ran, as James and Lange would have put it, but also because one had the *idea* of running. Binet's and Simon's claimed improvement appears very dubious indeed. Binet concluded with his definition of the manic-depressive psychoses:

> In the *folie* manic-depressive there exists a mental state of *domination* in which the subject keeps his consciousness, but lacks judgment, direction, or will with regard to its pathological stresses; that consists in an exterior manifestation of states of excitement or of apathy. . . . The attitude of the whole personality is very special: it is not at all separated from the troubles, it does not enter into conflict with them, but is rather suspended, allowing the troubles [or stresses] a free field [157, p. 214].

[13] The reference is to A. T. Beck's *Depression* (Harper and Row, 1967), p. 5. Perhaps Harold Klehr has resolved the difference by remarking that "the melancholic most often blames himself for his thoughts and impulses; in his own eyes he is generally innocent of deeds, but not of thoughts."

Looking briefly at the history of *systematized insanity*, or paranoia, Binet stated that Pinel had vaguely recognized it in his "melancholia," and Esquirol in his "monomania," and that both men correctly perceived it as a partial illness. However, since partial insanity may be said to exist in all categories of mental illness, he again insisted on the advantage of his own overview, which demanded the search for unique symptoms in each malady. The French psychiatrist, J.P. Falret, he said, had made some progress in the diagnostic area. He had been responsible for stressing the "systematization of ideas" in three progressive phases: incubation, that is "ideas characterized by the existence of an active and constructive delusion"; elaboration, that is a progression in the ideational work within a logical scheme; and finally, stereotypy, a relatively static condition without further elaborations.

Turning to Magnan's hypotheses, Binet pointed out that for this illness he stressed a regular pathological progression, from incubation, through delusions of persecution, to delusions of grandeur that terminated in dementia. All these patients harbored hereditary taints, according to Magnan, and when their symptoms did not fit the above progression, they did not disturb Magnan's theory but were simply called "atypical" and considered more degenerate than the others. It is not surprising that Binet again deplored Magnan's convenient artifices. Even so, this man's ideas were accepted almost universally, at least until Kraepelin's theories competed with them. They were even reproduced by Richard von Krafft-Ebing in Vienna and by Morselli in Italy. Yet, despite Magnan's elevated reputation, Falret and his students, with whom Binet delightedly agreed (6 March 1909), refused to accept Magnan's dicta that paranoid patients terminated in dementia or that their delusions were characterized by subject matter definite and progressive in its content.

Kraepelin included "true paranoids" in his classification of mental pathologies and contended that they neither terminated in dementia nor suffered from hallucinations, but exhibited coherent delusional interpretations of selected external events. For Binet and others, he muddied his overall classification by failing to include among these paranoids a group whom he called *"dementia paranoïdes."* Instead, he set the latter among the dementia praecoxes, thus in his opinion condemning them to a demential termination, which Binet and Simon did not find in agreement with their observations. Consequently they included the *paranoïdes* in the present systematized category, although the latter patients differed in the degree of their coherence and the cohesion to their false interpretations by showing weaker, less integrated delusional patterns than the true paranoids.

Binet reserved his most severe criticism for a very recent monograph by the Parisian psychiatrists, J. Capgras and P. Sérieux. He objected to their limited conception, which they called "a delusion of interpretation," and which he said was only a subdivision of the category, "hardly worth a whole monograph, purporting to establish a new entity." Also, he disagreed with their contention that these patients were not hallucinatory; he himself perceived scarcely a shade of difference between hallucinations and the paranoid misinterpretations.[14] Moreover, the doctors' claim that the condition was "constitutional in origin" was unacceptable because it was "entirely hypothetical and a priori." Lastly, and most damning in Binet's eyes, their inventory of symptoms of the disease did not differentiate *folie systematisée* from other insanities. The following year Capgras and Sérieux heatedly replied to these criticisms in an article in *L'Année.*

Binet and Simon found only two particular unique symptoms for the *folie systematisée*:[15] hallucinations,

[14] J. Capgras and P. Sérieux accepted the general medical opinion that hallucinations were the result of toxic conditions, like fevers, excessive alcoholic consumption, and other bodily "poisons"; since these conditions were not usually present in paranoids, the latter *could not* have hallucinations! Binet, on the other hand, was surprisingly modern in his opinion that the primary sources of hallucinations were "mental conditions based on the idea, the expectation, the delusional conviction."

[15] Again comparing this entity with others, Binet noted differences from other pathologies based on the *absence* of symp-

usually auditory and commonly excluding visual ones, and *organized* delusional conceptions that "represent [mental] work, effort, research, and elaboration tending toward organization. . . . They appear to become formed, not acutely, but rather very slowly" (158, p. 225). These patients, he indicated, are not detached from the outside world but present delusional, false interpretations of certain external data. It is characteristic that Binet also stressed the broad individual differences among the patients, in intelligence and in creative imagination: "Their delusional conceptions are as different as the productions of sane individuals . . . now manifested in ideas, now in action; in the latter case, the patient seeks to achieve some practical results, to transform society, to propagate a religion, to win a lawsuit, or very simply to kill an enemy" (158, pp. 227–28). Moreover, Binet and Simon noted that their mental state is almost completely made up of hostile interpretations: "In the asylum they isolate themselves; outside they cannot remain in any one place, but go from town to town following repeated dissensions. Their condition presents no periodicity, no remission; and they never judge themselves [harshly] or repent . . ." (158, pp. 255–56). The researchers found no evidence of a lowered intelligence (158, p. 228).

Binet and Simon themselves seem to have been guilty of a priori judgments when they hypothesized that while the delusions had a constitutional base, they were also probably set off by occasions "in youth or even in infancy . . . thus [apparently] mixing the acquired with the congenital" (158, pp. 260–61).

For dramatic contrast, Binet compared the *attitudes* of the manic and of the systematized patients:

In searching out the manics, one finds no personality, except one that is dissimulated, stuffed, paralyzed by the

---

toms: "One does not find here any amnesias as in hysteria, no disorders of general functioning, no impulsions, obsessions [sic], weakness of will, doubts, or bizarre perceptions as in lucid insanity; and no agitations, depressions, verbal incoherences, moral pains as in manic-depressives" (158, p. 224).

flowering of the symptoms. . . . Among the systematized insane, however, there is always someone there, and someone who acts like a normal person. . . . His words are sensible, he has a sensitivity for proprieties . . . his compositions are correct and abundant, even literary. He remains capable of directing his life, and he would not be hospitalized at all if his delusion did not make him likely to commit some dangerous acts. . . . These patients can still learn [e.g., new foreign languages and new vocations]; their character is intact, and they are sometimes even better integrated than normal persons [158, pp. 228–29].

Since some of the same things could be said for the lucidly insane, Binet added that the difference lies in the fact that there is no delusion among the latter. Moreover, the systematized are completely obtuse to arguments; where their fixed ideas are concerned, they do not perceive any incongruity, despite their otherwise constructive intelligence. It is for this reason that Binet applied the term *deviation* as the distinctive aspect of this illness: this patient *deviates* markedly from the truths of the exterior facts that are accessible to him (158, p. 231).

Some excellent illustrative cases follow, with long conversations and letters included. In discussion of differential diagnoses Binet again emphasized that the unique difference between a systematized delusion and those in other maladies lay, not primarily in the content, but in the degree of organization, the progression, and in their permanence.

Although current evidence indicated that paranoia was seldom curable, and although Binet believed that institutionalization might indeed exacerbate it because it was seen as "punishment" in the patient's eyes, he refused to be dogmatic about it. He concluded characteristically: "Experiment has not yet made a clear pronouncement about it. Let us leave the word to it" (158, p. 252).

For some time Binet had been very much aware of the role of the emotions and feelings in ideational processes and the acts that flowed from them. At this point he felt particularly the impact of the emotions and their overwhelming force among the *systematisés,* where the emotions "set" the patient to resist "with all his passionate energy" any arguments contrary to his misinterpretative, false judgments. In considering the "remarks for [normal] psychology," therefore, and for purposes of analysis, he discussed separately the emotions and judgments. He concluded that "emotion, passion, appetite, and need pose objectives for our activity . . . while intelligence [or judgment] serves to produce the means to these emotional ends—it carries out in some way what the emotion orders . . . we see the exterior world only through the dispositions of our whole subjective state." Among the paranoids, "their *émotion-passion* is like an organizing force inciting them to intellectual search [to satisfy it] . . ." (158, pp. 260–61). Likewise, among normal persons, love objects, religious fanaticism, conversions, and many other highly emotional experiences illustrate the intellectual search to fulfill emotional feelings and needs. In all of these could be found:

> the same foregone conclusions, the same weakening of the critical sense, the same adherence to incomprehensible truths. . . . A conversion is not produced by given ideas . . . but rather by a change in the affective disposition; new emotions surge up. The problems relative to the origin of the idea of God, and of belief in immortality, change their meaning completely when one considers them from this very interesting and new viewpoint. . .
>
> Likewise, love renders us blind to the dangers that may accompany it . . . [158, pp. 261–63].

Since love and religious feelings are normal, he sought to differentiate these attitudes from the delusional, and concluded:

> In our opinion what is specific to the delusional is the suppression of criticism, with the double effects of a proliferation of absurd ideas, and a failure to exercise control over this proliferation. This censored suppression [of criticism] exists in the systematized insane to an unbelievable degree; and there is no normal lover or fanatic to whom one can compare it [158, p. 263].

He continued with a brief description of normal attitudes,

which presaged distinctly and exactly his imminent answer to "What is an emotion? What is an intellectual act?" (163):

> At the base of mental life are tendencies to act, which . . . in moments of expectation, when action is suspended, are reduced to attitudes, or motor dispositions. . . . These attitudes, with accompanying sensations and emotions, are so commonplace in everyday life that one could almost say that our whole psychology is composed of representations and attitudes [158, p. 262].

Attention, will, generalizations, judgments: he listed all as "attitudes," with both intellectual and emotional aspects. Among normal people, the emotional aspects, the emotional pressures, are much more subject to self-criticism and control than among pathological patients (158, p. 263).

Binet's concluding definition of the *folie systematisée* was expressed as follows:

> Systematized insanity is a mental state of *deviation* in which the subject retains consciousness [awareness] but undergoes a perversion of judgment and of will with regard to the fervent [*passionnelle*] direction of his reasonings. What is unique to this affliction and what we have found nowhere else is that the troubles consist in a veritable intellectual work in which the whole intelligence and character participate, with conservation of the intellectual level and a complete loss of the critical sense [with regard to the patient's fixed idea] [158, p. 265].

It is clear that Binet's discussion does not go beyond descriptions and some loose hypotheses about heredity. Without the trappings of the so-called laws of learning and the dynamics of repression he was at a disadvantage. Even with these, however, the problems of etiology are still unsettled at the present time.

Binet's most arduous task in the whole project was easily that of presenting the *dementias*: general paralysis, senile dementia, and especially dementia praecox (159). Even by 1910 the difference between dementia and developmental retardation or amentia was frequently misunderstood, and the status of either category of patients was only vaguely and subjectively determined.[16] It was, however, urgent to specify the presence or absence of demential weakness, since it was posited as an optional symptom among all the categories of insanity and since its presumed degree and permanence were focal to the prognosis of the patient. In introducing the dementias into his schema of *alienation* Binet briefly recounted some of the early vicissitudes of these syndromes. While Philippe Pinel had failed to make any distinction between dementia and idiocy, Esquirol had done so, as had one long-forgotten Felix Plater some three hundred years before: "Sound ideas do not always germinate," was Binet's obvious comment (159, p. 268n.). After Esquirol, modifications continued. Binet affirmed that a Dr. A. L. J. Bayle in 1822 was the first to describe general paralysis as a dementia with diffuse lesions of the brain (syphilis had not yet been isolated in this disease) rather than the circumscribed lesions basic to other dementias. Binet thus offered general paralysis, or paresis, as a morbid entity among the dementias.

Psychiatrists were at that time quite generally claiming that dementia was a basic dimension of general paralysis, of senile dementia, of dementias based on circumscribed lesions, and of a pathological dementia called *démence vésanique,* within which all other cases were classified "if they ended in irremediable intellectual weakness." It was this last ragbag category that constituted Kraepelin's "dementia praecox," a term he borrowed from B. A. Morel and to which he gave status and popularity.

The curability of this so-called dementia became an important matter for debate: if some cases of mental

[16] Professor Starke Hathaway has bestirred me, much against my "overlearned" convictions, to consider that any clear dichotomy between amentia and dementia is "at best, an artificial issue." Thus he says that this, Binet's and Simon's "featured example of differentiated syndromes, is a 'has been' "; that it is as anachronistic as the other differential diagnoses with which the literature was replete until about 1950 (255). From this point of view, some of my own unregenerated observations will also appear anachronistic.

stupor were remediable, were they really cases of dementia? Some alienists asserted that dementia and incurability ought to be considered as synonymous, but Esquirol had confused the picture by speaking of "acute *curable* dementias." There was a long period of debate about the classification of "curable" cases. The term "mental confusion" was then introduced as a substitute for dementia and went in and out of style. In 1910 it was "in" again, but Binet felt that its vagueness, covering both organic and functional troubles and applied to all varieties of mental illness, made it unacceptable as a separate category.

Through a succession of arguments reported in the literature there finally seemed substantial agreement among alienists that dementia was an *acquired,* and *incurable,* weakening of intellectual faculties, which was frequently progressive as well as permanent. Binet wished to retrench on the "incurability" criterion, since he had seen remissions in general paralysis, and, strangely enough, "some cures of dementia praecox" (159, p. 279).[17] Omitting any mention of incurability, Binet set forth his own conditions for a true dementia: the intellectual weakening must be primary, isolated, and isolable from other psychological phenomena (like, for example, the emotions); it must be "fairly severe" as based on standards culled from the intelligence scale and other data; and it must be extended over a number of faculties so that the individual is incapable of directing himself (159, pp. 277–79).

[17] This must have meant to him that the diagnosis was wrong, since he contended that dementia praecox probably started and certainly terminated in dementia. Following Kraepelin, Binet and Simon were so adamant about the necessarily demential nature of dementia praecox that they were led into the following circular reasoning: a patient initially diagnosed as a dementia praecox who gave a correct answer to a comprehension question at the ten-year level was judged by them to be so nearly "normal" that they concluded that the diagnosis, rather than their hypothesis, was erroneous. They believed that she should be rediagnosed as a manic psychotic. Their suspicion, they said, was confirmed when she recovered and left the hospital some months later.

Since the diagnosis of intellectual status was so important, Binet saw the need for objective criteria to make it as precise as possible. While admitting that the patient's history and the intellectual residues of his former learnings gave useful clues, these could not be decisive. More significant were the signs furnished by his everyday hospital behaviors. Throughout the published articles Binet and Simon made detailed use of such "naturalistic" observations of the patients, but Binet's unpublished letters to Simon provide more penetrating clues to the special significance he gave to these. For example, he wrote in request:

> I need some notes now on the hospital life of all our dementia praecoxes . . . notes taken from time to time, indicating what they are doing just at the time you pass by, and whether they did some foolish things, extravagant acts, etc. Note, dear friend, that we are making too many examinations in the office [*de cabinet*], and it is too intellectual, too fragmentary.
>
> Make notes on their character. Does it still exist? Do they have tastes, requirements, aversions, desires, fears, affections? It seems that Bel——, a young patient, still has emotional traces, but the old chronics have the air of empty nuts. I believe that there are in this matter some researches that are *very important to carry out* [underlined thrice]. I feel the need of them in completing the article. If we leave the matter as it is, it would be a *gross* omission [6, 7 June 1909].

Again he wrote asking for more information on hospital behavior:

> I believe it good to judge the intelligence of patients by their hospital life; to dress one's self and to eat alone are good signs, perhaps superior to our tests of the [mental] level . . . [6, 15 June 1909].
>
> Ask the sisters [nurses] for some very detailed hospital notes about Lef——. Such notes are excellent. You know that I have told you that *they are another method* of getting the level, quite as good as ours; and from this point of view, what a contribution for the observations! [6, 20 June 1909].

Among the observations he explicitly requested were these: "How do they eat? Play cards? Must they be sought out for meals? For going to bed? Do they come when called from a distance?" Several times he listed a number of "tests" to be given that were not included in the scale and that he himself originated. His letters are replete with the names of patients about whom he wanted information, thus showing his personal acquaintance with them in the institution.

To assist others in making these evaluations of "daily behaviors" Binet and Simon provided a rough hospital scale in a table of behavior, paralleled with specifications of the general mental level they indicated:

Behavior	*General Mental Level*
Follow an object with the eyes Take an object when offered Obey a simple gesture	Idiot (up to two years of age)
Direct self in the institution Find one's place at table Feed self Blow one's nose Dress oneself Wash one's hands Keep clean Fasten underclothes or jacket Run a wheelbarrow or carry a load	Imbecile (two to four years of age)
Sweep Make one's bed Polish one's shoes	Imbecile (four to seven years of age)
Sew, make a hem, darn Mend or patch Comb and arrange one's hair Wash and iron Do simple cooking	Moron (over seven years of age and up to about twelve years)

[159, p. 283]

Of course this hospital scale was not very exact since it lacked standardization. For this reason Binet introduced the Binet-Simon test as an important adjunct; he commented: "Conceived in order to recruit classes of retarded children, it can equally well perform services [of diagnosis and prognosis] in mental illness. . . . Its proper function is to determine what the intellectual level is in states of emotional calm (*à froid*). Consequently it is the touchstone for determining the status of dementia" (159, p. 284).

Binet's remarks show clearly that the psychiatrists had given no attention to the scale. Nor did they do so after Binet recommended it, although his illustrations must have provided evidence that it could yield data more reliable than the usual subjective clinical examinations. He tried to interest these doctors by giving them a list of the test items in the scale by the ages they represented. He referred them to the more detailed 1908 publication in *L'Année*, and explained that the scale had been standardized on a population similar to that of the hospitalized patients, that is, on the laboring and small merchant classes. In this population, he added, a level of twelve years appeared to be the normal one, yet he insisted that careful consideration should be given to each individual patient's social class, level of education, and to the content and quality of his delusions, "which are related to the intellectual level." Although he added to his recommendations some cautions and delineated some difficulties in using the scale with these *aliénés*, he oversimplified them, since he himself fell victim to the erroneous conclusion that permanent mental deterioration was the touchstone of dementia praecox.

In his description of the *senile* and *paralytic dementias* Binet added little or nothing to his observations drawn a year earlier, except to integrate them into this general overview of mental pathology. *Dementia praecox* absorbed his attention. His remarks give painful evidence of this: "This study," he warned, "is a terrible one. The difficulties are multiple . . . there is such fluidity in its contours. . . . It is a delicate problem for it is an affliction whose nature and frontiers are still being debated . . ." (159, p. 291). Part of the confusion lay in the fact that dementia praecox victims show symptoms that imitate any or all the other insanities, although he felt that, beyond some marginal cases, "any experienced alienist can recognize it always and anywhere" (159, pp. 291–92).

Binet was not quite sure that Kraepelin had a theory of the real nature of the illness, since he was involved in presenting a rich and precise enumeration of all the symptoms, without recognizing any general unifying connection among them.[18] His admiration for Kraepelin, whom he called "the father of dementia praecox," apparently made him wish to exonerate the honored doctor from the banality of his symptomatology, for he pointedly inferred that Kraepelin would surely agree with his own (Binet's) conclusion that the multiplicity of symptoms stemmed from one primary factor: a deteriorated intelligence. Not finding a clear answer in Kraepelin's writings and being uncertain as to the timing of the onset of the dementia, he wrote to ask Kraepelin his opinion. The reply more than ever blunted the point: Kraepelin wrote that at the beginning of the disease he noted "a particular psychic weakness—in a certain emotional obtuseness and a dissociation of different psychic phenomena. . . . The intellectual functions in themselves are injured only much later, and only from the fact that they are no longer exercised because of disturbances of the will and attention." Since Binet had interpreted Kraepelin as having installed dementia almost at the onset of the disease, followed by a gradual but progressive worsening, he was "a little surprised that an absence of exercise appeared to Kraepelin sufficient to explain the intellectual lowering" (159, p. 304n.). Thus the reader becomes a spectator at one of the confused episodes in the history of medical thought.

Binet himself continued to assert that "all attitudes, gestures, and responses affirm dementia as the essential condition in dementia praecox." He did in fact deny any influence of the emotions on the symptoms of absorption, negativisms, automatisms, catatonias, and the rest, claiming that these were indeed, and uniquely, it appears, evi-

[18] Since Binet consciously avoided etiology in this series of articles, he hardly commented on Kraepelin's etiological hypotheses, which represented "the culmination of the neurophysiological approach" (257, p. 165). This was a completely organic theory ascribing dementia praecox to hereditary and/or autotoxic disturbances of body metabolism.

dence of "mental inertia," of intellectual deterioration. In all other instances of mental functioning Binet had become so insistent upon the interacting roles of intellect and emotion that it seems important to quote him directly on this point:

> It is true, in many mental maladies, that the intellectual trouble results from a disorganizing action of the emotions. . . . But not in the dementias. The dementias are maladies in which intellectual weakening is primary and not secondary. . . . The intelligence is found disorganized in itself, in its machinery [*rouages*], and not by a kind of induction, not from the effect of some general trouble comprising both intelligence and the affective life [159, pp. 295-96].

At this point he showed a surprising misunderstanding of the nature of the emotions by adding that, even under conditions "of calm, of tranquillity, where there are no [observable] emotions to trouble him" the patient continues to be incoherent and mentally disorganized, and therefore truly demential.

With regard to the emotions in dementia praecox, Binet objected strongly to the current contention that these patients showed an "affective indifference" as a pathognomonic sign of the illness. In many cases documented from direct observations he found continual apprehension, sudden changes from anger to calm, from sobs to smiles and laughter; even humor and solicitude for others (159, p. 293). "If affective apathy is the rule," he commented, "then it suffers many exceptions." He preferred to indict any "emotional incoordination or damage" as a secondary, not a primary, characteristic of dementia praecox.

These conclusions about the nature of dementia praecox had cost Binet an excessive effort that is reflected in his letters to Simon. It was of this chapter that he had remarked: "I have already recommenced it four times!" The first letter concerning it is dated 31 March 1909, in which he wrote:

> My dear friend, Everything is beginning to arrange itself in my head. I see in dementia praecox two conditions,

an active one, development of irritation, then a state of repose in which we must search for the sequellae of the active state.

If it is thus, we must use five methods:

1) physiological. To see if [for nearly two dozen listed conditions] there is not a difference between the active and the passive state. . . . We must not shut ourselves into psychology and forget this somatic aspect. [He wondered if they had not made this error in the study of imbeciles, adding: "Why the devil haven't we thought of this before?"]

2) Method of intellectual level, taking it in the condition of repose, and taking the *complete* level, which is essential.

3) and 4) Method of collecting observations of patients in their daily routines.

5) Method of Freud, to try it out; if possible, to see clearly into the delusions. . . .

After long reflection, it seems to me that this is the plan we should follow henceforth. Don't you find it more complete than a simple psychological analysis? I have a horror of restraining ourselves to one point of view as, for example, Janet has done. We should aim at syntheses as broad as possible . . . [6, 31 March 1909].

Obviously "1" and "5" were abandoned, but, "2," "3," and "4," much extended and supplemented by copious study of the pertinent literature, became the viable design.

The letters also furnish an opportunity to observe some of Binet's changed hypotheses about dementia praecox. Writing in March 1910, he wondered if "*absorption* rather than negativism and stereotypy" was not the cardinal symptom of dementia praecox. But later, probably after writing his chapter on the classification of abnormalities, (168), he brought himself up short and opted decisively for another hypothesis:

The sole criterion, in my opinion, is dementia—and dementia that is not only an intellectual weakening, but a *notable and progressive weakening*. . . . Every time we are not sure that this criterion applies, *it is so simple to abstain!* [from making the diagnosis]. You see how energetic I am, from my underlinings. I am strongly convinced that I am right. If I have said the contrary of what I am writing now, I renege and cover myself with ashes. We do not make the diagnosis with incoherence, absorption, catatonia, or negativism, but only with dementia. . . . All of that is going to upset the [previous] plan of our article . . . [letter undated; underlinings were doubled].

In making the analysis of the most characteristic *attitude* Binet introduced the use of the Binet-Simon scale in even greater detail,[19] because his conclusion was that the most generally applicable *attitude* of the dementia praecoxes was "less intellectual vigor" than among the nondements, or indeed among most other dements. For example, he compared a systematized patient with a *paranoïde* dement, finding the latter less logically devoted to his fixed idea. "The demential *paranoïdes,* although daughters of God or relatives of Charlemagne, apply themselves readily to most of the work they are asked to do, while the systematized refuse such duties [in line with their paranoid ideas]." He warned that natural differences in basic intelligence plus different stages of the disease confuse the picture and bring up serious questions about intellectual level in puzzling cases. It was here that he urged the employment of the intelligence scale. Clear examples of its value could be seen, he said: in its immediate testimony of deterioration in a former bookkeeper who never-

[19] If course, this was not the first application of tests to diagnostic problems of the mentally ill. For example, even more than a decade earlier the Tamburini school in Italy had used an extensive list, including tactile senses, dynamometer readings, suggestibility, reaction times, meanings of words, judgment, memory, and affectivity, which H. Piéron and E. Toulouse called "a very remarkable systematic effort." Guicciardi and Ferrari in 1896 had used fairly similar items. Kraepelin had used various tests to compare the sane and the insane and to search for standardized procedures for determining differences in certain mental tasks. In France, R. Masselon, a student of P. Sérieux, borrowed Binet's tests of attention for dements; and Toulouse and Piéron in 1902 published "Les tests en psychopathologie" *(Rev. de Psychiatrie et de psychol. expérimentale* 7 [1903]: 1–13)in which they proposed to test "all the operations of all the faculties of the mind," using some sane and some insane subjects.

theless could not count the money set before her; in a man who could speak an elegant sentence, but who failed very simple tests; in its surprising testimony that a catatonic who had remained immobile for weeks nevertheless, on coming out of her trance, finally gained a mental level of seven years. Moreover, there was another catatonic who had appeared to be "normal" on the basis of her charm, gestures, vocabulary, and grammar, but whose test responses forced a revision of this evaluation. Her responses to the pictures were a simple enumeration, her definitions of words were primarily utilitarian, and she could respond sensibly only to the easiest comprehension questions. When confronted with the absurdity "I have three brothers —Paul, Ernest, and me," she found no problem, and volunteered that she had three sisters, "Me, Virginia, and Rosalie" (159, p. 338). On the complete test Binet and Simon accorded her a mental level of almost nine years, and concluded that she might at that time have reached a relatively stable limit of deterioration, but a month later this possibility was destroyed, "for she had again fallen into the night" (159, p. 339). Carefully recorded responses, often verbatim, of three dementia cases fill thirty-four pages of *L'Année* (159, pp. 314–48). These and the other illustrative cases reported in *L'Année* appear to support the evidence for Binet's hypothesis of primary mental deterioration, which, of course, gave substance to his certainty.

Disorganization was the one-word characteristic that Binet attached to dementia. He concluded with the following summaries:

> Dementia is a mental state in which—outside of any phenomena of separation, of conflict, of domination, or of deviation—there exists an inferiority of the intellectual level with vestiges of a more elevated former level.
>
> General paralysis [paresis] is a dementia in which the destruction of intelligence is manifested particularly by tears, hitches, breaks *(accrocs)* of functioning.
>
> In senile dementia the intellectual lowering is less pronounced for the instinctive life, notably for [habitual] judgments, than for the intellectual life, notably memory.

Dementia praecox is a dementia that on the one hand does not present the characteristics of the two preceding forms, and on the other hand shows a clinical picture that borrows its particularities from manic, or paranoid, or lucid psychotic manifestations, which are, however, added to a demential base [159, p. 348].

From some current twentieth-century viewpoints about schizophrenia (the former dementia praecox) it appears that Binet and Simon were eminently correct when they attacked emotional indifference as a primary characteristic. And yet, they were far from the mark when they insisted upon incurable mental deterioration as the cardinal symptom. Apparently they had not read Carl Jung's dictum written in 1906: "The name dementia praecox is a very unhappy one, for the dementia is not always precocious, nor in all cases is there dementia."[20] Nor had they given attention to Eugene Bleuler who in 1908 wrote that the people ostensibly suffering from dementia praecox are not all demented, and also that they might recover.[21] Nor did they pay any heed to their critic M. Mignard's objection (213). In light of Binet's constant insistence on letting observation and experiment determine "the facts," it is surprising to note his dogmatism, his failure to distrust his own expectations or hypotheses. He seems to have been caught in the organic theories of the day and believed that "destruction" in the brain "caused" the mental weakening (167, p. 300). He also seems to have become a victim of his own certainty, based upon the convincing cases in his sample population, which limited his seeking a more representative sample, repeated testing, and proper experimental controls.

Binet's and Simon's short chapter on "Retardation" provided a restatement of their earlier accounts of this mental pathology with the advantage of looking at it within the more comprehensive overview of the whole subject of

[20] Carl Jung, "The Psychogenesis of Mental Disease," *Collected Works* 3 (Pantheon, 1960): 161.

[21] In 1911 Bleuler also coined the word "schizophrenia," which may be no happier than "dementia praecox."

"alienation." In the introduction they repeated their former complaints about alienists' subjectivity and inexactness in differentiating degrees of retardation. For example, even as late as 1909 E. Régis, in a book on psychiatry, discussed "light idiots who have practically no intelligence, profound idiots with a complete arrest of intelligence, and imbeciles with a very limited intelligence." Binet again commended Blin for pointing out the several diagnoses of a single case made by as many specialists, and he once more unleashed his sarcasm against such practitioners:

> Facing these contradictions, one can only admire the confidence of certain clinicians who have recently set up statistics and percentages of different degrees of retardation found in the schools, without having thought of the necessity of defining these degrees in an objective manner. Isn't this charming? [160, p. 351].

Moreover, many physicians insisted that in the mental condition of retardation there exists "a lack of some faculties altogether." Against this claim Binet asserted that "all functions are represented among the retarded—attention, memory, imagination, judgment . . . even abstraction and the aesthetic sense. But most of these remain rough or truncated [*frustes*]. It is only by practical, objective, measurable results . . . that the limits we seek will be determined . . ." (160, p. 351). Complaining that psychiatrists had neglected this topic, because "the idiot has not appeared worthy of their interest," Binet indicated that it was incumbent on them to utilize some objective means of making distinctions between normal and retarded intelligence, between the dements and the developmentally retarded, and among different degrees of retardation. His tests certainly could furnish a useful beginning.

Binet recapitulated his and Simon's general differentiation of idiots, imbeciles, and morons, claiming the limit of "gesture" for the idiot, of "simple speech" for the imbecile, and of at least elementary "reading and writing" for the moron. Furthermore, he added the warning that in addition to signs of inferior mental level, retardates also frequently manifest pathological emotional phenomena like extreme stubbornness, irritability, nightmarish episodes, violent rages, tendencies to run away, fugues, and so on—all expressed in line with their degrees of intelligence (160, p. 353).

To clarify differences, Binet proceeded to compare the retardates' intelligence with that of the nondemented insane, the demented insane, and finally with normal children. In the first comparison his main target was Pierre Janet. He particularly objected to Janet's statement that hysterical and psychasthenic patients exhibited "an arrest of development, without deterioration of functioning." In fact, he contended that only its vagueness and literary quality gave Janet's hypothesis its popularity, and that a comparison with characteristics of other maladies "makes it go up in smoke." In the first place, the characterization would be applicable to other insanities, except the dementias, and so would not be distinctive to hysteria and psychasthenia; and in the second place, what appeared to Janet as an *arrest* was simply a temporary and common manifestation of those who are mentally ill. For the time being they do not perform complicated, complex, or difficult operations, but return rather to simpler, easier tasks. As Binet stated it, "The patient becomes inferior to himself." It is the adult retarded who are *truly* "arrested" developmentally, since they lack a basic differentiation of thought. If Janet had looked over the whole field of mental pathology, he would have perceived that the intellectual shifts in mental functioning among hysterics and psychasthenics, which he called "arrested development," were only temporary manifestations of poor functioning (160, p. 356).

Although the deteriorated insane and the developmentally retarded might attain a similar mental level on the Binet-Simon scale, their differences were notable. The dement, who has had a previous "normal" development, displays residues like habits, voice tones, gestures, attitudes, turns of phrase that are absent in the imbecile (for example, "This is the whole story of my life" could not be said by the latter) ; the dement may almost daily show dissolution or deterioration, while the older retardate is practically static, arrested developmentally; the dements are frequently characterized by obscure, cloudy expressions, are somnolent, incoherent, excited, or excessively passive, all conditions usually lacking in the retarded.

Binet's next comparison was between five or six-year-old normal children and imbeciles of twenty-five to thirty years of age. Again Binet's literary skill suggests a quotation:

> Two trains, having started from A, now arrive at B. The one, that of the imbecile, has stopped at B, while the other, the child, is presently at B, but is going to continue the journey. . . . The difference between them lies in the profusion of activities in the child. Every being who is developing is like a wave that beats against a barrier; before a new structure is acquired, before a certain act has become definitive, the organism makes a multitude of efforts of apprenticeship. The child, like a young animal, . . . is active, turbulent. He feels the need of a surplus of activity; his cries, his angers, his movements that fatigue us help him to develop. . . . The child exerts himself to move his body, to take, to grasp, to run, to combine ideas, to defend himself against a danger, to move dirt, to discipline himself in games with several comrades. Now look at an imbecile adult; he has the same intellectual level as the child, that is, he will make the same childish responses to your questions, but he has no taste for play. If he does not play, that indeed is the sign that he is not in the process of developing [160, pp. 359–60].

Thus "the retarded, although able to achieve the same mental level in a series of tests, differs from the dement and from the normal child in the sense that he has not enjoyed the same past, and that he does not prepare for the same future" (160, p. 360). Binet added a succinct table, on one page, to summarize the "principal mental states of alienation." Regrettably its brevity both oversimplifies and confuses the issues (161, p. 370).

When these publications were in press for *L'Année,* Binet

wrote to ask Simon to send copies abroad, "for example, to Kraepelin, Vogt, Forel, Freud, Bleuler" (6, 7 February 1910), and also to alert "people worthy of responding to us" (6, 12 March 1910). Among the possible names for the latter purpose he mentioned Babinski, Janet, Freud, Séglas, and Kraepelin. His disappointment must have been great, because there is no evidence that any of them responded. Instead there were two articles by only moderately well-known French psychiatrists, one by M. Mignard and the other by P. Sérieux and J. Capgras who were obviously smarting from Binet's criticism of their work. Mignard busied himself with the whole bundle (213), while Sérieux and Capgras applied their critique only to *la folie systematisée,* the subject of their own monograph (179). Binet and Simon, of course, replied in the same volume of *L'Année* (166). Mignard's article strongly suggests that he had read only parts of the total work, or that he had read it with the blinders too frequently worn by reviewers who are assessing the theses of colleagues. He misstated or misinterpreted some parts and ignored others, notably any reference to the Binet-Simon scale. Even though his review suggested some measure of agreement, it also damned Binet's publications with faint praise.

Mignard, a convinced disciple of Pierre Janet,[22] could not agree with Binet's contention that Janet's theory of hysteria was "only a description." For him the proposal that hysteria was essentially "a lack of mental synthesis with manifestations of psychological automatism" was instead "a scientific hypothesis." He also criticized a point that must have occurred to the reader when Binet stated that in lucid insanity the patient suffers and agonizes over his doubts, anxieties, and compulsions without carrying

[22] My friend, Dr. Lucie Bonnis, knew Mignard well, since she took her first year of internship with him in 1922 at the Asile de Vaucluse. Her long letter about him provided the information about his devotion to Pierre Janet, and in the following quotation further highlighted the misfortune of having Mignard review the 1910 articles: "Mignard never used the Binet-Simon scale," she wrote. "The method absolutely did not interest him—in fact, it did not exist for him . . ." (246).

them out, without fulfilling their incitements. Mignard pointed out that Binet had undoubtedly been thinking only of obsessions, phobias, and psychasthenic phenomena, and ignored the morbid compulsions, like murder or suicide, that sometimes do end in the "complete realization" of the impulses. Binet and Simon readily agreed to this correction.

Mignard was willing to include only senile and paretic dementias among the demential regressions. Other incoherent delusional persons, even the so-called dementia praecoxes, "may occasionally sparkle with some poetic image or subtlety. As long as these spangles of human genius still shine," he wrote, "we must not despair" (213, p. 224). He refused, therefore, to subscribe to a necessarily demential condition, or even a demential finale, for these patients. Since he ignored the mental scale as a possible means of making these evaluations, Binet and Simon thought that his failure to gain precision by its use was responsible for this disbelief in dementia and so, unfortunately, they did not take seriously this difference of opinion. On the whole Binet and Simon concluded that they "tended to agree with Mignard more often than they disagreed."

The exchange with Sérieux and Capgras, psychiatrists for the institutions in the department of the Seine, was not so mellow; they were sarcastic and perhaps even scornful. They insisted that the scope of their monograph on the "delusion of interpretation" (*Les folies raisonnantes: Le délire d'interprétation*, Alcan, 1909), to which Binet and Simon had made reference, could be almost exactly superimposed on the Binet and Simon conception of "systematized insanity." They disagreed with many details, but they were most annoyed at Binet's insistence that his and Simon's account of the *folie systematisée* represented a whole category of mental illness when in reality they thought it as partial a syndrome as their own. Binet replied that "Facts deprived of all interpretation lose any value.... [Sérieux and Capgras] have confined themselves to [the phenomena of] a very specialized affliction omitting specific comparisons with others . . . and being criticized, they are obliged to go beyond their monograph. . . ." He added a characteristic tongue-in-cheek thrust: "According to them, the *folie systematisée* is an entity that corresponds to a vast group of which their delusion of interpretation is '*only one of the chapters*': that appears to be their definitive opinion and until there is proof to the contrary, it is also ours" (166, p. 277; emphasis added).

There must have been letters and verbal encounters that do not appear in the literature, because Binet stated that the two most important criticisms of their series on alienation were reproaches for failing to include "mental confusion" as a pathological unit and for omitting some kinds of maladies from their classification. Mignard had already unwittingly illustrated the uselessness of the amorphous term "mental confusion." Binet now called it a *caput mortuum,* "a pigeonhole into which everything that is embarrassing can be thrown pell-mell. . . . No expression has had as much vogue as this one; it occurs on every page of the journals on insanity; it resounds in all the discussions of the psychiatrists; it is used even by neurologists" (167, p. 278). He compared its popularity to that of the term "degeneration," and refused to give an account of its history, claiming that this would only add to the disorder: "History ordinarily clarifies questions; it beclouds this one" (167, p. 278). An example of this befuddlement was that the term "mental confusion" had become so elastic that at that time it might apply only to symptoms of a mental pathology or to a whole and distinct nosological disease! For Binet and Simon the principal significance of the term lay in the fact that as a symptom it highlighted the problems of patients' intellectual status, which was very important to diagnosis. "This diagnosis of dementia —or lack of it—is the most important problem of all mental illness," they asserted (167, p. 300). They themselves contributed to its perplexities, however, when they failed to recognize that emotional disturbances could occur in apparently calm patients, for they insisted: "In general, any time that mental confusion does not have the excuse of [noticeably uncontrollable] inhibitions, or of violent eruptions of the whole mind . . . it can persist only by virtue of destructions [in the brain] and it is demential . . ." (167, p. 300).

To round out his perspectives on alienation, Binet published several supplementary papers in *L'Année* for 1911. Two of these were practical and highlighted his crusading spirit. One, dealing with legislation about the mentally ill, emphasized two particular needs: the one to suppress risks of arbitrary and unjustified institutionalization in order to safeguard individual rights; the other to suppress premature discharges of dangerous patients (169). Binet had just completed the drama *L'Homme mystérieux* that poignantly illustrated the latter situation and provided extraordinary propaganda. In the other essay Binet compared criminals and the mentally ill in a way that strongly suggests that he had in mind the practical intention of enlightening court personnel and of improving their procedures. For example, he wrote that "it is absolutely exceptional that an insane person commits a crime for money; also, the insane are so isolated and alone that they will scarcely ever be found acting in groups or associations" (168, p. 322). Their usual irrationality easily freed them from being held responsible for their acts. On the other hand, even the philosophical determinists contended that criminals were in control of their behavior and voluntarily committed their criminal acts for personal gain or advantage. Nonetheless, in agreement with the "new" current sociological principles, Binet urged that court sentences should no longer be motivated by a vindictive desire to make the criminals suffer, but instead should be based upon the right of society to defend itself as well as upon treatment of the needs of the criminals. He commended the sociologists' support for "a new and rare treatment" in which prisons became treatment-centered institutions for the psychological rehabilitation of prisoners.

While many cases left no doubt of the proper diagnosis between criminality and insanity, there were, of course, ambiguous or marginal cases that were perplexing. "This is confused country," Binet admitted. The courts, he contended, must finally establish some limits: "After all, the law sets the moment when daytime is legally distinct from nighttime, and we must do the same [in the courts] to offset the complete arbitrariness of the judgments of individual experts." He suggested that these distinctions should be made on the basis of appropriate tests, to be determined by careful research, and his practical inclination induced him to argue also for "more research on the criminal beyond that of the conjectural work of the Italian school" (168, p. 328).[23]

Binet also added discussions of several theoretical viewpoints. He compared the views of alienation held by psychiatrists, sociologists, and psychologists. These comparisons are tedious and speculative, but they again give evidence of Binet's growing insistence on research studies to test psychiatric hypotheses, especially about hereditary etiology. They also included commendations for sociological hypotheses about the alleviation of insanity through attention to the environment and its heavy demands on personal adaptation.

Since Binet had given little recognition in his 1910 papers to a comparison of organic and functional psychoses, he now included a section on this topic (168, pp. 331–50). In view of the almost exclusive emphasis among psychiatrists on organic and constitutional elements in psychoses, and the unsettled and highly disputed territory between the two areas of organic and functional psychoses, Binet's treatment seems enlightened. He believed that the differences were often difficult to discern, and that they must be made "by a psychiatrist who thinks with psychological intuition" (168, p. 344). In general, those patients with primarily organic psychoses tended to manifest less regular evolution of their malady, were more often demential, and had less firm intentions, that is, they showed less adroit attempts at suicide or violence, "less pure, less typical symptomatology" (168, p. 349). He included in this organic classification all the dementias as

[23] Binet held Lombroso responsible for the widely held position that criminals show "degenerate hereditary stigmata." He claimed that the evidence was extremely unconvincing, and that Lombroso's work was "hasty and uncritical."

well as other persons whose cognitions were affected, even temporarily. "This group," he added, "is even richer than we supposed. . . . It could include all the physical maladies that present mental symptoms, like typhoid fever, grippe, respiratory and circulatory illnesses. . . . Any sickness could become a part of this category, for it is possible that no organ of the body can be injured by sickness without more or less affecting the mental functions" (168, p. 350).[24] The logical conclusion of this reasoning predicted the possibility that "the whole medical clinic might indeed invade the domain of alienation" (168, p. 350).

The collaborators also repeated and developed some of their earlier criticisms of the hypotheses of prominent and popular French psychiatrists. Their own work was more inclusive, more discrete in comparisons among the categories. It used unifying concepts rather than symptomatic "samples," permitted salient differentiations between mental *symptoms* and *attitudes,* compared organic and functional psychoses, and finally, it offered some means for evaluating diagnostic status as well as progressive changes during the course of an illness. The series was concluded with an expression of faith that, despite changes that would take place in the future, they had wrought well. They believed that their clinical and psychological divisions would "continue to be right and solid" and that "armed with some precise methods of research, the clinician could see more clearly into the troubles of his patients" (170, p. 388). While the disinterest of the contemporary psychiatric profession in these efforts was surely disappointing, it did not dampen their enthusiasm for this project. As witness to their confidence the following sentence appears in the *avant-propos* of *L'Année* for 1911:

Very soon we shall publish our ideas under the form of a treatise on mental alienation, in order to put this conception more within reach of doctors, especially of psychiatrists, and to accentuate its clinical character; for we

[24] Binet seems not to have turned the tables to discuss the possible effects of the emotions on organs of the body.

believe that this conception should supply great services to specialists—and thereby to their patients [162, p. x].

There is no available evidence that such a treatise was ever published.[25]

Perhaps Binet's and Simon's most significant contribution in this area was their comparative approach to mental pathology, which, although commonplace today, was not used productively by even the most outstanding psychiatrists like Janet, Kraepelin, and Magnan. The collaborators had offered more precision in the criteria for each syndrome, and therefore had demonstrated that the many "symptomatic samples" then in vogue could not satisfy any standards of specificity. While they did not, of course, "solve" problems of diagnosis, their criticisms, even including etiology, which they claimed to avoid, could have thrown wholesome doubt on leading hypotheses like Kraepelin's "autointoxication" and Magnan's "hereditary deterioration." To test these they called for the rigorous controls that are demanded by scientific research design. They tried to reduce subjectivism in the diagnoses of the mental states and the intellectual status of mentally ill patients. At a time when organic etiologies were "the order of the day," their discussions frequently suggested that they themselves thought in terms of psychological approaches to mental illness, that distressing emotional experiences might be as disturbing as organic or hereditary ones. In fact, Binet went as far as to say that in the case of functional mental disorders a psychiatrist must not be content with thinking in anatomical or physiological terms, but would find success only by using "psychological intuition" (168, p. 344).

Their findings on the intellectual status of psychotic patients are interesting, but they are also disappointing in their meagerness and in their failure to detail in any systematic way the difficulties involved in such testing.

[25] A letter from the Presses universitaires (successors to Alcan whom Binet mentioned) reports that no such volume appears in their publication list.

Even more distressing was their failure to use the Binet-Simon scale and the "hospital level" criteria to discredit rather than to support Kraepelin's prognosis for what he called "the psychosis with demential termination." A victim of the biases he so often warned against, Binet seems to have been "seized" by this hypothesis that dementia, based on organic destruction, was a necessary concomitant of dementia praecox, or schizophrenia. Of course, the subsequent unsuccessful search up to the present time to discover the true nature and etiology of this disorder is convincing evidence that Binet's and Simon's attempts were destined to be in vain. The very substantive nature of schizophrenia is so elusive that it still evades systematic and controlled research.

These attempts to bring some order out of the chaos of classification for the categories of alienation cost Binet much time and effort and in the end must have frustrated him greatly since they went unnoticed. He approached the problem as a psychologist with the same natural observations that had been characteristic of his other research. His letters to Simon are eloquent evidence of his methodology: observation, comparison, testing, and retesting. Unhappily, his methods did not provide adequate answers. Nonetheless, his evidence was enough to allow him to bring rational criticism to much of the work done by others and even to permit tentative suggestions for new categorization of mental pathologies. But he seemed to be dropping the results of his work into a well that gave no response. Binet was not a psychiatrist, nor even a medical doctor, and even though Simon could claim to be both, the tone and the form of the reports of their research were characteristically those of the psychologist. The psychiatrists ignored their work; the psychologists paid little attention to it. For a man with Binet's sensitivity (and stricken by a fatal illness), this treatment must have been devastating. Perhaps, however, it was inevitable, for work up to the present time on classification in mental aberrations seems to indicate that Binet and Simon as well as Kraepelin, Janet, and others devoted their efforts to questionable assumptions.

7 Experimental Pedagogue and Reformer

Alfred Binet should be remembered for his untiring efforts to bring the scientific method to bear on problems of education.[1] With his far-ranging inquisitive intelligence he struck out boldly in many directions and early became convinced that the schools of his day needed to be jolted by the application of the scientific method to teaching and learning. He devoted much of the last dozen years of his life to the work of an organization directly concerned with the problems of the schools. He was the leader and research director for this group of men and women: teachers, educators, and other professional persons who tried to influence the modernization of French education by the application of these methods to its problems. In the course of this work he also became a reformer making demands upon the French Ministry of Public Instruction. His efforts that brought him some recognition in France and

[1] G. Vattier of the University of Caen had written in his 1910 report of "Experimental Pedagogy in France": "This movement has seen much progress, due in large part to M. Binet . . . who is at present the uncontested chief of the new pedagogy in France . . ." (243, p. 402). At the time of Binet's death Ed. Claparède in Geneva wrote: "The name of Alfred Binet will remain among those of the creators of experimental pedagogy" (272, p. 379). Henri Piéron, Binet's successor as director of the Laboratory of Physiological Psychology at the Sorbonne and as editor of *L'Année,* affirmed: "Experimental pedagogy is in great part the work of Alfred Binet" (267, preface). R. Buyse, a distinguished educator in Belgium, remarked in 1935 in his *L'expérimentation en pédagogie* that he had been extensively inspired by Binet's work. Although F. Zuza (311) correctly avoided hailing Binet as *the* creator or *the* initiator of scientific pedagogy, he nevertheless portrayed him as the foremost practitioner in France and as significantly influential in the application of the scientific method to education. These are only a few testimonials to this area of his activities.

considerably more abroad make one of the more interesting chapters in the history of education at the turn of the century. Of course, Binet was not alone in this endeavor. Earlier psychologists had been concerned with the problem of applying psychological principles to education, and during the last decades of the nineteenth century stimulating educational reforms were progressing in England, Germany, and the United States (290, p. 106, and throughout the book). Yet Binet's approach, rather than being philosophical, theoretical, or intuitive, was more directly experimental than the others. He believed that the application of psychological principles offered only limited advantages and wished to concentrate on the possibilities of making direct experimental studies both of educational procedures and, especially, of the characteristics of the children who were being taught.

Binet's initial interests in pedagogy, although for many years tangential to his professional research, actually came early in his career. He undertook the education of his daughters at home. His studies in 1894 of blindfolded chess players and lightning-calculators (47) caused him to ask if their methods of memorizing might not in some way be useful in the schools. During this same year he and Victor Henri studied schoolchildren's memory for words and sentences (51, 52), and in 1896 they published their very fruitful proposal for the investigation of individual psychology in which children were among the categories of subjects who should be extensively studied (59). In 1897 Binet plunged into the study of individual differences in habitual cognitive modes, and reflected on their possible influences on children's ways of learning.

It was not until 1898, however, that Binet launched his decisive incursion into pedagogy. With the collaboration of Victor Henri he inaugurated *La bibliothèque psychologique et pédagogique,* which was intended to become a series of books combining psychology and pedagogy. The first volume in the series was their own *La fatigue intellectuelle*; two years later Binet's *La suggestibilité* completed this short-lived series. In these books as in all his articles in this area Binet's primary concern was with scientific psychological methodology rather than with attempts to translate or transfer the results of experimental psychology per se into the school programs.

The problem of intellectual fatigue that Binet and Henri proposed to analyze in their book was one that at that time occupied the attention of many Europeans. Compulsory education at the primary level was relatively new in 1898; in France it was less than twenty years old. Nonetheless, the problem of mental fatigue had become so important that the public authorities in many countries considered it worthy of general investigation. Indeed, in Germany no less a psychologist than Hermann Ebbinghaus had been commissioned to study it in the Breslau schools. Thus when Binet and Henri wrote *La fatigue intellectuelle,* mental fatigue had been carefully considered for more than ten years.

Binet was so imbued with the necessity for studying all human phenomena experimentally that he almost arrogantly dismissed other approaches. Consequently *La fatigue intellectuelle* opened with heated charges against both medical doctors and educators. His terse foreword in this book has been called "a veritable manifesto of experimental pedagogy" (311, p. 23). It was a scornful attack on the old pedagogy that its authors considered to be beyond reform, requiring instead "the creation of a new pedagogy." They were sure that the old one "was affected with a fundamental blight" that came from groundless assertions based on the authority of men like Quintillian and Bossuet. The pedagogues were thus blinded by "literary citations . . . by exhortations and sermons" that replaced facts. When these "revolutionary" authors, Binet and Henri, opened their accusations against such "verbiage," they chose a paper from the records of the Academy of Medicine for 1887 rather than any pedagogical publication. It is not at all clear why they took up the cudgels against a medical report almost a decade old unless it was the simple fact that the doctors had specifically addressed themselves to the problems of "mental fatigue" (*surménage*) in schools and universities, the subject which was also their own target. They pointed out that these physicians had indulged in "oratorical jousts" or in case reports and crude statistical analyses of pathological literature without even bothering to define their terms. They had presented schoolchildren as "victims," as "intellectual amputees," as "fit subjects for tuberculosis," as persons "condemned to forced labor"; they had called university education "homicidal." Without further ado they had also attributed cases of meningitis, typhoid fever, and tuberculosis to *surménage*—fatigue from overwork for examinations, daily assignments, and long hours. Probably this report of the physicians' meetings gained importance in the eyes of the collaborators because the doctors had forwarded their "weighty conclusions" as recommendations to the Ministry of Public Instruction. Their assertions, presented as facts although completely unsupported by tested evidence, became a natural target for Binet and Henri whose testy criticism smelled a bit of Molière's attitude toward the medical profession. Their contempt, at any rate, was rife: apparently they had found no pedagogical morsel as delectable as the published reports of these medical verbosities. Nonetheless they also pointed out similar inanities among the educators.

Although Binet and Henri considered "mental fatigue" a normal condition that could be righted after a short rest, or at least overnight, nevertheless in their opinion it interfered with optimum learning. It especially should concern the schools for its relation to programs of instruction, length of examinations, regulation of work, of recreation, of gymnastics, of age limits for admission to certain classes and schools, and even to suggestions for sleep. They indicated that in this book they would summarize the monographs that would be useful and pertinent, and then go on to suggest further research, with more emphasis on the methods used than on the results, still only very partial, that had been obtained. There was much to be done and they were interested in discovering it.

Indeed, the tone of this book gives the impression that Binet and Henri were making a bid to the French administrative authorities for their authorization to carry out in the French schools a "vast" study of mental fatigue.

Perhaps to mollify, and certainly to inform, these "authorities," who were suspicious of "psychological experimenters" and who even feared the use of suggestion and hypnotism on their pupils, the authors spelled out carefully the procedures that must be followed. The experimenter would ask the subjects to perform any of a number of mental tasks, like mental arithmetic, memorizing numbers or nonsense syllables, writing from dictation, and so on, and then would determine the effect of this work on their subjects' physiological and/or intellectual functions. A project in the schools might compare the effects of morning and of afternoon classes, or of an hour of hard exercise. The experimental conditions should first be tried out "many times" in the laboratory and in *one* class to avoid oversights and errors, and to evolve a practical and effective method of procedure (68, pp. 2, 226).[2] In addition to these trial runs the collaborators insisted on setting up expeditious procedures so that the pupil-subjects would lose only minimal time from their classrooms and also would not become bored or apathetic. Fifteen minutes once or twice a month, in each of several schools, should be sufficient: ". . . The administration ought energetically to encourage research of this kind, confiding it to trained experts." And yet they seemed pessimistic over this prospect, for "in France," they continued, "we regretfully report, the administration is little disposed to grant such authorizations . . ." (68 pp. 4, 5). Binet and Henri seemed indisposed to court the administration with soft words!

Instead of succumbing to their pessimism about immediately practical results, Binet and Henri proceeded to

[2] Pressing this point, Binet and Henri severely criticized H. Ebbinghaus's large-scale investigation in Breslau for his failure to do this. He had collected data from twelve thousand subjects without having set up a plan that could have prevented gross errors. For instance, he had failed to recognize the pollution of results by the effects of practice that masked those of fatigue in doing arithmetic problems; or, in using his sentence-completion tasks, he had ignored the problem of providing tasks of equal difficulty, thus contaminating his claimed measures of mental fatigue.

describe the experimental work that had been done by dividing it into two main categories: physiological and psychological effects of mental work. Binet himself had already researched with J. Courtier their effects on capillary circulation, and their reports from *L'Année* (volumes 2 and 3) were reported verbatim in *La fatigue intellectuelle* (68). Moreover, Binet and N. Vaschide had studied effects of mental work on blood pressure, which he now incorporated in this book. The other physiological dependent variables included effects on the heart, body temperature, respiration, muscular force, and nutritional changes. Under the last category Binet reported his very recent studies in four teacher-training institutions of the effect of mental work on "the consumption of bread." He had hypothesized that the long, demanding year of studies would decrease food consumption, presumably due to nervous tension or the like, and it appears that bread consumption was the only food for which regular records were available. After studying the monthly bread consumption for two consecutive years, from October to July, he believed that his hypothesis was upheld since the data showed a gradual decrease in the amount of bread eaten over the period, and especially in July, the month of nerve-racking final examinations. He was disappointed not to be able to find a control group "under similar conditions except for their freedom from mental work." This might have held the weather constant, but it could not have rescued such a loose-jointed and unconvincing project (61, 71, 73).[3]

Among the *physiological studies* the independent variables included the duration of the work, the nature of the tasks performed, age-grade differences, and so on.

[3] A detailed report of the study appeared in *L'Année* (67, 71, 73). Reviewers, especially the French pedagogue E. Blum, so mercilessly criticized it that one wonders at Binet's apparent enthusiasm for his evidence to which he devoted ninety-five pages in *L'Année*. He even cited supportive evidence of schoolchildren who showed increases in weight during vacation months—that is, "more vigorous health" in conditions free of hard mental work. The assumption equating weight and health was not questioned.

The general conclusion from Binet's and Henri's copious data was that

> . . . mental work produces modifications of varying degrees in the most important physiological functions of the organism. . . . Indeed, we can assert that *no mental work can be carried out without repercussions on the organism,* the duration and intensity of which vary according to the work done and the function studied [68, p. 328].

The authors freely admitted that, while these results were important, the methods used were not practicable for general use in the schools, both because the apparatus was necessarily complex and because the demands on the proficiency and knowledge of the experimenters would preclude its application by any except experts. Furthermore, since children tend to become excited and nervous even when their pulse is taken, their emotional state in such investigations would be likely to impair the results.

The *psychological effects* of mental work were measured largely by changes in the quality or amount of whatever work was in progress, over the time period agreed upon. Again, in many of the studies previously reported the subjects had been adults,[4] but Binet and Henri insisted that the results, and especially the method, were illustrative of their objective. In varying degrees the data showed effects of fatigue, but they urged and underlined the distressing feature of the experimental problem, also mentioned by Kraepelin and A. Oehrn, that *two* principal factors, fatigue and practice, influenced the products of mental work, *but in different directions.* Most researchers had neglected to note that one masks the other. Binet had no ready solution. "We cannot," he wrote, "get either of them alone."

The variables used in the school studies were hardly better. For instance, children wrote from dictation, did arithmetic computations and problems, or perhaps sen-

[4] One chapter was devoted entirely to the work of E. Kraepelin's student A. Oehrn whose name is not infrequently mentioned in the historical literature. Binet and Henri reported it in much detail with added calculations (68, pp. 229–61).

tence completions. Binet realized that the results were all contaminated by practice or by boredom, since the attitudes of the subjects underwent a change over periods of time. He and Henri thought that dictation was less affected by practice than were arithmetic calculations, but this posed the additional problems of scoring and of finding examples of equal difficulty to make valid comparisons of the hypothesized results of "mental fatigue."

Another tool, newly applied, seemed to offer relief from these troublesome issues of control, namely the esthesiometer, or the measure of two-point, tactile sensitivity.[5] A German physiologist, H. Griessbach, in 1895, and T. Vannod, a Swiss, in 1896, had studied separately the tactile thresholds of students to see if "the power of concentration of their attention would not vary after different school classes," which presumably would be shown by an increase in the size of the threshold. They believed that the converse should be true on Sundays, which, offering relaxation, hypothetically would produce a decrease in the threshold. Both studies "clearly" supported the hypotheses (68, pp. 320–24). Although Binet and Henri recognized the tentative and uncertain aspects of this work on tactile sensitivity, they looked at it as offering important possibilities for studies of mental fatigue.

After reading this long, minute, searching exposition and critique of the literature on mental fatigue, with its voluminous tables, graphs, and statistics, the reader wonders whether "members of the administration" would have had the necessary sophistication, or would have taken the time to read it, or, if they did, whether they would be moved to take any practical steps in light of its ambiguous conclusions. After all their discussion, Binet and

[5] As we have seen in chap. 3, this method was almost an experimental fad for many years, especially in Germany and the United States. In a long study toward his doctorate in philosophy in 1895 Victor Henri had worked under Wilhelm Wundt and Oswald Külpe, using this method with adult subjects, who were probably graduate students. Binet and Henri discussed the tentative and uncertain aspects of this work on tactile sensitivity.

Henri admitted that the research on mental fatigue had failed to produce evidence that could be put to practical use in the schools. They were sure, however, that they could set up projects that would fill in the lacunae and provide useful and authenic data. Their recommendations of "what remains to be done" have the sound of tintinnabulations to the ears of psychologists: more research and better, with many more subjects performing many more tasks for longer periods of time, under more varied conditions and in the awareness of the many experimental variables that can affect the outcomes. They knew that this must be done in an encompassing study in which "experts" were in control. In their opinion the educators would be interested in such a study, dealing with the most fatiguing times of day, the most fatiguing school subjects, the effects of physical exercise and exertion, the spacing of recreation and work, and the like. This apparent sole concern for "general results" may be puzzling in view of the image of Binet as the proponent of individual differences. Nevertheless, in almost every one of the research findings that he discussed, he mentioned the striking individual differences manifest in the data, but stressed the need to cloak these with large-scale studies in order first to arrive at group trends. His and Henri's very last paragraph is an appeal to "open the way" for these studies in the schools:

> The administration is too enlightened not to understand the high interest of these investigations, not to be persuaded that no educational problem can be resolved by discussions, by discourse and oratorical jousts. . . . May it, therefore, with all its power encourage research in the schools by means of experimental psychology [68, p. 336].

What were the results of this study?[6] Surely the "ora-

[6] James McKeen Cattell reviewed *La fatigue intellectuelle* in the *Psychological Review* (180). He first alerted his readers to the fact that it came from "the prolific laboratory of the Sorbonne . . . [where] according to the *Psychological Index* M. Binet had [produced] seventeen publications during the year 1897, leading, *longo intervallo*, Professor James M. Baldwin, who stands next in the list with eleven. . . ." He was not sure that the

torical jousts" and "the exchanges of imprecise opinions" among the physicians of 1887 had been discredited. But was it clear to "the administration" that practical tools were at hand, with experts ready to wield them? Evidently not. Binet's bid was not accepted. If he was to continue experimentation in the schools, it seemed destined to be irregular and fortuitous, without opportunities for prolonged research with relatively large numbers of children as regular subjects.

The Free Society for the Psychological Study of Children

Toward the end of 1899, however, opportunities to study children did appear, and Binet gave them hospitality. Simon's arrival as a collaborator offered at the Vaucluse hospital over two hundred retarded persons as subjects, and almost simultaneously Binet's work and reputation brought him an invitation to become associated with people connected with the school and university systems of Paris, and even in the provinces. He was invited to become a member of, and to act as an adviser to, *La Société libre pour l'étude psychologique de l'enfant*, henceforth referred to as *La Société*. It had been started in June 1899 by Ferdinand Buisson, occupant of the chair of the Science of Education at the Sorbonne,[7] at the urgent instigation of his students who were teachers, instructors, and professors, and who were enrolled in his course of Practical Lectures on Pedagogy. They had been stimulated by reading about child study associations abroad, notably those

---

title of the book was pertinent, but concluded: "For the psychologist it is the best existing summary of experimental work on certain of the relations of mental to bodily change." Binet's countryman E. Blum called it "a work of unique and opportune synthesis . . . an original and fruitful example to those who wished to contribute to *pédologie*" (176, p. 510).

[7] Formerly director of primary teaching in the Ministry of Public Instruction, Ferdinand Buisson had succeeded M. Marion in this chair and was himself replaced in 1906 by Émile Durkheim, who had been his substitute *(suppléant)* since 1902, when Buisson was elected a deputy of the 13th *arrondisement* in Paris.

initiated in the United States by G. Stanley Hall. *La Société* was organized in June, and, following the summer holidays, the next meeting was held on 9 November 1899 in the Amphitheater Richelieu at the Sorbonne. Alfred Binet joined the group at that time. Buisson, who knew Binet's work and interests, had asked him to participate in this November meeting. He obviously wanted to assure the quality of the research undertaken by *La Société* and therefore persuaded Binet to enter his candidacy for membership on the first advisory board (*bureau*) (262, p. 41). He was duly elected.

The word *libre* or "free" in the title of *La Société* indicated that it was open to anyone interested in the theoretical and practical aspects of education. This word had a significant meaning in those days when politics, religion, and private and public schools were sensitive issues in the French educational scene. Membership in *La Société* was thus open to lay and clerical persons, to those politically radical and conservative, to private and public teachers, to all professional people, and to parents. The early membership was largely made up of primary school teachers, principals, inspectors, divisional directors, directors of normal schools, and a few instructors and professors in the higher schools, colleges, and universities. It soon also included lawyers, doctors (Simon from the beginning), criminologists, sociologists (Tarde, for example); directors of special schools for the blind and deaf, a few priests, philosophers, and parents. Binet clearly showed his initial skepticism about its future in his announcement of its organization in *L'Année* (76, pp. 594–606), which even omitted any acknowledgment of his own authorship of the three questionnaires he printed there for *La Société*. All the same, he at once took a prominent part in the new organization. He was consultant for the studies undertaken, regularly attended meetings of the whole and of subcommittees, and also started publication of a *Bulletin* for *La Société*. The latter contained not only the minutes of the meetings, but also studies and notes of members and committees, pertinent news of foreign research, of books, and of reviews in psychopedagogy, and special addresses made to *La Société*, by their own members and by visitors.[8] It was a modest publication with a usual length of twenty-five to thirty pages. Binet seems to have been its chief editor, although there is no formal announcement to this effect. The first number appeared in October 1900, and it was issued four times a year until October 1904, when its popularity, plus a subsidy of five hundred francs granted by the Ministry of Public Instruction at Binet's request, made possible a monthly publication during the academic year, or eight times annually.

Primary school teachers, principals, and inspectors, both men and women, were the most active members. One of them later remarked, "I did not understand why a scholar like Binet could have need of us, poor teachers. Afterward I understood" (311, p. 54, n. 3). Some writers have falsified Binet's role, indicating that he was drawn to it by his "tenderness toward children," but Simon has dispelled this idea. In 1940 he wrote:

> Binet has sometimes been represented, because of his pedagogical writings, as having that sentiment—a little affected and watery—that so many authors believe they must display whenever they speak of children. I have never seen the least trace of this in him. He was truly preoccupied with achieving solutions to problems—with facts. Nothing turned aside his exclusively scientific direction and his concern for objectivity . . . [294, p. 35].

In 1899 he probably also saw the particular advantages in training teachers in the scientific method to make them distrust "imprecise opinions"; perhaps also in leading them to better observe their pupils. But it seems likely that Guy Avanzini came nearer the truth when he wrote the following for the celebration of the five hundredth issue of the *Bulletin* in 1968:

> [In 1899] he quickly understood that the proposed *Société* could eventually become the instrument he needed

[8] This practice was continued after Binet's death, and it is interesting to read a translation (into French) of J. M. Baldwin's "testimony to Binet's memory" (263) and Piaget's paper (284).

to assure him the collaborations he was seeking. It appeared so much the more opportune since the official patronage that it enjoyed[9] and its installation for meetings at the Musée pédagogique provided him with authorization to experiment in the classroms and at the same time granted him great freedom of initiative. Really there was a confluence between his own desire and that of these teachers and students who were interested in the psychology of the child, but who did not know how to approach it [261, p. 9].

The schoolchildren subjects who appeared in his investigations for *La suggestibilité* and in his extensive studies of cephalometry are evidence of the advantages that he received from these contacts. Very early, too, a primary inspector of the department of the Seine visited him at the Sorbonne laboratory and spontaneously offered to "support an inquiry on the conditions of intellectual superiority" in his school jurisdiction (78, p. 314). Binet gradually attracted other loyal and resolute collaborators among the school personnel.

From 1900 on, Binet's history and that of *La Société* became pervasively inseparable. By March 1901 he became vice-president, and in November 1902 he succeeded Buisson as president, when the latter entered politics. Buisson, thereafter named *président-fondateur,* admitted in several speeches reported in the *Bulletin* that Binet was the prime initiator of the activities of *La Société,* and generously called him *le véritable fondateur.* Binet continued as president until his death, and six years afterward (World War I having intervened) *La Société* was

[9] Professor Th. Ribot, at the *Collège de France,* and M. Bédorez, director of primary teaching of the *département* of the Seine, were honorary presidents; the treasurer was Dr. Galtier-Boissière, curator of scientific collections at the Musée pédagogique. Other officers were F. Buisson, president; Mme P. Kergomard, *inspectrice générale of les écoles maternelles,* and Dr. Léon Marillier, master of conferences at L'École des Hautes-Études, Sorbonne, vice-presidents; Mme Marie Fuster, professor at the Collège Sévigné, secretary-general; M. Bonzon, lawyer at the Court of Paris, and M. Devinat, director of the normal school of the Seine, were on the board (*Bull.,* 1900, No. 1, p. 1).

renamed in his honor *La Société Alfred Binet.* After Simon's death in 1961 it was again renamed, this time *La Société Alfred Binet et Théodore Simon.*

Avanzini, sometime secretary-general of *La Société,* and a resident of Lyon where the records are concentrated, has offered this expressive picture:

> From the time of his election [Binet] shows himself particularly active; presiding at all the monthly meetings, except when his health prevented it, he uses his energy as much in the domain of administrative management as in scientific work and deploys on the two planes the most remarkable qualities of perserverance and vigor; constantly supporting new initiatives, on the lookout to improve the methods, dreading passivity and routine, he is preoccupied especially in stimulating the zeal of his collaborators. . . . His high idea of the requirements of research is manifested by his rejecting any concession that appeared insufficient or contestable to him; not that he is ironical to any persons: witnesses agree in saying that his shyness, his courtesy, and his gentleness always make him keep an attitude that is friendly and kind. But one could not fail to recognize that he sometimes adopts a very rigid code [*formulation*] and that the energy and tenacity with which he directs the work led him to some authoritarian interventions, capable of provoking some belligerent reactions toward him . . . [262, p. 43].

Avanzini also went on to indicate Binet's ego involvement in the publications that he edited, almost considering them as belonging to him: " 'In *my Année psychologique,*' he writes; or again: 'Permit me to say how much I am attached to all *my* collaborators in *La Société.* . . . I feel that *I can count on them entirely* . . .' " (262, p. 43; the italics are provided by Avanzini).

With Buisson's help, Binet maintained close relationships with the high functionaries of the university and academic administration; the reports in the *Bulletin* frequently contain the names of supporters and collaborators like Bédorez, director of primary teaching of the Seine, of several general inspectors, of inspectors of primary teaching like MM. Baudrillart, Lacabe, and especially his long-time friend A. Belot, of principals like V. Vaney and J. Boitel, of directors of special education like Mme Kergomard, general inspector of the *écoles maternelles*, of primary teachers, and so on. Doctors, graphologists, and lawyers took some active roles, and the sociologist Tarde, then a professor at the Collège de France, had planned a piece of research with Binet that was cut off by Tarde's death in 1904. It is evident, therefore, that Binet, so frequently regarded as "timid and shy," was nevertheless able to build up a concerned and active clientele that was maintained throughout his own productive years.

Binet also set himself the task of increasing the membership. He sent letters and invitations to various educational societies, from student-teachers to inspectors. While the response was disappointing, in light of the numbers approached, the membership rose from approximately two hundred in 1900, three hundred in 1901, three hundred and fifty in 1902, four hundred and fifty in 1903, five hundred in 1904, six hundred in 1905, and up to seven hundred and fifty in 1911. An annual list of members shows something of the variety of professions represented—and maintained.[10] Branches were also formed in several cities and towns in France. The *Bulletin* showed

[10] The following table of categories presented to the General Assembly on 15 November 1903 is representative:

Group of universitaires:		*Group of non-universitaires:*	
General inspectors	7	Fathers and mothers	54
Rectors	2	Physicians and directors of scientific laboratories	27
Inspectors of the académie	2	Publicists	4
Professors of superior grades	7	Lawyers and judges	3
Provisors and principals	6	Editors	8
Professors of lycées and colleges	25	Chief of bureaus	1
Primary inspectors	34	Inspectors of children's welfare	3
Directors and professors of normal schools	52	Businessmen and bankers	5
Directors and professors of superior primary schools	50	Graphologist	1
Men and women primary teachers	145		
Societies or formal groups (mostly outside of Paris)	7		

J. Boitel, *Compte rendu moral, Bull.* 1904. *No. 14*, 352.

an increasing popularity, and it also reflected in general a reasonably harmonious ideological climate among the members of differing religious and political viewpoints.

The differences among the *sociétaires* regarding the methods and the content of the investigations they should pursue were not so easily settled. They wanted to work, but how and toward what? Binet's description of the first board meeting reflects their uncertainties:

> When the preliminary formalities had been accomplished according to the habitual rites . . . we looked around and asked: What are we going to do? It was a question of studying the psychology of childhood; but how, by what practical methods? . . . We had the feeling that our *Société* was going to play a role less passive than that [of many associations whose members simply read or listen to reports]. I recall very clearly the impression that I had during our first monthly meeting: everyone wanted to work, and to work together. It was understood that we had founded a kind of cooperative ["a scientific cooperative"]. . . . But what form could this collaboration take?
>
> There was no precedent for deciding this question. . . . These first members brought a touching zeal, and hopes . . . constantly stating the same request: we want to learn how to observe, we want to practice psychology, we want to do something scientific: How do we go about it? . . . I defy the most scholarly to reply in two words or a hundred to such questions, of this complexity. It is a great error to believe that the scientific method can be learned by reading or taking courses; it is learned by practice and personal effort . . . [110, pp. 548–49].

In the first issue of the *Bulletin* Buisson had pointed out that the members were divided into two lines of interest that were in some real opposition to one another: on the one hand, some wanted to carry out studies that would give their students better instruction, especially in morals, while on the other hand, others were more interested in studies aimed essentially at understanding children more objectively. Buisson himself, whose concerns were certainly influenced by Hall's Child Study Movement (290, chap. 15), belonged to the former group and it was probably his influence, plus the contagion of American societies of psychology and pedagogy, that made the board opt for the use of questionnaires to study aspects of character development. In fact, Buisson asked Binet at the outset to help with an investigation of three shortcomings that were characteristic of children: anger, misbehavior (*indiscipline*), and lying. Binet had used the questionnaire method previously, for example in a study of painters in collaboration with H. Beaunis in 1892. Moreover, in his *Introduction à la psychologie expérimentale* in 1894 he had even advocated its limited use. By 1900, however, he felt a considerable reserve about it, but he yielded to the fervor of the majority; he even composed the questionnaires and directed their distribution. The result was the amassing of thousands of responses for analysis. Enthusiasm for this first effort was responsible for three more investigations by questionnaire, this time on "children who are scolded," "their [children's] finest act," and "rewards for children." Forty thousand replies were returned for the last of these! Various members of *La Société* worked over the various results, with Buisson himself joining them to analyze the study of lying. The results were reported in the *Bulletins* of 1902, and even these reports betrayed the dubious value of the data.

For over two years the questionnaire was the primary method used by the *sociétaires*. Binet's own quiet dissatisfaction finally gained support among those who had from the beginning wanted to pursue individual observations: they criticized the ambiguous formulations of the questionnaires, their analyses, and the validity of the conclusions. Binet discussed the shortcomings at the general meetings, and noted that the advantage of large numbers of data was offset by a lack of precision ("numbers alone give only a mirage"). He felt that the questions were often inadequately stated and misunderstood, that the investigations were initiated without sufficient attention to underlying hypotheses, and, perhaps most important of all, that "complex and delicate information" was sought from respondents who did not know the subjects very well, and who also did not know how to observe their behavior. He wrote: "The study of thirty children by persons [who know them] and whom one knows as attentive, conscientious, intelligent, and instructed [observers] is incontestably worth infinitely more than vague, often equivocal, observations collected by some unknowns on three thousand children" (103, p. 341). He went on to admit that questionnaires might be useful in investigating matters that were not amenable to experimentation, like "the feelings," but even here he mistrusted observers' judgments and, hoping to improve reliability in later questionnaire studies, he proposed the use of two judges for each child in any group under consideration. He also used a pretest, without calling it that, and, after finding reliabilities among judges fairly high, he directed a correlational study to try to determine what particular traits appear to be associated in children's characters (*Bulls.* Nos. 14 and 16 in 1904; Nos. 21 and 24 in 1905). At almost the same time programmed observational and experimental studies began to replace some of the questionnaires: there were observations of age differences in children's drawings of the human figure, comparisons of the efficiency of memorizing by wholes and by parts, observations of children's morals, attempts to correlate children's physique and intelligence, and summaries of Binet's and Simon's multitudinous cephalic measurements.

In March 1903, shortly after Binet had assumed the presidency of *La Société*, the advisory board took the initiative to organize the work into what were called *commissions* or small working groups created on the basis of similar interests. Binet generously credited J. Boitel, the secretary-general of *La Société* and principal of Turgot school, with triggering this new procedure. Boitel had urged the introduction of more system into the work of *La Société:* the board, he suggested, should draw up at the monthly meetings a list of psychopedagogical problems in the order of their importance, and study each in its turn. While Binet agreed with Boitel in principle, his objections provided him an opportunity to interject some instruction about the scientific method:

A question does not become ripe for study solely by the fact of its importance; an investigation is ready to be made only after it has been submitted to a previous analysis. First an appropriate method must be found . . . in psychology it is necessary to give a question its experimental form before beginning experimentation. . . . You undertake your program only when you know exactly what you are looking for, when you can formulate in precise terms the question that you wish to pose to nature by experimentation or observation, when, finally, you have found the method, the procedure, the techniques capable of giving you a minimum of error. . . . This purely preparatory part of pointing up the problem often represents, in efforts expended and difficulties overcome, half the total work of the investigation [103, p. 337].

Out of the ensuing discussions came the idea of work teams or *commissions*, for each of which about twelve or fifteen interested persons would meet, outside of the monthly sessions, to plan the work and to carry it forward. Binet was a participant at most of these *commission* meetings. He assisted with plans as well as with the analysis of data. The first *commission* studied graphology. Realizing the surprise that this might arouse, Binet explained the reason: skepticism and interest among members of *La Société* had been aroused by claims of graphologists who had lectured to them, and they wanted to test these claims in studies made on their students. Another early *commission* concentrated on moral sentiments, others studied memory, abnormal children, individual aptitudes, especially in language acquisition, and school sociology that investigated the harmful effects of poverty on children.

Subsequently these *commissions* multiplied, and by October 1904, in a lengthy account of "the past and future of our society," Binet himself waxed verbose in his euphoria. The *commissions*, compared with the monthly meetings, "were more favorable to the precise, patient, sometimes meticulous work that experimental psychology exacts," he explained (110, p. 551). As he had written:

They meet to plan their studies. All of us penetrated

deeply into the fundamental idea that questions of psychology, of pedagogy, of education are not at all to be resolved by literary theories. . . . To observe and experiment, to experiment and observe, this is not only a good method, it is the only method that can obtain for us a particle of truth, in the moral as well as in the physical domain [103, p. 346].

The last sentence could almost be emblazoned as Binet's credo: "To observe and experiment, to experiment and observe. . . " He went on to assert that if questions arose that could not be settled by experimentation, there was really no useful reason to discuss them, "since they are not susceptible to the sole criterion of certainty that modern psychology can accept." With such affirmations he put himself squarely among the ever-increasing number of scholars who were then opting for the power of pure science to solve everything. He felt that in the *commissions* the members were aiming at this objective. His oratory "on the past and future of our society" continued in an almost lyrical paean of praise. In examining the reasons for such success he pointed to the feelings of accomplishment among the collaborators as they perceived the usefulness of their labors and the progress they made from one meeting to the next. They all entered actively into the planning and programming of the topic at hand: ". . . some with imagination, some with practical sense, some with know-how about statistics, about children, about bibliographies. . . . We insist that we thus succeed in making each one feel that he has the right to claim his part in the common work. It is this 'scientific cooperative' that is the whole secret of our policy" (110, p. 554).

Binet illustrated these general remarks by describing a new projected *commission* on the study of mental fatigue in the schools; he also enthusiastically commended the *commission* on the retarded for having sparked the administration to appoint a formal administrative commission to study problems of the mentally deficient. Furthermore, it appears in this speech that the more intimate relations within the *commission* teams inspired within Binet a closer feeling for the personal development of the school personnel who were now his frequent companions, his friends as well as his colleagues. But most of all he seemed to be pleased with the idea that this successful work in the *commissions* would result in "imbuing the teachers, and . . . the younger generations with the qualities of exactness and precision, with the feeling of what has been demonstrated [by evidence] and what has not, with the taste for disinterested research" that he believed necessary for real progress. He had confidence that they were developing the proper goal of an "intellectual and moral disposition that constituted the scientific spirit" (110, p. 555). Like so many of his fellow scientists at the turn of the century, Binet was sure that this spirit would lead mankind out of the darkness; that it was the proper educational goal despite the fact that his "experimental evidence" could not prove it.

During 1905 the programs undertaken by the *commissions* varied considerably; several of them even became "practical" in their relation to school instruction. Illustrations of one or two of them in some detail will describe the form of the process. The *commission* on mental fatigue, for example, met first on 25 November 1904 with fifteen members present, all professional people: teachers, principals, school inspectors, physicians, the director of a school for deaf-mutes, and others, including Binet and Simon. One of their number, Professor Charles Chabot of the University of Lyon, presented a summary of papers given at the Congrès d'Hygiène, which he had attended in Nuremberg the previous summer (181).[11] It was mainly concerned with the further work of Griessbach and Vannod, plus the report of similar experiments extensively applied by Dr. Sakaki of Tokyo; all three had

[11] Chabot called attention to its importance as "a problem that occupies scholars in laboratories, as well as hygienists and pedagogues . . ." (181, p. 622). In fact, the Congrès d'Hygiène had concluded that research on mental fatigue "should indeed be continued under a strict control of conditions and if possible *with an international organization*" (181, p. 628; emphasis added).

used the sensitivity to touch—the esthesiometer-compass—as the criterion of pupil fatigue. Binet indicated that this method had been under methodological fire[12] and that some results had not been very satisfactory; nonetheless, he encouraged the *commission* to proceed. He argued that since these "foreign promoters" at the Congress had not only *not* become discouraged, but had actually "brought to the Congress voluminous dossiers, full of tables and figures, and, since it is a problem that presents an incontestable pedagogical interest, we must not hesitate to take it up and examine it again" (110, p. 552). But he stressed the need for strict experimental controls. The *commission* met several times during November and December, enlarging its membership, and finally it divided into three groups to carry out the work in different schools. A further insight into the processes of these study teams comes from a note inviting a few doctors, interested in school hygiene, to join them. The three divisions also included groups of teachers whom Belot brought into the work. Sixty teachers in all became the experimenters. Binet met with them for over two hours at each school, both to instruct them in the methods of using the apparatus[13] and to warn them of the psychological errors that must be avoided. They should be careful to give equal weight to the two points of the compass and avoid making suggestions to the pupils or indicating by any gestures their own reactions to their responses. The pretests were made in the morning before classes, and then, to estimate fatigue, repeated after an hour or so of performing some task, usually arithmetical calculations and problems. Of

[12] The *Bulletin* (110, p. 552) omits any mention on Binet's part of his and Henri's book, or of his own masterly critique of tactile thresholds published in 1903, which we examined in chap. 3. One finds a number of such instances in which Binet's "modesty" appears exaggerated and surprising.

[13] In January 1905 M. Buzenet, a teacher and member of this *commission,* produced a new and "ingenious" modification of the apparatus, which Binet praised and adopted immediately. There is a picture and description of it in *Bulletin* No. 22, 1905, p. 634. It seems very simple but much more convenient than a compass that had to be regulated after each trial.

course, a considerable number of teachers had to be available at each of these trial periods in order to test each child "before and after." Each test lasted approximately ten minutes, and the whole plan required about a month to complete. All the documents were sent to Binet. After eliminating those that did not meet the conditions of the study, he found three categories of responses: "indifferent," that is, no change, and "more" and "less" sensitive after the work period. About half showed a difference in the expected direction, that is, less sensitive, but Binet was not unaware of causes of error due to states of health, attitudes (for example, girls who were afraid of being *piqued* by the esthesiometer), curiosity perhaps followed by boredom, and so on. To obviate the effects of possible timidity on the first trial, a subsequent sample of ten boys and ten girls were given a second set of "initial" trials on successive mornings. In a third experiment teachers gave twenty boys and seventeen girls hard mental work—oral and mental arithmetic—for two and a half hours without rest. Both of these sex groups showed a resultant lowering of tactile sensitivity, and therefore presumably the effects of mental fatigue.

As far as the *Bulletin* was concerned, Binet let the case rest there, and the *commission* was disbanded. There is, however, a diverting addendum in *L'Année* where similar work was also reported (114). Diplomatically asserting his faith in the conscientiousness of the teachers who had been the experimenters—"our coworkers," he called them—nevertheless Binet felt that "it is the duty of an experimenter to push skepticism to its limits." Therefore, with Simon and a trusted teacher, he repeated an abridgment of the test in a different school. To their "true satisfaction" they found results essentially the same as those of the teacher-experimenters. It is questionable whether any teacher who had happened to read *L'Année* found the same satisfaction.

The method had been illustrated, and the particularized applications to school planning presumably could be made. Binet cautiously suggested that the studies indicated that it "was possible to measure mental fatigue in the schoolroom, not individually, but collectively." He went on to say that pedagogy, not psychology, should "take up the consequences of the affair" (121, p. 652).

The story of another *commission*, which was studying the proper age to start the teaching of reading, whether in the kindergartens (*écoles maternelles*) or in the first grades, is extremely amusing. Mme Kergomard, director-general of the *écoles maternelles* in Paris, Vaney, and some first-grade men teachers got into a wrangle, and Mme Kergomard, apparently misunderstanding Vaney's discourse, indignantly gathered her teachers, all of whom were women, around her and defied what she thought was the men's lack of appreciation. All the data led to the conclusion that reading was more effectively accomplished in the first—or even the second—grade than in the kindergartens (*Bulls.* Nos. 46, 47, 49, 50, and 51 report the action almost "live"). She mistakenly thought that this was a reflection on her and her fellow teachers, although ironically they had supported the same reading-grade argument as the men!

New *commissions* continued to be formed; some persisted for several years and others dispersed. They are too numerous to be reported here, but the *Bulletins* reflect a humming activity, if not one impressive for experimental results.

"School Psychology": The First Pedagogical Laboratory

In 1905 an event occurred that in its own way is almost as noteworthy as the development of the first metric scale of intelligence. On 16 November 1905 at the general assembly of *La Société* Binet made an announcement that may have excited his audience as much as it did himself: he, with collaborators, had founded a Laboratory of Experimental Pedagogy in a primary school in Paris, rue Grange-aux-belles, where his friend Vaney was principal. It appears that this was the first such laboratory established in a school in Europe,[14] and it was a notable achieve-

[14] Zuza notes one established in 1904 in Petrograd, although not in a school; M. C. Schuyten founded "at Anvers, the first [non-school based] laboratory of pedology in Europe" (311, p.

ment. Its purpose was to provide a more permanent home for the systematic output of experimental research with children, to disseminate to teachers the results of pedagogical research, and shortly to provide instruction and consultations for persons who wanted to learn how to select and to teach retarded children, in which capacity it can be said to have initiated "school psychology." Binet had founded it without a subsidy of any sort. He had also furnished the pieces of apparatus, except the weight scales provided by *La Société*. Before the official authorization of October 1905 he and Simon had used the pupils at Grange-aux-belles as some of the subjects for their first intelligence scale, Vaney had used them in preparing his first "barometer" of achievement in arithmetic, and Binet and Simon were already using them to establish their optometric scale for schoolchildren.[15] Binet's speech to the assembly of *La Société* included a mention of these activities, and it was so exuberant that it deserves further attention. Typically, he began with criticisms of the physical and medical examinations recommended by doctors,

22) ; there was a Cabinet d'anthropologie pédagogique founded in Arona, Italy, in 1897, but with different objectives. Dewey's laboratory school in Chicago, 1896, was not "experimental" in the same way (311, p. 62n.). Binet's initiative was finally recognized by a ceremony in Paris on 5 June 1971 when a plaque commemorating the opening of the "first French laboratory of experimental pedagogy" was placed on the school of the rue Claude Vellefaux that had replaced that of the rue Grange-aux-belles. Speeches were made that described the circumstances in which Alfred Binet and his intimate collaborator Dr. Théodore Simon had organized the laboratory. Binet's granddaughters and Mme Simon attended the ceremony, and in her ninety-sixth year Mme Simon thanked those who were present and who had arranged the homage.

[15] Binet had gradually spent less and less time at the laboratory of the Sorbonne, and with the establishment of this pedagogical laboratory, the break seems to have been more distinct. It should be noted, however, that from May 1905 until July 1911 the inside cover of the *Bulletin* carried the following invitation: "M. Binet receives the members of *La Société* Thursdays from 2:00 to 4:00 o'clock in his laboratory at the Sorbonne and puts himself at their disposal for the psychological information that they need."

and then went on in oratorical style to plead the case for the priority of studies of individual differences in general intelligence and special aptitudes, information that would make a difference in the teacher's approaches to his or her pupils: he argued that "it becomes as ridiculous to oblige a child to learn by heart what is beyond his capacity as to oblige a man who has a bad stomach to digest a copious and indigestible meal" (122, p. 25). As early as 1905 he had seen and proclaimed the eminent necessity of measuring "memory and judgment; imagination, arithmetical ability, the aesthetic sense; and habitual ways of thinking." He asked his audience: "But how can we accomplish these things?" To this rhetorical question he replied:

> In my opinion it was necessary to choose a little primary school with an intelligent director, zealous personnel, inspectors who are friends of progress . . . and to say to them: I bring you some beautiful ideas that perhaps, even probably, will be very useful to children. . . . It is a question of performing some periodic tests and measurements on the physical and intellectual development of your pupils. The work will be long, meticulous, and fairly painful, we do not conceal this from you; and for the moment it will not be rewarding in the material sense of the word. You will not be rewarded for your efforts by anything except the satisfaction of having served the cause of education usefully [122, p. 26].

Binet played on the audience: what did they think would happen? Would such attempts be successful? Would they be understood? His hearers would be wrong to be skeptical, he said, for happily it had already been accomplished, on the condition stipulated by the administration that "we must not forget to do everything under private initiative." He went on to enumerate the instruments that were in place, "the methods ready to study attention, memory, imagination, judgment," and to speak of the teaching personnel who were trained and willing to carry on the work. He complimented the director of primary education, the inspector, and the principal of the school for their cooperation. In a burst of enthusiasm, and with an extraordinary optimism in light of the limited resources then available, he exclaimed: "Let all the teachers who want to learn . . . all the fathers who wish to have their children's intelligence and aptitudes studied more closely, and all who believe that our initiative is a good and fruitful thing—let them all come and knock at the door of this new laboratory where they can be sure of receiving the best of welcomes" (122, pp. 25–27).[16]

To clarify the particular research objectives of the laboratory, Binet brought the whole field of pedagogy within three principal categories: first, the subject matter that is taught and its programs, aims, and objectives; second, the methods used, the recruitment and training of teachers, the distribution and length of classes, and the like; and finally, the characteristics of the children who are taught, their aptitudes and abilities, so that instruction can be "cut to their individual measures." These are the same categories that he repeated four years later in *Les idées modernes sur les enfants,* and in both instances he indicated that he himself had chosen the third: individual pedagogy, to study scientifically the capacities—physical, intellectual, and moral or psychological—of children. His feelings ran deeply and persistently with this priority. "Pedagogy ought to have as its preliminary task a study of individual psychology," he insisted (142, p. 11). He later struggled unsuccessfully to integrate this conception with the needs and demands of society.

Of course, many of the *sociétaires*' studies fitted into the second category, and, under Binet's guidance, they continued to do so. In the fall of 1906, at the end of the first year of formal operations in the school laboratory, Binet, Simon, and Vaney prepared a report of the activities "to

[16] The laboratory had a rather distinguished *Comité de patronage* of over twenty persons (*Bull.* 34, 1906, pp. 10–24). In addition to its experimental and indigenous instructional role, it opened its doors to people from abroad. We know that one visitor was "Mlle Lilie Martin, Professor of Psychology from the University of Stanford" in 1906; that Baldwin, Burt, Decroly, Huey, Goddard, and others followed later, especially after the 1908 revision.

date" (128, 130). Its evident historical interest requires that this report be summarized in some detail, which will show the confluence of the work in the laboratory with that of the *commissions* in *La Société*.

In one study Binet and Simon fixed on the problems connected with children's vision, since their visits to the schools had disclosed pupils who were "slow" simply because they could not see the blackboard. They actually produced a standardized test of vision that the teachers themselves could use without waiting for physicians' visits to the schools. Once more, however, Binet irked some medical doctors by these incursions into their territory; they criticized this scale so that Binet felt obliged to put it to a test in the hands of ophthalmologists who in the end justified its effectiveness. The story of this beleaguered confrontation shows to what extremes Binet would go both to test and to support his recommendations (132, pp. 141 ff.; 130, pp. 239–54; 142, pp. 79–91). Subsequent reports and studies indicate that this optic scale became an important practical adjunct in many schools, in Paris and in Bordeaux. The two collaborators also tried to work out a scale for auditory acuity, but the results were somewhat disappointing because the acoustic controls were too difficult to solve adequately.

One *commission* examined the correct posture for writing and considered it related to the much debated question of whether "vertical or slanted writing" was more desirable. Instruments were used that indicated that breathing was diminished when the children leaned against their desks, until it was discovered that this constriction was compensated for by an increase in abdominal respiration. Binet concluded that the "battle" was specious, and the decision only a matter of taste, unrelated to hygiene.

A group of teachers worked with Binet to develop standard tables of children's height, weight, shoulder width, lung capacity, muscular strength, and head measures; both sexes were represented for the primary grades. Binet believed that such tables, related to age-grade-status, would be useful and important information for the school and the home, especially if cumulative results for each child were kept in a health notebook, a *carnet sanitaire*, which he urged.[17] He wrote out many suggestions for the use of such records, but warned that new averages must always be calculated when the comparison group was not very similar to his original one.

Another *commission* compared the physical development of six hundred children with the social and physical status of their parents, and found the not surprising evidence that physically retarded children tend to come from poverty-stricken homes. The objective seems to have been to have data with which to stir public concern.

Another series of studies can be grouped under the general rubric of "psychological investigations." In one of these an attempt was made to devise tests to evaluate the "degrees of instruction" in arithmetic, reading, and orthography, although by 1906 only the first had been accomplished. These tests were definitely the forerunners of current achievement tests even though the actual results suffered from crude standardization (238, 239). Binet gave Vaney, the principal at the laboratory school, most of the credit for the difficult task of developing the forms for these tests. Both of these men were indeed initiators in contributing more precise controls in this area of education that was "vague and fluid," although again they were and have been practically ignored even by Frenchmen like Henri Piéron who have been interested in the problem of "docimology," or measures in experimental pedagogy. It is this kind of lack of appreciation that made François Zuza exclaim: "New proof that no

[17] This *carnet sanitaire,* or individual health record, was so important in Binet's eyes that he wrote to the editor, Henri Piéron, suggesting that he would prefer to write for the *Revue Scientifique* "a twelve-column article" about this health measure than one on graphology, which had previously been agreed upon (5, 31 December 1906). He wanted school doctors and teachers to become immediately aware of his practical offerings, and he felt that an article has more rapid penetration than a book. It was for this reason that he also requested space in the same *Revue* to write about the diagnosis of abnormal children and asked in return fifty copies for his own distribution (5, March 1907).

one is a prophet in his own country—especially if he is a Frenchman!" (311, p. 111).

Vaney's first test in arithmetic covered the end of the first to the end of the seventh school year and included items that "ordinary pupils" should have acquired for each grade. His population sample consisted of three hundred pupils in seven grades in a milieu of workers and little shopkeepers or employees.

The French pedagogue Professor E. Blum had scorchingly criticized the content of these tests as representing "nothing more than rote memory," and, as Binet noted, "he followed his statement with two question marks and an exclamation point." Binet replied, however, that they were "tests of memory in use—comprising attention, application, sustained effort, comprehension, method, emulation—measuring [objectively] the child's output" or achievement (128, p. 19). Binet saw the advantages of evaluating pupil-achievement by these tests as "avoiding chance, the caprice of sudden inspiration, the surprises of the association of ideas." Tests of reading and orthography followed soon after.

Another study attempted to establish a relationship between physical and intellectual development. It was a question that had produced contradictory answers in studies made in Belgium and the United States. Vaney hoped to settle it by measurements on twelve hundred children. After much labor scoring three physical measurements, by the number of years in advance or retard or equality with average age-grade status, he found a correlation, but, disappointingly, "a weak one."

There was a controversy between A. Belot and a testy pedagogue named M. Payot over the proper method of teaching spelling, and revolving around the question of whether words should be spelled out loud or learned as a whole. Belot concluded from his data that the former, with visual presentation, was superior, but he did not convince Payot.

Binet had not even then given up trying to find physical signs of intelligence. He guided some studies in which teachers were asked to judge intelligence by physiognomy and the form of the hand. Although there was some success better than chance, it was not striking. Nonetheless, Binet remarked: "Although it is all intuition [on the untrained teachers' part] it merits attention because we have not proved one way or the other whether rational methods could improve on this intuition" (128, p. 21).

These early results from the pedagogical laboratory and the work of *La Société* did force Binet to reconsider some of his assumptions about education. He wrote that he had started the laboratory school ". . . to introduce the most recent results of pedagogical research—those that specialists alone know—into the schools," but he soon realized that he was wrong. "What the primary schools need," he stated, "is not the unpublished methods that we could provide, but rather to be reminded of facts acquired long ago, elementary methods, which should be universally known, but that are instead universally unknown!" (130, p. 239). This was an important, and probably very difficult, admission for the man whose first book on pedagogy had been an aggressive attack on the whole educational process because of its failure to apply scientific methods to the problems of teaching. Even when they had them available they were not ready to use them.

There was some discussion in this report (128, 130) of the work with retarded children that Binet and his colleagues had extended to the community, and for which they apparently employed the crude 1905 scale. The laboratory examination could end in nothing very practical since, as Binet reminded his readers, "special schools for the retarded do not yet exist in France." The ministerial commission of which he was a member, at the conclusion of its work in 1905, had recommended the creation of special classes or schools for the retarded (127). As a result of their efforts, and undoubtedly other influences, Aristide Briand introduced a bill in the Chamber of Deputies in June 1907 proposing the establishment of special educational opportunities, and finally in April 1909 a law provided for *classes de perfectionnement*, classes for educational improvement, a title that Binet had suggested to prevent offending sensitive parents of mentally deficient children. In August of the same year another law decreed that teachers of the retarded must obtain a diploma or certificate of specialization (262, p. 108). Thus four years after the ministerial commission had proposed the development of such classes, the government agreed to create them.

Binet could not wait for such formalizations; in 1906 he obtained permission from Bédorez to organize some experimental classes. The first one opened in January 1907 with nineteen boys; the second in April with seventeen girls; a third in June with nineteen pupils; and five other classes followed soon after. At the same time Rector Thamin opened two in Bordeaux, and C. Chabot took steps to establish one in Lyons (133). Both of these men were members of the Committee of Patronage of the new laboratory at rue Grange-aux-belles. Among the associates enthusiasm about these new classes was great; even the title of the report (133) was set in large black type in the *Bulletin*.

Binet and Simon undertook all the selections of pupils for the first special classes in Paris. It was a delicate task to select those who really needed this instruction, and who could profit from it. Teachers were asked to indicate candidates on the basis of pupils who were three years retarded in school grade after nine years of age, or two years retarded before that age, provided that their school attendance had been regular; there must have been many extended absences due to prolonged illness or to parental apathy to education, since Binet always made a point of this requirement. The final selection of children was made after Binet and Simon had studied the pertinent medical reports, had personally observed the children, and finally had given them both the Vaney achievement test in arithmetic and parts of the 1905 Binet-Simon scale that appeared to distinguish normals from morons (134, pp. 97–105). This work took many days of their time, but Binet and Simon thought that it was most important to make the proper selection of prospects for these classes if they were to succeed in convincing the country of their usefulness.

These early experiences provided the material for *Les*

enfants anormaux, "a practical guide for the admission of retarded children into special classes," which the commission had requested. It was published on 5 June 1907. This is a thin little book that showed the obvious hiatuses about the subject at that time, and yet its contents should not have been neglected as they have been in the literature about Binet, for it is history-making in its account of early work with the retarded.

In his short discussion of the early contributors to the subject, like J.-E. Esquirol, J.-M. Itard, and J. P. Falret, Binet added amusing cautions to his guarded praise of E. Séguin:

> One should not look too closely at Séguin's work. Those who extol it certainly have not read it. He has not succeeded in being clear in his books, which contain many absurdities. . . . Indeed, we would [in the case of Séguin] concur heartily with what Ingres, the painter, said to his students when they were passing through the Rubens gallery in the Louvre: "Hail and salute it, but do not look at it!" [134, p. 5n.].

Binet went on to describe characteristics of the retarded and unstable by pressing his favorite point, which he took "from the Americans," namely, that retarded pupils show natural aptitudes for sensory and manual tasks. "This fact," he wrote, "should be capitalized upon in teaching them." He clarified the different roles of teachers, of primary inspectors, of physicians, and of psychologists in the special programs; he discussed the recruitment of pupils[18] and the imperative necessity of individualizing their edu-

[18] Along with the warnings about pitfalls in selecting special class pupils, Binet added others of a completely different nature: there were teachers, he said, who would try to get rid of annoying pupils by recommending them for these classes; others who were unconvinced that the backward students were anything other than lazy; teachers of special classes who would retain pupils now ready to return to regular classes, in order to maintain their enrollment levels; parents who wished to "protect" their children, or, on the other hand, who wanted to take advantage of getting rid of them in special residential schools, and so on. In other words, he had found mixed motivations for the "identification" of children for special education.

cation, which included the use of a lengthy questionnaire by the teachers to make them well acquainted with each child and his background (134, pp. 120–22). He presented the importance of evaluating the results of the special classes by means of tests of instruction like Vaney's and, especially in the case of morons, of evaluating their subsequent "social achievements" in their job histories. Moreover, he added that special education should be maintained "only for the educable," which *certainly* included morons and excluded idiots, but which waited upon research in the case of imbeciles. As a general rule he cautioned that "all decisions about individuals for special class enrollment should be provisional" (134, p. 124), which meant constant reevaluation of the individual's accomplishments. He also insisted that the teachers and their classroom effectiveness should be tested regularly by evaluating their pupils' performances. The last sentence of the little book repeated Binet's now familiar refrain:

> The essential thing is that everyone understand that empiricism [subjective experience] has had its day, and that the methods of scientific precision must be introduced into all the works of education, to bring light and good sense to them from every direction [134, p. 211].

In his announcement of the opening of the pedagogical laboratory Binet had invited there teachers who wanted to learn the techniques of giving the tests—optical, pedagogical, and psychological. Since their traditional preparation for teaching had lacked any training with the retarded, he also offered discussions of pedagogical methods suitable for these pupils, including the importance of sensory and manual training. Furthermore, he encouraged the interchange of ideas and viewpoints among the teachers themselves. While it was Binet's influence that finally brought about the 1909 law requiring a certificate of merit for these special teachers, he also urged a flexibility in the early procedures that allowed for some experimentation, and many changes, "so that teaching may evolve and improve itself like a living organism" (134, p. 51).

Annual Reports of La Société

During these years when the main thrust of Binet's own work was concentrated on the development of the 1905 scale into a more effective instrument, he also continued to work with the *commissions* of *La Société* that were interesting themselves in many aspects of education. Annual reports in the *Bulletin* kept the members abreast of the work completed during the previous year. At the end of 1907 this report indicated that the earlier studies on the teaching of spelling, the correct posture for writing, and others were still important concerns that aroused disputes and provoked new investigations. The *commission* on language undertook to study children's vocabularies as well as other language problems. A physician reported on nervous maladies among schoolchildren, and there was discussion about "unhealthful air" in the classrooms and methods for testing it. One *commission* continued the testing of the Binet-Simon optical scale and reported on its use, and another, led by A. Belot, tried to work out a program by which "normal" girls acted as "big sisters" for retardates by systematic after-school tutoring and found considerable success with it.

Under Binet's guidance Vaney had prepared the early versions of the reading achievement test. These tests were very difficult to devise and even more so to grade. The investigators finally settled on five levels of proficiency that went from "subsyllabic" at six to seven years to "fluent with expression" at ten to eleven years. The development of the tests threw considerable light on the difficult process of learning to read, and the discussions of this process may have dissipated some of the annoyance of parents and teachers when children were struggling with the early stages.

In Binet's annual summary (136) he complimented *La Société* for its success in bringing the idea of measurement "for the first time" into pedagogy. He was undoubtedly largely thinking about his own efforts to improve the scale for he announced that there would be a revision, and added that he now had firm hope that there would be methods for "a direct measure of children's intelligence" that would not only recognize the retarded, but also provide an understanding of normal children. He expressed his enthusiasm and optimism for the project in the exclamation: "What services the measures of instructional achievement and of intelligence are going to render for all of us!" (136). Evidently most of the work of standardization must have been completed by the end of 1907.

During 1908 Binet was thinking about extensions for the use of the intelligence scale in its revised and greatly improved form. With it, and the addition of Vaney's arithmetic and reading achievement tests, and the orthography scale that was in preparation,[19] diagnoses could be made with more confidence. He had already recognized their application to "normal" children; now he began to hypothesize about the possibility of identifying the above-normal, the élite whom he considered as the "only creators" within any society. He also recommended the application of tests for military recruitment and selection, and approached the Minister of War to request the appointment of a special commission to work out test trials within regiments (139, p. 94). Binet has told us enough to know that some of these tests were carried out, yet it was in the United States Army in 1917 that these dreams of his saw their fruition.[20]

[19] The tests for orthography went through many changes. Tests and discussions can be found in 134, p. 81; 148, No. 54, pp. 99-100; 152, pp. 4ff. The dictation might be as follows: "*Les jeunes bergères des villages rentrent à la nuit noire avec leurs agneaux qu' elles ont menés tout le jour dans les champs.*" The average number of errors was given for each age (e.g., 20-24 between seven and eight years). Every error of the rule of grammatical agreement of adjectives, participles, and verbs counted for one point, every error in spelling and accent also, although two errors was a maximum for any one word. Binet underscored the point that every child should be judged on *not less than three dictations;* and he was to have an equal opportunity in arithmetic problems and reading tasks. He consistently recognized that a single performance of any kind is not reliable.

[20] Professor J. Mark Baldwin, speaking to the General Assembly of *La Société* on 28 November 1918, in what he called his "bad French"—which was actually "revised" by the editors

Work on the scale did not prevent Binet from taking an interest in the projects of the *commissions* of *La Société*. Their concerns were largely devoted to the practical problems of the classroom. The *commission* on language, using experimental and control groups, tried several methods of improving students' French composition, but had no firm results to report. Another *commission* studied the teaching of science in the primary grades; since they could discover no evidence that the pupils had learned either useful applications or scientific viewpoints, they recommended that teaching methods must be improved or that the subject should be dropped from the elementary school curriculum. Other *commissions* studied children's positive character traits, their shortcomings, and their feelings about the meanings of "justice" in their daily lives.

Binet took particular interest in an attempt to formulate "mental exercises" that would strengthen sensory and mental faculties much as "physical exercises" strengthen physical health. In 1908 he, along with Belot and Vaney, published their recommendations for this *orthopédie mentale.* These exercises are described in several places (see especially 142, pp. 147–54, p. 201), and are undoubtedly useful for normal children as well as for the educably retarded. Binet noted that they appeared to awaken the attention of "scatterbrained pupils"; that they effected a healthy competition in pupils' work and increased their self-confidence. The authors developed other exercises for improving judgment, memory, and reasoning, some of which are suggested in the later *Les idées modernes sur les enfants* (142).

Another by-product of *La Société*'s interest in everyday school problems was the extension of the Binet-Simon optical scale to include tests for small children who could

of the *Bulletin*—remarked: "I am moved by the memory of my friend Alfred Binet and am happy to bring testimony to his memory. His works and those of Ribot are very well known in America; his tests, developed with the collaboration of M. le Dr. Simon, serve as a basis for numerous experiments, even in the services of the Army . . ." (263, p. 4).

not yet read; even these little ones might fail to accomplish the desired objectives if their eyesight was faulty.

A primary inspector named Levistre, wishing to evaluate the results of some of the special classes for the retarded, compared his own familiar subjective methods with those from Vaney's tests and found the latter superior. But more importantly he discovered by both methods that the retarded in general had gained on the average almost a school grade in a school year, or surprisingly had made practically "normal" progress: the special instruction and attention were providing striking results.

Reports in the *Bulletins* during 1908 also indicated that Binet had talked with the *sociétaires* about the new book by William James, *Talks with Teachers,* which had been translated into French as *Causeries pédagogiques* (138, pp. 114–20, pp. 167–68). He had long been a great admirer of the American psychologist-philosopher, but now he was evidently ruffled by James's harsh criticisms of his own attempt to apply scientific psychology to pedagogy: ". . . all the useful facts from that discipline could," James asserted, "be held in the palm of one hand." Furthermore, Binet thought himself the target of James's lengthy objections to "teaching teachers how to undertake scientific research." "One is not made into a good teacher by knowing psychological facts," James declared. Binet took issue with both viewpoints: there was evidence of "useful applications" far beyond the capacity of any palm to hold, and, while readily admitting that he himself would have difficulty in directing a class, it did not follow that because knowledge does not make a good teacher, it is therefore useless, or even dangerous, for a teacher to have it! Once again in this dialogue Binet's belief in the objectives of *La Société* becomes clear:

> . . . A teacher who decides to do some experiments in psychology on his pupils never wastes his time . . . since he has reflected, has read, has broken the deadly daily routine. . . . Indeed, does not this work cultivate his mind? . . . He who has taken the pains to study in detail some psychological question has seen his pupils in a new light

[*sous un jour inédit*], he has learned to know better their ideas, their tastes, their characters. This insures a certain benefit guaranteed even to the least effective [research] studies [138, p. 167].[21]

The tone of this talk is very defensive, perhaps because Binet admired James so much that he was hurt to have his objectives misunderstood. There are fairly frequent references to James in Binet's writings, and, upon hearing of his death in 1910, Binet wrote: "It is truly a Master who has disappeared, a Master who inspired not only respect and admiration, but a sincere feeling of affection" (162, p. xi).

During the next year, which was 1909, the discussion of school problems in *La Société* took a new direction, probably as a result of Binet's interest in the effects of various environmental factors on children's achievements. His friend M. Limosin, school principal at Samois, had worked at a study in which he found a close relationship between school and adult "success," with the conclusion that "the primary school should be credited with the preparation of children for their later lives." At first Binet endorsed his friend's conclusion, but quickly saw the error: both of the "successes" were related to the same condition. The children of upper-class parents had lifelong learning opportunities that were denied the poor, and this fact was of primary importance in their life experiences. "Misery and poverty," he wrote, "produce a lowering of all physiological measures, as well as a measurable attenuation of intelligence among primary school children." He went on to say: "A sociologist cannot fail to understand the gravity of these facts. Despite the Revolution, social classes continue to exist. . . . Their influences are confirmed equally by physiology, psychology, and morals . . ." (148, pp. 105–

[21] It is here that Binet stated to the shocked reader that he had had a very long experience in the schools—"more than twenty-five years," he wrote. This would have located the first "experience" in 1883! Moreover, he repeated this error in *L' Année* in 1908, p. 407, where he changed the twenty-five years to thirty, or a beginning date of 1878! It probably seemed that long.

6). And yet there was little that could be done about it.

La Société's *commissions* continued their research, but it must be admitted that the results were small and indecisive. Binet probably was as impatient as anyone with this situation. These *commissions* worked on the problems of teaching French composition, on the right age to start the teaching of reading, on children's vision, and on the progress of the retarded in special classes. There were also studies of children's games, their feelings, and "a vast inquiry on laziness." *La Société* also extended itself to *filiales* or outlying branches, this year to Lyons and indicating that "a larger number of teachers are beginning to be interested in our work," as L. Roussel, a teacher and secretary-general of *La Société,* wrote in his report (223, p. 27). In spite of the mediocre results, there was some real satisfaction among the members in Paris for the part they had played in the passage of the laws on behalf of the retarded.

Binet himself found another cause for which he felt he must enter the lists: it was a dispute over the proper methods to be used to teach deaf-mutes to communicate with their fellows. Before the controversy broke out, Binet and Simon had devoted considerable time to a study of the two institutions in Paris that provided instruction for these handicapped persons, and they had published their findings based on home visits to the deaf-mute graduates of the special schools. They were openly critical of the method by which the pupils had been taught to "speak," that is to communicate orally, which had been quite unsuccessful in trying to prepare them for jobs or for social relationships. The article in *L'Année* (147) must have jeopardized any cooperation with the personnel of the institutions when Binet wrote: "[These teachers and directors] should be rigorously eliminated from the work of evaluation . . . because of their [biased] convictions, practices, and interests"! The teachers replied by asserting that "outsiders" simply did not understand, and they would not consent to any investigation. This meant that Binet's wish to compare the "oral" method with one combining writing, lip reading, gestures, signs, and the like could not be carried out. He had proposed the use of psychological tests for the selection of "characteristic" students for the experiments. The *Bulletins* carried letters and counter-letters between Binet's group and the teachers (1909, No. 58, pp. 32–33; 1910, No. 59, pp. 68–72; No. 61, pp. 11, 118–20; No. 63, pp. 166–168), but the latter, especially angry because Binet and Simon had approached their graduates without their permission, would not agree even to a planning meeting. It was a very unfortunate affair because one of the most active members of *La Société,* G. Baguer, was the director of the school for deaf-mutes at Asnières. Baguer had been one of the strongest advocates in *La Société*'s work to achieve special education for the retarded and had taken a continued interest in this group. Binet's intemperate remarks and the subsequent controversy led to Baguer's withdrawal from the board of *La Société* (223, p. 27). Unfortunately for the deaf-mutes, the encounter had produced more heat than results.

Binet's productivity for 1909, apart from his role as counselor and guide for the *commissions* of *La Société,* was astonishing. Not only did he edit *L'Année,* study "the mystery of painting" (145), and show solicitude for the teaching of deaf-mutes, but with Simon he published the pregnant article "L'intelligence des imbeciles" (144), and he wrote his very popular book *Les idées modernes sur les enfants.* The first striking fact for the reader of this latter book is the contrast between Binet's attitude toward pedagogy in this volume and that taken a decade earlier in *La fatigue intellectuelle.* The latter had been filled with invective against "the old pedagogy that should not even be remodeled, but done away with altogether." Now in *Les idées modernes . . .* he clearly showed a more seasoned, mellower frame of mind: instead of "a manifesto," the rubric for his new volume became "his pedagogical testament" (311, p. 34). In it he summarized the results of "the last thirty years of research, both abroad and in France,"[22] that he considered to be significant for education.

[22] In what can perhaps be considered an exaggeration, Zuza has remarked of *Les idées modernes . . .* : "Despite its small size and its aspect of popularization, it is a veritable balance sheet of modern pedagogy" (311, p. 34).

The "old pedagogy" now became a candidate for revision rather than for complete dismissal or oblivion. Binet gave it the high credit of asking the right questions, for being concerned with "real-life problems," and for truly containing the heart and essence of the issues that needed investigation. He could not, however, refrain from pointing out its enduring weaknesses:

> . . . It is too generalizing, too vague, too literary, too moralistic, too verbal, too preachy. . . . The ancient pedagogy, and that of the present day, has had an especially empirical [*expérientiel*] origin. Teachers, of course, have made some useful observations. . . . I would compare [the educational practices and programs] to an old wagon that creaks and moves very slowly, but nevertheless—it moves. . . . From time to time there have been . . . some excellent innovations, but the general flaw in these efforts [*tentatives*] is that they present no evidence, no control. . . . Its theory, its doctrine are so vague and nebulous—they are not precise enough even to be called false [142, p. 339].

Interestingly enough for current readers, Binet also made brief references to another kind of pedagogy, called "the new pedagogy," that was so scientific in a very technical way that its scope was contestable and its fragmentation and dismemberment defied efforts to put or to hold it together. "It was," he said, "like a machine thought up by people of the laboratory who have no feeling for school or for life, who seem never to have put their noses to the window of their laboratories" (142, p. 341). He provided no further identification of this "new pedagogy."

In *Les idées modernes* . . . Binet proposed to combine the two main viewpoints: the old pedagogy would present the problems to be studied, while the experimental pedagogy would provide the methods and processes for studying them. Conforming to this plan, he offered to his readers educational principles and usages based as much as possible upon experimental evidence, while at the same time he recognized the incomplete nature of many of its results. Of the three categories of pedagogical problems—programs, methods of instruction, and children's aptitudes—he reiterated his intention of devoting himself mostly to the third. The programs or objectives, which were not experimentally determinable, were outside of the proper scope of psychology. He felt that sociology should be closely involved in making recommendations about objectives, because they would differ with races, countries, groups, classes, children, and eras, and should be defined within the needs of these recognized differences. With regard to the second category—the methods—he was reporting the work of foreign investigators as well as of members of *La Société*. He himself, however, had stressed and would continue to stress individual psychology.

Binet had observed in countless schoolrooms and in "hundreds of books on education" a disregard of these differences, group and individual. Indeed, he objected, sometimes children were viewed as "little men," with their differences overlooked: differences in character, in ways of thinking and of feeling, in abilities and aptitudes, in physique and even in age, so that "when chance has brought together on the same school bench a child of nine years next to another of twelve years, the same effort is demanded of both, with unjust punishment for unequal performances." His own studies and observations led him to the conclusion that "pedagogy should have as a preliminary condition a study of individual psychology" (142, p. 11). This is hardly surprising in light of his research over the previous two decades.

In several chapters Binet suggested other criteria for a good school. There should be objective evaluations of everything possible, primarily to test the teachers' competence. Pupils in each grade could be tested by means of measures of their achievement in all school subjects; this could be accomplished by extensions of Vaney's work. Furthermore, the pupils should be followed in later life by reports of their vocational successes or failures. Finally there should be scientific tests to compare teachers' performances when they were teaching in similar circumstances, and also to evaluate various teaching procedures. He also advocated the analysis of anthropometric data, physical and physiological, to provide possible clues to individual differences in effort, attention, and even intelligence. He stressed the importance of measuring visual and auditory acuity. He also prescribed the determination of the global intelligence of pupils by using the Binet-Simon metric scale, which he surprisingly summarized in the book by listing the title of each subtest and then recommending it to parents as a means of estimating their children's intelligence. At that time it was practically inconceivable for most people to think of measuring anything as nebulous as "intelligence"; therefore, in this case we can assume that it is possible that he wanted to acquaint the public, by means of concrete examples, with the nature of such measurement, based on the average ages when children could perform certain mental achievements.

The book went on to recommend special classes for the retarded that should include *orthopédie mentale*, practice in everyday life activities like proper table manners and social greetings, and preparation for a modest vocation. All of these could be carried on in small groups, which was a necessary consideration for these pupils. Other lessons like reading would require individual attention. Binet advocated short and varied lesson periods, and again the principle of gradualness to distribute judiciously and progressively the difficulties of a subject. He believed that a child learns best when he is allowed to discover ideas rather than being told about them. He should be permitted to act spontaneously and to judge his own actions; to learn to evaluate his conversation, reading, and events of the day because he would thereby learn to be a person on his own account (142, p. 158). This general principle of "active learning," he insisted, was as applicable to the retarded as to normal children.

Binet's concern for these deficient children continued to be manifest. He pointed out that at least the educable need not be condemned to useless and barren lives if society would only take an interest in them. He had nonetheless an important caveat. In Germany for about fifty years special classes for the retarded had been common, but very little or no progress had been made either in the manner of identifying pupils, in controlled studies of the relative effectiveness of various teaching methods, or in investigations of their postschool destinies. He suggested that the basic reason for this fact was that, in spite of the galaxy of psychological talent in the German universities, "none of the foremost psychologists—like Müller, Kraepelin, Ebbinghaus, Külpe, Meumann, or Wundt—had ever [profoundly] studied the retarded child . . . especially the moron, to discover his mental apparatus" (137, p. 59). He obviously believed that he and his *confrères* in *La Société* were doing a better job and would continue to do so. Small wonder that in his *Les idées modernes* . . . he should persist in urging special education for the retarded and special studies of them. In the same year of its publication he and Simon had published as profound a study of imbeciles as had yet appeared (144).

But Binet was not solely concerned with the retarded, the deaf mutes, those with optical difficulties, and the like. At the other extreme of the classroom population he found another group that should have special education: the gifted. He may have been one of the first to urge the organization of special classes for the "above-average." He argued that it is "through the élite, and not through the efforts of the average that humanity invents and makes progress," and therefore children with superior intelligence should "receive the education that they need" (142, p. 109).[23] He had no recommendations for educating these children, but wished to press the importance to society of this "source of strength."

Binet's close and careful observation of individuals made him aware very early of individual differences in special aptitudes that must become the concern of the school in order to meet the needs both of the individual and of society.[24] The scale was, by contrast, a measure of

[23] Binet and Simon also urged the importance of gifted children when they addressed a society of medical doctors and recommended the use of their test to help in discovering these children (143, p. 2).

[24] It is not clear whether Binet used "faculties" and "aptitudes" interchangeably. In his writing he frequently used the former word, as we have noted; as early as 1904 a *commission* of *La Société* organized a study of "individual aptitudes" to investigate imagination, natural language development, and

general, of global intelligence that brought out *degrees* of difference with only slight or ancillary distinctions of a sensory and verbal nature. In *Les idées modernes . . .* he turned to this question of special aptitudes and ruminated at length about it, giving attention especially to aptitudes for drawing, music, foreign languages, composition, and mathematics. Predictive measures would be important for the selection of and preparation for career or job situations, and should underlie instructional methods. His discussion took on the attributes of wishful thinking since he acknowledged that the study of aptitudes was "scarcely sketched out," that the necessary application of correlations "is still badly understood," and finally that "on this point we are in the science of tomorrow" (142, p. 343).

Yet in 1909 Binet was writing for parents and teachers who should be concerned about educational methods and their relation to occupational choices. With scientific measurements so wanting, was there anything to be suggested to lead to possible insights? Binet replied affirmatively. In the matter of the retarded, for instance, their sensory and manual abilities were usually greater than their verbal or abstract ones. Manual training and parallel activities should therefore be stressed in their education, while at the same time society must be persuaded to abandon its snobbish preferential acclaim of verbal intelligence (142, p. 288). In the case of normal children, parents and teachers should talk with them, observe them, and note whether their stated interests accorded with their actual actions and accomplishments. For example, if the child has a choice of activities, to which one does he return most often? If he reads only science or mechanics, or spends his

aptitude for naming objects in pictures. This vocabulary test of fifteen words was given to two hundred and six children, six to eight years of age, and the results were analyzed according to sex and residential locales (104). This early search was obviously for "special" aptitudes. "Aptitudes" or "faculties" by whatever name, Binet continued to recognize that their determination was an important adjunct to the global evaluation of intelligence by means of the Binet-Simon scale.

Sundays drawing, his interests and perhaps his abilities would lie within these orientations rather than within literary ones. He also advocated studying children's play, for, he said, "A school yard is a marvelous field for observation" (165, p. 175). He offered particular minor case studies to discuss and to serve as warnings against too hasty conclusions, and indicated that the matter of vocational choice was further complicated by the fact that there had been no analyses of various occupations that would enumerate their particular requirements. Here again, however, one could judge some vocations by ordinary, natural observations. The point was that teacher, parent, and child should "work on the matching" between abilities and interests.

Although measurements fell so short, Binet proposed that more could be done by teachers to estimate abilities. Many studies had shown how "memory," for example, could be measured; how habitual modes of thought could be judged; how *results* or performances and achievements could be utilized as indications of aptitudes. And yet there were difficulties to be avoided. He analyzed the suggestion then being made by educators for *l'école sur mesure*, that is, a school made to order for each child. He felt that although "homogeneous classes could give partial assistance," such specialized, individualized education, if carried too far, might lead to too narrow an education. There are certain viewpoints and bodies of knowledge that all children should learn, for their own edification and to become useful members of the community. Furthermore, since society is in a continual process of change, its demands also change, which makes too narrow a specialization disastrous.

Nonetheless, Binet declared that, as far as possible, the individual should fulfill himself, his aptitudes, his natural orientations of thought, his interests. On the other hand, this self-fulfillment must be satisfied within the framework of society's demands. He so fully realized that the latter were imperious that he urged, for example, that even retarded children must, if at all possible, be taught to read and write. For some this would be a very painful process, but the effort must be made and new teaching methods developed to attain these objectives, since reading and writing play such an important role in social living, especially in large cities (142, p. 12). There were, therefore, cultural and societal demands that must attenuate, perhaps even complement, any all-out individualization of *l'école sur mesure*. From the present perspective there seemed little danger, however, that the pendulum would go too far in a school system mired in rigid and unindividualized procedures.

It was these considerations that have given Binet both the credit of being the first "educator" to make clear and insistent this distinction between the individual and society, and also of failing to solve this conundrum. The latter criticism seems unjust since the problem still plagues us today.

Another topic on which Binet wrote a long chapter in *Les idées modernes* . . . was that of "the education of memory," which is related, of course, both to special aptitudes and to instruction at home and in school. He included an explanation of the principal "laws of learning" that had been developed "over a period of about thirty years of laboratory studies" in various countries, notably in Germany and America. "To learn how to learn" was his springboard, and his illustrations of the principle of gradualism are homely and pleasing (pp. 209–32). Binet shows almost a romantic respect for "memory" in the following case that he makes for its significance in complicated intellectual activities:

Certainly memory is one of the most powerful mental faculties, and if one examines its distribution . . . one will see that it is proportional to intelligence. . . . Among the average types of humanity, all faculties present only small variations; but for the accomplished types, like a Leibnitz or a Goethe, one sees that all of these admirable intelligences had an encyclopedic memory. . . . To make their grand syntheses, they had to know much, to retain much, and consequently, to possess a great memory. . . .

Memory is like a great animated and intelligent book that opens its pages to the necessary places. Let us say more precisely that memory furnishes the abundance of materials on which thought works. The more the critical spirit is refined by comparisons, the more the imagination is enriched in its developments. Memory, without perhaps augmenting the profoundness of intelligence, gives it richness, mass, quantity; it is like a multiplication of its products [142, pp. 163-64].

If Th. Simon was correct, Binet was personally acquainted with the ramifications of memory, for he reported that Binet's memory was "phenomenal." He was certainly convinced that training was significant to its performance, and made many practical suggestions in this direction.

His final chapter in *Les idées modernes* . . . was on the subject of "laziness and moral education." It is almost an exposition in parent education, built out of intuition, the psychology of learning, and common sense. There is little to quarrel with in its emphasis on letting natural consequences influence children's behavior, on the use of "social sanctions," on a minimum of punishment for undesirable behavior and a maximum of reinforcement of desirable behavior through "centers of interest," qualified approval, appropriate material rewards, and practice, as in altruism, for example. And yet he must have recognized the subjective, wordy, opinion-weighted nature of this chapter, for François Zuza reports that "Binet admitted to Dr. Simon that his book *Les idées modernes* . . . included weak spots. Among them, he was the first to criticize the chapter on 'moral education' and to be astonished that this one brought him the most praise" (311, p. 46, n. 1).

In conclusion, in *Les idées modernes* . . . Binet seems to have come to the point of talking about pedagogy without strong distinctions of "old," "new," and "experimental." He saw himself in the advanced wing of the field. There are several possible hypotheses about the influences at work on him during the decade between his attack on "the old pedagogy" in 1898 and his mellowed appreciation of it in 1909. It is unquestionably his close relationship with educators—teachers, principals, inspectors, supervisors, directors of education, and university professors in *La Société*—and with hundreds of children and their parents that furnished him many moving experiences within the educational process, increased his sensitivities, and influenced and forged his own attitudes both as scientist and as crusader.

The last two years of Binet's life continued to be busy ones. His crusading spirit led him to try a second time to establish an international and permanent committee of pedagogy, with the aim of providing substantive, informational exchanges among experimental psychologists and educators and of disseminating educational developments among those interested in many countries. He had first made the proposal in 1905, but "for reasons of health" he had at that time excused himself from making the plea in person, and had sent his friend Professor J. J. Van Biervliet of the University of Ghent to present his plans to a congress meeting in Liège, Belgium. The proposal was adopted with few changes, and Binet was elected president with Van Biervliet as vice-president. The whole project, however, was stillborn. Zuza believes that some political considerations might have become obstacles, but Piéron suggested that Binet's personality was a significant factor: after all, he "never" attended meetings in other countries, and, consequently did not know personally many people abroad (256).

Five years later, in 1910, when a competitive group organized by M. C. Schuyten of Antwerp met in Paris, Binet and Van Biervliet had also revived their organization and urged the fusion of the two groups. Schuyten, however, vigorously protested (225) on the grounds that the Binet-Biervliet project emphasized applications, while, in contrast, he and his colleagues had a "purely scientific objective." Once again the Binet plan was dropped. There could be several reasons for the failure; the Belgians' refusal to share their programs may have dulled the enthusiasm of the Paris-based program, or it may have been that Binet's personality became an obstruction. He was able to function easily in *La Société*, but seems never to have been at home in the presence of his peers at international congresses. Even though very little actually came of his proposal, it has been credited as a project that anticipated the *Association internationale de pédagogie expérimentale de langue française* formed in 1958 (262, p. 226); such claims are dubious. The only certainty is that Binet envisioned the possibility of an international society that could keep current the educational insights being developed in all countries active in the field.

During these last two years Binet also maintained close contact with the work of *La Société*. The *commissions* considered introducing American projects of student self-government into authoritarian France, investigated possible improvements in school hygiene, and considered the influence of parental alcoholism and of fatherless families on pupil morality. Vaney used the Binet-Simon intelligence scale to test a gifted child and, probably for the very first time, published an item-by-item analysis of the interesting results (*Bull.* 1910, No. 63, pp. 160–65). Binet entered the fray to discuss the current debate concerning the maintenance of "religious neutrality" in the schools, and, unable to provide evidence of its consequences in the adult lives of the pupils, he remained undecided and claimed that others must do so also (150). He also offered more evidence to convince teachers that their judgments of their pupils would be sharpened and enlightened by the use of objective measures—of intelligence, of memory, of physique, and so on (151). Another *commission* extended the earlier studies of children's "use" and "comprehension" vocabularies by adding an investigation of developmental changes in grammatical syntax (*Bulls.* 1906, No. 30; 1910, No. 61; 1911, No. 72).

When *La Société* celebrated its tenth anniversary, its secretary-general, L. Roussel, happily reported that its efforts had shown the educational world the "necessity for breaking with a routine pedagogy." Its activities, Roussel insisted, "had shown them the child, no longer as a passive being whom we force into acquiring a mass of knowledge, but as a personality whose faculties must be known and developed." As more and more of the teaching personnel were adopting these new ideas, he saw the usefulness of the work of the *commissions* on French education in "a real cultivation of the critical spirit . . . and an enlarged inclination toward, and love for, the child" (223, p. 31). Binet, as president, added another dimension to the importance of *La Société* when he informed its members that almost daily he "received from France and abroad evidence that we are noticed: . . . teachers, publicists, scholars, political men write to me to ask information about our work and projects, to request consultations on difficult cases, or to let me know that they approve heartily of the precise, experimental, and disinterested work that *La Société* pursues . . ." (150, p. 87). He regarded this correspondence as "comforting testimonials" to *La Société*.

The optimism about *La Société's* work and place in the European educational world may have been somewhat exaggerated, and yet it surely was true that this little group of men and women were in the forefront of a movement that was remolding the educational institutions of France and other countries of the Western world. They were identifying problems that laws requiring universal education presented to society at large as well as to the people who were responsible for the teaching of the young. Surely Binet and his *confrères* can be pardoned if their achievements had not kept pace with their aspirations.

Binet was not to see much more of *La Société*'s work for death overtook him and ended his career. The *Bulletin* for August/October 1911 (212) carried in a black frame the announcement of his death on 18 October, "following a cerebral apoplexy," a diagnosis that is much in doubt. It also recorded Professor P. Malapert's words spoken at Binet's graveside in Montparnasse cemetery in Paris. He emphasized his relation to *La Société*:

> . . . When he came to us as our President . . . he did so with the firm intention of dedicating to us a great part, perhaps the best part, of his activity. . . . What happy stimulation he gave to our work, how much time and effort he reserved for us, this great worker; with what sureness of method he directed, supported our research, with what modesty he made us profit from his own, how well he knew how to combine with the most scrupulous demands of

> scientific investigation the lively, penetrating feeling of pedagogical realities, the constant and judicious concern for practical applications. . . . Those who have worked with him have been especially able to judge his indefatigable zeal over long years, his reliable character, the cordiality of his welcome, the smiling good grace that never abandoned him. All these qualities made him, not only the most venerated of presidents, but a friend, very sure and very dear . . . [212, pp. 1-2].

This encomium must have come from the heart, for members of *La Société* long remembered Binet as the man who taught them to be more critical of "authoritative" or "expert" opinions and more appreciative of their pupils' problems and individual needs. Teachers, administrators, parents, and public officials alike saw him as their leader as in 1917 they proudly renamed *La Société libre pour l'étude psychologique de l'enfant* as *La Société Alfred Binet.* He had left his mark on educational activities because his crusade embraced the practical needs of his time and also presented a vision of educational psychology to bring it within the purview of the social sciences.

8 Epilogue

This book has been the story of the growth and accomplishments of an eminent scientist who, as his friend and colleague Théodore Simon once remarked, "attempted to penetrate the human mind, to analyze its wellsprings, to understand [it as] a complete whole" (296, p. 357). It was an ambitious program, impossible to achieve even if death had not prematurely ended Binet's labors. Binet obviously believed that he could not arrive at his goal by single-mindedly following one aspect of his problem to the exclusion of all others, and furthermore his restless curiosity was not attuned to such an objective. Therefore, his life work really was a *carrefour* with roads extending in many directions, all of them unfinished. He tried to penetrate too many aspects of the human personality to be able to reach many conclusions about them, and yet we must allow him his own modest claim that he did "achieve some fragments of the 'truth.'" Perhaps even more important, however, is the fact that his efforts to solve the puzzles of psychology have provided the base for much research since his death; if more students had been willing to dig into his voluminous writings, there probably would have been much more work inspired by his insights. Even so this man of ideas, of projects, of imaginative research programs has earned a secure place in the history of psychology even though he left so much of his work incomplete.

The question of priorities in science is a very delicate one, and yet it seems obvious that Binet has never been given sufficient credit for his original contributions. His work on imageless thought and the method of systematic introspection should merit at least equal consideration to that of the Würzburg school. His experimental work and discussions of the psychology of legal testimony should be recognized as having preceded those of Stern and his coworkers who built on it without appropriately crediting Binet's earlier investigations. His approaches to the "experimental" study of children, begun as early as 1890, should be included in any account of the history of child psychology, at least as precursors to experimental studies of children's cognition and perception. His large volume on suggestibility is, for that time, a model of originality and inventiveness. His creative, strong, and continued advocacy of experimental pedagogy, including the development of achievement tests, and his conspicuous, original efforts on behalf of retarded children should have earned for him a prominent place in the history of education. Further, one finds in his publications adumbrations of introversion-extroversion, of the importance of individual modes of thinking, of levels of aspiration, of small-group social psychology, of comparative psychology. In fact, the reading of Binet's voluminous publications in the Bibliothèque Nationale, where he himself began his studies of psychology, produces a strong impression that if a subject-index of his publications were made, many doctoral candidates and postdoctoral researchers in psychology would find a pertinent reference there. His work indeed illustrates "the spiral of history" in psychology.

It would be impossible to state categorically the reasons for Binet's eclipse. Without much doubt he would have been more visible and more fully recognized if he had confined his labors to a narrower or at least a less-dispersed field. Probably an investigator draws more attention if he concentrates and focuses his problem range. Moreover, French psychology itself lacked focus in the absence of any French "school" of psychology (34, p. 8). Again, Binet lost opportunities to attract a wide psychological audience by his failure to publish some of his significant, integral concepts in a coordinated series, instead of scattering them in media serving different readers. He also jeopardized his reputation by several articles in *L'Année* that showed regrettable proof of careless, hurried preparation. Yet these seem to be insufficient reasons for the lack of attention given to his work.

It appears plausible to seek further insight by comparing Binet's career with that of his German contemporaries, especially Wundt, who has been so much more celebrated in the history of psychology, despite the fact that Binet's work is clearly more closely related to the directions of current psychology. Wundt's advantage surely cannot rest on any assumed difference between an experimentalist and a nonexperimentalist, or between a student of the normal versus the pathological, for Binet also regarded measurement as the necessary condition for the growth of psychology, and his concern for pathology per se was primarily as a means of providing more insights into so-called normal personality. Indeed, in the framework of twentieth-century psychology it is Binet who has the advantage. While he frequently used the language of faculty psychology, his conceptions were clearly those of a functionalist, and he was very critical of structural approaches. Again, while Wundt's subjects were mostly university men studied within a laboratory setting, Binet's were varied in sex, age, and status and his settings were diverse. Moreover, instead of Wundt's studious attempts to reduce the troublesome results of individual differences, Binet cannot be denied a foremost place among those who have made these individual differences a key problem of psychology. This was, in fact, his theme-with-many-variations.

There seems to be little doubt that a really important deterrent to the actualization of Binet's influence and reputation lay in the university climate of France as compared with that of Germany. Under the German university system, for example, Wundt was able to institutionalize his position at the University of Leipzig, both with a professorship and the founding of a laboratory from which a generation of followers expanded and extended his work. In contrast, Binet was not able to achieve a professorship at the Sorbonne, for neither his background, his education, nor his social and political predilections fitted the pattern of French institutional requirements; and he was not even honored by a chair at the Collège de France, for which the above requirements were not as rigid. This failure to achieve a professorship restricted his prestige and influence, abroad as well as in France.

It was not only this fact, however, that undoubtedly limited the number of his students. French students were discouraged by the fact that the field of psychology did not offer them employment in the lycées, since it was not included in the curricula, and American students, who were then seeking training in Europe to prepare themselves for professorships in the United States, were unable to obtain a diploma at the Sorbonne. Unlike the German universities, the Écoles des Hautes-Études in the Sorbonne, which included Binet's laboratory, were not authorized to award certificates to mark the successful completion of graduate programs. The students, then, would have to return empty-handed to the campuses in the United States. Binet's attempts to change this situation were entirely unsuccessful. Therefore, as Wundt's influence continued to expand through his students both in Europe and especially in the new laboratories in the United States, French publications became less and less read abroad. Thus it is not surprising that German psychology simply overwhelmed the almost single-handed efforts of the first and foremost experimental psychologist in France.

With the advent of the intelligence scale, however, fame came to Binet; probably to his own astonishment, his name rocketed into prominence. A few months after his death an unsigned necrologist in the *Bulletin* of *La Société* exclaimed that "beyond the frontiers of France there has been for a long time agreement in esteem and praise [for Binet's work]. In Switzerland, in Belgium, in Germany, in England, in Holland, in Italy, in the United States, and even in Japan, Alfred Binet is a name . . ." (*Bull.*, 1911, No. 74, p. 4). Nor was this judgment wrong, for among other newspapers in Europe the Brussels *Soir* and the *Journal de Genève* carried laudatory articles about him. Most of his admirers did not know the full extent of his interests and work, but the intelligence scale had catapulted him to international status and established his reputation as a psychologist.

The Binet-Simon scale, though imperfectly, had accomplished an objective that had been sought all over the

Western world, namely, a reasonably brief and convenient means of estimating degrees of intelligence. It offered assistance to many pressing social and educational needs, and unquestionably was a breakthrough of high importance. Ever since its introduction scholars have, in superlative terms, expressed their appreciation of it. One specialist in the field of individual differences summed it up with the remark that "probably no psychological innovation has had more impact on the societies of the Western world than the development of the Binet-Simon scales" (J. J. Jenkins and D. G. Paterson, *Studies in Individual Differences*, Appleton-Century-Crofts, 1961, p. 81). Its use has become worldwide, both for practical and research purposes.

Unquestionably this instrument has been justly esteemed, but there is reason to doubt whether its later development has continued in the spirit characteristic of its discoverer. Binet's last revision was dated 1911; it is astonishing to see how negligible have been the changes in substance or in scope since that time. There are weighty reasons for this conservative development. Large investments in time and money have been devoted to standardizations and restandardizations, and also there are hundreds or even thousands of investigations where it has been used as a comparative research instrument. This means, however, that the scale is in danger of becoming an unexamined fixture in the psychological armamentarium, rather than representing a developing conception of the growth and measurement of intelligence. Had he lived, Binet very probably would have continued to improve the scale; he would have added studies of special and general aptitudes to complement it, and, since he had a "passion to understand the human mind," he would surely have observed its operations in more investigations. In fact, he might have agreed completely with Piaget's comment:

. . . Binet, a subtle analyst of thought processes, was more aware than anybody of the difficulties of arriving, through his measurements, at the actual mechanism of intelligence. But precisely because of this feeling of doubt,

> he had recourse to a kind of psychological probabilism. . . . It is indisputable that these tests of mental age[1] have on the whole lived up to what was expected of them: a rapid and convenient estimation of an individual's general level. But it is no less obvious that they simply measure a "yield" without reaching constructive operations themselves . . . [*Origins of Intelligence in Children,* pp. 153–54].

These "constructive operations" were nonetheless characteristic of Binet's thinking. For example, his 1890 studies of his daughters' number sense, perceptions, and other cognitive functions; his subtle investigations of individual modes of thinking; his resolute and persistent analyses of language and thought, of images and thought, and of the dynamics of the mental functioning of imbeciles that led him to his proposed dimensions of intelligence: all of these were directed toward his objective of "understanding the human mind." There is good reason to assume that his work was an inspiration to Piaget's own ingenious investigations of "constructive operations." Furthermore, Binet's work on intelligence measurement, with its deep and intrinsic foundations in experimental psychology, should be considered as an essential progenitor of current investigators and theorists like the late L. L. Thurstone, like J. P. Guilford, A. Anastasi, D. Wechsler, and others. Binet will always be remembered for mental measurement, but in his own writing he constantly warned that such measurements oversimplify the complexities of the human mind and indicated that understanding or explanation must go far beyond the possibilities of the measurements of that day—or perhaps of any day.

Binet's own spectrum was broad, probably too broad in those early stages of the discipline called psychology. He stressed the need to carry on investigations under conditions as natural as possible, urging observations beyond the walls of the laboratory. He was interested in human

[1] Here we find even Piaget making the mistake of attributing the phrase "mental *age*" to Binet. See chap. 5 for a discussion of the important contrast between "mental *age*" and "mental *level*."

behavior in all its forms; his subjects included infants, children, adults—normal, retarded, mentally ill, criminal, and representative of all classes of society. He utilized as subjects his collaborators and students, his family, visitors to his laboratory, friends, and servants, and he took his paper, pencil, and usually simple instruments to the laboratory, to military caserns, to schools, to institutions for the mentally abnormal, and into his own study at home. By traveling into so many avenues of the *carrefour*, his diverse efforts, his multifarious interests, his many substantive objectives may suggest superficiality. Since all of his publications are not of equal value, and a few are surprisingly crude, some of them undoubtedly fall under this rubric. Yet a careful reading of his original articles and books reveals a truly productive and fruitful record.

Binet's approach to problems was inventive and original. His systematic variations of stimuli, for example, in his studies of memory and suggestibility, of visual illusions, of touch thresholds, and of individual modes of cognition; his incredible tenacity in trying out age-appropriate items for the intelligence scale—all show a sensitive and trenchant insight into the diversity of possible independent variables. In many of these cases the reader can follow his reasoning almost step by step as he tried to clarify his strategies. He reported his failures, his hesitations, his changes from one experimental condition to the next, his quandaries about interpretations.

Binet's wide-ranging intelligence did not even stop at the frontiers of psychology. The "General Reviews" in *L'Année* included extensive representations of learned disciplines that were even remotely related to psychology; and the same can be said about the short-lived *L'intermédiare biologique*. Furthermore, although he felt that metaphysics and psychology must be carefully differentiated, he specifically warned against proscribing the validity of the former. At a time when sociology was striving for recognition he maintained that psychology depended in large measure upon this discipline, that is, that the study of man's place in society is necessary to an understanding of his behavior. He even credited sociology with enlightened and significant viewpoints about the nature and alleviation of "insanity."[2]

Because Binet did not theorize even to the extent of giving a definition of intelligence for fear of "setting" or imposing only a priori concepts, and because he attacked some theorists who ignored relevant evidence, he was sometimes reproached for being an enemy of theory. Once he answered this charge in the following way:

> This reproach is unjust. We encourage discussions of theory, *before* experimental researches, to prepare them, and *after*, to interpret them; what we reject with all our might are theoretical discussions that replace the exploration of facts. . . . The ideal scientific method should, in our opinion, be a collaboration of theory and experimentation, a collaboration well summarized in the following formula: a prolonged meditation upon the facts collected at first hand [139, p. 1 n.].[3]

It was this gathering of facts at first hand that he always emphasized. Joseph Peterson underlined this characteristic a half-century ago when he wrote: "Binet has shown a master's hand in discovering realities in human nature and in letting facts lead rather than being determined by prejudice and theories" (283, p. 149). Binet's remarks about the metric scale provide an excellent example:

> It was constructed slowly, with the help of studies made not only in primary and preprimary schools on children of all ages . . . but also in hospitals and hospices, on idiots, imbeciles, and morons, and finally in all sorts of milieux—even the regiment—and on adults, literate and illiterate. After some hundreds of verifications and improvements,

[2] Any suspicion that such an acceptance of sociology was quite general at that time should be corrected by the reminder that Paul Janet told Durkheim that sociology would surely lead one to insanity (273, p. 66).

[3] Mary Henle has provided me with a very nice parallel to this statement in Darwin's *Autobiography*, where Mrs. Darwin quoted her husband as saying: "It is a fatal fault to reason whilst observing, though so necessary beforehand and so useful afterward" (*Autobiography*, edited by Nora Barlow [London: Collins, 1958], p. 159).

my opinion, ripened and more definitive, is not that the method is perfect, but that it is indeed the one that must be used; and if, after us, others improve it, as we certainly hope they will, they will do so only by using our own procedures and by drawing profit from our experience [142, p. 125].

Such apparent self-assurance, however, is belied by other observations that indicate Binet's real ambivalence and uncertainty. Time and again, he was so critical of his own work that Fr. Paulhan once wrote that "to criticize Binet I have almost always applied his own testimony to his work" (216, p. 308). Sometimes, in fact, "his own testimony" was so critical that he almost denied the value of an enormous labor, for example, in his conclusion to *L'étude expérimentale de l'intelligence.* In this instance, and others less flagrant, he showed that characteristic pattern of first harshly criticizing the work of others, following this with some high claims for his own improvements, only then to disparage his accomplishments by calling them "simply a bare sketch," "only descriptive," and therefore scientifically inadequate and quite incomplete. This is undoubtedly the basis for one critic's disappointment in Binet, when he wrote: "However, after a marvelous exposition . . . one waits avidly for some conclusions—but he swerves from them. . . . Binet, so to speak, never comes to a conclusion . . ." (279, p. 17). It is true that this caution about drawing conclusions was characteristic of Binet, even, or especially, with regard to the nature and measurement of intelligence. He had become sensitive to the possible influences of suggestion, on subject and experimenter alike, cautioning that "it is always necessary to give a good reception to facts that are in disagreement with our own theories" (90, p. 130), or "that which one does not understand well, one ignores" (*L'Année*, 1910, 16, p. 487). Probably more important was his recognition of, and concern with, the overwhelming complexities of the nature of man.

Simon's move from Paris in 1908 deprived Binet of their daily collaboration in investigations with school children. Perhaps it was this situation that prevented him from concentrating his research efforts on the aptitude measurement that fascinated him. At any rate, instead he turned his major attention to an attempt to bring order into the chaotic classifications of mental abnormalities, with Simon assisting him from Rouen. He was entering a field in which he was considered an alien: a psychologist in the psychiatrists' domain. Still an uneasy relationship at the present time, in 1910 many must have thought him mad to dare to criticize existing formulations and even to suggest programs for theoretical and/or practical reforms. Binet was either unaware of, or unresponsive to, such attitudes. His letters to Simon indicate that he proceeded with the confidence that important psychiatrists would listen to him. He did not realize how mistaken he was.

The unique contribution that Binet brought to this problem of mental abnormalities was a fresh perspective, since he viewed them inclusively as one broad field, focusing on similarities and differences among the various categories in order to highlight the particular nature of each. Although he made some egregious errors, notably in the case of dementia praecox, he did pose useful questions. Certainly Binet was not as successful as he had hoped to be with his psychiatric collaborator and friend, Simon, but, considering the disorder and confusion in the psychiatry of that time, his suggestions for systematization were definitely not without value. Nonetheless, while he urged the psychiatrists to bring psychological insights to their perceptions of the mentally ill, he failed in a measure to use them himself in his discussions of these contemporaries. It is almost incredible that he did not understand that his attacks, his harsh, pointed criticisms of leading theorists and practitioners like Janet, Kraepelin, and Magnan as well as of lesser men would either arouse heated counterattacks or receive the cold, icy disregard that they did. Thus, although he did succeed in casting doubt upon the theories and classifications of leading contemporary psychiatrists, he made little impression upon them or on their followers. Perhaps the time was not ripe for a psychologist to invade this domain, surely not one with Binet's acid pen.

Binet the psychologist unquestionably deserves a place in the field of education, or, as it was called, pedagogy. Here too he was a reformer, an activist, a crusader of high spirit. The reformer and scientist are both evident in his activities within *La Société* that he directed and in the pedagogical laboratory he established. His own work on the intelligence scale, assisted as it was by his entrée into the schools, led him inexorably to the problems of measuring special and general aptitudes. While he failed to find a solution for this problem, he did stimulate the production of usable "achievement tests" for the primary grades. In this guidance of teachers and parents he pleaded for the recognition of individual differences among schoolchildren, at the same time that he insisted upon the necessity for applying scientific methods to the problems of pedagogy. He also was among the first in France to recognize the need for differentiating retarded schoolchildren from the "normal," and to provide special classes for them. Indeed, he stimulated the progress of legislation that made mandatory their instruction by qualified teachers.

Although within the limits of the crude instruments that Binet had forged he may have instituted a kind of "school psychology," it cannot be claimed that his efforts produced many substantive results for education other than his tests of intelligence. His insistence upon scientific goals, viewpoints, and methods did give substance to the educational psychology of the men and women whose lives he touched in *La Société*. There, hundreds of teachers and school administrators learned through his teachings to be more critical of the opinions thrust upon them and more appreciative of the individual differences among their pupils. In this milieu the experimental psychologist and the educational reformer found a place for satisfying and fulfilling labors that were to influence the work of educators in France and elsewhere long after his death.

Since the French have often been criticized for their failure to honor and recognize Alfred Binet appropriately, perhaps it is fitting to allow an appreciative Frenchman to have the last word. On the occasion of a modest celebration of the one hundredth anniversary of Binet's birth, the psychologist Paul Fraisse observed:

> My conclusion? Alfred Binet has been honored throughout the world for his inspired contribution to the method of tests. But in my opinion this renown has wronged him, for the trees have hidden the forest. Binet enriched psychology far beyond the practical application that he drew from his fruitful research [275, p. 112].

Fraisse then supported this statement by a quotation from Ed. Claparède who called Binet "the Paganini of psychology" and praised his "original virtuosity and fecund genius." Both men concluded that Binet would not only remain among the greats in psychological science, but also that his reputation would be augmented in time. In this second century after Binet's birth it is still too soon to say how true this prediction will becomc. Nonetheless, it must be evident that Binet was an important figure in the history of experimental psychology in the early years of its development.

Appendix
Binet's Flight into Metaphysics

The discursive nature of Binet's writings is nowhere better illustrated than in his several attempts to discover the relationship between mind and body, between consciousness and the brain. These projects, written between 1904 and 1906, would appear as a certain anomaly in his work if they were not rooted in psychological data, since he drew his hypotheses and his illustrations primarily from the psychology of perception. Moreover, at the turn of the century it was popular for psychologists both in the United States and Europe to invade the metaphysical domain as they felt the need to integrate the two disciplines or to seek out their interrelationships.[1] Although Binet had decided this problem for himself in 1894 by advocating their unequivocal separation (48), a decade later he admitted that he "had been taken with an irresistible need to make a study in metaphysics" (112, p. 74) and shortly afterward announced to his friend, Larguier des Bancels, that he was ". . . preparing with [Victor] Henri [such] a little study" (4, 1904). It appears, however, that Henri was neither in Paris nor very communicative, for Binet lamented: "I shall be obliged to do this metaphysics article alone. This would wear me down a good deal. Comfort me a little, and write me often" (August 1904). By September he had finished it and sent it on to Larguier for his "fearless criticism," since he said

[1] Dorothy Ross vividly discusses the philosophical fervor that permeated the thinking and writing of psychologists at the turn of the century. See particularly the latter chapters of Part I and most of Part II in her *G. Stanley Hall, The Psychologist as Prophet* (290).

that he had no shame about making errors in this field (12 September 1904). At the same time he requested Larguier to recommend "guides" to the writings of several philosophers, especially to those of Kant, which he was about to read seriously. A month later, while Larguier still had the manuscript, Binet wrote of his impatience to receive it back again: "This article is like the cider that we have just made here: it continues to ferment in my head, and, without changing the principal ideas much, I see their nature better." In his brash self-confidence he added: "The readings that I am pursuing show me particularly in what ways my thinking differs from others' . . . with the curious consequence that the reading of other authors makes me [seem] more original . . ." (12 October 1904). By December he had completed this first paper to be presented before the Société française de philosophie (112), whose membership included the philosopher Bergson. Binet felt that the members "appeared interested" (6 January 1905).

For two more years metaphysics continued actively to ferment in Binet's head. He published a book (113) and an article (115) in 1905 and three more articles during 1906 (124, 125, 126). It appears that in writing the book his attempts to solve the mind-body problem stirred up more questions and doubts about metaphysical solutions than he had dreamed of. At one point he seems to have come to the position of equating psychology with philosophy, for he wrote to Larguier: "I do not see at all how philosophy differs from psychology, and I feel altogether bewildered that I cannot see it" (March 1906). Yet he recognized that the observations and experiments that provided "verifications of all sorts" would be interpreted differently by different people. This relativity undoubtedly bothered this man who wanted answers in science provided by "facts." Nonetheless, he did recognize this personal equation and called metaphysics "an intellectual form given to an emotion" (3 April 1906). Furthermore, at the very end of *L'Âme et le corps (The Mind and the Brain)* he asserted that each person will choose his metaphysics "as his heart desires and needs." After two years of intellectual struggle with materials that defied neat and convincing solutions he confessed to Larguier: "The essential thing [in this kind of venture] is not to discover a hypothesis that really stands up, but to arrive at the perception of some fragments of the truth" (May 1906).

Whether or not Binet thought he had done even this is uncertain, since his last papers on the subject indicate his agonizing irresolutions. In fact, these articles and the book on metaphysics are so difficult to puzzle out that they are open to many misinterpretations and misunderstandings. They harbor lacunae, inconsistencies, and, of course, many open-ended questions, which is not surprising since the mind-body problem has not yet received a convincing philosophical treatment. Binet's wrestling with these enigmas should not be omitted from an account of his work, for they represent not only a strong intent on his part to break into naïve conceptions of mind and matter—and likewise of soul and body—but also indicate Binet's awareness of some of the weaknesses of psychophysical parallelism, of spiritualism, idealism, interactionism, and radical materialism. He was careful not to label his own position with any certainty, although once he called it a monism. This appears to be what he *wanted* to achieve, but perhaps his own perplexity is indicated by the fact that Bergson asked whether Binet's viewpoint was different from psychophysical parallelism (112), while Piéron dubbed it a dualism (218), and Martin claimed that "Binet was an idealist without knowing it" (279). The discussion and quotations that follow will allow the reader to form his own opinion. It has been correctly said that Binet's position was similar to that of Mach.[2] Essentially he contended that the nature of the

[2] Of course Ernst Mach wrote decades earlier, although it seems that Binet became acquainted with him only after his own early writings. This is uncertain, however, since Mach's *Contributions to the Analysis of the Sensations* (with original preface dated 1885, Prague), was translated by C. M. Williams for the Open Court Publishing Company in 1896. Mach also wrote for *The Monist,* which the omnivorous reader Binet might very probably have read. In this article Mach actually stated

two so-called worlds of the mental and the physical are one and the same, since we can "know" the world only by means of our sensations. His long and tortured discussions fall generally into three categories: first, the definition or nature of matter; second, the definition or nature of the mind; and third, the union of mind and body.

The Definition or Nature of Matter

Binet believed in the reality of a world of objects that persists even when unperceived, for he claimed that to follow Berkeley in making consciousness the condition for the existence of real external objects is, in the last analysis, "to make living matter the condition for the existence of brute matter." He admitted, however, that the real world, which he called "world X," was, like Kant's *noumena*, unknowable in itself. It is known only as its own "real properties" are transmitted through the specific energies and the chemical and anatomical particularities of our nervous systems. "Thus, the optic nerve, whether stimulated by a luminous ray, an electric current, or a mechanical blow, always makes the same response, which is a sensation of light" (112, p. 75). Thus, despite the physicists' claim that they are analyzing *the real world of matter*, they are actually "seeing and analyzing only the world of our sensations." He went on: "Of the exterior world we know only one thing, our sensations . . . we perceive only the modifications that the exterior object, as an excitant, sets up in this system" (112, p. 75). "When we believe we are perceiving the external world, we are perceiving only our ideas, so that when we take a train to go to Lyons, we are stepping up into one state of consciousness to attain another state of consciousness" (115, p. 103).

In the intermediary role that the nervous system plays, Binet argued, each of our senses must have equal weight;

---

in capsule form Binet's primary viewpoint: "I see no opposition of physical and psychical, no duality, but simply identity" (210, p. 207). Binet could have absorbed this viewpoint without recognizing its apparent origin.

that is, we cannot give special sanction to particular sensations, as physicists do who claim that the external world is basically movement. They arrive at this "demonstration" only through the senses of sight, touch, and kinesthesis. We have no right to extract the data from these senses alone and claim that they give us access to the-world-as-it-is. We can admit only that the data from these senses give us *sensations* about our surroundings, a combination of the nature of the real objects as they affect and pass through parts of our nervous systems.

Binet went on to argue that because of the brain's invisibility, which causes us to ignore it, and even more because physiologists think of the-brain-as-we-know-it as a real, exterior object, we have come to conceive of it as separate and different from our thoughts or sensations; that is, in a dualistic error we tend to think of the cerebral processes as objective and material, the psychic ones as mental, when actually they are of the same nature. Binet metaphorically suggested that the reader should imagine him as he looks at a flock of sheep, while at the same time another person, "armed with a microscope à la Jules Verne," looks into his brain while he is observing the sheep, "discovering there a certain dance of molecules that accompany the visual perception. The naïve would remark: 'How little the one perception resembles the other!' " Binet, on the other hand, stressed the resemblance: both perceivers have a visual perception and, despite the difference in content, we have no right to conclude that one represents a material phenomenon and the other a psychological one. "Really, each of these perceptions has a double value, psycho-physical; physical by way of the object to which it is applied, and psychical as an act of perception or consciousness . . . There is as much psychical as physical in both," he wrote. That is, the perception of the flock of sheep is as material as the perception of the activities in the brain" (112, p. 81; 113, pp. 267–68). And the nervous system contained both perceptions "rolled up in it."

Apparently Binet put up with considerable good-humored bantering and censure from friends and critics who asked ignorant questions about how he could get a four-meter street lamp into his brain; or even from Bergson who declared that, the smaller not being able to contain the larger, it was impossible for the small brain to contain the material idea of the great big outer world. Binet pointed out the pertinence of the psychology of perception to this problem. But he added:

> There must exist, though unperceived by our senses, a sort of kinship between the [real] qualities of external objects and the vibrations of our nerves. . . . The specific property of our nerves does not prevent our knowing [something of] the form of the excitant. . . . The nervous undulation expresses both the nature of the object that provokes it and that of the nervous apparatus that is its vehicle. It is like the groove traced in the wax of the phonograph that expresses the collaboration of an aerial vibration with a stylus, a cylinder, and a clockwork movement. This engraved line resembles, in short, neither the phonograph apparatus nor the air-waves, although it results from a combination of the two [113, pp. 242-43].
>
> We perceive only the modifications that the external object, acting as an excitant, provokes in this system. . . . Sensation, therefore, should be considered as a physical phenomenon in the sense of a thing felt . . . [113, p. 257, 261].

The Definition or Nature of Mind

Binet had suggested that a sensation should be considered as a physical phenomenon in that it is affected by an unknowable external object through the transmission in the nervous system. Thus "sensation is not a *means* of knowing these properties of matter; *it is these properties themselves*" (112, p. 79; emphasis added). This seems to make sensations a part of physical matter, and thereby to constitute the monism. But Binet went on to say that sensation and consciousness must be differentiated; they are "two orders of elements, united in our perceptions, but that must be considered separately," and hence present a dualism. "The sensation as the thing felt, *that* is the physical part, *there* is matter; the sensation as a fact of feeling, of judging, *there* is the mind. . . . The mind is the act of consciousness; it is not a thing that has consciousness, but rather, like form, that can be realized only in its application to matter of some kind. . . . As form cannot be devoid of matter . . . it is impossible to understand a consciousness existing without an object. . . . Mind and matter therefore are correlative terms . . ." (113, pp. 262, 264–65). He then asked the reader to try to imagine a landscape without any clouds, trees, atmosphere, and so forth, that is, a mental event without the content represented by external objects. But he had obviously not resolved the relationship between physical sensations and consciousness.

The Union of Mind and Body

What of the union of mind and body, of consciousness and matter? As Binet approached this problem the crucial question seemed to be whether or not consciousness could be considered as a sensation, and therefore physical. It becomes apparent that he could not answer this question. He pondered at length various theories of the nature of consciousness and the many problems incurred, including the fact that if it is not within the physical world it cannot fit the law of the conservation of energy, which it had to do if it were to *influence* or *act upon* the physical world. He asked: Is it, then, a useless luxury, an epiphenomenon? But he left open the question. Whatever might be the answer, he considered parallelism and interaction impossible to conceive, since they required two worlds that can have no intercourse with one another. Among attempts to get out of the dilemma he considered a suggestion that consciousness might be a *directing* force; since it did not change in quantity, but only in the *direction* or *form* of energy, it would still meet the demands of the law of the conservation of energy. This represented a change from his position in 1904 when he spoke of "the work of consciousness," of its "expenditure of energy," and added:

> Having established that there exists a single series of phenomena, which is physical, we are led logically by this monist conception to give to consciousness a place in the physical series. . . . It analyzes nerve currents . . . it provokes representations and judgments, which create new

connections, and give a wiser direction, a more perfect adaptation to the activity of being [112, pp. 85, 86].

Here consciousness had a dynamic character, but in *L'Âme et le corps* and a later article (125) he altered his opinion and wrote: "it clarifies, reveals, but changes nothing" (125, p. 118). In *L'Âme et le corps* he hypothesized that we become conscious only through change; that the brain's actions are so constantly similar, as background stimuli, that we have no consciousness of them. Therefore, the change that counts in consciousness takes place in the external objects, and it is subsequent to these changes that we are conscious, that we experience the sensations. In the later article (125), however, his final paragraph demonstrated his ignorance and dismay before this phenomenon of "consciousness." While he recognized and agreed essentially with Kant's proposition that the-object-in-itself is unknowable, he believed that this "real" object is *partially* knowable by means of its "capture" (*prise*) by perception and consciousness. Nonetheless, two years later he had concluded that "the really inaccessible frontier, the limit of knowledge, the truly unknowable—is consciousness itself" (125, p. 136).

It is probably because Binet could not place consciousness with any certainty within the physical world of matter and sensations that at the end of *L'Âme et le corps* he left the reader with a curious choice. He wrote: "There must exist a sort of kinship between the qualities of the real external objects and the vibrations of our nerves . . . thus, we admit a kind of parallelism between the consciousness and the object of cognition; these two series, however, are not independent, but united and fused together to complete one another . . ." (113, p. 251). Nonetheless, he could not clarify this fusion any better than to conclude:

In order to form a true phenomenon, there must be at one and the same time a consciousness and an object. . . . Now one and now the other is stressed. . . . If we had to give our final verdict we would say: "Consciousness and matter have equal rights," thus leaving to every person the power to choose as the more significant that one [of these equals] of which his heart has the need . . . [113, p. 255].[3]

He knew that it was a specious choice, and one that he could not himself resolve. He was driven to write one last word about the nature of consciousness. He "knew" that "it is of the utmost necessity to put psychic and cerebral material in the same world," that "they are different not in their nature, but only in the difference of their objects" (126, p. 25). As he had earlier referred to the unknowable objects-as-they-are as "objects-X," he now referred to other even more challenging unknowables as "the brain-X," "the consciousness-X." The objective of his poignant search had not been reached, but he never returned to this problem again.

L'Âme et le corps was reviewed in France, England, and America, with some praise and more criticism. Henri Piéron felt that it indicated that too much attention was being given to philosophy, and urged that "we agree to being unable to know what the brain cannot know, and then go ahead making science. . . . I say, let her go—these problems have not made a step forward since Hume . . ." (218, p. 112). P. Malapert (211) and L. Dugas (195) presented some balanced criticism of an "excellent, suggestive book." H. H. Bawden of Vassar (172) and H. N. Gardiner of Smith College (199) decided that Binet had given a satisfactory definition neither of mind nor of matter. Nevertheless, *L'Âme et le corps* was at least successful from the "materialist" point of view, for Bertrand reported that by 1918 ten thousand copies had been sold (267, p. 49).

[3] The outcome "of what the heart has need" referred, of course, to biased conclusions. Binet was much aware of these. He had written: "One could say of every metaphysician: 'Tell me what you are looking for, and I will tell you what you will find. Tell me the needs of your heart, and I will tell you the solutions of your reasoning' " (124, p. 600).

References

For convenience the journals used most extensively have been abbreviated as follows:

Bull. *Bulletin de la Société libre pour l'étude psychologique de l'enfant.*

R. Ph. *Revue philosophique.*

L'A. P. *L'Année psychologique.* In this book citations to this journal indicate the volume numbers and dates provided by the publisher on the title pages.

In instances where the quotation is brief and the source used only once, the reference is indicated in parentheses in the text and not cited in the following bibliography.

PRIMARY SOURCES

I. Letters:

1. Binet, Alfred, Letter in papers of Alexander Dumas fils, Salle des manuscrits, Bibliothèque Nationale, 21 March 1893.
2. ———, Letters in papers of Gaston Paris, Salle des manuscrits, Bibliothèque Nationale, 1895, 1899.
3. ———, Letters in papers of Louis Havet, Salle des manuscrits, Bibliothèque Nationale, 1899, 1901, 1902, 1904, 1906, 1907.
4. ———, to J. Larguier des Bancels, Lausanne, Switzerland. Approximately one hundred and thirty-four cards and sixty letters, 1900 to 1911, microfilmed from his papers by permission of his niece, Marie Garibaldi. Originals now available at the Bibliothèque Cantonale, Lausanne.
5. ———, Letters and cards to Henri Piéron, from October 1903 to July 1911: twenty-nine pieces.
6. ———, Letters and postcards to Théodore Simon, 1904 to 1911: sixty pieces.

II. Unpublished Manuscripts:

7. Binet, Alfred, "Images de lecture." Undated.
8. ——— "La psychologie et la pédagogie." Undated.

9. ——— "L'éducation psychologique de l'instituteur." Undated.

III. Publications:

Alfred Binet (and Binet with collaborators). These publications are listed in chronological order.

10. Binet, Alfred, De la fusion des sensations semblables. *R. Ph.* (1880) 10: 284–94.
11. ———, Du raisonnement dans les perceptions. *R. Ph.* (1883) 15: 406–32.
12. ———, and C. Féré, Les paralysies par suggestion. *Rev. sci.* (1884): 45–49.
13. ———, L'hallucination, *R. Ph.* (1884) 17: a) Recherches théoriques, 366–412; b) Recherches expérimentales, 473–502.
14. ———, and C. Féré, L'hypnotisme chez les hystériques: le transfert. *R. Ph.* (1885) 19: 1–25.
15. ———, and C. Féré, Hypnotisme et responsabilité. *R. Ph.* (1885) 19: 265–79.
16. ———, and C. Féré, La polarisation psychique. *R. Ph.* (1885) 19: 369–402.
17. ———, L'image consécutive et le souvenir visuel. *Rev. Sci.* (1885) 2: 805–8.
18. ———, and C. Féré, Hypnotisme et responsabilité. *Rev. Sci.* (1886), 2: 626.
19. ———, *La psychologie du raisonnement.* Paris: Alcan. 1886.
20. ———, and J. L. R. Delboeuf, Les diverses écoles hypnotiques. *R. Ph.* (1886) 22: 532–38.
21. ———, Analyses L. Bernheim, *De la suggestion et de ses applications à la thérapeutique.* *R. Ph.* (1886) 22: 557–63.
22. ———, and C. Féré, *Le magnétisme animal.* Paris: Alcan. 1887.
23. ———, La perception extérieure. Séances et travaux de l'académie des sciences morales et politiques (Institut de France), 47th Année, T. (1887) 28: 624–66.
24. ———, and C. Féré, Recherches expérimentales sur la physiologie des mouvements chez les hystériques. *Arch. de physiol. normale et pathol. 3rd série* (1887): 320–73.
25. ———, Note sur l'écriture hystérique. *R. Ph.* (1887) 23: 67–70.

26. ———, L'intensité des images mentales. *R. Ph.* (1887) 23: 473–97.
27. ———, Le fétichisme dans l'amour. *R. Ph.* (1887) 24: 142–67, 252–75.
28. ———, La vie psychique des micro-organismes. *R. Ph.* (1887) 24: 449–89, 582–611.
29. ———, Sur les illusions de mouvement. *R. Ph.* (1888) 25: 335.
30. ———, Le problème du sens musculaire, d'après les travaux récents sur l'hystérie. *R. Ph.* (1888) 25: 465–80.
31. ———, La responsabilité morale. *R. Ph.* (1888) 26: 217–31.
32. ———, Résumé of Balbiani's lectures on "Les théories modernes de la reproduction et de l'hérédité." *R. Ph.* (1888) 26: 529–59.
33. ———, Sur les rapports entre l'hémianopsie et la mémoire visuelle. *R. Ph.* (1888) 26: 480–88.
34. ———, *On double consciousness.* Chicago: Open Court Publishing Co. 1889. (This book was not published in French.)
35. ———, La vision mentale. *R. Ph.* (1889) 27: 337–73.
36. ———, La concurrence des états psychologiques. *R. Ph.* (1890) 29: 138–55.
37. ———, Revue de *L'automatisme psychologique,* par Pierre Janet. *R. Ph.* (1890) 29: 186–200.
38. ———, Recherches sur les mouvements chez quelques jeunes enfants. *R. Ph.* (1890) 29: 297–309.
39. ———, La perception des longueurs et des nombres chez quelques petits enfants. *R. Ph.* (1890) 30: 68–81.
40. ———, Perceptions d'enfants. *R. Ph.* (1890) 30: 582–611.
41. ———, L'inhibition dans les phénomènes de conscience. *R. Ph.* (1890) 30: 136–56.
42. ———, Sur un cas d'inhibition psychique. *R. Ph.* (1891) 32: 622–25.
43. ———, *Les altérations de la personnalité.* Paris: Alcan. 1892.
44. ———, Les maladies du langage. *Rev. des deux mondes* (January 1892) : 116–32.
45. ———, Les grandes mémoires: Résumé d'une enquête sur les joueurs d'échecs. *Rev. des deux mondes* (15 June 1893) : 826–60. (This was a popularization of

several articles on rapid calculators and chess players published in *R. Ph.* and *Travaux du laboratoire.*)

46. ———, Contribution à l'étude du système nerveux sous-intestinal des insectes. Thesis presented to the Faculty of Sciences of the Académie de Paris to obtain the doctor's degree in natural sciences. December 1894. (Bibliothèque Nationale.)
47. ———, and L. Henneguy, *La psychologie des grands calculateurs et joueurs d'échecs.* Paris: Hachette. 1894.
48. ———, with J. Philippe, J. Courtier, V. Henri, *Introduction à la psychologie expérimentale.* Paris: Alcan. 1894.
49. ———, and V. Henri, Recherches sur le développement de la mémoire visuelle des enfants. *R. Ph.* (1894) 37: 348–50. Also reported for *Rev. gén. des sciences pures et appliquées* (1894) 5: 162–69. Translated in R. H. Pollack and M. W. Brenner (287).
50. ———, and V. Henri, De la suggestibilité naturelle chez les enfants. *R. Ph.* (1894) 38: 337–47.
51. ———, and V. Henri, La mémoire des mots. *L'A. P.* (1895) 1: 1–23.
52. ———, and V. Henri, La mémoire des phrases. *L'A. P.* (1895) 1: 24–59.
53. ———, and J. Passy, Notes psychologiques sur les auteurs dramatiques. *L'A. P.* (1895) 1: 60–118.
54. ———, M. François de Curel (Notes psychologiques). *L'A. P.* (1895) 1: 119–73.
55. ———, La mesure des illusions visuelles chez les enfants. *R. Ph.* (1895) 40: 11–25. Trans. in Pollack and Brenner (287).
56. ———, and J. Courtier, La circulation capillaire de la main dans ses rapports avec la respiration et les actes psychiques. *L'A. P.* (1896) 2: 87–167.
57. ———, Recherches graphiques sur la musique. *L'A. P.* (1896) 2: 201–22.
58. ———, La Peur chez les enfants. *L'A. P.* (1896) 2: 223–254. Translated in Pollack and Brenner (287).
59. ———, and V. Henri, La psychologie individuelle. *L'A. P.* (1896) 2: 411–65.
60. ———, Connais-toi toi-même. *Rev. des Revues* (1896) 19: 419–24.
61. ———, with J. Courtier and N. Vaschide. Five articles

on the influence of several conditions on capillary circulation and blood pressure. *L'A. P.* (1897).
62. ———, Psychologie individuelle—La description d'un objet. *L'A. P.* (1897) 3: 296–332.
63. ———, Analyse de J. H. Leuba: "A Study in the Psychology of Religious Phenomena." *L'A. P.* (1897) 3: 548–52.
64. ———, with N. Vaschide, La psychologie à l'école primaire. *L'A. P.* (1898) 4: 1–14.
65. ———, with N. Vaschide, Corrélation des épreuves physiques. *L'A. P.* (1898) 4: 142–72.
66. ———, with N. Vaschide, Corrélation des tests de force physique. *L'A. P.* (1898) 4: 236–44. (Summary of pp. 1–235, Vol. 4.)
67. ———, La consommation du pain pendant une année scolaire. *L'A. P.* (1898) 4: 337–55.
68. ———, and V. Henri, *La fatigue intellectuelle.* Paris: Schleicher Frères. 1898.
69. ———, La mesure en psychologie individuelle. *R. Ph.* (1898) 46: 113–23.
70. ———, La suggestibilité au point de vue de la psychologie individuelle. *L'A. P.* (1899) 5: 82–152.
71. ———, Note relative à l'influence du travail intellectuel sur la consommation du pain dans les écoles. *L'A. P.* (1899) 5: 332–36.
72. ———, with N. Vaschide, Historique des recherches sur les rapports de l'intelligence avec la grandeur et la forme de la tête. *L'A. P.* (1899) 5: 245–98. Unsigned, but its co-authorship with Vaschide is mentioned in (78).
73. ———, Nouvelles recherches sur la consommation du pain dans ses rapports avec le travail intellectuel. *L'A. P.* (1900) 6: 1–73.
74. ———, Attention et adaptation. *L'A. P.* (1900) 6: 248–404.
75. ———, Review of Stella E. Sharp, "Individual Psychology. A Study in Psychological Method." *L'A. P.* (1900) 6: 583–93.
76. ———, Revue générale sur la pédagogie expérimentale en France. *L'A. P.* (1900) 6: 594–606. (Signature designated 6: 774.)
77. ———, *La suggestibilité.* Paris: Schleicher Frères. 1900.

78. ———, Recherches sur la technique de la mesure de la tête vivante. *L'A. P.* (1901) 7: 314–68.
79. ———, Recherches préliminaires de céphalometrie sur 59 enfants d'intelligence inégale, choisis dans les écoles primaires de la ville de Paris. *L'A. P.* (1901) 7: 369–74.
80. ———, Recherches complémentaires de céphalometrie sur 100 enfants d'intelligence inégale, choisis dans les écoles primaires de Seine-et-Marne. *L'A. P.* (1901) 7: 375–402.
81. ———, Recherches de céphalometrie sur 50 enfants d'élite et arriérés des écoles de Seine-et-Marne. *L'A. P.* (1901) 7: 403–11.
82. ———, Recherches de céphalometrie sur 60 enfants d'élite et arriérés des écoles primaires de Paris. *L'A. P.* (1901) 7: 412–29.
83. ———, L'observateur et l'imaginatif. *L'A. P.* (1901) 7: 519–23.
84. ———, Nouvelles recherches de céphalometrie. *L'A. P.* (1902) 8: 341–44.
85. ———, La croissance du crâne et de la face chez les normaux, entre 4 et 18 ans. *L'A. P.* (1902) 8: 345–62.
86. ———, Corrélation des mesures céphaliques. *L'A. P.* (1902) 8: 363–68.
87. ———, Les proportions du crâne chez les aveugles. *L'A. P.* (1902) 8: 369–84.
88. ———, Les proportions du crâne chez les sourds-muets. *L'A. P.* (1902) 8: 385–89.
89. ———, Analyse de H. Bergson: Note sur la conscience de l'effort intellectuel. (IVe Congrès. intern. de Psychol., Paris, 1901.) *L'A. P.* (1902) 8: 471–78.
90. ———, *L'Étude expérimentale de l'intelligence.* Paris: Schleicher Frères. 1903. (Costes edition, 1922, used.)
91. ———, La mesure de la sensibilité. *L'A. P.* (1903) 9: 79–128.
92. ———, Les simplistes: enfants d'école et adultes. *L'A. P.* (1903) 9: 129–68.
93. ———, Les distraits. *L'A. P.* (1903) 9: 169–98.
94. ———, Les interprétateurs—Théorie et portraits. *L'A. P.* (1903) 9: 199–234.
95. ———, Influence de l'exercise et de la suggestion sur la position du seuil. *L'A. P.* (1903) 9: 235–45. Translated in Pollack and Brenner (287).

96. ———, Le seuil de la sensation double ne peut pas être fixé scientifiquement. *L'A. P.* (1903) 9: 247–52. Translated in Pollack and Brenner (287).
97. ———, La pensée sans images. *R. Ph.* (1903) 55: 138–52.
98. ———, De la sensation à l'intelligence. *R. Ph.* (1903) 56: 449–67, 592–618.
99. ———, La création littéraire: Portrait psychologique de M. Paul Hervieu. *L'A. P.* (1904) 10: 1–62.
100. ———, Questions de technique céphalométrique d'après M. Bertillon. *L'A. P.* (1904) 10: 139–41.
101. ———, Graphologie et ses révélation sur le sexe, l'âge et l'intelligence. *L'A. P.* (1904) 10: 179–211.
102. ———, Analyse de P. Malapert: *Le caractère. L'A. P.* (1904) 10: 492–507.
103. ———, Nos commissions de travail. *Bull.* (1904) No. 14, pp. 337–46.
104. ———, and G. Vaillant, Commission des aptitudes individuelles: Contributions à l'étude du développement du langage. *Bull.* (1904) No. 15, pp. 397–405.
105. ———, Addition à l'article de M. Boyer. *Bull.* (1904) No. 15, pp. 412–14.
106. ———, Les frontières anthropométriques des anormaux. *Bull.* (1904) No. 16, pp. 430–38.
107. ———, and "J. B.," Report of Commissions. *Bull.* (1904) No. 17, pp. 465–66.
108. ———, Note relative à la communication de M. Parison (Commission de la mémoire) *Bull.* (1904) No. 17, p. 488.
109. ——— Avis. La Commission ministérielle pour les anormaux. *Bull.* (1904) No. 18, p. 506.
110. ———, Le passé et l'avenir de notre Société. *Bull.* (1904) No. 19, pp. 547–55.
111. ———, Réflexions à propos de deux communications de M. Boyer et de Mme. Meuzy, *Bull.* (1905) No. 20, pp. 563–64.
112. ———, Esprit et matière. Séance du 22 Décembre 1904. *Bull. soc. franç. de philosophie* (1905) 5: 73–101.
113. ———, *L'Âme et le corps.* Paris: Flammarion. 1905. (English edition also used; London: Kegan Paul, 1907.)

114. ———, Recherches sur la fatigue intellectuelle scolaire et la mesure qui peut en être faite au moyen de l'esthésiomètre (given in table of contents as "du dynamomètre"). *L'A. P.* (1905) 11: 1–37.
115. ———, Étude de métaphysique sur la sensation et l'image. *L'A. P.* (1905) 11: 94–115.
116. ———, La science du témoignage. *L'A. P.* (1905) 11: 128–236.
117. ———, with Th. Simon, Sur la necessité d'établir un diagnostic scientifique des états inférieurs de l'intelligence. *L'A. P.* (1905) 11: 163–90.
118. ———, with Th. Simon, Méthodes nouvelles pour le diagnostic du niveau intellectuel des anormaux. *L'A. P.* (1905) 11: 191–244.
119. ———, with Th. Simon, Application des méthodes nouvelles au diagnostic du niveau intellectuel chez des enfants normaux et anormaux d'hospice et d'école primaire. *L'A. P.* (1905) 11: 245–336.
120. ———, Analyse de C. E. Spearman, "The Proof and Measurement of Association between Two Things" and "General Intelligence Objectively Determined and Measured." *L'A. P.* (1905) 11: 623–24.
121. ———, Expériences sur la mesure de la fatigue intellectuelle scolaire, au moyen du sens du toucher. *Bull.* (1905) No. 22, pp. 628–32; No. 23, pp. 644–52.
122. ———, Allocution de M. Binet à l'Assemblée générale de la Société, 16 Novembre 1905. *Bull.* (1905) No. 27, pp. 21–27.
123. ———, and Th. Simon, Méthodes nouvelles pour diagnostiquer l'idiotie, l'imbécillité et la débilité mentale. *Atti del V Congresso internazionale di psicologia* (held in Rome, 26–30 April 1905) (Rome: Forziani, 1906), pp. 507–10.
124. ———, Les premiers mots de la thèse idéaliste. *R. Ph.* (1906) 61: 599–618.
125. ———, Pour la philosophie de la conscience. *L'A. P.* (1906) 12: 113–36.
126. ———, Cerveau et pensée. *Arch. de Psychol.* (1906) Nos. 21–22, pp. 1–26.
127. ———, Travaux de la Commission ministérielle pour les anormaux. *Bull.* (1906) No. 28, pp. 57–61.
128. ———, with Th. Simon and V. Vaney, Le Laboratoire de la Rue Grange-aux-belles: Travaux du lab-

oratoire en 1905–06. Première année de sa création. *Bull.* (1906) No. 34, pp. 10–24.
129. ———, *Les révélation de l'écriture d'après un contrôle scientifique.* Paris: Alcan. 1906.
130. ———, with Th. Simon and V. Vaney, Recherches de pédagogie scientifique. *L'A. P.* (1906) 12: 233–74.
131. ———, À propos de la communication de M. Vaney sur les degrés de lecture. *Bull.* (1907) No. 37, pp. 82–83.
132. ———, La valeur médicale de l'examen de la vision par les instituteurs. *Bull.* (1907) No. 40, pp. 146–63.
133. ———, Les nouvelles classes de perfectionnement. *Bull.* (1907) No. 41, pp. 170–83.
134. ———, with Th. Simon, *Les enfants anormaux.* Paris: Armand Colin. 1907.
135. ———, Une expérience cruciale en graphologie. *R. Ph.* (1907) 64: 22–40.
136. ———, Allocution du président. *Bull.* (1908) No. 43, pp. 37–52.
137. ———, Allocution du président sur les enfants anormaux. *Bull.* (1908) No. 44, pp. 59–60.
138. ———, Un livre récent de William James sur l'éducation: *Causeries pédagogiques.* Translated from *Talks to Teachers* by Pidoux. *Bull.* (1908) No. 46, pp. 114–20; No. 48, pp. 167–68. Also, *L'A. P.* (1908) 14: 405–31.
139. ———, Le développement de l'intelligence chez les enfants. *L'A. P.* (1908) 14: 1–94.
140. ———, with Th. Simon, Langage et pensée. *L'A. P.* (1908) 14: 284–339.
141. ———, Essai sur la chiromancie expérimentale. *L'A. P.* (1908) 14: 390–404.
142. ———, *Les idées modernes sur les enfants.* Paris: Flammarion. 1909. (1911 edition used.)
143. ———, with Th. Simon. La mesure de l'intelligence chez les enfants (avec démonstrations). *Bull. de la soc. clinique de médecine mentale* (1909) No. 9, pp. 1–10.
144. ———, with Th. Simon, L'intelligence des imbéciles. *L'A. P.* (1909) 15: 1–147.
145. ———, Le mystère de la peinture; La psychologie artistique de Tade Styka. *L'A. P.* (1909) 15: 300–56.

146. ———, with Alice Binet, Rembrandt. *L'A. P.* (1910) 16: 31–50.
147. ———, with Th. Simon, Peut-on enseigner la parôle aux sourds-muets? *L'A. P.* (1909) 15: 373–96.
148. ———, L'école primaire, comme préparation à la vie. *Bull.* (1909) No. 52, pp. 58–66; No. 54, pp. 101–8.
149. ———, with Th. Simon, Nouvelle théorie psychologique et clinique de la démence. *L'A. P.* (1909) 15: 168–272.
150. ———, La neutralité scolaire. *Bull.* (1910) No. 60, pp. 87–89.
151. ———, Comment les instituteurs jugent-ils l'intelligence de l'écolier? *Bull.* (1910) No. 64, pp. 172–82.
152. ———, Mesure du degré d'instruction d'après les recherches nouvelles. *Bull.* (1910) No. 66, pp. 1–14.
153. ———, Avant-propos: le bilan de la psychologie en 1909. *L'A. P.* (1910) 16: i–ix .
154. ———, Les signes physiques de l'intelligence chez les enfants. *L'A. P.* (1910) 16: 1–30.
155. ———, with Th. Simon. Introduction: Définition des principaux états mentaux de l'aliénation. I. L'hystérie. *L'A. P.* (1910) 16: 60-122.
156. ———, with Th. Simon. La folie avec conscience. *L'A. P.* (1910) 16: 123–63.
157. ———, with Th. Simon. La folie maniaque-dépressive. *L'A. P.* (1910) 16: 164–214.
158. ———, with Th. Simon. La folie systématisée. *L'A. P.* (1910) 16: 215–65.
159. ———, Les démences. *L'A. P.* (1910) 16: 266–348.
160. ———, with Th. Simon. L'arriération. *L'A. P.* (1919) 16: 349–60.
161. ———, with Th. Simon. Conclusions. *L'A. P.* (1910) 16: 361–71.
162. ———, Avant-propos: le bilan de la psychologie en 1910. *L'A. P.* (1911) 17: v–xi.
163. ———, Qu'est-ce qu-une émotion? Qu'est-ce qu'un acte intellectuel? *L'A. P.* (1911) 17: 1–47.
164. ———, with Th. Simon. Les classes pour les enfants arriérés. *Bull.* (1911) No. 68, pp. 53–150.
165. ———, Nouvelles recherches sur la mesure du niveau intellectuel chez les enfants d'école. *L'A. P.* (1911) 17: 145–201.

166. ———, with Th. Simon. Réponse à quelques critiques. *L'A. P.* (1911) 17: 270–77.
167. ———, with Th. Simon. La confusion mentale. *L'A. P.* (1911) 17: 278–300.
168. ———, with Th. Simon. Définition de l'aliénation. *L'A. P.* (1911) 17: 301–50.
169. ———, with Th. Simon. La législation des aliénés. *L'A. P.* (1911) 17: 351–62.
170. ———, with Th. Simon. Parallèle entre les classifications des aliénistes. *L'A. P.* (1911) 17: 363–88.

Publications about Binet before 1911, Listed Alphabetically:

171. Baird, J. W., Proceedings of the First Congress of Experimental Psychology. *Psychol. Bull.* (1905) 2: 81–86.
172. Bawden, H. H., Review of *L'Âme et le corps*. *Psychol. Bull.* (1906) 3: 350–53.
173. —Belot, A., Rapport au nom de la commission de Graphologie. *Bull.* (1904) 18: 510–22.
174. Bernheim, L., Correspondence—Réponse à la critique de M. Binet sur le livre de M. Bernheim. *R. Ph.* (1887) 23: 93–98.
175. Blin, Dr., Les débilités mentales. *Rev. de psychiatrie* (1902) 8: 337–45.
176. Blum, E., Analyse des livres sur la pédagogie; includes *La fatigue intellectuelle*, by Binet and Henri. *R. Ph.* (1898) 46: 504–18.
177. Boyer, J., Essai de céphalométrie chez les enfants idiots. *Bull.* (1904) No. 15, 408–12.
178. Buchner, E. F., Review of *L'Année psychologique*, (1900) vol. 6, including Binet's "Attention et adaptation." *Psychol. Rev.* (1901) 8: 535.
179. Capgras, J., and P. Sérieux, Le délire d'interprétation et la folie systématisée, *L'A. P.* (1911) 17: 251–69.
180. Cattell, J. McK., Review of Binet and Henri, *La fatigue intellectuelle*. *Psychol. Rev.* (1898) 5: 428–30.
181. Chabot, C., Les nouvelles recherches esthésiométriques sur la fatigue intellectuelle. *Bull.* (1905) No. 22, pp. 622–28.
182. Claparède, E., Report of First German Congress for

Experimental Psychology. *Arch. de psychol.* (1904) 3: 315–16.

183. Commission des anormaux. *Bull.* (1904) No. 15, pp. 406–8; No. 16, p. 429.
184. Damaye, H., *Essai de diagnostic entre les états de débilités mentales.* Thèse pour le Doctorate en Médecine (Paris: Steinheil, 1903) pp. 160.
185. ———, Rapport de "la méthode d'examen et de classement des enfants anormaux": presented by Piéron at Ve International Congress of Psychology. *Rev. sci.* (1905) 4: No. 3, p. 70.
186. Decroly, S. O., and Mlle J. Degand, Les tests de Binet et Simon pour la mesure de l'intelligence: contribution critique. *Arch. de psychol.* (1907) 6: 27–130.
187. ———, La mesure de l'intelligence chez des enfants normaux, d'après les tests de Binet et Simon. *Arch. de psychol.* (1910) 9: 81–108.
188. Decroly, S. O., Revue annuelle des anormaux. *L'A. P.* (1906) 12: 498–524. (See especially reviews of M. Ganguillet, pp. 504–6; and Philippe and Paul Boncour, pp. 505–7.)
189. Delboeuf, J. L. R., La mémoire chez les hypnotisés. *R. Ph.* (1886) 21: 441–72.
190. ———, Influence de l'éducation et de l'imitation dans le somnambulisme provoqué. *R. Ph.* (1886) 22: 146–71.
191. ———, Une visite à la Salpêtrière. *Rev. belg.* (1886) 54: 121–47, 258–75.
192. ———, *Le magnétisme animal à propos d'une visite à l'école de Nancy.* Paris: Alcan. 1889.
193. ———, Correspondance: La personnalité chez l'enfant. *R. Ph.* (1891) 31: 106–7.
194. Demoor, J., and S. O. Decroly, Revue de pédagogie des anormaux. *L'A. P.* (1904) 10: 317–27.
195. Dugas, L., Review of *L'Âme et le corps. R. Ph.* (1906) 61: 435.
196. Flournoy, Th., Influence du milieu sur l'idéation. *L'A. P.* (1895) 1: 180–90.
197. Franz, S. I., Review of *L'Année psychologique,* 1898, vol. 4—specifically the series of articles by A. Binet and N. Vaschide. *Psychol. Rev.* (1898) 5: 665.
198. Ganguillet, M., Nachträgliche Bemerküngen zum Sickingerschen Vortrag am der V. Schweizer. Con-

ferenz für das Idiotenwesen in St. Gallen. Review by O. Decroly. *L'A. P.* (1906) 12: 504–6.
199. Gardiner, H. N., Review of *L'Âme et le corps. Am. J. of Psychol.* (1906) 17: 422–23.
200. Gruyelle, L., La céphalométrie et la pédagogie. *Bull.* (1907) No. 42, pp. 8–18.
201. ———, Exercises d'orthopédie mentale. *Bull.* (1908) No. 49, pp. 174–82.
202. Henri, Victor, Les laboratoires de psychologie expérimentale en Allemagne. *R. Ph.* (1893) 36: 608–22.
203. ———, Revue générale sur le sens du lieu de la peau. *L'A. P.* (1896) 2: 295–362.
204. ———, et C. Henri. Enquête sur les premiers souvenirs de l'enfance. *L'A. P.* (1897) 3: 184–98.
205. Janet, Pierre, Revue de *La psychologie du raisonnement* by A. Binet. *R. Ph.* (1886) 21: 188.
206. Kostyleff, N., *La crise de la psychologie expérimentale.* Paris: Alcan. 1911.
207. Larguier des Bancels, J., La psychologie judiciaire. *L'A. P.* (1906) 12: 157–232.
208. Lévèque, Ch., Séances et travaux de l'académie des sciences morales et politiques (Institut de France). 1887, 47th année, T. *28,* 2d semestre. 624–66.
209. Levistre, Classes de perfectionnement. *Bull.* (1908) No. 50, pp. 18–23.
210. Mach, E., Facts and Mental Symbols. *The Monist* (1892) 2: 198–208.
211. Malapert, P., Review of *L'Âme et le corps. L'A. P.* (1906) 12: 580–89.
212. Malapert, P., Mort de Binet. *Bull.* (1911) No. 74, p. 1–5.
213. Mignard, M., Fonctions psychiques et troubles mentaux. *L'A. P.* (1911) 17: 202–32.
214. Müller and Wilbert, Étude sur la mémoire des enfants *Bull.* (1905) No. 25, pp. 703–6; No. 26, pp. 10–16.
215. Parison, Rapport de la commission de la mémoire. *Bull.* (1904) No. 17, pp. 471–88.
216. Paulhan, Fr., Review of *La suggestibilité. R. Ph.* (1900) 50: 290–310.
217. Philippe, J., and Paul Boncour, Analyse de *Les anomalies mentales chez les écoliers.* Paris: Alcan.

1905. Review by O. Decroly; *L'A. P.* (1906) 12: 506–7.

218. Piéron, Henri, Analyse de *L'Année psychologique,* 1906, vol. 12. *Rev. sci.* (1906) 6: 112.

219. Procès-Verbal: Séance du 2 juin, 1904 sur "la Mémoire." *Bull.* (1904) No. 18, pp. 507–8.

220. Réunions mensuelles (de *La Société*) *Bull.* (1904) No. 15, pp. 386–92.

221. *Revue internationale de pédagogie comparative:* The contents are brief, often only comments or résumés, and so they will be noted only by authors and dates:
   a. W. S. Munroe (1899) 1: 2–6.
   b. W. S. Munroe (1899) 1: 70–78.
   c. J. Demoor (1900) 2: 209–21.
   d. G. Hellstrom (1901) 2: 161–66.
   e. M. Manheimer-Gommès (1903) 4: 42–48.
   f. Cercle pédagogique (1899) 1: 100–101.
   g. G. Baguer (1900) 2: 29–38; 3: 117–22; 4: 169-78.
   h. P. Malapert (1903) 3: 161–64.
   i. Third Congress (1903) 3: 311–12.

222. Roussel, L., Compte-rendu moral des travaux pour l'année 1908–9. *Bull.* (1909) No. 58, pp. 26–29.

223. Roussel, L., Compte-rendu des travaux de *La Société. Bull.* (1911) No. 67, pp. 27–31.

224. Schallenberger, M., Discussion: Professor Baldwin's Method of Studying the Color-Perception of Children. *Amer. J. of Psychol.* (1897) 8: 560–76.

225. Schuyten, M. C., Comités internationaux de pédologie. *Arch. de psychol.* (1910) 9: 139–43.

226. Scripture, E. W., *The New Psychology.* New York: Scribners. 1897. Binet's chapter on French psychology, pp. 464–69.

227. Seashore, C. E., Review of Binet's *La suggestibilité. Psychol. Rev.* (1901) 8: 610–16.

228. Sharp, Stella E., Individual Psychology: A Study in Psychological Method. *Amer. J. of Psychol.* (1899) 10: 329–91.

229. Simon, Th., Recherches anthropométriques sur 223 garçons anormaux âgés de 8 à 23 ans. *L'A. P.* (1900) 6: 191–247.

230. ———, Le développement du corps et de la tête chez

les enfants anormaux. *Bull.* (1901) No. 5, pp. 109–14.

231. ———, Recherches céphalométriques sur les enfants arriérés de la colonie de Vaucluse. *L'A. P.* (1901) 7: 430–89.

232. ———, Résumé clinique d'aliénation. *L'A. P.* (1904) 10: 328–47; (1905) 11: 531–72.

233. Spearman. C., "General Intelligence" Objectively Determined and Measured. *Amer. J. of Psychol.* (1904) 15: 201–93.

234. ———, Note on the First German Congress for Experimental Psychology. *Amer. J. of Psychol.* (1904) 15: 447–48.

235. Taine, H., *De l'intelligence.* 1883 edition; Paris, Hatchette. (first published 1870).

236. Tarde, G., Revue de Delboeuf: *Magnétiseurs et médecins. R. Ph.* (1890) 30: 93.

237. Tawney, George, The Perception of Two Points not the Space-threshold. *Psychol. Rev.* (1895) 2: 587–93.

238. Vaney, V., Nouvelles méthodes de mesure applicables au degré d'instruction des élèves. *L'A. P.* (1905) 11: 146–62.

239. ———, Nouvelles méthodes de mesure. *Bull.* (1905) No. 23, pp. 653–60.

240. ———, Développement physique et intellectuel. *Bull.* (1906) No. 33, pp. 195–202.

241. ———, Les degrés de lecture. *Bull.* (1907) No. 37, pp. 77–82.

242. ———, Le développement physique des arriérés d'école. *Bull.* (1908) 46: 108–14.

243. Vattier, G., Experimental Pedagogy in France. *J. of Educ. Psychol.* (1910) 1: 389–403.

244. Warren, H. C., Review of Binet's *L'introduction à la psychologie expérimentale. Psychol. Rev.* (1894) 1: 530–31.

Secondary Sources

I. Interviews with T. H. W.:

245. Binet, Mlles. Géraldine and Georgette, granddaughters of Laure and Alfred Binet, daughters of Madeleine and Edgard Binet. October 1963.

246. Bonnis, Dr. Lucie, 1959 through 1969.
247. Piéron, Professor Henri, May 1960.
248. Simon, Dr. Théodore, November 1959–May 1960.

II. Personal letters to T. H. W.:

249. Anastasi, Dr. Anne, 25 August 1970.
250. Anderson, Dr. John E., 14 September 1962.
251. Binet, Mlles Géraldine and Georgette, 1963–72.
252. Bonnis, Dr. Lucie, 1960 through 1972.
253. Boring, Professor E. G., 1964, 1965, 1967.
254. Burt, Sir Cyril, 5 August 1969.
255. Hathaway, Dr. Starke, August 1970.
256. Piéron, Professor Henri, May 1960.

III. Publications after Binet's Death in 1911, Listed in Alphabetical Order:

257. Alexander, F. G., and S. T. Selesnick, *The History of Psychiatry*. New York: Harper and Row. 1966.
258. Anastasi, Anne, Psychology, Psychologists, and Psychological Testing. *Amer. Psychol.* (1967) 22: 297–306.
259. Anderson, John E., Child Development: an Historical Perspective. *Child Development* (1956) 27: 181–96.
260. Angell, J. R., Imageless Thought. *Psychol. Rev.* (1911) 18: 295–323.
261. Avanzini, Guy, Le 500e numéro. *Bull.* (1968) No. 500, pp. 6–16.
262. ———, *Alfred Binet et la pédagogie scientifique: La contribution de Binet à l'élaboration d'une pédagogie scientifique.* Paris: Vrin. 1969.
263. Baldwin, J. M., Allocution à la Société, November 1918. *Bull.* (1918) No. 124, pp. 4–5.
264. Beck, A. T. *Depression.* New York: Harper and Row. 1967.
265. Bejat, Marian, S. Alexandru, and R. Anatol, Alfred Binet Professeur à l'Université de Bucarest. *Rev. roumaine des sciences sociales* (1965) Série de Psychologie, 9: No. 1, pp. 109–21.
266. Bejat, Marian, Une Correspondance inédite d'Alfred Binet, *Rev. roumaine des sciences sociales* (1966) Série de Psychologie, 10: No. 2, pp. 199–212.
267. Bertrand, François-Louis, *Alfred Binet et son oeuvre.* Paris: Alcan. 1930.

268. Boring, E. G., *A History of Experimental Psychology.* New York: Appleton-Century-Crofts. 1950.
269. Burt, Cyril, The Inheritance of Mental Characters. *Eugenics Rev.* (1912) 4: 168–200.
270. ———, Apports de Binet aux tests d'intelligence et développement ultérieur de cette technique. *Rev. de psychologie appliquée* (1957) 7: No. 4, pp. 231–48.
271. *Centenaire de Th. Ribot, 1839–1939: Jubilé de la Psychologie Scientifique Française.* Paris: Agen. 1939. (Includes some papers and other references to Binet.)
272. Claparède, E., Alfred Binet. *Arch. de psychol.* (1911) 11: 37–88.
273. Clark, Terry N., Émile Durkheim and the Institutionalization of Sociology in the French University System. *European J. of Sociol.* (1968) 9: 37–91.
274. Courtin, G., Étude expérimentale des facultés de l'enfant. *Bull.* (1912) No. 81, 185–91.
275. Fraisse, Paul, L'oeuvre d'Alfred Binet en psychologie expérimentale. *Psychol. française* (1958) 3: 105–12.
276. Goodenough, F. L., *Mental Testing.* New York: Rinehart and Co. 1949.
277. Kite, Elizabeth S. (trans.), "The Intelligence of the Feeble-minded" by A. Binet and Th. Simon. Vineland, N. J.: Vineland Press, 1916.
278. Maier, N. R. F., Maier's Law. *Amer. Psychol.* (1960) 15: 208–12.
279. Martin, Robert, "Alfred Binet." Thèse complémentaire, presentée à la Faculté des Lettres de l'Université de Paris, 1924, 122 pp.
280. Munthe, A., *The Story of San Michele.* London: John Murray. 1959. See chap. 18 for dramatic episodes about Charcot at the Salpêtrière.
281. Packe, M. St. J., *The Life of John Stuart Mill.* New York: Macmillan. 1954.
282. Paterson, Donald G., *Physique and Intellect.* New York: Appleton-Century-Crofts. 1930.
283. Peterson, Joseph, *Early Conceptions and Tests of Intelligence.* New York: World Book. 1925.
284. Piaget, Jean, La psychanalyse et la pédagogie. *Bull.* (1920) No. 131, pp. 18–34; Nos. 132 and 133, pp. 41–58.

285. Piéron, Henri, Histoire succincte des congrès internationaux de psychologie. *L'A. P.* (1954) 54: 397–405.
286. ———, Quelques souvenirs personnels de Binet. *Psychol. française* (1958) 3: 89–95.
287. Pollack, R. H., and M. W. Brenner (eds.), *The Experimental Psychology of Alfred Binet: Selected Papers*. Translated by F. K. Zetland and C. Ellis. New York: Springer. 1969.
288. Postman, L., Hermann Ebbinghaus. *Amer. Psychol.* (1968) 23: 149–57.
289. Ribot, Th., Le problème de la pensée, sans images. *R. Ph.* (1913) 76: 50–68.
290. Ross, Dorothy, *G. Stanley Hall, The Psychologist as Prophet*. Chicago: Univ. of Chicago Press, 1972.
291. Simon, Th., Le problème des aptitudes. *Bull.* (1911) No. 76, pp. 84–94.
292. ———, Étude expérimentale des facultés de l'enfant. *Bull.* (1912) No. 81, pp. 215–24.
293. ———, Alfred Binet. *L'A. P.* (1912) 18: 1–14.
294. ———, Alfred Binet. *Bull.* (1940) No. 365, pp. 29–36.
295. ———, L'étude psychologique de l'enfant. *Bull.* (1948) No. 381, pp. 173–85.
296. ———, Souvenirs sur Alfred Binet. *Bull.* (1954) No. 415, pp. 342–60.
297. ———, L'échelle Binet-Simon et l'intelligence. *Bull.* (1954) No. 418, pp. 409–20.
298. ———, Notes sur La Société de psychologie du sud-est. *Bull.* (1958) No. 443, p. 78.
299. ———, *Inédits d'Alfred Binet* (avec une page autographe hors-texte). Cahors: Coueslant. 1960.
300. Terman, Lewis M., *The Measurement of Intelligence*. Boston: Houghton Mifflin. 1916.
301. Tuddenham, Read D., The Nature and Measurement of Intelligence, pp. 469–525, in Leo Postman, ed.: *Psychology in the Making*. New York: Knopf. 1962.
302. ———, Jean Piaget and the World of the Child. *Amer. Psychol.* (1966) 21: 207–17.
303. Varon, Edith J., *The Development of Alfred Binet's Psychology*. *Psychol. Monogs.* (1935) 46: 1–129.
304. ———, Alfred Binet's Concept of Intelligence. *Psychol. Rev.* (1936) 43: 32–58.
305. Wolf, Theta H., An Individual Who Made a Differ-

ence: Théodore Simon. *Amer. Psychol.* (1961) 16: 245–48.
306. ———, Alfred Binet: A Time of Crisis. *Amer. Psychol.* (1964) 19: 762–71.
307. ———, Intuition and Experiment: Alfred Binet's First Efforts in Child Psychology. *J. of Hist. of Behav. Sciences* (1966) 2: 233–39.
308. ———, The Emergence of Binet's Conception and Measurement of Intelligence: A case history of the creative process. Parts I and II. *J. of the Hist. of Behav. Sciences* (1969) 5: 113–34, 207–37.
309. Zazzo, René, Alfred Binet et la psychologie de l'enfant. *Psychol. française* (1958) 3: 113–21.
310. Zazzo, R., M. Gilly, and M. Verba-Rad, *Nouvelle échelle métrique de l'intelligence.* Paris: Armand Colin. 1961. Chap. 1, "Historique et Méthodologie," by R. Zazzo, pp. 9–66.
311. Zuza, F., *Alfred Binet et la pédagogie expérimentale.* Louvain: E. Nauwelaerts. 1948.
312. Larguier des Bancels, J., L'oeuvre d'Alfred Binet. *L'A. P.* (1912) 18: 15–32.

Index